COMPARATIVE P

Political Parties

COMPARATIVE POLITICS

Comparative politics is a series for students and teachers of political science that deals with contemporary issues in comparative government and politics. As Comparative European Politics it has produced a series of high quality books since its foundation in 1990, but now takes on a new form and new title for the the millennium—Comparative Politics. As the process of globalization proceeds, and as Europe becomes ever more enmeshed in world trends and events, so it is necessary to broaden the scope of the series. The General Editors are Max Kasse, Professor of Political Science, University of Mannheim and Research Professor Wissenschaftzentrum Berlin, and Kenneth Newton, Professor of Government, University of Southampton. The series is published in association with the European Consortium for Political Research.

OTHER TITLES IN THIS SERIES

Coalition Governments in Western Europe
Edited by Wolfgang C. Müller and Kaare Strøm

Parties without Partisans: Political Change in Advanced Industrial Democracies
Edited by Russell J. Dalton and Martin P. Wattenberg

Political Institutions: Democracy and Social Change
Josep H. Colomer

Mixed-Member Electoral Systems
Edited by Matthew Soberg Shugart and Martin P. Wattenberg

Divided Government in Comparative Perspective
Robert Elgie

Political Parties

Old Concepts and New Challenges

edited by

RICHARD GUNTHER, JOSÉ RAMÓN-
MONTERO, AND JUAN J. LINZ

OXFORD
UNIVERSITY PRESS

OXFORD
UNIVERSITY PRESS

Great Clarendon Street, Oxford OX2 6DP

Oxford University Press is a department of the University of Oxford.
It furthers the University's objective of excellence in research, scholarship,
and education by publishing worldwide in

Oxford New York

Auckland Cape Town Dar es Salaam Hong Kong Karachi Kuala Lumpur
Madrid Melbourne Mexico City Nairobi New Delhi Shanghai Taipei Toronto

With offices in

Argentina Austria Brazil Chile Czech Republic France Greece
Guatemala Hungary Italy Japan South Korea Poland Portugal
Singapore Switzerland Thailand Turkey Ukraine Vietnam

Oxford is a registered trade mark of Oxford University Press
in the UK and in certain other countries

Published in the United States
by Oxford University Press Inc., New York

British Library Cataloguing in Publication Data

Data available

Library of Congress Cataloging in Publication Data

Political parties: old concepts and new challenges/edited by Richard Gunther,
José Ramón Montéro, and Juan J. Linz.
p. cm.–(Comparative politics)
Includes bibliographical references.
1. Political parties 2. Democracy. I. Gunther, Richard. II. Montero, José R., 1948-
III. Linz, Juan J. (Juan José), 1926- IV. Comparative politics (Oxford University Press)
JF2051.P578 2002   324.2—dc21   2001055475

ISBN 0-19-829669-X
ISBN 0-19-924674-2 (Pbk.)

5 7 9 10 8 6 4

Typeset by Hope Services (Abingdon) Ltd.
Printed in Great Britain
on acid-free paper by
Biddles Ltd., King's Lynn, Norfolk

For Linda, Pilar, and Rocío

Acknowledgements

Our deepest debt of gratitude is owed to the Center for Advanced Studies in the Social Sciences (CEACS) of the Instituto Juan March of Madrid. The CEACS is a unique and outstanding institution dedicated primarily to the postgraduate education of young Spanish social scientists. Over the course of the past decade, it has become an important point of reference for the international social science community. Without its support, this book would not have been possible. In the spring of 1994, the Steering Committee of the CEACS proposed the convening of a major international conference dedicated to the systematic exploration of political parties by many of the world's leading experts in this field. This meeting, held between 15 and 17 December 1994, brought together forty prominent scholars from eleven countries. The wonderful staff and facilities of the CEACS helped make it possible for our discussions of political parties, party organizations, party elites, party linkages, and party images to take place within an extremely pleasant and congenial atmosphere. CEACS personnel also provided invaluable assistance during the editing and preparation of this manuscript.

Among those at the Instituto Juan March who are deserving of special praise are José Luis Yuste, its Managing Director, whose support for this multi-year project made it possible; José María Maravall, now the Academic Director of the CEACS; and Leopoldo Calvo-Sotelo, who served as its Secretary General at the time of the conference, and was an active and valuable collaborator in this project during the first several years of work on the manuscript. His successor, Javier Gomá, has also helped to bring this project to fruition. Andrew Richards was an excellent collaborator in the selection and revision of those conference papers that ultimately appeared in this volume: his comments, criticisms, and suggestions were invaluable. Ignacio Molina also helped with the revision of some chapters, and Martha Peach served as an inexhaustible source of suggestions and insights, and made available the enormous resources of the excellent CEACS library which she directs. Luis Díaz and Magdalena Nebreda also provided considerable assistance. But the person who devoted the most time and effort to this enormous project was Jackie de la Fuente, who laboured through many revisions of these manuscripts over the years with a smile, a good sense of humour, and a tireless willingness to help.

The editors would like to thank the contributors to this volume, not only for the high quality of their respective chapters, but also for their patience throughout the protracted processes of manuscript revision and editorial refinement of this book. We must also acknowledge the important roles played by prominent Spanish and foreign scholars (too numerous to be listed here) who presented papers and made invaluable contributions to the lively intellectual discussions at the conference. We would have liked to include in this volume many more of those fine conference papers, but space limitations made it necessary to publish only a handful of them here. Fortunately, several of those other papers were published by the CEACS in its Working Papers series.

Dominic Byatt of Oxford University Press has been extremely supportive of our efforts, and we greatly appreciate his forbearance during what must have seemed like a never-ending project. Amanda Watkins, assistant editor at OUP, has been an impressive collaborator in moving this manuscript through the copy-editing and production stages in record time, while maintaining the highest scholarly and stylistic standards throughout. We are also grateful to the copy editor, Jane Robson, for both correcting our mistakes and, at the same time, respecting the varying styles of expression of our contributing authors, and to Frank Pert, for his excellent work in preparing the index. Our respective academic institutions (the political science departments at Ohio State University and the Universidad Autónoma de Madrid, and the department of sociology at Yale University) also provided considerable assistance over the course of this extensive project. In addition, the Mershon Center of Ohio State University and the Spanish Comisión Interministerial de Ciencia y Tecnología (through grant SEC95–1007) provided substantial financial support at crucial times.

Our final words of thanks go to our wives, Linda, Pilar, and Rocío, to whom this book is dedicated. Over the course of several decades, they have provided the support—not to mention forbearance and understanding—that has made it possible for us to pursue our academic objectives.

R.G., *Ohio State University;*
J.R.M., *Instituto Juan March and Universidad Autónoma de Madrid*
J.J.L., *Yale University*

Contents

List of Figures   xi

List of Tables   xii

Contributors   xiv

1. Introduction: Reviewing and Reassessing Parties   1
   José Ramón Montero and Richard Gunther

I. Reconceptualizing Parties and Party Competition

2. Parties: Denied, Dismissed, or Redundant? A Critique   39
   Hans Daalder

3. Still the Age of Catch-allism? *Volksparteien* and *Parteienstaat* in
   Crisis and Re-equilibration   58
   Hans-Jürgen Puhle

4. Electoral and Party Competition: Analytical Dimensions and
   Empirical Problems   84
   Stefano Bartolini

II. Re-examining Party Organization and Party Models

5. The Ascendancy of the Party in Public Office: Party Organizational
   Change in Twentieth-Century Democracies   113
   Richard S. Katz and Peter Mair

6. Beyond the Catch-All Party: Approaches to the Study of Parties
   and Party Organization in Contemporary Democracies   136
   Steven B. Wolinetz

7. Party Organization and Party Performance: The Case of the
   French Socialist Party   166
   Serenella Sferza

8. A Crisis of Institutionalization: The Collapse of the UCD in Spain
    Richard Gunther and Jonathan Hopkin   191

III. Revisiting Party Linkages and Attitudes Towards Parties

9. Party Government, Patronage, and Party Decline in Western
    Europe   233
    Jean Blondel

10. Anti-Party Sentiments in Southern Europe   257
    Mariano Torcal, Richard Gunther, and José Ramón Montero

11. Parties in Contemporary Democracies: Problems and Paradoxes   291
    Juan J. Linz

References   318
Index   345

List of Figures

4.1. The structure of voters' preferences   96

6.1. Primary emphases or orientations of political parties   151

6.2. Vote-seeking, policy-seeking, and office-seeking political
parties   161

8.1. Intra-party clashes, economic conditions, and support for
UCD and PSOE as incumbent parties, 1977–1986   226

9.1. The two dimensions in the government–party relationships   239

10.1. Cohorts and cultural anti-party sentiments in Spain, 1985–1997   271

10.2. Cohorts and reactive pro-party sentiments in Spain, 1985–1997   272

List of Tables

4.1. The dimensions of electoral competition: a summary   105

6.1. Cadre versus mass party distinction: a revised version   144

6.2. Panebianco's distinction between mass-bureaucratic and electoral-professional parties   147

6.3. Policy-, vote-, and office-seeking parties: operational measures   155

8.1. Proportional representation of political families with UCD, 1979–1988   211

8.2. Identification with political families by the Spanish electorate, 1975–1993   216

10.1. Factor analysis of anti-party sentiments in Southern Europe, 1985–1998   264

10.2. Indicators of cultural anti-party sentiments in Southern Europe, 1985–1998   265

10.3. Indicators of reactive pro-party sentiments in Southern Europe, 1985–1998   266

10.4. Reactive anti-party sentiments in Southern Europe, 1985–1998   267

10.5. Cultural anti-party sentiments in Southern Europe, 1985–1998   268

10.6. Anti-party sentiments and political efficacy, interest, and awareness in Spain, 1995   274

10.7. Anti-party sentiments and conservative or reformist attitudes towards Spanish society, 1995   276

10.8. Anti-party sentiments and educational attainment in Spain, 1995   279

10.9. Anti-party sentiments and exposure to political information in
Spain, 1995 281

10.10. Anti-party sentiments and support for democracy in Spain,
1995 282

10.11. Correlates (Tau-b) of cultural anti-party sentiments in
Portugal, Italy, and Greece, 1985 283

10.12. Correlates (Tau-b) of reactive anti-party sentiments in
Portugal, Italy, and Greece, 1985 284

10.13. Relationships between cultural antipartyism and forms of
political participation in Southern Europe, 1985 286

10.14. Relationships between reactive antipartyism and forms of
political participation in Southern Europe, 1985 287

11.1. Belief in the need for parties and confidence in parties in Latin
America, 1997 295

11.2. Trust in various institutions in selected South American
countries, 1997 296

11.3. Readiness to contribute economically to a party in Spain in
general elections, by party voted, 1997 308

11.4. Confidence in parties and attitudes towards democracy in
Spain, Chile, and Ecuador, 1997 314

Contributors

Stefano Bartolini (1952) is Professor of Comparative Political Institutions at the European University Institute, Florence. He was previously professor at the Universities of Florence, Trieste and Geneva, and visiting professor at the Instituto Juan March. His most recent publications include *The Class Cleavage. The Electoral Mobilisation of the European Left 1880–1980* (2000); 'Collusion, Competition and Democracy', in *Journal of Theoretical Politics* (1999–2000); and 'Franchise Expansion', in Richard Rose (ed.), *Encyclopedia of Elections* (2000).

Jean Blondel (1929) was educated at the Institut d'Études Politiques in Paris and at St Antony's College, Oxford. He was the founding Professor of the Department of Government of the University of Essex and one of the co-founders and first Executive Director of the European Consortium for Political Research. He has been professor at the European University Institute in Florence, to which he remains associated, and is current visiting professor at the University of Siena. His field is Comparative Government and his recent publications include *Governing Together* (co-edited with Ferdinand Müller-Rommel, 1993), *Comparative Government* (last edn., 1995), *Party and Government* (1997), and *The Nature of Party Government* (2000) (both co-edited with Maurizio Cotta).

Hans Daalder (1928) was Professor of Political Science at Leiden University from 1963 to 1993, and visiting professor at the Instituto Juan March. One of the founding members of the European Consortium for Political Research, he was the first Head of Department of Political and Social Sciences at the European University Institute. One result of the latter was the book edited with Peter Mair, *Western European Party Systems: Continuity and Change* (1983). More recently he organized and edited a volume of intellectual (auto)biographies of comparative politics scholars entitled *Comparative European Politics. The Story of a Profession* (1997). He is working on a biography of the leading post-1945 Prime Minister of the Netherlands, Willem Drees (1886–1988).

Richard Gunther (1946) is Professor of Political Science at the Ohio State University. At Ohio State, he has also served as Director of the West European Studies Program and Executive Director of International Studies. He is founder and co-chair of the Subcommittee on Southern Europe of the

American Council of Learned Societies and the Social Science Research Council. He has also been the Peace Fellow at The Hoover Institution, visiting professor at the Instituto Juan March, Madrid, and visiting lecturer at Wuhan University, Hubei Province, Peoples Republic of China. His principal publications include *Public Policy in a No-Party State: Spain After Franco* (with Giacomo Sani and Goldie Shabad, 1986); *Elites and Democratic Consolidation in Latin America and Southern Europe* (with John Higley, 1992); *Politics, Society and Democracy: The Case of Spain* (1993); *The Politics of Democratic Consolidation* (with P. Nikiforos Diamandouros and Hans-Jürgen Puhle, 1995); *Democracy and the Media* (with Anthony Mughan, 2000); and *Political Parties and Democracy* (with Larry Diamond, 2001).

Jonathan Hopkin (1967) is Lecturer in Political Science at the University of Birmingham. He is the author of *Party Formation and Democratic Transition in Spain* (1999) and has published articles on political parties in Southern Europe in edited collections and journals such as the *Revista de Estudios Políticos, Crime, Law and Social Change*, the *European Journal of Political Research, West European Politics*, and *Party Politics*. His current research focuses on rational-choice theory and comparative political economy.

Richard S. Katz (1947) is Professor of Political Science at the Johns Hopkins University, Baltimore, and has held faculty appointments at Queens College of the City University of New York and at the State University of New York at Buffalo. He is the author of *A Theory of Parties and Electoral Systems* (1980) for which he received the George H. Hallett Award in 1998, and *Democracy and Elections* (1997). He is also co-author and editor of *Party Governments: European and American Experiences* (1987) and co-author and co-editor of *The Patron State* (with Milton C. Cummings, 1987), *Party Organizations* (with Peter Mair, 1992), *How Parties Organize* (with Peter Mair, 1994), and *The European Parliament, the National Parliaments, and European Integration* (with Bernhard Wessels, 1999).

Juan J. Linz (1926) is Emeritus Sterling Professor of Political and Social Science at Yale University. He is recipient of the Premio Príncipe de Asturias and the Johan Skytte Prize, and has received honorary degrees from the Universidad de Granada (1976), Universidad Autónoma de Madrid (1992), Georgetown University (1992), Universität Marburg, and Universiteit Oslo (2000). He has taught previously at Columbia University, and was visiting professor and member of the Scientific Council of the Instituto Juan March. Among his many publications are several studies of political parties; *The Breakdown of Democratic Regimes* (1978); *Informe sociológico sobre el cambio político en España, 1975–1981* (1981); *Conflicto en Euskadi* (1985); *The Failure of Presidential Democracy* (1994); and *Problems of Democratic Transition and Consolidation* (1996).

Peter Mair (1951) is Professor of Comparative Politics at Leiden University is co-editor of the journal *West European Politics*. His most recent books are *Party System Change* (Oxford University Press, 1997) and *Representative Government in Modern Europe* (McGraw Hill, 3rd edn., 2000, with Michael Gallagher and Michael Laver). He is co-editor of *Political Parties in Electoral Markets* (Sage, forthcoming).

José Ramón Montero (1948) is Professor of Political Science at the Universidad Autónoma de Madrid and at the Instituto Juan March, Madrid. He has taught at the Universities of Granada, Santiago, Zaragoza, Cádiz and Complutense de Madrid, and has been Visiting Fellow at Harvard and the University of California at Berkeley, and visiting professor at Ohio State University. He has been Secretary and Dean of the School of Law at the Universidad of Cádiz, and Deputy Director of the Centro de Investigaciones Sociológicas. He is member of the Standing Committee for the Social Sciences, European Science Foundation, and has also been Director of the Economics and Social Science Programme, Comisión Interministerial de Ciencia y Tecnología. His publications include *La CEDA: el catolicismo social y político en la II República* (1977), *El control parlamentario* (with Joaquín G. Morillo, 1985); *Crisis y cambio: electores y partidos en la España de los años ochenta* (with Juan J. Linz, 1986), *Elecciones autonómicas en Aragón* (with Ricardo Chueca, 1995), and *El régimen electoral* (with Richard Gunther *et al.*, 1996).

Hans-Jürgen Puhle (1940) is Professor of Political Science at the Johann Wolfgang Goethe Universität Frankfurt am Main (since 1990), and previously at the Universities of Münster and Bielefeld. He has been a Fellow of Harvard and Oxford University, and a visiting professor at Cornell, Stanford, Universidad de Chile, University of Tel Aviv, FLACSO Buenos Aires, and Instituto Juan March, Madrid. He has published extensively in the fields of comparative social and political history of the Western world, problems of modernization, comparative government and political theory, state functions in welfare capitalism, political parties, pressure groups and social movements, nationalism and regionalism, regime change and transitions to democracy. His books include *Politische Agrarbewegungen in kapitalistischen Industriegesellschaften* (1975); *Preussen im Rückblick* (with Hans-Ulrich Wehler, 1980); *Bürger in der Gesellschaft der Neuzeit* (1991); *Staaten, Nationen und Regionen in Europa* (1995); *The Politics of Democratic Consolidation. Southern Europe in Comparative Perspective* (with Richard Gunther and P. Nikiforos Diamandouros, 1995); *Von der Diktatur zur Demokratie* (with Wolfgang Merkel, 1999).

Serenella Sferza (1951) is currently visiting assistant professor at the MIT Political Science department; she is also affiliated with the Minda de Gunzburg Center for European Studies and co-ordinates the MIT–Italy program. Sferza's primary interests are in long-term processes of political change, with particular emphasis on party formation and renewal, and her ongoing research focuses on the historical evolution of cleavage structures and party types. For an overview of her approach, see S. Sferza, 'What is Left of the Left?: More than One Would Think', *Daedalus* (Summer 1999).

Mariano Torcal (1962) is Associate Professor in Political Science at the Pompeu Fabra University, Barcelona. He has been Associate Professor at Universidad Autónoma de Madrid, and visiting professor at the University of Michigan, Instituto Juan March, and the Kellogg Institute at the University of Notre Dame. He has published articles on political culture and political behaviour in major international journal such as *Comparative Political Studies, British Journal of Political Research* and *International Journal of Public Opinion Research*. The American Political Science Association awarded him with the runner-up to the best article in Comparative Politics in 1997. He is about to finish a manuscript on political disaffection in new democracies.

Steven B. Wolinetz (1943) is Professor of Political Science at Memorial University of Newfoundland. His publications include *Parties and Party Systems in Liberal Democracies* (1988), *Political Parties* (1998), and *Party Systems* (1998), and several articles on continuity and change in party systems.

Introduction:

Reviewing and Reassessing Parties

José Ramón Montero and Richard Gunther

Students of democratic politics may have mixed feelings about the value of yet another book on political parties. Some scholars may have concluded that the existing literature on parties is sufficient, and that there is little more that can be learned through additional study in the aftermath of a century of scholarly research on the topic. Others may be led to dismiss further empirical study of parties on the grounds that parties are becoming increasingly irrelevant, since they are failing to respond successfully to a series of challenges, and many of their functions are performed better by less formally organized social movements, by direct contact between politicians and citizens through the broadcast media or the internet, or by innovations in direct democracy. In the view of this group of scholars, parties may be seen as in an inexorable process of 'decline'. Finally, there may be some who have concluded that scholarly research on parties has failed to advance the task of developing rigorous and persuasive theory, and that further efforts along these lines are doomed to fail. Such an assertion might be especially appealing to those scholars who have embraced analytical approaches that place little value on the study of complex organizations or political institutions and who may simply dismiss the study of parties as irrelevant to the development of a more universalistic theory of politics.

We shall begin this introductory chapter by reviewing each of these assertions. It should not surprise the reader to find that we conclude that such negative views are unwarranted. We shall argue that political parties in the early twenty-first century are confronting a number of new challenges, many of which had neither been anticipated nor adequately addressed by the existing literature on parties. And while we acknowledge the general weakness of theory-building efforts regarding political parties, we believe that the continuing importance of parties in all democratic systems, in combination with the extent to which challenges facing contemporary parties have raised a wide variety of new questions crying out for empirical research, make it all the more important to continue to push towards the formulation and systematic testing of more sophisticated and empirically grounded hypotheses, with the ultimate objective of developing a more compelling set of middle-range theories. While such advances have been made with regard to the study of party systems, we believe that a critical reassessment of traditional concepts and models of parties *per se* is long overdue, particularly concerning their capacity to deal adequately with recent developments and the new challenges that have confronted parties over the past two decades. Both the empirical and the more purely theoretical chapters included in this volume address these issues.

This introductory chapter will conclude with a brief overview of the contributions made by the authors of the following chapters to the literature on political parties, especially with regard to core concepts that have guided empirical research on parties, their organizational structures, and the changing and sometimes problematic nature of their relations with citizens in democratic political systems.

THE GROWING LITERATURE ON PARTIES

We must begin by conceding to the first hypothetical group of sceptics that there is no shortage of books and articles on parties. As Strøm and Müller have noted (1999: 5), 'the scholarly literature that examines political parties is enormous'. Indeed, parties were among the first subjects of analysis at the very birth of modern political science, as exemplified by the classic works of Ostrogorski (1964 [1902]), Michels (1962 [1911]) and Weber (1968 [1922]). Over the following years, a number of extremely important works were published (e.g. Merriam 1922; Schattschneider 1942; Key 1949), but it was really in the 1950s, 1960s, and 1970s when studies of parties fully blossomed as a subfield in political science. Such works as those of Duverger (1954), Ranney (1954), Neumann (1956), Eldersveld (1964), Sorauf (1964), La Palombara and Weiner (1966, which included Kirchheimer's seminal contribution), Epstein (1967), Lipset and Rokkan (1967*a*) and Sartori (1976) established the conceptual and empirical bases for countless studies in comparative politics. In terms of the sheer number of publications, the growth of this subfield has been spectacular. Since 1945, approximately 11,500 books, articles and monographs have been published that deal with parties and party systems in Western Europe alone (Bartolini *et al.* 1998).[1] Isn't that enough?

The contributors to this book would reject such a conclusion. Contrary to assertions that 'the golden age of party literature may now have passed' (Caramani and Hug 1998: 520), we believe that it is more important than ever to study political parties and the roles they play in modern democracies. To begin with, parties have always been among the handful of institutions whose activities are absolutely essential for the proper functioning of representative democracy. Given the centrality and fundamental mission of political parties, it is not surprising that students of democracy have, since the very beginnings of modern political science, recognized the importance of constantly monitoring and analysing their evolution and the quality of their performance. Bryce (1921: 119), for example, argued 'that parties are inevitable: no free country has been without them; and no one has shown how representative government could work without them'. In the early 1940s, Schattschneider (1942: 1) succinctly summarized their importance by stating that 'modern democracy is unthinkable save in terms of political parties'. Several decades later, similar words were used by other scholars to illustrate the central role played by parties. As described by Stokes (1999: 245), parties are 'endemic to democracy, an unavoidable part of democracy'. Americanists have long believed that 'political parties lie at the heart of American politics' (Aldrich 1995: 3). Not to be outdone, West Europeanists have asserted that 'European democracies are not only parliamentary democracies but also party democracies' (Müller 2000*a*: 309). As one might expect, the chapters in this book also recognize the importance of parties, and present illuminating discussions of the roles played by parties in various dimensions of democratic political life.

Following several years in which scholarly interest in political parties appeared to have waned, there has recently been a notable revitalization of the subfield of party studies. The appearance in 1995 of the journal *Party Politics*—which is devoted explicitly to the systematic examination of parties and party systems from a variety of perspectives—has been accompanied by a substantial outburst of comparative studies of parties.[2] In the aggregate, the reawakening of interest in political parties has been so considerable as to make the temporary decline of this subfield following its 'golden age' appear as a puzzling aberration.[3] As Peter Mair (1997: p. vii) has pointed out, 'little more than a decade ago, students of party politics were often accused of being engaged in a somewhat *passé* branch of the discipline; today it is a field which is brimming with health and promise'. Far from declining in importance, we believe that a re-examination of both the prevailing theories of political parties and their actual behavior in a variety of political systems should continue to occupy a prominent place on the research agenda of political science.

ASSESSING PARTY DECLINE

Paradoxically, this revitalization of scholarly interest in parties has coincided with frequent assertions that parties have entered into an irreversible process of decline. Indeed, if the 'decline of party' hypothesis were found to be substantiated in many contemporary democratic systems, one might conclude that new studies of political parties would be increasingly irrelevant. We believe that the exact opposite is true. Rather than assuming that an alleged decline of parties should imply a decline in the literature on parties, we think that the confrontation of new challenges suggests a reassessment of parties and the contemporary relevance of some aspects of the traditional party literature. As several of the following chapters will demonstrate, in recent years these venerable organizations have been forced to confront a wide variety of new challenges. What is not at all clear is the extent to which parties have failed to meet these challenges and have therefore begun to decline in importance as institutionalized actors in democratic politics. As Strøm and Svåsand (1997*b*: 4) have noted, 'doom-and gloom treatises on political parties have become a growth industry over the past two decades. But this gloomy picture of contemporary parties is far from self-evident.' Thus, one set of research questions arising out of this line of speculation concerns the extent to which parties have, indeed, declined organizationally, as objects of citizen loyalty, as mobilizers of votes, and as key actors in democratic politics. All of these are empirical questions, answers to which should not be assumed or generalized excessively.

Accordingly, a second line of potentially fruitful research that emerges from speculations about party decline concerns the nature of the challenges facing contemporary parties, as well as their reactions to those challenges. Some of these challenges have their origins in the changing nature of society. In many countries, levels of affiliation with parties and with allied mass-membership organizations upon which many mass-based parties have depended for support have declined significantly, thereby calling into question the viability of mass-based institutional structures that had their origins in earlier times. Trends towards secularization have sapped the strength of denominational parties, at the same time that increasing affluence and expanding middle classes have shrunk the potential electoral base of working-class parties. The greater participation of women in the labour force has both placed new demands on the policy agendas of parties, and created a transformed constituency in need of party representation. Massive international migration has introduced many individuals into societies who had not been represented by previously established parties, and in some quarters has given rise to xenophobic reactions feeding the growth of new kinds of right-wing parties.

Other challenges to parties have emerged as consequences of higher levels of personal resources possessed by citizens. Better educated individuals who had never experienced economic deprivation have tended to adopt post-materialist values that both conflicted with the traditional ideologies of many parties and have given rise to participatory expectations better suited to new social movements, single-issue interest groups, and unconventional forms of political involvement. Better informed citizens are also able to enhance their participatory capabilities, expand the range of their access to independent channels of information, and develop their own attitudinal orientations towards politics and parties independent of guidance from secondary associations or 'opinion leaders'. Some of these trends have weakened the structural and psychological linkages between citizens and parties, as reflected in lower levels of party identification, and increases in feelings of political dissatisfaction, cynicism and even alienation.

Still other challenges have their origins in technological developments. The mass-communications media have opened up new channels for direct access between citizens and their political leaders that need not pass through traditional partisan channels. The rapid spread of access to the internet has created massive and complex networks of direct horizontal communications among citizens, while at the same time establishing a potential basis for 'narrowcasting' messages between politicians and specific if not highly specialized sectors of society. The downside of these communications advances involves the enormous cost of establishing such networks, paying consultants for the purpose of crafting messages and attractive images of politicians, and in some countries (especially the United States) purchasing television or radio time for the broadcasting of commercial advertisements. Dramatic increases in the cost of campaigning has compelled parties to seek massive volumes of revenue from both public and private sources, and this has sometimes spilt over into the adoption (or suspicion) of corrupt practices of various kinds. Finally, the trend towards devolution of governmental authority from centre to regional or local levels of government in several countries has posed new challenges associated with electoral competition at both the national and subnational levels.[4]

The cumulative effects of these challenges have given rise in some Western democracies to a literature characterized by its somewhat fatalistic analysis of the organizational, electoral, cultural, and institutional symptoms of party decline (e.g. Berger 1979; Offe 1984; Lawson and Merkl 1988*a*). Some scholars regard these challenges as so serious as to threaten the very survival of parties. As Lawson and Merkl (1988*b*: 3) have noted, 'it may be that the institution of party is gradually disappearing, slowly being replaced by new political structures more suitable for the economic and technological realities of twenty-first-century politics'.

Parties in new democracies have had to confront an additional set of challenges, in addition to those described above. With the 'third wave' of democratization, party institutions have been born or re-established in dozens of political systems that had either lacked a tradition of democratic stability or never experienced truly democratic governance. Not only do they have to perform the standard functions of political parties in established democracies (including the recruitment of candidates for public office, the mobilization of electoral support, the structuring of policy agendas, and the formation of governments), but have also been key actors in the establishment and consolidation of new democratic regimes, at the same time that they must institutionalize themselves as viable partisan organizations.[5]

These challenges have often been quite severe, and have forced parties to undertake considerable efforts to adapt to the changing conditions of political competition. They have also affected politics in Western democracies by facilitating the emergence of new types of parties associated with social movements. But in no instance have they led to the disappearance of parties and/or their replacement by other types of organizations (such as interest groups or social movements) or institutionalized practices (such as those of direct democracy). Thus, much of the alarmist literature regarding the decline of parties must be reassessed. As Tarrow (1990: 253) has pointed out, the literature on the relationship between parties and new social movements has been undermined by an overestimation of the distance between those two sets of actors, as well as an underestimation of the ability of parties to adapt to the demands of the New Politics. Aldrich (1995: ch. 8) is even more sweeping in his reassessment of this literature, suggesting that studies dealing with 'the three *Ds*' (party decay, decline, and decomposition) should be replaced by 'the three *Rs*' (party re-emergence, revitalization, and resurgence), in light of the profound changes in the functions and objectives of contemporary American parties.[6] To an even greater extent, Western European parties have been, and still seem to be, able to successfully meet these challenges through processes of adaptation over the past three decades.[7] Indeed, Kuechler and Dalton (1990: 298) have suggested that the principal (and clearly unintended) impact of the emergence of new social movements has been to force parties to adapt and initiate evolutionary processes of change that have helped to guarantee the long-term stability of the political system. This may very well be true, but if it is, it certainly suggests that the literature on party decline should be substantially reformulated in several ways. First, it should abandon the deterministic quality of its assessment of the negative impact on parties of a wide variety of causal factors. Second, it should acknowledge the important roles played by party elites in adopting strategies to meet external challenges and in successfully maintaining reasonably cohesive and electorally competitive organizations (see Rose and Mackie 1988). To date, the net effect has been that, despite suffering through periods of electoral dealignment over the past three decades, most available indicators suggest that 'parties are alive and well within the governing process' (as described by Dalton and Wattenberg 2000*b*: 273). And contrary to predictions of party decline in the 1980s, parties remain the most important actors in democratic systems. In the words of Peter Mair (1997: 90),

parties continue to matter. Parties continue to survive. The old parties which were around well before Rokkan elaborated his freezing proposition are still around today, and, despite the challenges from new parties, and new social movements, most of them still remain in powerful, dominant positions. . . . Following Rokkan, the party altern-atives of the 1960s were older than the majority of their national electorates. Thirty years on, these self-same parties still continue to dominate mass politics. . . . Nowadays, in short, they are even older still.

To some extent, all of the chapters in this volume examine the factors that have contributed to the extraordinary continuity of parties, and they do so from complementary perspectives that have not been well explored in the existing party literature. Some of these chapters focus on the themes of party decline and public cynicism towards parties. As we will discuss at greater length in this introduction, Hans Daalder's critical review of the party-decline literature brings to light the analytical biases and value-laden assumptions that underpin many such studies. Similarly, Juan J. Linz presents empirical evidence suggesting that many of the criticisms of parties by ordinary citizens may be derived from the holding of attitudes that are inherently contradic-tory, or from expectations of party performance that are impossible to meet, particularly in light of the increasing number of demanding roles that parties must perform in democratic systems. Mariano Torcal, Richard Gunther, and José Ramón Montero also examine the nature of citizen attitudes towards parties and politicians, and conclude on the basis of survey data from Southern Europe that anti-party sentiments are of two fundamentally differ-ent types—one fluctuating cluster of attitudes linked to satisfaction with the performance of the incumbent party, and another strikingly durable set of orientations rooted in the political cultures of these countries and the anti-party socialization experienced by older citizens under previous authoritarian regimes or prior unsuccessful democratic regimes.

Other chapters in this volume re-examine current conceptualizations of par-ties and the functions they perform in democratic systems. Stefano Bartolini undertakes a rigorous analysis of the complex dimensions that underpin the basic concept of party competition, and persuasively argues that this com-plexity defies the simplifying (if not simplistic) assumptions that underpin many rational-choice analyses of parties, party systems, and electoral behav-iour. Steven B. Wolinetz examines the existing typologies of parties, particu-larly from the standpoint of party organizational characteristics, and reformulates some of them in an effort to better capture the extreme diversity of parties and reconcile that variation with specific analytical criteria. Richard S. Katz and Peter Mair argue that analyses of parties must acknowledge changes that have occurred with regard to their different *faces* (the party in public office, the party on the ground, and the party in the central office), and pay greater attention to the connection between the ascendancy of party in public office and some symptoms of party decline. In a similar manner, Jean Blondel introduces into the literature on party decline a series of observations about the ways in which differing practices regarding party patronage may affect public satisfaction with parties and their performance in public office. In

short, these chapters explore, from a theoretical perspective, the current conceptualizations of parties and party functions, and propose modifications in
the ways in which analysts should approach these questions.

Three chapters present empirical comparative studies or case studies of the
ways in which parties have attempted to cope with these challenges and adapt
to changing circumstances. Hans-Jürgen Puhle presents a broad overview of
the manner in which party elites were able to develop strategies that enabled
them to adapt their organizational structures and mobilizing capacities to the
new circumstances of the last decades of the twentieth century. In doing so,
he raises important questions concerning the tendency of analysts to indiscriminately apply the term 'catch-all' to a wide variety of party types that
depart in significant ways from Kirchheimer's original formulation of that
concept. Serenella Sferza systematically analyses the changing fortunes of the
French socialist party over the past several decades. She also derives a number of broader theoretical implications from her case study, in particular in
her criticism of 'externalist' approaches that have dominated the literature on
party performance and party decline. Parties are not passive objects, she
argues, and several aspects of their internal dynamics and the models of
parties that are adopted have an important bearing on their capacity to successfully adapt to changing circumstances. Finally, Richard Gunther and
Jonathan Hopkin present a detailed analysis of a once-powerful governing
party that failed to meet various kinds of challenges, and, as a result, ceased
to exist in the aftermath of destructive internal conflicts at the elite level. They
concur with Sferza concerning the important role played by seemingly
abstract models of parties, and conclude that fundamental conflicts over such
models can destabilize a party and preclude its successful institutionalization.

STRENGTHENING PARTY THEORY

A third possible source of scepticism about the value of a new book on political parties might be rooted in disappointment over the underdevelopment of
theory concerning parties, and in pessimism that it will ever culminate in a
persuasive body of middle-range theory that might serve to orient future
research in a coherent and consistent manner. While we acknowledge the
general weakness of theory in this field (certainly compared with the broader
consensus regarding concepts, terminology, and operational indicators which
underpin research in some other related subfields of political science), we
regard some of these criticisms as excessive, and we do not share their pessimism about the future evolution of this literature. First, it must be noted
that the literature on political parties has, from the very beginning, sought to
rise above the level of mere description (see Daalder 1983). Over the past half-
century, in particular, many students of parties have attempted to generate

broad, theoretical propositions regarding the behaviour of parties, have proposed a number of typologies in an effort to make sense of the extraordinary variety of parties in existence, and/or have sought to establish concepts that might serve as the cornerstones of middle-range theoretical propositions. As Caramani and Hug have documented (1998: 507), over a third of the publications they surveyed concerning European parties are of a theoretical or analytical nature.[8] Given the prominent role played by parties in democratic politics, the continuing impact of the classic contributions to this literature that we cited earlier, and the considerable volume of publications that have appeared in recent decades, one would have expected that by now there should have been some scholarly convergence on a systematic theoretical framework. Despite the potential presented by this rich and complex aspect of democratic politics, however, no such consensus has emerged. Much of the theorizing concerning parties has been unpersuasive, so inconsistent as not to have served as a basis for systematic hypothesis-testing or cumulative theory-building, or so divided among diverging research traditions as to have impeded cumulative theory-building.

This theoretical weakness was first noted by Duverger (1954: p. xiii). In the very first paragraphs of his classic book, he called for a breaking of the vicious circle that afflicted the parties literature: on the one hand, a general theory of parties must be based upon empirical studies; on the other hand, empirical studies should be guided by hypotheses derived from some putative body of theory, or at least a commonly accepted set of theoretical propositions. In actuality, neither of these conditions was met, to the detriment of the development of this field of research. A generation later, Sartori (1976: p. x) began his book with a criticism of the imbalance resulting from the continuing weakness of a theory of parties and the abundance of empirical materials which were not easily cumulative or comparable. And today, widespread dissatisfaction with this literature appears to have continued, in so far as it has made little progress towards the development of theory built upon systematic comparative empirical analyses, general and testable hypotheses, and valid explanations of key phenomena (Wolinetz 1998*c*: pp. xi and xxi; Crotty 1991).

Over the past several decades, there have been some noteworthy attempts to build theory based upon approaches that were sometimes complementary, and sometimes competing and even incompatible. These various approaches have been categorized by many authors as historical, structural, behavioral, ideological, and functional-systemic (for instance, Lawson 1976: ch. 1; Ware 1996: ch. 6). Other overviews, more centred on party systems than parties *per se,* classified them as genetic, morphological, competitive, and institutional (Bartolini 1986*b*; Epstein 1975). It is clear from this brief enumeration that such efforts have been both numerous and diverse.

One of the most significant of these efforts towards theory-building occurred in the midst of the great outpouring of party studies in the 1960s.

Since at the same time structural-functionalism was the most attractive paradigm in comparative politics, it is not surprising that many such studies were closely tied to its core premisses. This approach had a substantial impact on the study of parties in part because this was a critical period for the definitive institutionalization of parties in Western democracies, and it coincided with the appearance of many new parties in the short-lived democracies that emerged from decolonization in Africa and Asia (see Kies 1966). Under these circumstances, characterized by the proliferation of greatly divergent types of political institutions in societies at greatly different stages of socio-economic development, adoption of a common structural-functional framework offered an ambitious promise of serving as the basis for the scientific and comparative study of politics. It was claimed that theorizing about parties and other important political phenomena would be advanced by the identification of common attributes and functions played by parties in all political systems irrespective of their institutional, social, and cultural diversity. To facilitate comparison, or at least to try to discern common themes among widely diverging developmental trajectories, it was posited that parties are the principal performers of the functions of interest articulation and aggregation, and, to a lesser extent, political socialization, recruitment, and communication. It was thought that this common ground could serve as the basis for the elaboration of concepts, deductive reasoning, and ambitious theoretical propositions.[9]

For a variety of reasons, that analytical approach became extinct. Its disappearance may have been partly attributable to the disconcerting, anticumulative (and therefore non-scientific) trendiness that has too often led to radical paradigm shifts in the discipline of political science. But its extinction was also a consequence of flaws that were inherent in the approach itself—particularly its static quality, its ethnocentrism, and the tendency of many of its practitioners to stress equilibrium, stability, and the functionality of institutions over conflict and change. More radical criticisms focused on its tautological character, its confusion over basic definitional dimensions, and the often weak and tangential link between the theory's core propositions and the actual empirical analysis carried out in its name, with this latter deficiency a logical outgrowth of its lack of operationalized concepts and testable hypotheses.[10] In any event, this attempt to establish a universalistic framework for the analysis of politics in general, and parties in particular, disappeared as a guiding force for empirical analysis by the mid-1970s.

A second significant effort to develop a universalistic theory of party politics is the emergence over the past decade of a number of studies analysing parties from a rational-choice perspective. Following the classic book by Anthony Downs (1957), the various currents of rational-choice scholarship have sought to formulate compatible sets of highly stylized hypotheses based upon a common set of assumptions about individuals and their goals. In the

United States, this perspective has, since the mid-1960s, progressively transformed the study of American political parties. Previously, as Aldrich (1995: ch. 1) points out, American parties were seen as coalitions among numerous and diverse groups whose interests are aggregated around a platform that is attractive to the majority of voters, and which seek to advance those interests through their presence in government (see Key 1964; Sorauf 1964). A second earlier focus of the literature on American parties adopted a more normative tone in proposing the need for parties to be responsible by offering voters sets of policy commitments which they would implement when they are in office, or serve as alternative sets of choices when they are in opposition (see Ranney 1975; Epstein 1968). Beginning in the 1970s, the unfolding of a number of propositions derived from the works of Schumpeter (1942) and Downs (1957) served as the basis of a new phase in the study of American parties increasingly dominated by the rational-choice perspective.

This third phase, based upon an analogy between the functioning of economic markets and the so-called political market, has reduced parties to groups of politicians competing for public office. While party models thus focusing on electoral competition have facilitated an extraordinary growth of studies by distinct schools of rational-choice scholars, they are problematic for the purpose of generating a theory of parties beyond the extremely formalized model of the American two-party system. To be sure, the definition of party set forth by Downs (1957: 25) presents clear advantages over the functionalist approach in its characterizations of parties as goal-oriented, of politicians as rational actors, and of their objectives as ranked according to preferences which can be achieved through access to government posts. But this approach is also problematic in so far as its analysis is based on a series of highly simplifying assumptions whose correspondence with reality is most questionable. One of these conceives of the party as a unitary actor or a unified 'team'. As Downs explained (1957: 25–6): 'By team, we mean a coalition whose members agree on all their goals instead of on just part of them. Thus every member of the team has exactly the same goals as every other . . . . In effect, this definition treats each party as though it were a single person.' Also problematic are simplifying assumptions about the motivations of politicians. Again as described by Downs (1957: 28), 'We assume that they act solely in order to attain the income, prestige and power which come from being in office. . . . [T]heir only goal is to reap the rewards of office per se. They treat policies purely as a means to the attainment of their private ends, which they can reach only by being elected.' Accordingly, 'parties formulate policies in order to win elections, rather than win elections in order to formulate policies'. This extremely reductionist characterization ignores the organizational complexity of parties (but see Schlesinger 1984, 1991), interactions among party members, the obvious existence of party preferences over policies, and their sometimes conflicted stands regarding objectives and preferences.[11] It also focuses its attention exclusively upon interparty electoral competition, which it portrays as competition between candidates.[12] Parties have virtually disappeared as significant actors in rational-choice analyses.[13] Indeed, most analyses of this kind go so far as to avoid explicit references to 'parties', subsuming the concept of party under the rubric of 'candidates'. And when such references do appear, they are often subjected to oversimplifications that run counter to reality and give rise to hypotheses that are of dubious validity.[14] As Roemer (forthcoming, Introduction) contends, the Downsian model and many of those who have adopted it make a grave error when they simplify these dynamics to the point of eliminating politics from political competition.

As a product of these conceptualizations and core assumptions, the contribution of the rational-choice literature to the development of theory regarding parties has been notably weak (notwithstanding the exceptions noted below). The criticisms of rational-choice applications in political science (such as by Green and Shapiro 1994) have been particularly pertinent to the study of parties: the universalistic claims of the axioms and assumptions of this approach have improperly and arbitrarily ignored the great variation in types of political parties; the method-driven (rather than problem-driven) selection of their hypotheses have greatly restricted their applicability and even relevance to many actual facets of party behaviour; and the explanatory capacity of the interactions between parties and voters or with other parties is also weak. Thus, the very same consistency and simplicity of the assumptions underpinning this approach that are allegedly so beneficial for the purpose of launching complementary, mutually compatible and potentially cumulative theory-building and hypothesis-testing are also sources of weakness when applied to the study of political parties, particularly with regard to their inability to capture the complexity, multidimensionality, and interactive nature of the objectives parties and their leaders pursue, the strategies they adopt, and their actual behaviour in the real world of politics. As has been noted, the analysis of party competition is a good case in point. In this volume, Stefano Bartolini carefully analyses the problems inherent in the one-dimensionality and ambiguity of the concept of competition, borrowed initially from economics and applied, often uncritically, to the political arena. As he demonstrates, many of the simplifying assumptions inherent in that economic approach do not fit with important aspects of actual competition in the world of politics. Accordingly, theory-building concerning political parties has been undermined by the poor fit between an often complex, messy, and multidimensional empirical reality, on the one hand, and an 'elegant' but often simplistic and unrealistic theory-building enterprise, on the other. Given these incompatibilities between simple models and a highly complex reality, doubts even arise concerning the extent to which these efforts to establish a single common framework for the deduction of hypotheses and the construction of a cumulative theory of politics may, in the end, prove to be counter-productive.

Fortunately, over the past several years some scholars have employed 'soft' rational choice approaches in their studies of parties. They acknowledge that the reduction of 'parties' to individual candidates in their models of electoral competition has weakened empirical analyses of parties. As Strøm concludes (1990*b*: 565), 'rational choice models of political parties . . . have failed to generate a simple, coherent theory of competitive party behavior or to produce robust results that apply under a variety of environmental conditions'. In contrast, these 'soft-rational-choice' studies have relaxed many of the core assumptions of the more rigid applications of this approach in their empirical analyses; their representations of the rationality of political actors are much more plausible (albeit still quite stylized); they have broadened the range of objectives pursued by politicians, and included in their analysis considerations of the constraints imposed on party behaviour by varying contexts; and they have paid more attention to empirical data in developing theoretical propositions regarding parties.[15] These studies have been based on systematic empirical analysis, and have sought to improve theory-building by taking into account the organizational complexity of parties, distinctions among party goals (differentiating among vote-seeking, office-seeking, and policy-seeking parties), and the interaction between the demands of voters and the nature of the offers extended by parties. Accordingly, they treat parties as endogenous variables whose organizational, ideological, and institutional characteristics are conditioned by the strategies pursued by party leaders (functioning as rational actors), and by the various contexts of the political systems within which they act. This literature has made significant advances towards establishing a common framework for theorizing about the behaviour of parties, the preferences of their leaders, and the conditions which affect the formation of governments in polities with distinct institutional structures. In our view, they have much greater prospects for making significant contributions to theory-building relevant to parties than do applications of simplistic economic models to the study of complex party organizations, and their interrelationships with distinct set of actors in society and government. Some problems remain, however, particularly with regard to the ability of this approach to integrate assumptions about the behaviour of the leaders of different kinds of parties within similar political systems, or of parties with common organizational characteristics in different systems. In this sense, it is noteworthy that the chapter in this volume by Wolinetz makes an effort to connect the classificatory schemes based upon the differing objectives pursued by party elites with operational criteria better suited for the generation of testable hypotheses and theory-building with regard to parties.

A third intellectual tradition is one that seeks to generate theoretical insights by employing an inductive approach to the study of parties. This more traditional and time-honoured school has elaborated large numbers of models and typologies of political parties. While much has been learnt about the structure, strategies, and behaviour of parties based upon middle-range hypotheses derived from these party types, this effort has also fallen short of expectations for the development of party theory. This is for a variety of reasons. First, most typologies of parties were based exclusively on the historical experiences of surprisingly few West European democracies during the first six decades of the twentieth century. This generally static conceptualization has limited applicability to parties in other countries (even in established democracies like that of the United States), is in many respects incapable of coping with the new challenges confronting parties that we noted earlier, and has become increasingly irrelevant to studies of the large numbers of parties that have emerged from the Third Wave of democratization that has swept across many parts of the world. Neither the classic (e.g. Duverger 1954; Neumann 1956) nor the more contemporary categorizing schema (e.g. Kirchheimer 1966; Panebianco 1988; Katz and Mair 1995) have been able to capture the full range of variation in the extremely large number of parties in the world today, particularly given the very small number of party types elaborated in each of these contributions.

Neither has this approach led to cumulative theory building, or even consensus on a categorization of parties according to a consistent set of criteria. Indeed, as Gunther and Diamond (2001) have pointed out, the various typologies have differed substantially with regard to the fundamental nature of the criteria used to distinguish among party types. Some (e.g. Neumann 1956; Kitschelt 1989*a*; Katz and Mair 1995) of these categorizations are based upon functional criteria, differentiating among parties on the basis of an organizational *raison d'être* or some specific goal that they pursue; others (Duverger 1954; Kitschelt 1994; Panebianco 1988) are organizational, distinguishing between parties that have thin organizational structures and those that have developed large infrastructures and complex networks of collaborative relationships with other secondary organizations; while others (e.g. Michels 1962 [1911]; Eldersveld 1964) have adopted sociological criteria, implicitly or explicitly basing their work on the notion that parties are the products of (and ought to represent the interests of) various social groups. Finally, there are some prominent scholars who indiscriminately mix all three of these sets of criteria, such as Kirchheimer (1966), who posits four party models: bourgeois parties of individual representation; class-mass parties; denominational mass parties; and catch-all people's parties.

As useful as these typologies are in identifying distinguishing characteristics of political parties, they are not inherently explanatory. Their greatest utility, as Rokkan (1967: 174) noted, is when multidimensional criteria have been employed to capture complex configurations of features, including elements that may be significant in a particular political context but at the same time allowing for comparative analysis on various dimensions. When misapplied, however, these typologies can induce scholars to fall into a methodological trap based upon the implicit assumption that a particular party type will become dominant and will characterize an entire phase in a long-term process of historical evolution, only to be followed by its displacement as the prototypical party by a different type in a subsequent period.[16] Moreover, a superficial and inappropriate use of party models can actually weaken both empirical studies and theory-building by leading to gross oversimplifications of party characteristics, unwarranted assumptions of commonalities (if not uniformity) among parties that are in fact quite varied, and the inappropriate application of labels (such as 'catch-all') to parties whose organizational, ideological, or strategic characteristics differ significantly from the original prototype. In short, scholars may feel compelled to attempt to cram round pegs into square holes because the available options are insufficient in number and variety to capture the essential nature of many real-world political parties. This leads, in turn, to inattention to potentially significant differences among parties, or strains and evolutionary tendencies within parties, that might have considerable theoretical relevance.

WHERE DO WE GO FROM HERE?

The study of parties should not be fundamentally different from other subfields of political science. As a scientific enterprise, it should reverse the vicious circle mentioned earlier into a virtuous circle, in which theoretical propositions help to stimulate and structure empirical research, and will, in turn, be validated, rejected, or modified on the basis of the findings of that empirical research. Accordingly, the basic canons of science reserve important roles for both inductive and deductive analytical processes. Induction is most appropriate for the generation of theoretical propositions that accord with the reality that they purport to explain. Deduction is necessary in order to derive from putative theoretical propositions testable hypotheses that can either be supported or rejected on the basis of empirical evidence. To date, this dialogue between the inductive and deductive phases of theory-building has been inadequate with regard to the study of political parties.

We have briefly surveyed two predominantly deductive efforts to establish a general theory of parties (if not of politics, more broadly construed): one of them, structural-functionalism, was imported from the fields of anthropology and sociology; the other, rational-choice analysis, from economics. In our view, neither has achieved its objective of establishing a common analytical framework, generally acknowledged by a consensus among scholars within the discipline as an acceptable if not fully valid basis for research and for theory-building.[17] The paradigmatic status of structural-functionalism in political science lasted less than a decade before it was virtually abandoned as a framework for analysis. Rational-choice approaches have been much more persistent: with regard to the study of parties, they have been employed by a minority of scholars over more than four decades. But by the end of the twentieth century, the more rigid and orthodox versions of rational-choice theory had failed to approach remotely paradigmatic status in the field, or even to convince a majority of scholars working in this area that it provided a valid, or even useful, way of framing both theoretical and empirical studies of party behaviour. To be sure, much of value has been derived from 'soft' applications of this approach, which rigorously test selected rational-choice-generated hypotheses using empirical data. Given the advances made by practitioners of this related approach, it is unlikely that there will be many scholars who choose to employ the more orthodox, overwhelmingly deductive, and non-empirical versions of rational-choice theory: indeed, for the reasons also stated above (and more elaborately in the chapter by Stefano Bartolini), we have doubts about the validity of the fundamental analogy between simple economic models of profit-maximizing individuals, on the one hand, and complex, multidimensional parties, pursuing a variety of objectives within widely varying contexts, on the other. Indeed, we question whether it is reasonable to strive for the formulation of *a* single, all-encompassing theory of parties, let alone of politics in general. We share this scepticism with a number of other scholars who reject the notion that a general theory could be constructed that would explain, through a series of inter-related propositions, such diverse phenomena as those ranging from the organizational features of parties to the impact of party activities on the lives of citizens. In short, we fear that the search for a general theory of parties (or politics) may prove to be as fruitless as the search for the Holy Grail.

This is not to say that the predominantly inductive, empirically based studies that dominate the parties literature have culminated in the development of a satisfactory body of middle-range theory. While many interesting theoretical insights can be gleaned from this enormous literature, and many rich empirical studies represent significant contributions to political science, this field of study is excessively cluttered with concepts, terminologies, and typologies that are either unnecessarily redundant (with different terms used to describe the same basic phenomena) or not comparable or cumulative (being based on fundamentally different classificatory criteria). While 'let a hundred flowers bloom' may be an excellent strategy for encouraging the proliferation of novel developments in a new field, at a certain point it becomes desirable to remove the weeds from the garden and concentrate on the cultivation of the more fruitful offspring. Thus, we believe that the study of parties would benefit from adopting analytical strategies solidly based on the middle ground between the deductive and sometimes excessively simplifying, method-driven and barely empirical approaches, on the one hand, and the empirically driven studies that have occasionally culminated in a cacophony of sometimes compatible but redundant, sometimes incompatible and non-cumulative concepts, typologies, and models, on the other. As Janda (1993: 184) has proposed, 'Our challenge is now to assimilate, develop, and extend existing theory rather than to wait for a general theory to descend on high.'[18]

What kinds of steps could be taken to strengthen middle-range theories and testable hypotheses concerning political parties? One approach (as proposed by Beyme 1985; Wolinetz 1998c) is to develop partial theories dealing with specific aspects of parties, but which go well beyond mere schematic description or empirical generalization. This approach has been effectively utilized in closely related subfields in political science. In the subfield of electoral behaviour, for example, this kind of approach is best exemplified by 'social cleavage theory', in which a coherent set of explanatory hypotheses (based upon a common set of assumptions and concepts, and consistently using a common vocabulary and generally compatible empirical methodologies) have been systematically tested over more than four decades. This body of theory has not only been able to reach broad consensus in its empirical findings, but it has also generated fruitful theoretical innovations, and has been highly sensitive to changes in the strength of the cleavage-anchoring of the vote over the past several decades.[19] A second approach would be to further lower the barriers between predominantly deductive approaches, such as rational-choice theory, and more inductive traditional approaches. Such a course of action has been endorsed by prominent scholars in both camps. Barnes (1997: 135), whose roots are in the more traditional inductive-empirical camp, has, for example, called for the development of general theories through the integration of what he calls inductive islands of theory and the principal achievements of rational choice. In many respects, the gaps between the two approaches are not that great, as the recent flourishing of 'soft rational-choice' studies would attest. From the rational-choice camp, Schlesinger (1984: 118) has argued that claims concerning the absence of theory on parties are simply overstated, since there exists a common framework underpinning the majority of monographs on parties, even though it may be necessary to polish, systematize, and empirically test this theoretical framework. Relatedly, Müller and Strøm (1999b: 307) call for much more frequent engagement between research traditions characterized by formal modelling and by more empirical and inductive approaches. While such an approach would entail an abandonment of the universalistic pretensions based upon strict assumptions of rationality, which often preclude systematic empirical testing, it could also push otherwise atheoretical descriptive studies of parties towards the more conscious generation and testing of hypotheses oriented towards theory-building.

A third approach would be to maintain a largely inductive/empirical stance but to facilitate hypothesis generation and testing by consolidating the myriad existing typologies, and adopting a standard terminology to describe fundamentally equivalent models of parties that are currently grouped under different labels. This, in turn, would require a standardization of the criteria upon which parties are categorized and, if necessary, elaboration of additional models to capture the essence of parties that have emerged in some of the new Third Wave democracies outside of the heavily studied West European and North American regions, or in the long-established democracies since the traditional typologies were formulated.[20] The benefits of such an approach can be seen in another two closely related subfields, the dynamics of party systems[21] and the effects of electoral systems:[22] both have been greatly facilitated by a common set of concepts, vocabulary, and formulas for calculating their main operational indicators. General agreement on the meaning and operationalization of these concepts has made it possible to compare consistently and precisely democratic party systems with one another, and to monitor their evolution over several decades. No such standardization of concepts, terminology, or operational indicators has taken place yet with regard to the study of political parties, *per se.*

Another, more modest but necessary approach, which is adopted in this volume, is to re-examine critically these old typologies, concepts, and the assumptions underpinning them. The ultimate development of more comprehensive, systematic, and coherent models of parties, for example, requires an understanding of the strengths and weaknesses of the existing typologies. This book also explores some of the standard criticisms of political parties, with the objective of identifying common errors in empirical studies based upon these concepts, as well new questions upon which empirical research could profitably be focused. The chapter by Hans Daalder, for example, discusses the analytical biases and value-laden assumptions that undermine the credibility of many contributions to the party-decline literature. Similarly, Hans-Jürgen Puhle criticizes the misapplication of the term 'catch-all' to parties very different from those Kirchheimer had in mind when he formulated that concept. The chapter by Richard S. Katz and Peter Mair also goes beyond the traditional approach to the use of party models by analysing the interrelationships among different models of party organization (the cadre, mass, catch-all, and cartel parties) and among different 'faces' of parties.[23] In a similar vein, Jean Blondel argues that the differing roles played by party patronage within various institutional settings have important implications for party performance and decline. Steven B. Wolinetz critically re-examines the existing classificatory schema and proposes that we focus our attention on the distinction among vote-seeking, policy-seeking, and office-seeking parties. And Stefano Bartolini rigorously explores the assumptions underpinning the application of simple economic models of competition to the study of electoral competition. The chapters by Serenella Sferza, and Richard Gunther and Jonathan Hopkin undertake analytical case studies of particular parties, and demonstrate the extraordinary importance of different party models for their performance and even survival. Finally, comparative analyses of survey data enable Juan J. Linz and Torcal, Gunther, and Montero to challenge common assumptions about the meaning, the origins, and the behavioural consequences of anti-party attitudes among the general public. Linz concludes by raising a number of issues that he believes should serve as the basis of future empirical analysis.

RECONCEPTUALIZING, RE-EXAMINING AND REVISITING PARTIES

The principal objective of this book is to lay the groundwork for future theory-building efforts regarding political parties by re-examining some of the established concepts, models, and linkages that have underpinned this field for the past five decades, and by further exploring their applicability to parties today. The book is divided into three parts. It begins with chapters devoted to a reconceptualization of basic aspects of political parties. In the second part, our contributing authors re-examine party models based upon a set of organizational criteria. Finally, the last group of chapters revisit several significant dimensions of party linkages. From a variety of perspectives— both conceptual and empirical—these ten chapters are intended to contribute to the refinement of cumulative knowledge about political parties, to the formulation of testable hypotheses that can serve as the basis for the building of middle-range theory, and to theoretical propositions with greater explanatory power.

Reconceptualizing Parties and Party Competition

In the first part, Hans Daalder systematically analyses writings since the beginning of the twentieth century that have dealt with an alleged 'crisis of parties', or, as described since the 1970s, 'party decline'. Daalder criticizes the normative or ideological pseudoconcepts used implicitly or explicitly in this literature with extraordinary frequency in generally negative assessments of the status of parties in Western Europe. The term 'crisis of parties', he finds, was commonly used as a euphemism to reflect a rejection of parties in general, or a party in particular. This is most clearly the case with the first of the four varieties of this literature, which he calls 'denial of party'. Shortly after the appearance of mass parties, studies by Ostrogorski (1964 [1902]) and Michels (1962 [1911]) denounced the subordination of individual to organization, and of the latter to party leaders. Daalder identifies two distinct sets of arguments under this critical common rubric: one was articulated by those who were nostalgic for a traditional and supposedly harmonious political order; and the other by individualists and liberals who conceived of the party as a tyrannical and antidemocratic organization. The subsequent establishment of the

Parteienstaat (analysed in greater depth by Hans-Jürgen Puhle in this volume) conferred legitimacy on parties, but this did not preclude a second type of criticism, focusing on certain types of parties or party systems. Among European scholars, catch-all parties were the targets of this new round of criticism, while in the United States parties were criticized on the grounds that they were not 'responsible' (with the American Political Science Association passing a resolution in favour of a 'more responsible two-party system': APSA 1950). A third type of criticism, based on highly idealistic impressions of the British two-party system, focused on multi-party systems. Even though only a small minority of democracies have a two-party system, it was seen by some as the 'natural' party system by those who either preferred majoritarian electoral principles or preferred to analyse partisan competition from a rational-choice perspective. The fourth group of critics are those who view parties as 'redundant', having fulfilled their basic function of mobilizing the mass electorate, or having degenerated into mere electoral machines. In their view, parties are likely to disappear or, at least, continue to decline as a consequence of the emergence of new social movements and the acquisition of new personal resources by citizens. These waves of criticism in the literature are problematic from two perspectives, Daalder argues. The first is that each of these normative arguments is linked exclusively to a particular party, to a particular historical epoch, or to a particular country. Daalder warns that those engaged in concept-building should take care to avoid such normative biases, and should be specific in stating the criteria underpinning their formulation. And he concludes by noting that more a rigorous analysis of key concepts can debunk easy 'generalizations' or conventional wisdoms that commonly circulate within various academic circles or the general public, and, in turn, can yield more refined concepts and facilitate theory-building.

While Daalder critically re-examines the pseudoconcepts that have appeared in the 'crisis of parties' literature since the beginning of the twentieth century, Hans-Jürgen Puhle focuses his analysis on the 'crisis' of the catch-all party since the 1970s. He discusses in great detail the restructuring that Western catch-all parties have undergone in response to new challenges arising out of changes in society and in the *Parteienstaat* within which they function. Puhle's chapter displays a rich combination of theoretical, typological, conceptual, and empirical elements in its analysis of the evolution of the catch-all party. He also presents a critical re-examination of theorizing about European political parties. In a manner similar to arguments set forth by Katz and Mair in their chapter, Puhle's analysis distinguishes among three waves of party-building, culminating in four types of party that have emerged over the past century in Europe. And also like Katz and Mair, Puhle cautions us that these historical phases are merely suggestive: models of parties are 'ideal types' that do not neatly correspond to real-world political parties. Instead, most parties contain a mix of characteristics of different types, although usually one or another is sufficiently pronounced as to allow the analyst to characterize parties as close enough to one or another as to be placed within the typology. Both because the historical phases he identifies are illustrative rather than definitive, and because most real-world parties only roughly approximate the defining criteria of the ideal types of parties that make up most typologies, it would be particularly inappropriate to assume that any one type of party was dominant within any given historical phase. Party types, argues Puhle, usually overlap the boundaries of historical periods, and the simultaneous interaction among parties of different types helps to drive the evolution of parties.

These caveats notwithstanding, Puhle makes three important points. The first is to remind us of that the catch-all party, as defined by Kirchheimer (1966), was an outgrowth of the mass-integration party, as described by Neumann (1956). Accordingly, this concept included certain specific criteria that make many misapplications of this term inappropriate: it is much more than simply a residual category to describe the full panoply of parties that have emerged since the heyday of the mass-based party. Second, he claims that most of the major parties of Europe are still predominantly catch-all. But, third, he points to a widespread tendency since the early 1980s towards lower levels of organization and societal penetration of parties. Social demo-cratic, Christian democratic, and conservative parties in Western Europe have adapted to the challenges of the past two decades by re-equilibrating (not by breaking down or declining) on the basis of a new type of party, which he calls the 'catch-all plus' party. This new kind of party has a smaller and less structured organizational base, and is more flexible in its efforts to remain electorally competitive. The negative aspects of these characteristics, how-ever, include a 'short-termism' and 'ad-hockery' in their programmatic and electoral appeals, coupled with a reduced capacity for social integration and mediation. Overall, this development is suggestive not of 'party decline' in the face of new challenges, but of adaptation and continuity, albeit in a somewhat different organizational form and with different behavioural characteristics. More broadly, Puhle concludes that this process of adaptation underlines the importance for scholars of continuing to study parties, to reconsider their fundamental conceptualizations whenever they cease to conform to com-monly accepted party models, and to avoid the conceptual paralysis that has too often characterized the study of parties. While parsimony remains a desir-able characteristic of typologies, reconceptualization and the development of new models may be necessary in order to cope with new challenges in future historical periods and in different kinds of democratic systems that are emerg-ing in other world regions.

The chapter by Stefano Bartolini focuses on the concept of electoral and party competition as the key mechanism leading party elites to respond to the preferences of voters.[24] While competition is of central importance in both democratic theory and in empirical studies of party behaviour, the concept (as operationalized in many studies) is vague and ambiguous. In particular, it has very different meanings in the real world of electoral and parliamentary behaviour, on the one hand, and in the formal models of rational-choice scholars, on the other. Bartolini presents a rigorous critique of the problems inherent in applying this import from economic theory to the study of competition between political parties. One significant problem (which we discussed earlier) is that this approach requires an excessive simplification of political reality. Perhaps even more fundamental are problems resulting from differences between the economic and political markets, to the extent that the analogy between the two breaks down in several important respects. Following an overview of its intellectual origins (e.g. Simmel 1955 [1908]; Schumpeter 1942; Downs 1957), the bulk of the chapter is dedicated to an impressively original criticism of this approach based on a detailed consideration of the basic nature of competition in these two different spheres of human and institutional interaction, or 'markets'. Bartolini focuses his attention on several key dimensions of competition, not to mention of democracy itself—contestability, availability, decidability, and vulnerability. He further argues that these four crucial dimensions of competition interact with one another in ways that are fundamentally incompatible with the simplifying assumptions upon which the economic model depends. Each of the dimensions of party competition impinges on the others in an interactive, if not sometimes contradictory manner. A decrease in availability can create disincentives for electoral competition, while an increase can lead to high levels of electoral volatility. If decidability is low, parties are presented with powerful incentives to engage in collusive practices on the basis of their minimal differences regarding issues and policies; but if it is high, it can lead to ideological polarization. And if vulnerability is low, it can make parties unresponsive in so far as they feel secure; but if it is too high, it can culminate in a decisional paralysis by parties out of fear of alienating voters. As a result of these multidimensional interaction effects, party competition cannot be conceived of as a linear process that unfolds between minimum and maximum points on a single continuum, but rather as a moving point shifting about in a four-dimensional space within which no equilibrium point can be identified. Accordingly, electoral preferences cannot be regarded as exogenous to party competition, but are decisively influenced by parties and party elites.

In combination with the findings of the two previous chapters, these conclusions have important theoretical implications. Most importantly, they suggest that competition cannot be treated as a unidimensional phenomenon whose optimal conditions can be quantified. Instead, it is a multidimensional phenomenon in which the maximization of preferences on one dimension has direct and often negative repercussions for another dimension. Analyses of policy stands or electoral appeals can only be based upon a study of decisions made by political elites, acting within particular historical contexts and weighing conflicting considerations of trade-offs among these various dimensions of party competition. This does not imply that generalizations cannot be made about various combinations among these dimensions of competition; nor does it preclude the systematic study of elite strategies and decision-making. But it does argue that analytical frameworks must stand up to the test of feasibility, and must take into consideration those factors that have empirically and theoretically significant impact on the behaviour of parties, candidates, and voters. The fact that party competition is affected by the interaction among several different dimensions is not symptomatic of imperfections in the market; it is, instead, a reflection of the true context within which party elites must make their strategic decisions.

Re-examining Party Organization and Party Models

The second part of this book reexamines various facets of party organization. As one might imagine, the literature on party organization is considerable. Many of the classic works on parties—such as Michels (1962 [1911]), Duverger (1954), Neumann (1956), Eldersveld (1964), and Kirchheimer (1966)—dealt extensively with typologies of party organizations and the problems associated with different party types. Subsequently, however, attention was shifted away from a concern with party organization, *per se*. Many studies focused on the relationship linking parties with citizens, especially through analyses of voting behaviour, or with governmental institutions, in public policy analyses. The abandonment of concern with parties as organizations is most extreme in the case of rational-choice studies, whose conception of the party as a unitary actor explicitly ignores its organizational complexity (Daalder 1983: 21). To be sure, there were significant exceptions to this trend.[25] But we are far from achieving the goals of the research agenda set forth by Mair (1997: 41–4) to go beyond simplistic classifications of party organization, to develop empirical indicators regarding the internal life of parties, to monitor the relationships between organizational change and electoral volatility, and to test hypotheses accounting both for the diversity of, and change within, party organizations. The four chapters included in this part of the book address some of the questions arising out of this agenda, and make significant contributions to advancing this theory-building enterprise.

The chapter by Richard S. Katz and Peter Mair examines the interactions among models of party organization and the shifting internal balance of power over the course of the twentieth century. Specifically, it links four different models of party organization (the cadre or elite party, the mass party, the catch-all party, and the cartel party) with the three 'faces' of parties: 'on the ground,' 'in the central office', and 'in public office'. They argue that the strategies of party elites, in combination with the institutional processes of party competition in advanced democracies, have led to the ascendancy of 'the party in public office', and a commensurate subordination of the other two faces of parties.[26] Consistent with the line of argument advanced by Puhle in this volume, Katz and Mair warn against simplistically linking party models with the developmental trajectory of parties: the basic nature of parties is not determined by a particular historical state, and various party types may coexist simultaneously in democratic party systems. Instead, over the course of history, organizational 'inventions' may appear, providing party elites with a new addition to the available repertoire of institutional forms that may be emulated. Inertia, contradictory developments, and mixes of factors help also to determine the more distinguishing features of the type of party at any one point in time. They further argue that each of these party models may be more compatible with one or another of the various roles played by parties. The catch-all party, for example, fits better with the role of the party-in-central-office, the elite party with the party-in-public-office under liberal regimes, and the mass party model with the nexus between the party-on-the-ground and the party-in-central-office. However, since the 1960s, when the catch-all party model crystallized, there have been significant changes, particularly with regard to the privileged position of the party-in-public-office. These conditions are associated with the emergence of the 'cartel party' (see Katz and Mair 1995, 1996), the electoral-professional party (Panebianco 1988), and the modern cadre party (Koole 1994, 1996). Among the factors that have facilitated these developments are public financing of parties and election campaigns (which are primarily allocated by party elites who also control public offices), as well as the increasing use of party staff by public office-holders, the personalization and centralization of election campaigns, and the increasing importance of professionals with expertise regarding campaigns and mass communications (also see Müller 2000*a*: 317–19). In turn, the privileged position of party elites, the cartelization of parties, and practices regarding party patronage or corruption have contributed to a delegitimation of parties, the growth of anti-party sentiments among citizens, and general dissatisfaction with party performance.[27] As we will see below, the chapters by Blondel, Torcal, Gunther and Montero, and Linz explore these themes in greater detail.

The chapter by Steven B. Wolinetz approaches the subject of party organization from a complementary perspective: where Katz and Mair re-examine party organization on the basis of interactions among party models and the various 'faces' of parties, Wolinetz uses party organization as the basis for criticizing the validity of existing typologies of parties, and to propose new classificatory criteria. Among the sources of his dissatisfaction with the existing typologies are the inability of the strikingly small number of party models to capture the essence of the extremely wide variety of parties that exist today, the fact that these party models are in some cases primarily oriented towards describing parties as they existed over a hundred years ago, and that they are largely limited in their applicability to West European parties. The net result is that they have largely been incapable of capturing the variations among the many new parties that have appeared since the beginning of the Third Wave of democratization in the 1970s. The homogenizing biases implicit in the static nature of the relatively few categories used to typologize parties, moreover, tends to give rise to an appearance of 'convergence' among parties, overlooking basic differences in their principal objectives, their strategies for achieving those goals, and their responses to constraints or opportunities arising from the contexts within which they function. He points out that these limitations are particularly noteworthy even with regard to their application to parties in France, the Netherlands, Canada, and the United States, let alone those in new democracies, with more recently formulated party types (such as Ware 1987a; Koole 1994; Grabow 2001). The criteria set forth by Kirchheimer (1966) defining the catch-all parties, for example, cannot differentiate between American and Canadian parties despite their manifold divergences. Panebianco's (1988) contribution remedies some of these shortcomings, but it is substantially weakened by its assumptions of homogenizing trends among Western parties: he believes that his electoral-professional party is a type whose features will be adopted by all parties, irrespective of their distinct origins or basic organizational features. Finally, the cartel party of Katz and Mair (1995) is useful for identifying some features of parties that have emerged over the past two decades, but it is not clear that this is a model of a distinct type of party or a description of dynamic interactions between parties in a party system (see Koole 1996; Katz and Mair 1996). Given the limitations of these other classification schemes, Wolinetz proposes that we focus on the distinctions among policy-seeking, vote-seeking, and office-seeking parties, which he believes will make it possible to study significant questions regarding party behaviour and party organization. Wolinetz then discusses how operational indicators of these different orientations might be developed (see Müller and Strøm 1999a and 1999b; Strøm and Müller 1999). The development of this approach would, it is hoped, facilitate the formulation and testing of hypotheses concerning the behaviour of parties, cross-national comparisons among parties—especially with regard to how parties have responded to the challenges that have arisen over the past two decades—and, overall, in the enrichment of potentially cumulative theoretical propositions about parties.

Serenella Sferza's study of the French Socialist party since the 1970s goes well beyond typical case studies of parties by explicitly analysing a series of theoretical propositions concerning party organizational behaviour. She begins with a criticism of the literature on party decline, particularly on 'externalist' interpretations of party development that portray parties as 'passive takers' or as actors who merely react to developments arising out of their social-structural or institutional environments. Sferza argues that the behaviour of parties must be analysed both from 'within' and 'without'. Particularly important factors relevant to explanations of strategic choices and party performance are the specific organizational form adopted by the party, the relationship between intra-party resources, and inter-party politics (see also Kitschelt 1989*a*; 1994). In the case of the French Socialist party, she argues that a series of internal changes in the 1970s helped the party to win two impressive electoral victories in 1981, electing François Mitterand as President of the Republic, and securing a Socialist majority in the National Assembly. But by the mid-1980s, a number of problems of internal origin coupled with electoral defeats dramatically reversed the fortunes of the party. Sferza argues that the factionalism explicitly organized and recognized following the party's 1971 congress greatly facilitated its growth and electoral success. But this same institutionalized factionalism made it difficult for the party to adapt flexibly to new challenges emerging from altered environmental circumstances during the following decade. Thus, the same organizational feature that proved to be such an asset under one set of conditions proved to be a liability when it faced different kinds of challenges. Sferza undertakes a detailed empirical analysis of her hypotheses both at the national level of French politics and in two strategically chosen provincial branches of the party. She begins with an exploration of the advantages and drawbacks of the traditional territorial format for party organization versus the factional structure that the party adopted in the 1970s. Among the advantages she notes are the contributions of a factional structure to ideological revitalization, to recruitment of party activists, to leadership renewal, and to party governance. Once the party was elected to large numbers of important public offices at all levels of government in the 1980s, however, factions abandoned their previous competitive stance and adopted a more collusive pattern of interaction, converting factionalism into a source of destabilizing paralysis. Three sets of theoretical implications emerge from this analysis. First, the adaptive capacity of parties depends to a considerable degree on the organizational forms adopted. Second, the substantial impact of the particular organizational form adopted by the party further illustrates why oversimplified party typologies do a disservice to comparative analysis by ignoring an important factor that so powerfully influences party behaviour. And third, the challenges that faced the Socialist Party in the 1970s when it was out of power were fundamentally different from those when it governed France in the 1980s, underscoring the importance of party–government relations.

Richard Gunther and Jonathan Hopkin also examine the impact of various organizational models on party performance in a detailed case study.[28] They conclude that the demise of the UCD is attributable to the party's lack of institutionalization. While invocation of this concept as an explanation of party failure could be construed as tautological, they break down the concept of institutionalization into its key component parts and carefully document how one aspect of institutionalization, in particular, proved to be so important. The UCD's institutionalization was not at all deficient with regard to the development of an extensive organization or to its penetration into Spanish government institutions at all levels. Instead, the failure of institutionalization affected interactions among the party's top-ranking leaders in Madrid, far too many of whom saw the party in purely utilitarian terms as merely a vehicle for achieving their short-term objectives, and who failed to 'infuse with value' (to cite Selznick's [1957] classic definition of institutionalization) or to develop a sense of abstract loyalty to the party. This lack of institutionalization was also manifested in fundamental and unresolved differences of opinion over the model of party that should guide its organizational development, its electoral strategies, and, most importantly, its norms of internal governance. The party's founder, Prime Minister Adolfo Suárez, favoured development of a classic catch-all party under strong presidential leadership. But the party's 'barons' had very different models in mind. Several of them implicitly favoured development of the party along 'factional' lines, which would be governed through collective decision-making processes by the leaders of the various factions, and which would allocate both party and governmental posts proportionately, in a quasi-consociational manner (see Huneeus 1985). Other party leaders demanded that the party establish strong institutional ties to, and stoutly defend the interests of, specific social groups (such as the Church and big business), virtually reducing the party to the status of a 'holding company'. Differences over these party models were manifested in various aspects of the party's performance in government, leading to an unseemly series of public squabbles, and ultimately schisms and defections of prominent leaders, that had the net effect of thoroughly discrediting the party. While tensions and conflicts are produced inside of all parties whenever there are differences of opinion regarding personnel appointments, the formulation of government policy, or the adoption of an electoral strategy, the lack of commitment to the party in the abstract, coupled with a lack of a common understanding of behavioural norms and intra-party decision-making processes—all of them aspects of institutionalization—made it impossible for the party to contain these struggles successfully. Accordingly, it abruptly disappeared in the aftermath of the single most disastrous electoral defeat in West European history.

Revisiting Party Linkages and Attitudes towards Parties

The three chapters in this third part of the book deal with two distinct sets of questions. What these have in common is that they explore the extent to which the progressive weakening of party linkages has contributed to party decline in Western Europe. The first of these questions deals with linkages between governments and parties in parliamentary democracies, specifically, the extent to which party government is based in some European systems upon patronage and corruption. The second set of questions involves linkages between parties and citizens, in particular, the extent to which these ties have been undermined by the widespread emergence of anti-party sentiments. Those two distinct sets of questions have both been largely ignored in the comparative literature on political parties. Inattention to patronage or corrupt practices within the party–government literature has often meant that an important determinant of party or government performance is either not dealt with analytically, or is attributed in an ad hoc manner to spurious factors. And most studies of political behaviour by voters restrict their analytical focus to the act of voting, *per se*, or to positive linkages between citizens and parties, such as their psychological attachments to their preferred party in the literature on party identification or their membership in party organizations. This excessively narrow view of these relationships therefore neglects more generic orientations of voters towards parties, party politics, and politicians which have an important impact on their involvement in political life. The three final chapters in this book are oriented towards filling this gap in the literature on party linkages: the chapter by Jean Blondel explores party government, patronage, and party decline within Western European parliamentary systems; and the chapters by Mariano Torcal, Richard Gunther, and José Ramón Montero, and by Juan J. Linz, present preliminary analyses of anti-party sentiments, and their attitudinal and behavioural correlates, as well as empirically grounded speculation about the origins of such attitudes.

Blondel approaches the question of party decline from a novel perspective. His starting-point is a simple question: 'To what extent is party decline a product of semi-legal or illegal practices adopted by parties?' At first glance, the answer should be positive: the discovery of corruption or the distribution of favours by parties has made them the target of attacks of the mass media that have fed into increasing citizen dissatisfaction with or disaffection from parties. Blondel, however, adopts a more cautious and conditional stance: negative electoral consequences of illegal or semi-legal practices have been inconsistent among countries with significant levels of corruption. He therefore develops a series of analytical distinctions and empirical generalizations focusing on the concepts of party government and patronage.[29] Starting from the notion that the most basic linkages between governments and their supporting parties involve policies and appointments, he notes that traditional parliamentary theory neglects patronage as one important aspect of these linkages. While these interactions are often regarded as unappealing if not distasteful, patronage does exist, is increasing in some countries, and is manifested in many different forms (see also Müller 2000*b*; Cotta 2000). In an effort to speculate about the origins of cross-national differences in the extent of patronage, Blondel develops a classification scheme based upon two dimensions. The first is derived from the various types of party-government relationships as described in the classic studies by Lijphart (1984, 1999), which distinguish among 'adversarial,' 'consensual', and 'conciliatory' types of interaction. The second dimension involves the extent of parliamentary support for the government, ranging from minority government to oversized coalitions. In addition to these dimensions, it is important to distinguish among those parliamentary settings in which parties are, in general terms, dependent upon the government (as in Britain, France, and Spain), those in which parties predominate over the government (as in Belgium, Austria, and pre-1992 Italy), and those in which the government and its supporting party/ies are linked in a situation of mutual interdependence (such as the Dutch and the Scandinavian cases). These typologies enable Blondel to analyse the extent of patronage within differing institutional contexts. He finds that patronage is extensive and widely distributed in 'partitocratic' countries, is less common in Westminster majoritarian systems, and is greatly reduced in 'conciliatory' systems. Since the 1980s, there has been a notable growth in patronage, but only in the first two of these categories. Blondel suggests that this increase is the result of the predominance of governments with extremely ambitious programmes which would be difficult or impossible to implement; as a partial substitute for these unfulfilled programme commitments, favours, bribes, and corruption are utilized in an effort to maintain smooth and conflict-free party–government relations.

Blondel further argues that an assessment of the effects of patronage also requires a differentiation among types of party government. Given the extent to which patronage has always been widespread within partitocratic systems, it could not be argued that this factor can account for the decline in public support for parties in recent years. But given the significant differences in party performance among the partitocratic systems of Italy, Belgium, and Austria, some kind of explanation is still called for. In the majoritarian, Westminster type of parliamentary system, patronage has increased, but its contribution to party decline does not extend beyond some limited impact upon the short-term fortunes of the major parties. Blondel concludes with a note of caution. Even though it does not appear that patronage has contributed directly to party decline, it certainly poses considerable problems for the parties of Western Europe which vary depending upon the specific institutional framework of party–government relations. While some level of patronage is inevitable in any democratic system, a heavy reliance on favours, shady deals, corruption, and the like as a principal linkage between governments and their supporting parties poses significant problems with regard to the accountability of politicians and the responsiveness of parties.

The chapter by Torcal, Gunther, and Montero analyses, using survey data collected in Spain and (to a lesser extent) other Southern European countries

over the past three decades, the nature, evolution, and behavioural consequences of anti-party attitudes among citizens. It addresses one of the most
uncontestable aspects of the 'decline of party' literature—that is, that large
and increasing numbers of citizens in Western democracies have attitudes
towards parties that are negative if not downright cynical (see for instance
Poguntke and Scarrow 1996a). But it does so in a much more nuanced manner than is typical of this literature, which is often characterized by sweeping
and undocumented assertions about the 'crisis of parties', if not a broader
'crisis of democracy'. Empirical analysis of a number of the most commonly
used survey items tapping into public attitudes towards parties reveals that
such orientations are to two distinct types, which the authors call 'reactive
antipartyism' and 'cultural antipartyism'. *Reactive antipartyism* is a critical
stance adopted by citizens in response to their discontent and/or frustrations
with the performance of party elites and institutions. To some extent, it may
be the product of the inability of parties to meet the unrealistically high expectations of voters. But it may also arise out of actual failures of party performance, particularly with regard to a lack of success in managing the economy
or in enacting promised policies. It is also likely to emerge in reaction against
corruption scandals. In any event, aggregate levels of such attitudes should be
expected to fluctuate over time, in accord with citizens' varying levels of satisfaction with the performance of parties, particularly the party or parties in
government. The authors find that, indeed, the evolution of such attitudes
accords with this prediction. The second kind of anti-party attitude, *cultural
antipartyism*, in contrast, is more durable over time. The authors find that this
set of beliefs is rooted in the core values and historical traditions of a political
culture, and independent of short-term changes in a country's political conditions. Accordingly, such attitudes are acquired at a particular stage in an
individual's socialization process, and remain generally stable throughout the
life of the individual citizen. As several cohort analyses confirm, there are
systematic differences among age cohorts that reflect differences in their
respective socialization experiences during that particularly intense state of
political-attitude development.

The authors argue that much of the literature on antiparty attitudes has
produced inconsistent and unpersuasive conclusions as a result of an analytical inattention to the differences between these two varieties of attitudes.
They point out that reactive and cultural antipartyism have distinctly different attitudinal and behavioural correlates. Respondents with cultural anti-
party attitudes tend to avoid the development of a sense of identification with
parties, shun involvement with organized secondary associations, vote for
anti-system parties, and abstain from both conventional and unconventional
forms of political participation and protest. Reactive antipartyism is part of
an attitudinal domain that is both conceptually and empirically distinct from
the political disaffection syndrome. These attitudes are very much a function

of the respondent's degree of satisfaction with the performance of the incumbent government, which is, in turn, strongly influenced by his/her own partisan preferences. Accordingly, it is not surprising to find that in Spain and Greece (but not Portugal or Italy) a principal behavioural consequence of holding reactive anti-party attitudes is to vote against the incumbent party. The authors conclude from this empirical analysis that much greater caution should be exercised in extrapolating system-wide implications from the presence of anti-party attitudes than is typically the case in the 'decline of parties' literature. Reactive anti-party attitudes are quite limited in their behavioural ramifications, and do not imply any significant threat to support for democracy. In so far as such sentiments periodically increase, they tend to culminate in mass behaviour that is perfectly consistent with democratic theory—votes for the incumbent party (but not support for democracy) tend to fall. Cultural antipartyism has more negative implications for the quality of democracy in so far it is associated with the marginalization of a sector of society from active participation in political life.

In the last chapter of this volume, Juan Linz examines the same theme of anti-party sentiments among the general public, but from an entirely different perspective. Supporting his speculative hypotheses with survey data from Spain and Latin America, he suggests that the increase in negative attitudes towards political parties may be less attributable to the behaviour of parties themselves than it is to inconsistencies or outright contradictions among relevant beliefs held by citizens, to unrealistic expectations concerning the extent to which parties can achieve a series of demanding objectives, or to the increasing number of the functions that parties must play in representative democracies (see also Linz 199, 2000). Linz notes, for example, that people tend to give high marks to non-partisan figures who represent national unity. In part because they are 'above politics' and they do not pit segments of society against one another, heads of state in parliamentary systems are highly valued, while parties, which divide people and compete with one another for office, are consistently given lower marks. The unsolvable problem that parties face in this respect is that the basic function they are supposed to serve in democratic system is to represent the interests of one or another segment of society, and seek to advance those interests through victory in electoral competition. Large majorities of citizens in most countries acknowledge that 'Without parties there can be no democracy', but those same individuals often criticize parties for their 'divisive' behaviour. Another striking inconsistency is that most citizens in democratic systems want parties to represent 'their interests'; at the same time, they criticize parties in the abstract for representing 'special interests'. This seemingly self-contradictory stand is usually rooted in one simple pair of assumptions. When they affect the individual's own group, there are regarded as 'our interests' or 'the interests of people like me'; but when these same kinds of issues involve the interests of others, they are pejoratively regarded as 'special interests'. Similarly, many of them simultaneously complain that 'parties are all alike', while they also castigate parties for creating 'conflicts that don't exist'. These are just a few among the many inconsistencies and incompatibilities in popular attitudes that have often led to criticism of political parties that are explored by Linz in his provocative essay. Parties can thus be seen as stuck 'between a rock and a hard place'. Citizens acknowledge that democratic systems require that parties perform certain roles, but then criticize them for performing those roles on the grounds that this would conflict with a different and incompatible set of values. The result has been the widespread adoption of anti-party attitudes among both old and new democracies. But what does this imply for the future of democracy? Apart from the occasional adoption of populist reforms (as in the case of the mandatory implementation of term limits in many American states in the 1980s and 1990s or the several proposed reforms which Linz examines in his essay), which may hinder party performance, the consequences and implications of the emergence of such attitudes has remained relatively benign to date. Unlike in the earlier decades of the twentieth century, anti-party attitudes have not been linked to support for anti-system parties or movements, or to a weakening of support for democracy *per se*. Thus, it appears from this chapter and the one preceding it that the ominous long-term implications of a 'decline of party' may have been substantially overstated.

NOTES

1. Of these publications, about half have appeared in journals, one-quarter in books, and the others in edited volumes; see Caramani and Hug (1998: 512); for two different and more limited databases, see Norris (1997); Karvonen and Ryssevik (2001).

2. Among the many such books that have recently appeared are Katz and Mair (1994); Kalyvas (1996); Scarrow (1996*a*); Ware (1996*a*); Mair (1997); Boix (1998*a*); Müller and Strøm (1999*a*); Dalton and Wattenberg (2000*a*); Diamond and Gunther (2001); Farrell, *et al.* (2002). In addition, Wolinetz has edited two very useful volumes (1998*a*, 1998*b*) reprinting noteworthy journal articles on parties and party systems that have appeared since the 1960s.

3. Moreover, over the past two decades, the study of political parties has emerged as a clearly identifiable field within the discipline of political science. Accordingly, chapters specifically devoted to political parties have been published in several systematic overviews of this academic discipline; see Epstein (1975, 1983); Crotty (1991); Janda (1993).

4. See the systematic exploration of these themes in Strøm and Svåsand (1997*b*). While that volume was focused on the case of Norway, its findings have broader implications for democratic political systems throughout the industrialized world; see also Dalton and Wattenberg (2000*b*); Bartolini and Mair (2001).

5. These arguments are developed more extensively in several recent volumes dealing with parties in the new democracies of Southern Europe (Pridham and Lewis 1996; Morlino 1998; Ignazi and Ysmal 1998; Diamandouros and Gunther 2001), Latin America (Mainwaring and Scully 1995), Central and Eastern Europe (White *et al.* 1993; Evans and Whitefield 1996; Hofferbert 1998; Hermet *et al.* 1998; and Kitschelt *et al.*, 1999), and East Asia (Stockton 2001).

6. For similar reassessments of party-decline arguments by Broder (1972), Crotty (1984) and Wattenberg (1990), see Schlesinger (1991) and Coleman (1996).

7. For critical reassessments of the party-decline literature, see Strøm and Svåsand (1997*a*); Reiter (1989); Beyme (1993: ch. 2); Schmitt and Holmberg (1995); Mair (1997: chs. 2 and 4); Dalton and Wattenberg (2000*b*); and the special issue of the *European Journal of Political Research* (29(3), 1996) edited by T. Poguntke and S. E. Scarrow and devoted to 'The Politics of Anti-Party Sentiment'.

8. Another third of this literature has been dedicated to the study of party organization, to their participation in the electoral process, or to their bases of electoral support. The remaining third have dealt with studies of party ideologies, the formulation of public policy, and their roles in parliament and in government. Also see Bartolini *et al.* (1998).

9. Among the many classical contributions in this genre, see Almond (1960); Almond and Powell (1966: ch. 5); Holt (1967); and several of the chapters in La Palombara and Weiner (1966).

10. See Meehan (1967: ch. 3) and Flanagan and Fogelman (1967) for two critical evaluations of the basic approach, and Lowi (1963), Scarrow (1967), and King (1969) for specific criticisms of functionalist studies of political parties.

11. E.g. Gunther (1989) found through an extensive series of interviews with Spanish party leaders that their behaviour was often not guided by calculations of short-term electoral advantage. Instead, they sometimes formulated strategies and oriented their behaviour in efforts to achieve two other objectives—to consolidate fully Spain's new democratic regime, and to establish durable party organizations—both of which proved to be incompatible on several notable occasions with short-term vote maximization.

12. The electoral process is conceptualized as a model of competition based upon the voter's perception of the issue positions of candidates, with the voting decision based upon the perceived proximity among these issue stands; a party is therefore little more than the aggregation of issue stands by its candidates in a given election (see, e.g. Davis *et al.* 1970: 426 and 445). For a subsequent treatment of these themes which used formalized conceptions of parties, see Hinich and Munger (1997).

13. In the textbook of Shepsle and Bonchek (1997), for example, parties are notably absent from explanations of interactions among political actors, processes, and institutions. Parties only appear in the penultimate chapter on 'Cabinet government and parliamentary democracy [in Western Europe]'.

14. Brennan and Lomasky (1993: 121), for example, assume as one of the premises upon which they base their research 'the existence of a stable two-party system in many Western democracies'.

15. See, for instance, Strøm (1990*a*: ch. 2); Budge and Keman (1990); Aldrich (1995); Laver and Shepsle (1996); Müller and Strøm (1999*a*, 1999*c*); and for case studies of two specific families of parties, Koelbe (1991); Kalyvas (1996).

16. As Bartolini has observed (1986*b*: 259), in no historical phase has there been a homogenization of parties. On the contrary, several different types of parties have coexisted throughout the history of multi-party democratic competition, with pre-existing parties overlapping with newly emerging types. This has continued to the present day: even though there has been a general trend towards 'organizationally thin' parties, a number of very different types of parties can be found in most democratic systems.

17. This stands in contrast with the discipline of physics, where a broad consensus has existed for decades concerning which kinds of phenomena can be adequately explained by hypotheses derived from the Newtonian paradigm, which phenomena entail dynamic processes best captured by relativistic physics, which require analysis rooted in the precepts of quantum physics, etc.

18. Also see Janda (1980, 1983), where the author contributes to comparative theorizing by empirically testing and analysing the concepts originally advanced by Duverger (1954).

19. See, for instance, Lipset (1960*b*, 1981); Lipset and Rokkan (1967*a*); Rose (1974*a*); Bartolini and Mair (1990); Franklin *et al.* (1992); Evans (1999); Bartolini (2000*a*); Karvonen and Kuhnle (2001); Gunther and Montero (2001).

20. See Gunther and Diamond (2001) for one such effort.

21. Among the many noteworthy analyses of party systems over the past five decades are Duverger (1954); Lipset and Rokkan (1967*a*); Sartori (1976); Merkl (1980); Daalder and Mair (1983); Beyme (1985); Wolinetz (1988); Ware (1996); Mair (1997); Pennings and Lane (1998); Broughton and Donovan (1999); Karvonen and Kuhnle (2001).

22. A continuous line of development of theory and operational indicators in this subfield can be traced from Duverger (1954) to Rae (1971); Nohlen (1984); Grofman and Lijphart (1986); Taagepera and Shugart (1989); Lijphart (1994); and Cox (1997). Although still in Spanish, an excellent recent contribution is Penadés (2000).

23. As already mentioned, these three 'faces' are those of the party on the ground, the party in the central office, and the party in public office, as restated in their earlier work (Katz and Mair 1993), and as originally formulated by Key (1964) and Sorauf (1964); see also Beck (1996); Dalton and Wattenberg (2000*a*). Aldrich (1995: ch. 6) has added as a fourth 'face', that of party in elections, and Blondel and Cotta (1996, 2000) have respecified the party in government inside the party in public office.

24. See Bartolini (1996, 1999, 2000*b*) for a more extensive exploration of these issues.

25. Notable among these are Mayhew (1986), Schlesinger (1991), Aldrich (1995) in the USA; Panebianco (1988), Katz (1990), Kitschelt (1994), Scarrow (1996*a*), Mair (1997), Katz and Mair (1992*a*, 1994) in Western Europe; for Central and East Europe, Lewis (1996).

26. See also Thies (2000), Kopecký (1995), and Biezen (2001) for different conclusions regarding most new democracies. For recent analyses on party membership as the most visible dimension of the 'face' of the party on the ground, see Scarrow (2000) and Mair and Biezen (2001).

27. Kitschelt (2000), however, presents a different interpretation of these phenomena.

28. This analysis of the demise of the UCD is the product of two different research projects (one carried out by Gunther between 1979 and 1984 [see Gunther 1986*b*;

Gunther *et al.* 1986], and the other by Hopkin in 1992–3 [see Hopkin 1999]), based upon over forty-three hours of interviews with the party's former leaders. Despite the completely independent origins of their two research projects, they reached a remarkable consensus in their interpretations of the dramatic collapse of what was once Spain's governing party.

29. For more extensive analyses along these lines, see Blondel and Cotta (1996, 2000), and particularly Blondel (2000), Cotta (2000), Strøm (2000). For the related topics of parties in legislatures and of parties as parliamentary groups, see respectively Bowler (2000) and Heidar and Koole (2000).

Part I

Reconceptualizing Parties and Party Competition

Parties: Denied, Dismissed, or Redundant?
A Critique

Hans Daalder

We all speak about the crisis of party. But are we clear what we mean? *A priori* normative positions often cloud both our diagnoses and prognoses. In the debate on the crisis of party, I will argue, at least four different bodies of writing are intermingled which should be clearly distinguished:

1. The persistent body of thought which denies a legitimate role for party, and sees parties as a threat to the good society. Such thoughts were nurtured from two sides: lingering authoritarian ideologies on the one hand, and naïve democratic beliefs on the other. I will call these views *the denial of party*.
2. The views of those who regard certain types of parties as 'good' but other types parties as 'bad'. These writings may be summarized under the label *the selective rejection of party*.
3. The proposition that certain party systems are 'good' and others are 'bad'. This view will be dealt with under the heading *the selective rejection of party systems*.
4. The affirmation by those who regard parties as a transient phenomenon, products of a period of mass mobilization which is now a matter of the past. According to this argument, parties are becoming increasingly irrelevant in democratic politics as other actors and institutions have taken over the major functions which parties once played. That body of literature will be analysed under the rubric *the redundancy of party*.

THE DENIAL OF PARTY

We must first recognize that, comparatively speaking, organized and legitimate political parties are a relatively new phenomenon. David Hume, for instance, could still speak of parties of principle as 'the most extraordinary and unaccountable phenomenon that has yet appeared in human affairs'. In

the Britain of his day, 'factions' and 'parties' were not yet clearly distinguished from one another; and while 'factions from interest' and 'factions
from affection' were to him and his contemporaries perfectly understood
phenomena, this was not true of 'parties from principle'.[1] But the situation
was changing in the eighteenth century, at the very time Hume wrote. The viscount of Bolingbroke drew up the first explicit argument in favour of formal
opposition as a political good, and Edmund Burke (1861 [1770]: 372) defined
parties as 'a body of men united, for promoting by their joint endeavors, the
national interest, upon some particular principle in which they are all agreed'
(see also Sartori 1976). Parties increasingly came to be understood as legitimate actors, and the institutionalized competition of parties as a valuable
characteristic of an open polity.

It was no accident that such thoughts developed first in Britain of those
days. For two fundamental conditions for the rise of party were already were
well understood in that country by the eighteenth century: first, the acceptance of the inevitability of pluralist forces in any society; and second, the
importance of political representation. For parties to become the modern
institutions we know today, two further conditions had to be fulfilled, however. First, Burke's argument that people could honestly differ on the common good, and might legitimately organize to seek representative office on
that basis, had to be accepted; and secondly, the manner of representation
had to be altered so that, instead of the principle of sending 'delegates' on
behalf of particular social orders, regions, or cities, representatives would
depend on recognized bodies of individual voters. Once the latter became
increasingly numerous, the modern party became not only legitimate, but a
matter of necessity. First local, and then increasingly nationwide, organizations had to be formed to fill the gap between individual representatives and
expanding numbers of voters.

The rise of the modern party produced the first articulate analyses of the
role of party in modern society. In 1902, the Russian *émigré* Moisei
Ostrogorski published his two-volume book on *La Démocratie et les parties
politiques* which was a detailed, if highly critical, comparative study of the
building of 'caucuses' in modern city centres in Britain and the United
States.[2] Ostrogorski did not like what he saw. He ended his book with a
strong plea to substitute ad hoc, single-issue associations (which would allow
the full play of individual will) for mass parties which in his view denied individuals their sovereign right to decide. And Ostrogorski influenced that other
great, early theorist of party, Robert Michels. The latter's *Zur Soziologie des
Parteiwesens in der modernen Demokratie: Untersuchungen über die oli-
garchischen Tendenzen des Gruppenlebens*, which appeared in 1911,[3] was
based on a trenchant analysis of decision-making within the German Social
Democratic Party of his time. Starting from the belief that the political influence of members within organizations should be direct and equal, he in fact

showed the inevitability of rule by political elites. Parties were thus seen by both Ostrogorski and Michels as subordinating individuals to organizations, the latter being inevitably dominated by party leaders. Hence Michels's paradox that masses were capable of revolution, but not of self-rule, as all they could achieve was to substitute new elites for old ones, oligarchy being so inevitable as indeed to represent 'an iron law'. If Ostrogorski was to conclude with a preference for ad hoc associations over durable parties, Michels was to turn his diagnosis of unavoidable elitism into a romanticist advocacy of fascism.

On closer analysis, the source of such a rejection of party can be found in two, at first sight, very different bodies of thought. On the one hand, there were the proponents of a traditional political order who saw in the rise of party an unwanted invasion of the terrain of the state, which as the guardian of long-term transcendental interest threatened to fall victim to private interests of a short-term nature. On the other hand, there were those who cherished a belief in the 'sovereign', free individual and thus opposed what they regarded as the tyranny of party, which would do away with freedom of individual action and thought for the sake of collectivist organizations led by irresponsible elites.

The first of these arguments logically gave rise to the frequent assertion that there was danger in a *Parteienstaat*. To those using this notion, parties (which on closer analysis were nothing but the instruments of political elites covering private interests under a cloak of ideology) encroached on the mainsprings of decision-making in the state which should remain immune from such attempts at 'colonization'. In the second view, parties were regarded not as genuine instruments of representation, but as barriers between individuals and the general interest. In either case, this led to a wish deliberately to restrict the scope of party. Thus, it was thought necessary to immunize certain sectors of government from the stranglehold of party (notably the judiciary, but also the bureaucracy and to some extent the supreme executive itself). At the same time, it would be vital to maintain direct links between 'the' people and their leaders, so as to preclude the complete dominance of parties in that relationship. This might be achieved, for instance, by assuring the direct election of presidents or prime ministers, and by maintaining or introducing other plebiscitary instruments, including referenda which could be used by government if need be also against a Parliament increasingly monopolized by self-seeking parties.

If such reasoning had its origin in older, autocratic traditions, newer beliefs in direct democracy could be turned to the same direction. Did not Rousseau's notion of the general will imply that no special place should be given to 'partial societies', that anything which would come between individuals and the general will was bound to infringe on the general interest, and that citizens should themselves remain free and autonomous rather than allowing their right to decide to fall in the hands of 'parties' which denuded them off their right to decide for themselves?

The two arguments (the older authoritarian one and the one favouring a direct expression of individual will) might at first sight seem to be at opposite poles. Yet, on closer analysis, they had certain features in common. In both one finds the postulate of a pre-existing harmony which should not be jeopardized by the divisive battle of competing parties. In both there was a clear distaste for modern forms of organization. Both also rejected the idea of a mandate for elected representatives, as likely to impair the formation of genuine will and 'objective' interest, whether residing in the state or in the people. One can formalize this argument. For parties to exist and to acquire legitimacy, there should be a clear acceptance that men might honestly differ, that all might organize to repeat Burke's words 'upon some particular principle' to promote 'the national interest', that all may vote equally, and that government must rest on what Schumpeter (1942) would term the 'competitive struggle for the people's vote'. Modern parties, in other words, presuppose the conditions of representative democracy. Typically, parties are rejected by those who do not accept such underlying principles, either because they believe the state to have legitimate claims beyond electoral expression and democratic representation, or because they see in parties the 'associations partielles' *par excellence* so much rejected by Rousseau as infringing on the formation of a (mythical) general will.

THE SELECTIVE REJECTION OF PARTIES

Unlike those who doubt the legitimacy of organized parties altogether, others reject certain *types* of parties, but not all. In well-known typologies of political parties, such as those of Maurice Duverger or Sigmund Neumann, one finds the assumption that there is an inevitable, but one suspects sometimes regretted, transition from what Duverger (1954) called the *partis-comité* or caucus parties to the *partis de masse* or mass parties and Neumann (1965) a shift from 'parties of individual representation' to 'parties of integration', with the implicit danger of a slide towards 'parties of total integration' characteristic of totalitarian regimes. This reflects a definite ambiguity in the appraisal of mass parties. On the one hand there is widespread recognition of their emancipatory and democratic potential. To the extent that they structure the vote and make for reasonably unified actors, they can be seen to contribute to political stability and to allow for both the exercise of leadership and permit accountable government. One can see the force of such arguments amongst critics of 'fluid politics' as exemplified in the United States, in many of the states of the Third World, and now in Central and Eastern Europe. A famous normative statement on the need for coherent mass parties was the seminal report drawn up more than forty years ago by the Committee on Political Parties of the American Political Science Association, under the title *Towards a More Responsible Two-Party System* (APSA 1950). And one finds the same line of reasoning amongst those who plead for the need for more structured party systems as a condition of viable democracy, in the extensive literature on democracy and political development.

But there is no denying another body of thought which betrays a definite distancing from the notion of the mass party. Mass parties are accused of being heavily ideologized 'fighting machines', seeking to subject both voters and the state to a combination of dogma and elitist self-interest. Their party discipline is held to destroy the conditions of free debate which is regarded as the hallmark of the parliamentary system. Mass parties in particular are thought to 'penetrate' beyond the legitimate terrain of competitive electoral politics into the sanctity of the state, or in another view they are thought to submit the social order to unwanted 'colonization'. Such ideas, I must repeat, are nurtured strongly by idealized views of alternative ways of ordering the body politic: a romanticized traditionalism, beliefs in a monolithic state, a hallowed notion of a 'golden age of parliamentarism', in which unfettered deputies debated until *'du choc des opinions jaillit la vérité'*, a naïve hope in communitarian direct democracy: views which on closer analysis tend to a denial of parties altogether rather than to a selective acceptance of some parties and a rejection of others.

THE SELECTIVE APPRAISALS OF PARTICULAR PARTY SYSTEMS

The literature on party systems is equally replete with normative statements which extol certain party *systems* but damn others. Thus one often finds, among political scientists as among historians and constitutional lawyers, the assumption that 'my country is best'. But one also finds the reverse position: critics of a given party system seek inspiration in comparing it with the assumed 'better' system of another country. I shall review such arguments in four successive steps (for a fuller statement, see Daalder 1987).

The Once Dominant Model of the British System

Until relatively recently, the dominant model for many critics and reformers in other countries was undoubtedly 'the' British party system—the little word 'the' is put between quotes to indicate that it referred to an idealized, stylized version of the British system as much as to the realities of British politics at any particular period of time. I shall not seek to define that all too familiar model. But one should note its pervasive influence in a number of ideas:

1. There is a widespread conviction that one can engineer a two-party system by the introduction of the single member district system.[4]
2. There is the idealization of single-party government and its logical opposite: the undesirability of coalition governments.
3. The idea of a 'front benchers' constitution',[5] implies a specific, normative reading of the relationship between elites and followers. Such thinking gives a clear verdict in favour of leadership won in a constant battle among rival contenders seeking to 'climb the slippery pole of politics'. It underlines the merit of 'amateurs' changing from one ministerial post to another and thus exercising a genuine 'political control' over specialized departments and bureaucrats. And it takes an unmistakable position on the need for control by parliamentary leaders over politicians fulfilling roles in the party outside Parliament as presented in the seminal study on *British Political Parties* by McKenzie (1955).
4. The concept of the political mandate: even though British voters technically vote, not for a government but for a Member of Parliament in the district in which they live, the strength of the two-party system makes voting in practice a matter of direct choice of alternative prime ministers. This endorses both the idea of absolute majority rule and the assumption of clear, accountable government.

The ideal-type British model has not only influenced much of our normative thinking about the working of party systems, it has also for long determined prevailing typologies and models in comparative politics. It was one reason why originally German critics of Weimar (e.g. Hermens 1941; Friedrich 1941) held up the British system as the best guarantee of ensuring stable democratic government in a larger state. The stark two-party system mesmerized Duverger (1954) whose belief in the 'naturalness' of dual forces was so strong as to make him deduce even multi-party systems from a '*superposition des dualismes*'. Even in the more sophisticated writings of Duverger's ardent critic, Giovanni Sartori, one can easily trace the impact of the British type. This appears not so much in his analysis of two-party systems, which he recognizes as being rare in practice, but in his analysis of systems of moderate pluralism, where rival coalitions of parties dance a British minuet around the centre (Sartori 1976; for a critique of both Duverger and Sartori, see Daalder 1984). In the rather different typology of Gabriel Almond (1956), it is again the British system which is the prototype of the 'Anglo-Saxon system' which in stark contrast to the 'continental European system' is characterized by a homogeneous political culture and a highly differentiated role structure which permits the political process to function with characteristic moderation and an efficient, non-ideological style of pragmatic bargaining. Even when the tables were turned, and a new generation of researchers began to oppose what they regard as a rather superficial

view of 'Europe'—witness the writings of the consociational democracy
school (e.g. Lijphart 1968*a*)—the British model was retained as at least one
polar type.

The British model was also very much at the basis of the construction of
formal models which have played a powerful role in the literature on parties
and party systems, and on the functioning of democracy generally. Thus, it
served Schumpeter with the material from which to fashion his 'alternative
theory of democracy'. Since Schumpeter published his *Capitalism, Socialism
and Democracy* in 1942 writings on democracy have been suffused with views
about rival elites competing for the people's vote. In practice, rather different
assumptions went with such views. Some thought it possible to maintain a
confident belief in the sovereignty of the electorate—for example, through
reifying the notion of a 'mandate' as bestowing full power on the majority
party for the limited period of one Parliament, and discounting the dangers
of that notion by suggesting that governments were really controlled not by
the last but by the next election. Others followed Schumpeter more closely,
stressing the fact that electoral will was really the product rather than the
source of the political process. In either version the assumption remained that
politics was above all a dualistic conflict between rival groups, a group in
power and a group of opposition forces which would seek replace it.

Schumpeter undoubtedly strongly influenced the later elaboration and for-
malization of models of party politics by Anthony Downs (1957). In his book
on *An Economic Theory of Democracy,* the 'normal' model of politics is very
much that of two actors being forced to compete with one another for the
same voters in the centre of a political system, and thus being necessarily
drawn to a moderate—and, in its logical conclusion, identical— position at
the centre. In reverse, Downs depicted a multi-party system as lacking by definition some of that 'rationality', parties now having the choice not to compete at large irrespective of ideological positions, but on the contrary carving
out a special ideological position on which they might 'particularize' their
appeal to specific groups of voters.

The Rejection of Multi-Party Systems

A logical corollary of the strong normative value of the British two-party system was the wholesale rejection of multi-party systems. Such a rejection is not
difficult to document. Three major examples are the traditional treatment of
the politics of the French Third and Fourth Republic, Weimar Germany, and
post-1945 Italy.

A wholesale rejection of the 'instable' politics of the French Third (and
later Fourth) Republic formed the traditional tune of French as well as
British observers. It sounded the theme of the fragmentation of will represented by the French Parliament—thought to be the inevitable consequence

of a large number of constantly regrouping parties—which was responsible for executive instability. That view led many in turn to the assumption that such stability as there was, was due to the force of the Napoleonic state which provided permanent strength in a system in which the party system was ineffective. This of course meant an acceptance that *la fonction publique* should remain free from the encroachment of parties. In contrast, parties were easily seen as instruments of self-seeking politicians, rising to power in a *République des camarades* (De Jouvenel 1914). Specific explanations were thought to account for the weakness of parties in France. Some found this in an excessive role for ideology which kept voters apart and the Republic divided. Others emphasized the individualist recruitment of French members of Parliament which, as long as they nurtured their local constituencies, were really free to do as they wished in the Paris *Assemblée*, which was described as a *maison sans fenêtres*.

Such arguments, taken from debates in the early part of the twentieth century, were strongly reinforced by events in the 1930s and the Vichy experience which were to give rise in the Fourth Republic to the groping for solutions which were thought to lie in institutional reforms as diverse as introducing an effective right of dissolution to strengthen Cabinets against the 'irresponsible maneuvrings' of Parliament, the introduction of a special mandate for a prime minister relying on a clear *vote d'investiture*, the manipulation of the electoral system, or beyond this the search for an independent electoral mandate for the executive. Such debates were to reach a feverish state in 1958 when the Fourth Republic succumbed, and France was to be given a new constitution under the decisive control of that ardent critic of the Third and Fourth Republic alike, General Charles de Gaulle. Parliament during the last gasps of the Fourth Republic put certain conditions when it agreed to a wholesale transfer of authority to De Gaulle. Among them were the insistence on the maintenance of free elections and the principle of a parliamentary system. But there is little doubt that the framers of the Constitution of the Fifth Republic intended specifically to reduce the power of Parliament, to circumscribe the role of traditional party groups, and to rely for good government instead on a president who in both his personal and constitutional capacities would be very much the arbitrator of political life and institutions. One finds in French legal and political writings a strong distaste for a multi-party system which entrusted government to constantly shifting, ineffective, and immobilist coalitions at the centre, *cet éternel marais* in Duverger's words. As a corollary one finds a strong belief in the need and possibility of institutional tinkering with political systems, rather than a recognition of the value of a stable, functioning party system.

French writing is as nothing compared to the effect of the even greater *Kladderadatsch* of Weimar. The Weimar Constitution had been hailed as the epitome of democratic politics, but was seen within a decade and a half to be powerless to stop Hitler's *Machtübernahme*. Already before 1933 a vigorous debate had been opened on the appropriate role of parties and party systems. I have already signalled the habitual rejection of a *Parteienstaat* by constitutional thinkers in Germany. One major problem of government under Weimar was the inability of parties to form lasting government coalitions and to prevent the rise of a new totalitarian party which was to conquer power later. Again, as in France both in the interwar period and later, the presumed malfunctioning of the political system was attributed to a faulty party system. That argument might be directed against all parties and their tendency to encroach on the mainsprings of government which should remain free from their grip. It could also be turned against specific parties, whether those organized too strongly, as many non-socialists argued thinking of socialists or communists, or not strongly enough, as those were to argue who held the 'democratic' parties of Weimar to have been too timid and too weak to grasp real power, and to subordinate the state apparatus (including the bureaucracy, the military, and even the courts) to real democratic control.[6] It was in this climate that Hermens (1941) could formulate his influential indictment of proportional representation as a major cause of the fall of Weimar: it was to that factor, so the argument went, that one should ascribe the nefarious ideologization and fragmentation of politics which proportional representation engendered. If one were to point to smaller European countries which seemed to be able to work democratic politics more effectively under one kind of proportional representation or other, that argument could easily be discounted with the *riposte* that larger states could not afford the inability to act as the realities of the international world inevitably charged larger states with responsibilities not resting on small countries. Such arguments, brought over to Britain and the United States by influential writers, including Hermens himself, could not but reinforce the conviction that 'Anglo-Saxon' two-party systems were superior, and that 'continental' systems of government suffered a congenital defect in lacking the ability to combine the realities of party politics with the need for unmistakable executive government.

The indictment of excessive multipartism has also been a constant feature in the criticism of Italian politics after 1945. Even before the drastic changes in the early 1990s the spectre of Weimar hung over much of the political debate about the chances of democracy in Italy. There were undoubted similarities between Sartori's (1976) model of extreme or polarized pluralist party systems on the one hand, and Hermens's (1941) interpretation of the fall of the Weimar Republic, on the other.[7] Thus, Sartori's notion of 'ideological stretching' resembles Hermens's argument, as does his view that 'centrifugal' forces will benefit 'irresponsible oppositions', which through a 'policy of outbidding' and 'outflanking' threaten the heart of responsible democratic politics. And for all his criticism of Duverger, Sartori's strong disavowal of centre parties—which by occupying the centre ground induce centrifugal forces in the system—is not so different from Duverger's fundamental rejection of the centre. One of the major contributions of Sartori's typology of party systems is his deliberate distinction between 'moderate' and 'extreme' pluralism—'moderate' pluralist systems differing fundamentally from 'extreme' multi-party systems in having a mechanics of 'blocs' of parties in a system with two poles that are not too far apart on an ideological dimension. One need not deny the merit of that model yet to notice that such a 'moderate' pluralist system apparently has some 'British' virtues, although it presumably remains a poor relation of the Westminster family.

The failure of alternation was a constantly recurring theme in the writings also of other Italian political scientists. The impact of such reasoning was so strong that a growing distaste for the ruling system parties could lead to a wholesale overhaul of the electoral system, intended not only to throw the rascals out, but also to secure the blessings of alternating governments, so it was thought. Disappointment with the ensuing polarization would, however, soon make many a one-time proponent of such reforms seek desperately for ways to strengthen moderate forces at the centre.

The Re-evaluation of Multi-Party Systems

The preceding literature generally shares a dichotomous view of party systems: it opposes, in one form or another, a meritorious two-party system found in the Anglo-Saxon world to a rather less successful multi-party system characteristic of party systems on 'the' European continent. This simple dichotomy has since withered, as a result of at least two changes: first, the discovery that not all multi-party systems resembled Weimar, a Third or Fourth Republic France, or post-1945 Italy; and second, a growing criticism of the archetype of the two-party system as practised at Westminster itself. Of course, some had always recognized that certain states seemed to have stable politics notwithstanding somewhat 'quaint' institutions and party divisions. Switzerland was generally accorded a special status, and so to a lesser extent were Scandinavian countries. Yet, there was an unmistakable touch of surprise in discoveries in the 1950s and later that not all continental European systems resembled France (e.g. Wheare 1963), and that there were such things as 'working multiparty systems' (Rustow 1956). I have already noted the earlier argument which clearly sought to explain away the examples of many a smaller democracy which apparently could afford the luxury of a 'divided' (not to speak of 'fragmented') system because unlike larger states they were not called on really to act in the world of international politics. However, a more fundamental re-evaluation was also taking place.

One factor was the growing tendency to draw up comparative tables as various new international organizations (notably the OECD and the EU) came to collect a variety of social indicators to assess the policy performance of different countries. Such tables hardly suggested a better record for Britain than for other European countries. In the process even countries long regarded as the 'sick cases' of Europe began to be seen in a new light. This happened first to the Federal German Republic, then to France, and for a time even to Italy. Although there remained considerable room for debate whether performance on economic or social indicators should be attributed to governments and their policies, or rather to successes scored irrespective (or even notwithstanding) of these governments or policies, it at least made clear that there was a problem which needed study.

A second factor was the growing internationalization of political studies. Notably through the powerful impact of American political science, younger political scientists in country after country began to have a new look at their own systems. If they learned to reject too narrow historical and institutional approaches which had traditionally dominated the study of their own countries, they also could not help reacting more or less strongly to what to them smacked as often naïve, and on closer analysis parochial, theories and typologies framed from the perspective of the United States, or Britain for that matter. If this initially implied little more than an insistence that one's own country was somehow different and did not really fit the place assigned to it on the as yet overly general map of comparative politics, it resulted eventually in the growth of a large body of monographic literature on which future comparative study could draw. And in certain cases it led to the deliberate development of counter-models.

Thirdly, an increasing sophistication of research methodology also led comparative scholars to look for more 'cases' with which to confirm or falsify particular hypotheses. Thus, a growing literature developed seeking to test hunches about a variety of phenomena, including the effect of electoral systems, the salience of particular cleavages in party systems, the measure of fragmentation, the duration of cabinets, and the validity of coalition theories. In such approaches one country might be as 'good' as another for empirical analysis. To some extent the complexity of multi-party systems might serve sophisticated analysts even better than the overly simple, and also somewhat rare, case of two-party polities.

The movement away from the one-time normative dominance of the British two-party systems was further strengthened by increasing criticism of the model in Britain itself. One could see this in the growing rejection of adversarial government (in this respect one should note the very considerable influence of the writings of Finer [1975, 1980]), the increased protest against a total sovereignty of Parliament which allows unrepresentative single-party governments absolute power, a renewed fear of the power of extra-parliamentary party organizations, and so forth.

The Consensus Multi-Party Model

The tables were definitely turned in the writings of my one-time compatriot, now an American citizen, but always admirable colleague Arend Lijphart who developed first the so-called 'consociational democracy model' and later the 'consensus model' of politics as a deliberate counter-model to the 'Westminster type politics' or 'majoritarian government'.[8] Lijphart (1968a, 1968b, 1969) began by way of deviant case analysis, using the Netherlands as a special case to criticize the assumptions of Almond and others that there was an unavoidable negative relationship between plural societies (characterized by a fragmented political culture) and democratic stability. He then generalized the consociational democracy model (systems in which elites consciously chose cooperation to counter the divisions of countries in different subcultures) to other European countries (notably Belgium, Austria, and Switzerland). From there, he went further to distinguish between 'majoritarian' political systems, 'logically based on the principle of concentrating as much power as possible in the hands of the majority', from their opposites, 'based on the principle of sharing, dispersing, and limiting power in a variety of ways'. In an analysis of twenty-one countries (actually twenty-two cases as he treated the French Fourth and Fifth Republic as separate cases) Lijphart (1984) found that one major dimension separating these two models was composed by features clearly related to differences relevant to the party system. 'Majoritarian' systems differed from 'consensual' systems on each of the following five characteristics: (1) concentration of executive power versus executive power-sharing; (2) executive dominance versus executive–legislative balance; (3) two-party versus multi-party system; (4) one-dimensional versus multidimensional party system; and (5) plurality election versus proportional representation. Lijphart then constructed a nine-cell table formed by three categories on this dimension and three on a second dimension composed of three other variables (unitary and centralized versus federal and decentralized government; unicameralism versus strong bicameralism; and unwritten versus written and rigid constitutions). He found that only one European country (Britain) was clearly majoritarian on both dimensions. But most European countries fell clearly on the consensual end of the continuum on the parties dimension, while only a few occupied intermediate places, and only Ireland, Austria, and Germany were closer to the ideal-type 'majoritarian' case.[9]

Lijphart's analysis went far to confirm earlier views that, far from representing the 'normal' model, the British case was rather the exception in European politics. Moving beyond this he also questioned its value as a 'normative' model, clearly arguing that what he termed the 'consensual' model was in many ways superior also as a prescriptive model, at least for countries which knew sharp social divisions as so many European countries historically did. If one surveys this rather considerable shift, away from a two-party model to an empirical—and in the case of Lijphart undoubtedly also normative—'consensus-model', one cannot but feel that we are in the presence of a great many a priori views about the functioning, or not-functioning, of particular type of party *systems*, and hence in the presence of a literature which needs thorough rethinking.

THE REDUNDANCY OF PARTIES

Finally, another trend of thought emerged which questions the very function of parties and party systems themselves. Such views were argued from a variety of perspectives. One view stated that parties played a historically specific role in mobilizing new groups of citizens and integrating them into the body politic; but once this historically unique task had been performed, parties would be proven to be transient phenomena only. Another view—somewhat less deterministic—held that parties which once represented distinct policies and groups fell increasingly under the working of market forces; in the process they came to resemble one another as tweedledeedee and tweedledeedum, losing their virtue with their specificity. A third argument emphasized not so much the role of parties themselves, but the increasing role of other political actors which singly or jointly went far to remove the substance of function and power from parties, and thus caused parties no longer 'to really matter'. A short review of each of these positions should be enough to indicate their impact and intent.

Political Parties as Passing Agents of Mass Mobilization

This school of thought attributed to parties a historically specific role in the process of democratization. As shown particularly clearly in the seminal writings of Stein Rokkan (1970), many European parties crystallized around the expansion of the franchise, and played a historical task in incorporating new groups into the body politic (see also Rokkan and Svåsand 1978). From this some observers drew certain rather fargoing conclusions (not drawn by Rokkan himself, one should hasten to say). One of these conclusions was that parties indeed fulfilled a specific historical task in drawing new citizen groups into the body politic. Having done this, parties no longer serve a real need, as other actors take over their role of mobilization and articulation.

Such a view could be reinforced by those who gave a particular interpretation to Lipset and Rokkan's famous *freezing proposition* (see also Mair 2001). Rokkan's emphasis on the crucial role of past political alignments could be read as a proposition that parties which represented such alignments no longer reflect the 'new politics' of another era so that they must increasingly and inevitably lose their relevance in the contemporary world. Whether they do is an empirical question. For the present argument it suffices to state that such a conclusion *could* be construed on the basis of the freezing proposition.

Parties as Market Forces

Such thinking comes unexpectedly close to a second view which holds that parties are giving up their historical function and *raison d'être*, and are instead turning into mere market forces. One finds this argument to some degree in Schumpeter's (1942) theory of democracy, but it is made more explicitly in Downs (1957), and particularly in the work of Otto Kirchheimer (1966), who coined the term catch-all party. I shall take their arguments as read, emphasizing merely that in such views parties are no longer thought of as representing 'bodies of particular principle', but rather as vote-maximizing agents without any real ideologies of their own, in a time when ideologies come to an end anyhow and a new cynical realism takes over. One may note that here again we are in the presence of a somewhat normative statement (although Kirchheimer disliked his own creation) rather than of a fully proven empirical statement.

The Waning of Parties

A more definite step towards the view that parties are really redundant was made by those who came to query the role of party in modern society altogether. That view has been argued in a variety of ways: studies on whether 'parties really matter'; theories about neocorporatism; a neopluralist perspective which sees 'action groups' as replacing parties as chief agents of political representation; and a renewed call for the introduction of new direct democracy instruments, c.q. the increased use of such instruments already in place.

Doubts about the extent to which parties really mattered had their origin in American political science. Students of comparative state politics came to ask the question whether policy outcomes in different American states could be attributed to peculiarities of their party system (for example, whether Democrats or Republicans were in charge, or whether states were clearly competitive between them), or to the more general social conditions prevailing in any one state which threw up their own problems for whatever party happened to be in charge. This type of analysis was taken over by students of comparative public policy using European data. One major line of analysis concerned the expansion of the welfare state, and of particular policies within it. Such analyses tied in closely with older studies of 'political economy' or 'public finance', which ever since Wagner (1892) held that the increase of state tasks and expenditures was a function not of ideology but of objective social and economic changes accompanying industrialization. And one particular variant of this kind of analysis centred on the degree to which socialists could have a differential impact in societies which some described as having a 'mixed' economy but others preferred to call essentially 'capitalist'. If some found that the participation of socialists in government did matter, others found the opposite. The latter view was in consonance with Marxist and neo-Marxist critics who saw in *Stamokap* (a conjunction of state and monopoly capital) yet another stage in the development of capitalism—seeing in the close linkage between state and economic interests an explanation why capitalism had not yet come to its close as a crisis-model would inevitably have it.

The elaboration of more detailed neocorporatist theories took place very much against a similar background of left-wing hopes being destroyed by the harsh realities of social structural developments. Many proponents of the neocorporatist approach did not care to discuss the role of parties, or tended at most to treat them as surface phenomena.[10] They clearly held that the importance of what Rokkan called 'the partisan-electoral channel' was greatly overwhelmed by the realities of 'corporate pluralism'.[11] Neocorporatist writers pointed to the rapid and reciprocal expansion of state agencies and specialized interest groups which settled policies between them in a direct give and take without party actors interfering. Clearly, roles that parties were thought to play (and possibly had once played) in determining government policy were thus fulfilled by institutionalized interest groups intertwined with sections of officialdom. Being side-stepped in policy-making and policy-implementation, parties also became less functional in their traditional role of articulation and aggregation.

A third school of thought about an inevitable waning of parties based itself on the increased role of ad hoc 'action groups'. If special interests had specific *institutionalized* channels which gave them direct access to government, so other groups learnt that the interest of policy-makers was often secured more easily by direct action tactics and media exposure than by working through the more tortuous channels of party decision-making. Paradoxically, therefore, the traditional role of parties as intermediaries was thought to be eroded by two seemingly opposite processes: the increased institutionalization of sectional interests *and* the attempt by such groups as well as single-interest groups and ad hoc media interests to short-circuit the road to the government agenda through direct action tactics.

Finally, there is the deliberate use of direct democracy instruments to side-step the role of parties. Such tendencies can be seen in a variety of political expedients and reforms. Thus, ever since the adoption at the beginning of the French Fifth Republic of the 1958 Constitution and the ensuing (unconstitutional) 1962 referendum which introduced the direct election of the French president, the wish for a directly elected executive has exercised an unmistakable lure in other European countries as well. In parliamentary elections, there has been a marked increase in the role of communication specialists who tend to package politicians rather than seek a mandate for party platforms. One can signal an increased call for and use of referenda, precisely to take specific decisions out of the hand of party-controlled parliaments, not to speak of possible regime change. And of late, there has been the new hype of a presumed teledemocracy which should restore the 'democratic city-state' through new electronic media which purportedly would allow its citizens to share directly in political debate and to take binding decisions without having to rely on party intermediaries.

CONCLUSION

The preceding survey—which is partly an inventory of theoretical propositions, partly a sketch of changing political moods in the wake of fargoing political and social changes which have taken place in European societies— should make clear that a great many often a priori arguments enter into any discussion of the role of party in European politics. As we saw, the period began with a denial of party and of lingering doubts about the extent to which parties might properly intrude on government. Once parties came to be more accepted there were still doubts what parties were to be preferred: looser parties of representation or mass parties representing groups formed on specific cleavages. In all such cases the spectre of more totalitarian parties (whether fascist or national-socialist, or communist) hovered as a portentous presence. Furthermore, parties came to be accepted much more easily in certain societies than in others. They were greeted with most reluctance in states which had a powerful tradition of authoritarian government represented most distinctly by dynasties and their bureaucracies. Wherever more pluralist traditions had prevailed in processes of state making, older traditions of representation and conceptions of politics in terms of balanced estates or interests was to facilitate the eventual legitimation of parties. Modern parties formed mainly as existing or aspiring elites mobilized an expanding number of voters: as Rokkan (1970: *passim*) taught us, the cleavages which were salient at the time of the advent of universal suffrage were to have a very strong impact on later divisions, and hence on the format of party systems.

Much of the writing on parties and party systems was inspired by individual country experiences. Notably the British system was long held up as an enviable model, both in Britain itself but also among critics of existing party systems elsewhere. In contrast, notions about multi-party systems were for a long time heavily coloured by experiences in countries which saw their party system end with their democratic regime, as in Fascist Italy, Weimar Germany, and to some extent 1940 or 1958 France. The situation began to change when the British two-party system came increasingly under criticism, while at the same time multi-party systems began to have a more favourable image, first through greater knowledge of the politics of smaller European democracies, then also in the increasingly rehabilitated larger continental European countries. The turn towards more empirical styles of comparative political science research greatly facilitated this development.

But at the same time the political relevance of parties and party competition was increasingly questioned. Some six lines of argument which contributed to that line of argument have been reviewed: the view that parties are by nature the product of a historical period of initial mass mobilization, but have now become become largely irrelevant for present-day political choices; the catch-all proposition which argued that the pull of the market led parties to give up their once distinct functions of articulating and aggregating policy positions; the debate on whether parties really mattered in the elaboration of policies which in reality are determined by objective structural requirements of modern society; neocorporatist theories which see in the interaction of specialized state agencies and interest groups the real arena of political decision-making, while parties appear to become mere surface phenomena; the view that parties lose out increasingly as the primary channels of articulation and aggregation in favour of 'direct action' groups and media contacts; and the renewed advocacy of direct democracy instruments which would 'free' the citizen from party control. Again, this survey should make clear that 'general' statements about parties frequently contain highly a priori assumptions. Often, the assumed 'crisis of parties' is mainly a euphemism for a dislike of parties. The debate is shot through with speculative statements about 'inexorable' trends: towards mass parties, towards catch-all parties, towards a 'waning' of parties as other political actors take over. There is much less in the way of detailed study of the actual role of parties.

If we want to do better, what should we do? First, we should seek to query the presence of possible, normative biases in the literature, and our own thought and writings. Some of these have been spelt out in the preceding pages. Secondly, we should attempt to detail the different criteria by which the working of parties and party systems may be judged. Any such attempt is likely to reveal the existence of conflicting criteria. If so, such conflicts should be clearly faced rather than left unanswered. Thirdly, one should carefully specify the particular roles and functions which parties play. It may well be that parties are losing certain functions, but gaining others (notably in political recruitment). The assumed 'crisis of party' may result from a one-sided focusing on some functions to the possible neglect or exclusion of others.[12] This may lead us to write off parties rather than to analyse their actual functioning and possible changes in them.

Once we have faced possible biases (and hopefully discarded them), once we have replaced such biases by a clear specification of normative criteria (even though these may be mutually conflicting), and once we have realized fully the manifold functions which parties and party systems fulfil in democratic societies, we must turn towards a full study of the empirical record. This will force us to investigate the actual functioning of parties and party systems in relation to other political actors, most notably the voters, interest groups and action groups, the media, and the various actors within government ranging from Cabinets and Members of Parliament to different levels of the bureaucracy. In doing so, we are likely to find considerable differences, from time-period to time-period, from country to country, from one possible function of parties or party systems to another, from one site of decision-making to another. This should force us to give up many easy generalizations, and instead to grapple with very complex developments. If this will disillusion us of popular certainties, it will undoubtedly make for more realistic comparative insights.

NOTES

This chapter is a reworked version of my 1991 Stein Rokkan Lecture, published as 'A Crisis of Party?' in *Scandinavian Political Studies*, 15(4): 269–88.

1. Excerpts from his famous essay, 'Of Parties in General', reprinted in Hendel (1953: 81).
2. Published in Calman-Lévy in Paris. There is a critical introduction to an English trans. in Lipset (1964).
3. Published in Leizpig in Dr. Werner Klinkhardt, *Philosophish-soziologische Bücherei*, 21: 191–401. See the excellent critical introduction written by Linz (1966) to the Italian trans. The English trans. was published by the Free Press in New York in 1962 as *Political Parties: A Sociological Study of the Oligarchical Tendencies of Modern Democracy*.
4. I am of course referring to the old debate on whether electoral systems 'make' party systems, or whether inversely party systems are likely to 'make' electoral systems to suit their needs—a subject with which, one would have thought, Stein Rokkan (1968) dealt with conclusively in his famous article on 'Electoral Systems'.
5. This is the happy term used by Wheare (1954).
6. This line of reasoning may have been an important factor in the deliberate upgrading of parties in the Federal German Republic after 1949, not least by massive financial support given by the state.
7. One should note that in his younger days Giovanni Sartori was assistant to G. Maranini, Professor of Political Science in Florence. Maranini shared Hermens's belief that proportional representation caused the downfall of democratic politics and thus inexorably paved the way for fascism. See his intervention in the debate about electoral politics in Heckscher (1957).
8. For a review of authors who tended to arrive at similar conclusions, often independently from Lijphart, see Daalder (1974).

9. In his most recent book on democracies, Lijphart (1999) enlarged the sample of cases to thirty-six, and included more variables and characteristics.
10. Parties are notably absent, for example, from the writings of the major initiator of the concept of neocorporatism, Philippe Schmitter; they are given greater prominence in the writings of his fellow editor Gerhard Lehmbruch; cf. Schmitter and Lehmbruch (1979); Lehmbruch and Schmitter (1982).
11. Rokkan (1966) was often uncritically annexed as a precursor of neocorporatism on the basis of this distinction, as well as on that of the happy title of his contribution: 'Norway: Numerical Democracy and Corporate Pluralism'.
12. In this regard, see for instance the analyses undertaken by Mair (1997), particularly in ch. 6.

3

Still the Age of Catch-allism?

Volksparteien and *Parteienstaat* in Crisis and Re-equilibration

Hans-Jürgen Puhle

Political parties are at the core of democracy. Unlike interest groups and even the institutions of interest intermediation, they do not merely represent a specific sector of the polity. Along with the voters (or the citizens as the sovereign 'people'), parties and their elected representatives are the key actors in the most basic procedure that essentially constitutes democracy: the election of the legislature and (directly or indirectly) the government.[1] In a democratic regime, political parties are the principal mediators between the voters and their interests, on the one hand, and the institutions of decision-making, on the other. They are the channels of political interaction between 'civil society' (in its broader Lockean sense) and 'the state'. Hence the study of political parties is an essential contribution to the study of democracy, and theories on political parties, in particular, can contribute to democratic theory. As these theories focus on structures and processes of intermediation, they not only involve the specific problems of a particular type of democracy, but speak more generally to current interpretations of the relationship between state and society, and therefore are also linked to the debates in social theory and theory of society.[2]

Political parties have also played a crucial role in the transitions from authoritarian rule during the 'third wave' of democratization in the twentieth century (Huntington 1991), which began in Southern Europe in 1974, and spread subsequently to Latin America and East Asia, and finally, in 1989, to post-communist transformations of a 'fourth wave' in Eastern and East Central Europe. Here parties have in many ways been different from parties in longer established 'Western' democracies. They have followed different patterns of development and behaviour, and have fulfilled additional functions in extraordinary constellations usually characterized by uncertainty, a low degree of democratic institutionalization, and a relative weakness of the groups of 'civil society'. They have often been the principal founders of democracy. Where the new democracies have finally become consolidated, and democratic persistence or normalcy has set in—as in Southern Europe and some countries of East Central Europe—the situation of political parties has also become 'normalized', in the sense that they have begun to share more of the characteristics and the problems of parties in the older, established democracies. Observers have noted that the more democratic the countries in transition or consolidation have become, the more their parties and party systems have faced the same kinds of problems as in the established democracies of the West in recent decades (see Puhle 2001).

The more recent experience of modern political parties during the last fifty years can be briefly summarized under two headlines: the rise of the catch-all party after the Second World War (earlier in the United States), and the 'crisis' and restructuring of the catch-all parties under profound challenges and severe 'stress' since the late 1970s. Both processes have been interrelated as it often seems that the 'crisis' has been due in part to a number of inherent characteristics and weaknesses of catch-all parties, and that the 'pure type' of catch-all party has been somewhat transitory in structure despite its apparent longevity. My analysis of the character and the potential outcome of the perceived present 'crisis' will begin with a description of the principal dimensions of the problem at hand. I will then move on to a careful reassessment of the *Gestalt*, the meaning and the 'confining conditions' of the catch-all type within its appropriate broader context.

THE DIMENSIONS OF THE PROBLEM

The discussion of the present 'crisis' of the catch-all parties has been conditioned by a number of factors, of which at least four deserve to be mentioned here: (1) the traditions and trajectories of the more general and mostly European 'theories' on political parties (which have often been no more than typologies); (2) the broad variety of different paradigms of and approaches to the analysis of parties and party change; (3) a relative consensus on 'stages' and periodization; and (4) the limitations and problems of the 'catch-all' type from its beginning.

In contrast to the earlier Anglo-Saxon normative tradition (of the Federalists, Burke, *et al.*), research on political parties over the last hundred years has largely involved the development of a broad variety of descriptive and analytical categories for classification. These have focused on such factors as the parties' membership, elites, organization, decision-making processes, programmes and policies, electoral campaigns, and the composition of their respective electorates. Research has also focused on party change and on party systems. Before the First World War, Max Weber started to write more systematically on the characteristics and functions of the different types of parties, particularly the (European) *Weltanschauungsparteien* (Liberals, Conservatives, and others), (American) patronage parties, class parties, and interest parties, in addition to some older terminology on parliamentary parties of representation, caucus parties, elite or notable parties (*Honoratiorenparteien*), or the particularly German and Dutch brand of the *Konfessionspartei* (denominational party). All of these party types more or less corresponded to the typical nineteenth-century 'liberal' or representational type, which Duverger later labelled as 'cadre parties'. Weber also analysed the rise of a new and different type of political parties since the 1890s: the better organized and more mobilized 'mass party' that was to dominate large parts of the twentieth century.[3] The analysis of the prewar German Social Democratic Party inspired Robert Michels (1962 [1911]) to find the 'iron law' of the 'oligarchic tendencies' of party life and decision-making, even in categorically democratic organizations; and Emil Lederer (1973 [1912]) has emphasized the 'economic' elements of party formation and performance.

Since the 1930s, two German emigrants, Sigmund Neumann (1956) and Otto Kirchheimer (1966, 1969), were among those who have conducted the most important research on the evolution of political parties in the twentieth century: they pointed to the emergence of the 'mass-integration party' (Neumann) early in the century, and its transformation into the 'catch-all party' (Kirchheimer) after the Second World War. The difference between these two subtypes of mass party is that the older mass-integration party represents a particular class, religion or a 'socio-cultural' or 'social and moral milieu' (Lepsius 1993 [1966]), as did the German Social Democrats or the Catholic Center Party, whereas Kirchheimer's younger catch-all party has transcended the boundaries of class, religion, or milieu. In contrast to the United States where they had different origins, in Europe the catch-all parties have mostly developed out of mass-integration parties.

Since the 1950s and 1960s, Maurice Duverger (1954) and Seymour Martin Lipset (1959, 1960*a*, 1960*b*, 1994) have systematically studied the socio-structural and institutional aspects of political parties. Lipset and Stein Rokkan (1967*b*; Rokkan 1970) have analysed the social and political cleavages and the interactions between party systems and voter alignments. Gabriel Almond and Sidney Verba (1963, 1980; also see Muller and Seligson 1994) have focused on the attitudinal dimensions of democratic politics and the particular trajectories of the respective 'civic cultures', and Giovanni Sartori, in his influential book of 1976, has provided a comprehensive formal and analytical typology classifying the parties and the seven types of party systems according to their number and interaction. This typology has been modified by Klaus von Beyme (1985, 2000), who added a historical dimension of ten different 'familles spirituelles'. Theories and research on the parties have, of course, also been influenced by the trends and changes in democractic theory, particularly those emphasizing the mechanisms of competition (Schumpeter 1942), pluralism (Fraenkel 1964), of inclusion and exclusion (Dahl 1971, 1989), consociationalism (Lijphart 1968a, 1969, 1977) and corporatism (Schmitter and Lehmbruch 1979; Lehmbruch and Schmitter 1982), and by the more general contexts of an economic theory of politics (particularly of democracy), or of theories on 'value change' or on politics as ritual and symbolic action.[4] On the other hand, the increasing professionalization and specialization in the social sciences, from the 1970s on, have taken their toll: theories and research on the political parties have become more and more segmented, methodologically sophisticated, and compartmentalized, hence narrower. Electoral studies, in particular, and research into the attitudinal aspects, into cleavage formation, issue voting, party identification, etc., have become a booming growth industry of their own.[5]

One of the consequences of the high level of specialization in the social and political sciences is that different aspects and dimensions of party performance and party-system change have usually been analysed by different approaches linked to different theoretical traditions. This corresponds to the multidimensional character of political parties as office seekers, vote seekers, and policy seekers (a distiction which has also inspired different typologies),[6] and organizations. The most important factors affecting a party's performance and evolution appear to be the following six:

1. *The electoral dimensions,* including the volatility of the vote (total and inter-bloc), the composition of the electorate, reflections of social and political cleavages, regional strongholds, the values, attitudes, and preferences of the voters, party identification. This has been a field for a great number of psychological and sociological theories on individual and group behaviour, mechanisms of cognitive dissonance, rising expectations and disenchantment, traditional attitudes and 'milieu' -relatedness, but also for theories of rational choice or value change, such as from 'materialist' to 'post-materialist' orientations.

2. *The interests of the party constituency*: studies of this type tend to focus on the size, social, and regional composition of the party's membership; the members' preferences and interests in relation to the cleavages, organized interests and 'milieux' of the civil society; links with interest groups, associations, or institutions (like the Church); and the extent of the party's entrenchment or encapsulation within society. Here an important set of general theories of society comes in, from pluralism and conflict theories (including Marxist ones) to a number of theories on interest intermediation like (neo)corporatism or regulation theory. The issue of interests and institutionalized channels and mechanisms of interest intermediation is also related to Lipset's (1959, 1994) discussion of the economic and social requisites of democracy.

3. *Party organization*: the recruitment of the elites and the processes of decision making are frequently analyzed, as are issues of unity versus factionalism, problems of leadership and/or a 'political class', the role of the parliamentary group within the party, mobilization strategies, public and private sources of party financing, the party's bureaucracy, and the implementation of responsiveness and accountability. Sociological theories of organization, bureaucracies, elites, and decision-making processes are most appropriate for such studies, including both actor-centred and structural or institutional approaches. Rational choice might also apply.

4. The *party system* and public institutions more generally: studies of this variety analyse constitutional and electoral systems. Among the more specific focuses of these studies are legislative/executive relations, especially those pertaining to the differences between presidential or semi-presidential systems, on the one hand, and parliamentary systems, on the other; the number of parties and the traditions of the social milieux behind them; and patterns of interaction among parties (especially regarding competition and alliances, see Laver and Hunt 1992; Strøm 1990*b*), between parties and other organized groups, and with the state (for example, whether or not these include significant elements of corporatism or of a *Parteienstaat*).

5. *Policy formulation*: many scholars have studied the programmes of parties, their ideologies and belief systems, their strategies of propaganda and mobilization, and their capacity for setting priorities, for concertation and for integration. Here we need concepts capable of relating particular interests and cleavages to particular ideologies.

6. *Policy implementation*: the roles and capabilities of parties in formulating and implementing defined policies—either from their positions in government or from the opposition benches—have also been the object of much scholarly research. Particular attention has been given to the analysis of whether or not all parties are capable of forming coalitions with all other parties (the problem of *allgemeine Koalitionsfähigkeit*). Questions of cabinet stability (when multi-party coalition governments are involved), interactions between government and opposition, patronage and the mechanisms of distribution, partyness, and government-ness, the degree of party control of agenda setting, the capacity of parties and the party system to adapt to change, and the capacity of civil society to control the parties and the 'political class', the quality of party government and political style have been analysed extensively.[7] Here a whole range of theoretical approaches might be in order, including those focusing on structures or institutions, the roles of political actors, social cleavages, the dynamics of social movements, and on state–society relationships in a broader sense.

Despite the great variety of theoretical, typological, and methodological approaches, a consensus has emerged with regard to a periodization of stages of party-building and development in Europe over the course of the last century and a half. Specifically, three waves and four types of party structuring have been identified. The first wave of adaptation and modernization spanned the interval between the 1890s and the First World War (in some cases later). This period entailed a shift from the traditional liberal nineteenth- century type of loose representational parties (called elite or 'cadre' parties by Duverger 1954) to more organized mass parties.[8] The second wave, which was set in motion after the Second World War, featured the emergence of the catch-all party, using the term coined by Kirchheimer in 1965 (and published in English in 1966). The third period of party change started during the 1970s and so far has led to a variety of modified or post-catch-all parties for which we still seem to lack a generally recognized term, or, in fact, still have too many competing or complementary terms, as we shall see later in this chapter. What is most noteworthy is that the direction in which this third wave is moving parties is in an opposite direction to the first two waves: for the first time in a century, change is primarily characterized by a lesser instead of a greater degree of organization. This has, of course, been part of a secular trend that has also affected many other sectors of politics and society.

The important thing, however, is that the sequence of the three waves and four types cannot be considered to be more than a general rule. The scene of political parties, more than many other scenes in the social sciences, has always been and continues to be under the spell of *die Gleichzeitigkeit des Ungleichzeitigen* (the overlap of features stemming from different historical periods). That means not only that parties in real life almost never correspond to a 'pure type' but usually reflect a mix of characteristics, though with recognizably dominant typological features. It also implies that, in more cases than not, parties belonging to different types and 'stages' may interact simultaneously, and, what is more, that different typological features corresponding to different stages of the party's development may prevail, at the same time, in different regional and sectoral units or partial constituencies of one and the same party. As political parties essentially reflect a complex ensemble of processes of interaction rather than a static organizational or institutional blueprint, the clear lines and terms of a typology necessarily become blurred when used in the context of empirical analysis. The 'pure type' of a party tends to be extremely short-lived. Hence it might be wise to refrain from overstating the typological side as well as from inventing too many new types which, like the older ones, would immediately become subject to change and modification once they have been established.

When Otto Kirchheimer, more than thirty-five years ago, first introduced the notion of the 'catch-all party' (or catch-all mass party, or catch-all 'people's' party), and pointed to the functional and organizational changes that had taken place within major parties in many Western democracies following the Second World War (in the United States even before), his seminal paper ended with a question: 'Will this limited participation which the catchall party offers the population at large, this call to rational and dispassionate participation in the political process via officially sanctiomed channels, work?' And Kirchheimer (1966: 200) left no doubt that he could imagine serious problems when he continued:

The instrument, the catch-all party, cannot be much more rational than its nominal master, the individual voter. No longer subject to the discipline of the party of integration—or, as in the United States, never subject to this discipline—the voters may, by their shifting moods and their apathy, transform the sensitive instrument of the catch-all party into something too blunt to serve as a link with the functional power-holders of society.

He added that we might even come to regret the passing of the class-mass party and the denominational party 'even if it was inevitable'.

Indeed, it appears that this instrument of 'limited participation', though it has survived a number of decades and still appears to be very much alive, has not fully satisfied the voters. From the 1970s on, substantial numbers have turned away from catch-all parties either in disappointment and frustration or in search of new forms of mediation and linkage between the grass roots and organized institutional politics that might again perform the functions of expression and integration which the old mass-integration party had satisfied. Change and even 'crisis' of the catch-all party was inevitable, as Kirchheimer had noted. Some have regarded this as a crisis of 'modernity' entailing a number of changes: phenomenological, organizational, and functional; in dimension, scope, and weight; and in their interactions and linkages with the state and with the various interests and groups of civil society.

Whether or not it is appropriate to refer to these developments as a 'crisis' (see Daalder 1992 and Chapter 2 above), it is undeniable that there have been important changes that may even have reached a categorical threshold. These changes have affected the widely established mechanisms of the *Parteienstaat* (or of *partitocrazia*), and, more broadly, interactions between the so-called political class and citizens at the grass-roots level, as well as the channels of interest intermediation. The symptoms of the crisis have usually shown in higher rates of protest votes or abstention,[9] in a decline (at least temporarily) in the vote for catch-all parties from about 90 per cent in the 1960s to about 70 per cent in the 1990s,[10] in a reduction in the societial 'presence' of parties and in their overall influence, and in increased fragmentation and competition. This syndrome has variously been described in terms of dissatisfaction and disenchantment, *desencanto*, or *Parteienverdrossenheit* and *Politikverdrossenheit*.[11] Does this mean that the age of the catch-all parties and of the *Parteienstaat* is over? Or could the crisis lead to re-equilibration?

I shall argue that we still live in the age of catch-allism and, where it applies, of the *Parteienstaat*, but that a number of important modifications of the original type have taken place (in addition to those Kirchheimer had already mentioned as constituting the partly divergent and mixed empirical cases as compared to his real type), and significant mixes and overlappings of typologically different phenomena have been produced simultaneously which make Kirchheimer's type eventually look outdated in many ways. I will also argue that we may best understand the twentieth-century evolution of the major party types as a continuous and often gradual two-step process in which we can identify more continuities than have been suggested by the usual typological differentiations. For example, numerous features that have been ascribed to the catch-all party could also be found in the mass-integration party, while others usually believed to be products of the more recent crisis of the catch-all party have been inherent in the type from the beginning. Many class-based or denominationally based mass parties already had a latent or manifest tendency towards catch-allism, and many declared catch-all parties, like the Italian Christian Democrats or the German Social Democrats, have often shown a tendency towards preserving some residual characteristics of their earlier denominational or class orientations, particularly in regions whose social milieux are compatible with such characteristics.

I shall also argue that there seems to be a more pronounced threshold between Kirchheimer's catch-all party and the modified present-day catch-all party than there was between the catch-all party and the earlier mass-integration party. The classic European catch-all party still followed the twentieth-century pattern linking political modernization with more and denser organization; it was still recognizable as a *Gestalt*; and it still retained patterns of cleavage anchoring, particularly with regard to the left/right cleavage that had been established at the birth of the mass-integration parties around the turn of the century (see Puhle 1977: 340–77). The crisis of the late twentieth century, in contrast, has apparently reversed the secular trend toward greater organization: the present-day catch-all party, which has been considered to be more 'vulnerable' by many authors, has been characterized by less organization, by increased segmentation and fragmentation, a decline of cleavage anchoring, and by an interaction between the left/right cleavage and a more categorical in/out cleavage in which there are greater similarities among the 'ins' (whatever their ideological orientation) and the 'outs'.

In light of these observations, one might even contend that Kirchheimer's catch-all party is actually an extension of the mass-integration party, and reserve the term 'catch-all' for the less systematic, less structured, less well organized, and less well defined modified catch-all parties that have emerged in recent years, which I will refer to as 'catch-all parties plus'. A number of scholars have already moved in this direction, though often implicitly and in a somewhat meandering fashion: Peter Mair (1990) has used Kirchheimer's original term for the catch-all-party-in-crisis; Gordon Smith (1990) has distinguished between a pre-crisis catch-all party and a crisis-affected 'people's party' (using two terms differently which Kirchheimer had used synonymously). And von Beyme (2000) has recently borrowed Panebianco's (1988) term of the 'electoral-professional party' in order to give it a new meaning and to label, against Panebianco's intentions, a categorically new type which apparently goes even beyond 'catch-all plus'.[12]

Even if the terminology may be confusing, the symptoms seem to indicate a clear diagnosis: catch-allism, in essence, is considered to be still prevailing, in one way or another, but Kirchheimer's term has taken on so much patina over the years that it no longer seems to be adequate in itself to the purpose of characterizing present-day tendencies of party change.

Before we can analyse this crisis and the emergence of the 'catch-all party plus', we have to be as clear as possible about the definition, the characteristics, the constellations, and the historical context of the catch-all party. This cannot be separated from the respective constellations of the party systems and from the emergence of another European invention which came to be known as the *Parteienstaat* (party state).[13]

CATCH-ALL PARTIES AND THE *PARTEIENSTAAT*

Otto Kirchheimer's article on the rise of the catch-all party and Gerhard Leibholz's (1966) new interpretation of the *Parteienstaat* both date from the mid-1960s, though the authors could and did rely on their previous work dating back to the late 1920s. The rise of the catch-all party (also *Volkspartei*) in Western Europe after the Second World War was a product of the second wave of organizational modernization in contemporary politics. It had been preceded by a first wave of modernization about half a century earlier that had triggered the rise of what later came to be known as the mass or mass-integration party (out of which the catch-all party subsequently emerged). This first wave had produced, among other things, a new type of aggressive pressure group; technically efficient, well organized, and disciplined, often bureaucratic political machines (*Apparate*); an extension of political participation; and a decisive change in the relationships among parliaments and governments, parties, interest groups, and the public at large. In this process the traditional liberal dichotomy between 'the State' and the autonomous associations and agents of the 'civil society' became increasingly blurred and (in some respects) was replaced by an explicit left/right cleavage. Parties on both sides of that cleavage drew support equally from civil society and from the state. Typologically, it was a step from less organized nineteenth-century representative or notable politics to organized mass politics consistent with the logic of organized capitalism, and the beginning of a secular trend that was to last until the last quarter of the twentieth century. While this general process affected all of Western Europe, its particular manifestation in any given country or region was affected by the differing political, social-structural, economic, and cultural contexts (Puhle 1973, 1995; Habermas 1990).

The extension of the suffrage, growing social and political polarization, technological and organizational innovations, strong competition, and the need for better organized and coordinated mass campaigning made the traditional 'parties of representation'—of particular interests, classes, elites, beliefs, programmes or *Weltanschauungen*—increasingly transform into class- or denominationally based 'mass-integration parties' (Neumann 1956). Organizational modernization weakened the influence of individual members and local or regional groups vis-à-vis the central party organization, while it emphasized the party's integrative functions and enabled the party elite and bureaucracy to act more autonomously. The trend towards 'oligarchic' rule noted by Robert Michels (1970 [1911]) in the German SPD as early as 1911 was also detected in other working-class, Catholic, conservative, or nationalist mass-based parties before and after the First World War. As mass-integration parties sought to expand their constituencies, their pro-grammatic, religious, or class character was diluted. Accordingly, it could be argued that the very founding of the mass-integration party was accompanied by the first steps toward the rise of the catch-all party about half a century later.[14]

The second wave of organizational modernization of the European parties began after the Second World War and, notwithstanding exceptions and many parties which include features derived from a mix of party types, it has produced as a dominant pattern what became to be known as the 'catch-all party' (Kirchheimer) or *Volkspartei*.[15] When class and religious conflicts (with some notorious exceptions) became less entrenched in post-war Western Europe, and as the mass consumer society became more widespread (making European societies in some respects more 'American'), the major political parties found it not only desirable and necessary but also feasible to expand and go beyond the traditional constituencies of the mass-integration parties, and hence began to give first priority to the goal of maximizing votes. In contrast to the United States where the mass-integration party had never existed, this implied a number of specific changes including (as described by Kirchheimer 1966: 190) a

drastic reduction of the party's ideological baggage . . . [, a f]urther strengthening of top leadership groups, whose actions and omissions are now judged from the view-point of their contribution to the efficiency of the entire social system rather than identification with the goals of their particular organization . . . [, d]owngrading of the role of the individual party member, a role considered a historical relic which may obscure the newly built-up catch-all party image . . . [, d]eemphasis of the *classe gardée*, specific social-class or denominationally clientele, in favor of recruiting voters among the population at large . . . [, and s]ecuring access to a variety of interest groups.

It should be noted that some (but not all) of these changes represented a continuation of tendencies that had already been inherent in the mass-integration party. But Kirchheimer's emphasis was on the discontinuities, particularly the fact that, of the three vital functions of parties (nomination of candidates, integration, and expression) only the first would be satisfactorily fulfilled by the catch-all parties. They would try to differ from one another only in so far as that was necessary to make themselves recognizable. In light of the downgrading of the expressive function of parties and the loosening of their ties to voters, parties would perform poorly with regard to identification and integration. Accordingly, many of the characteristics later regarded as evidence of the 'crisis' of the catch-all part were integral aspects of the new type from the beginning.[16]

In the real world, political parties have never completely conformed to all elements of Kirchheimer's real type, and not all of them have become catch-all parties. The extent to which they did approximate this type depended on a number of factors, including the size of the parties and the country in question, electoral systems and the institutional structure of democracy, the cleavages existing in each relevant society, historical legacies, and the specific trajectory of modernization of the social and political system in question (see Puhle 1995). Here the relationship between the (strong or weak) state and (a strong or weak) civil society, and the links among citizens, organizations, and government are of a particular importance. And in almost no case did the membership or electorate of a catch-all party exactly reflect the overall composition of society as a whole; the party's clientele was also shaped in part by its historical background and residual traditions. Similarly, subunits or affiliated organizations of the party often significantly departed from the new type: numerous residua or enclaves of Catholic (or otherwise denominational), working-class, or regional subcultures have remained, for example. Finally, the structure and dynamics of the party system has also substantially influenced the kinds of alternatives presented to voters by individual parties (see Sartori 1976).

Catch-All Mechanisms

The transition from mass-integration party to catch-all party by and large entailed the following basic trends. The parties' programmes, milieux, religious and class connotations have become less important, although they still seem to correspond to a persistent left/right cleavage in the perceptions of the voters. Their societal links and hence their 'rootedness' have weakened, as has the representation of particular interests by the parties. Parties have adopted a market-related strategy intended to maximize votes (and in some instances, members), and steps to foster short-term identification with and loyalty to the party. Political issues and proposed solutions had 'to be sold', and how to sell them has often turned out to be more important than the issues and solutions as such; accordingly, image has often counted more than competence. Campaigns have become more commercialized and more professionalized, and hence, with the exception of the United States, more centralized, and the pervasive issue of 'credibility' has personalized them further. Focusing their campaigns on the small segment of shifting votes near the centre of the polit-ical spectrum, parties have become more centrist, more moderate, and more similar to one another—except in those cases where there are deeply rooted controversies or ethno-national cleavages (like in Catalonia, the Basque provinces, or Northern Ireland) or the party system has been generally more *verzuilt* (like in the Netherlands). At the high point of catch-allism (the 1950s through 1970s, when they collectively captured over 90 per cent of the vote), the number of alternative political positions was reduced, as was the degree of respective cleavage anchoring. *Allgemeine Koalitionsfähigkeit* became more of a reality.

Catch-all politics has been further strengthened by the emergence of tele-vision as the dominant medium of political communication, beginning in the United States with the 1960 presidential campaign, and spreading over the fol-lowing decade and a half throughout Europe. Television has revolutionized electoral campaigns, greatly increasing the role of the national party leaders and their advisers (who are increasingly professionalized and media-savvy), and often marginalizing local and regional party elites. The political use of television has also influenced the criteria for the selection of party leaders, and it has contributed to a further personalization and simplification of political issues. In combination with the increasing reliance upon public opinion poll data, it has also strengthened the affirmative mechanisms of identity and loy-alty building at the expense of traditional or new forms of political particip-ation. These trends have been particularly strong in Portugal and Spain, which returned to democracy in the mid-1970s, by which time access to television had become almost universal (see Gunther *et al.* 2000; Pasquino 2001). While much systematic comparative research on the impact of television on politics has yet to be undertaken, there are indications that similar processes have been at work elsewhere in Western Europe, North America, and Latin America.[17] In the case of Western Europe, it is interesting to note that the heyday of the catch-all party corresponded with the predominance of public broadcasting systems, with particular mechanisms of control in different countries, while the crisis of catch-allism began in the 1980s, at about the same time that pri-vate-sector, commercial channels were beginning to proliferate.

The Emergence of the Parteienstaat

Catch-all parties and television campaigns were American inventions that proliferated throughout Europe, albeit with adaptations to certain characteristics of the European context. The development and evolution of the *Parteienstaat*, however, was entirely different. It came to flourish first and particularly within the post-fascist democracies of West Germany, Austria, and Italy, and among the latecomers transiting from authoritarian rule in the late 1970s, notably in Greece and, to a much lesser extent, Spain. The strength of the market, private businesses, and commercial broadcasting systems prevented these government/party practices from spreading to the United States. Nor did they take root in the United Kingdom, due to the tradition of a politically neutral civil service and state broadcasting system, nor in France, due to the *grands corps*, to the strong residua of notable politics and the prevailing role of the state conceived as being 'above' the parties. Statist and absolutist traditions also existed in many continental European countries, including the post-fascist democracies, but the memory of the breakdown of earlier democracies in these countries, the prominent roles played by party leaders in the fight against fascism, and the defeat of dictatorial regimes which had suppressed the democratic parties helped establish the new political parties as the most important vehicles and actors in a parliamentary democracy and even recognized in a number of constitutions. The positive new attitudes towards the parties and the traditions of a relatively 'strong' state were to combine and find a new *Gestalt* in what was to become the *Parteienstaat*. It is important to note that all cases of a *Parteienstaat* have been parliamentary not presidential systems, and all had a dominant element of proportional representation in their electoral systems. Evidently the institutions, the concrete type of a democratic regime, and its history do matter.

Parteienstaat basically means the same as *partitocrazia*: a situation in which the political parties dominate the state and 'colonize' important segments of its institutions and society, like public administration (at all levels), public enterprises, education, the media, etc. (see Leibholz 1973; and Beyme 1993b). Even if the concept may have been exaggerated since its invention and in many sectors could be better understood in terms of approximation than as a full-fledged real type, the amount of reality behind it is impressive. It came into existence in a context in which the rise of the mass consumer society and a relatively long period of economic prosperity coincided with the extension of the bureaucratic social and welfare state, of the mechanisms of corporatist or semi-corporatist concertation, and with a first wave of new communication technology (television still being overwhelmingly public). It amounted to much more than just an explicit recognition of the parties (as had been written into a number of West and South European constitutions after the Second World War), and to more than the traditional patronage practices exercised by a majority party or a coalition in government.

The privileges and the services of the *Parteienstaat*, first of all, go to *all* significant parties, including the opposition—a mechanism that has been further intensified in Germany by federalism, in Austria by the long-standing practice of Great Coalitions, and in Italy by the broad *arco costituzionale*, the antifascist consensus, and a long tradition (until 1993) of an almost equal distribution of the local and regional strongholds between the two major parties. Including the opposition in the dispensation of patronage helped to reduce the potential for effective parliamentary control of the government and of the parties participating in the game. Here the *Parteienstaat* comes close to some earlier Latin American experiments in *co-gobierno* (like in Uruguay). In spite of their competition for the votes, in many sectors the parties form an oligopolistic cartel that commands important institutions and resources of the state (and whose privileges have eventually been written into law, like in the German *Parteiengesetz*[18]). One of the most prominent features of these practices since the late 1950s has been the financing of parties out of the state budget. Public financing of parties has usually favoured the parliamentary group of the party, and currently covers about half of the budgets of the major parties in most European countries (with the exception of the Netherlands).[19]

One of the products of the *Parteienstaat* has been a structural proximity and overlapping between the parties and the state which differ markedly from the nature of this relationship in liberal times. The parties (represented by the party elites) are no longer representing societal interests vis-à-vis the government and the bureaucracy; instead, they form part of the state, primarily representing themselves as a power elite or 'political class', as it has often been called since the 1980s. This has made it necessary for societal interests to be represented by different groups and organizations, which, in turn, approach the parties in their function as representatives of the state.[20] The tendency to incorporate societal organizations and interests into state institutions and channels, as is inherent in systems characterized by organized capitalist or (neo)corporatist arrangements, also fits with recent patterns of executive dominance over parliament, for various reasons, and, when party leaders are also heads of government (for example, Helmut Kohl and Felipe González), over their respective parties. The new proximity (or symbiosis) between the party establishment and the state—the counterpart to which is distance between party leaders and citizens—may eventually limit the parties' capacities for reform and their effectiveness as mediators, and favour corruption, clientelism, and lack of imagination. The problem here is that a party's fortunes, even life and death, are no longer determined by the mechanisms of the political market alone, because the *Parteienstaat* provides for additional means for survival, delaying or blunting negative sanctions that might otherwise have been imposed when a party no longer delivers. The quality of the

Parteienstaat depends on the quality of the parties, and the partiess' crisis will affect the state.

We now turn to the various symptoms of the perceived crisis of the catch-all party and the implications of the 'third wave' of politico-organizational modernization in the final decades of the twentieth century. As we shall see, this has led to numerous 'catch-all plus' phenomena and a search for new terms to describe a 'fourth type' of party, the contours of which are still not sufficiently clear.

THE CRISIS OF CATCH-ALLISM AND TENTATIVE NEW TYPES

Since the late 1970s and the 1980s the catch-all parties and the *Parteienstaat* have both entered into 'crisis', raising questions about whether this crisis will lead to breakdown or re-equilibration. Given the similarities (if not inter-changeability) among the policy positions of the major conservative or social democratic European catch-all parties and the lack of clear alternatives, some critics have asked: 'do parties matter?'[21] Symptoms of the crisis have been seen in the higher rates of protest votes and abstention; in a significant decline of the vote for the catch-all parties; in the fragmentation of political issues and preferences; in lack of leadership, imagination, and capacity for integration; and in corruption, clientelistic practices, and pervasive 'disenchantment'.

The critical diagnosis has inspired demands for a number of therapies which have not always been easily compatible with one another. Parties are urged to act forcefully and in a united manner, but, at the same time, to resist oligarchic temptations and promote democratic decision-making, particip-ation, and control from below within the party. They are expected to rep-resent the interests of their constituency, but also to be able to formulate coherent policies 'above' special interests. They should provide leadership, but not be dominated by their leaders. They should not be financed by the state (at least not to the present extent), but nor should they be dependent on the contributions of wealthy donors, corporations, or interest groups. They should not be represented and led by 'professional' politicians, nor, at the same time, should they be led by amateurs or inexperienced elites. The parties are, however, not only victims of a catalogue of 'rising (and sometimes unreasonable) expectations'; their structure and performance has also con-tributed to their 'crisis'.

The Challenge: Crisis and Gradual Delegitimation

The crisis has been caused by three different sets of factors. The first involves the inherent structural weaknesses of the catch-all party identified earlier: catch-all parties are weak in in their integrative capacities, policy articulation, and leadership, and, hence, in their ability to retain the support of a stable core of members and voters during bad times. Second, they were forced to confront an odd type of economic crisis ('stagflation') that the standard Keynesian policy responses could not effectively address, in addition to the need to embrace a wide range of economic and social reforms at a time of diminished resources. The economic crisis of the 1970s demonstrated not only the limits to growth but also the limits of the welfare-oriented policies of distribution that had been the key instrument and principal source of legitimation of the *Parteienstaat*. The parties could no longer 'deliver' as expected. This economic crisis was further complicated by rapid technological change and growing international competition, as well as by a political climate that increasingly delegitimized the social-welfare state and big government in general, and made neoliberal ideas of deregulation, 'destatization', decentralization, and privatization popular. 'Small' became 'beautiful' and fashionable. This challenge to the social-welfare state and Keynesian interventionism came not just from the neoliberal right: there was also a populist groundswell, articulated by the 'new' social movements, against bigness, intermediary institutions, and professionalization, and in favour of more direct participation from the grass roots and a better control of governments and bureaucracies. The net effect of these developments was to produce a third dimension of the crisis of the catch-all party: the reactions of the voters and the political parties to these changes.

Even if the (neo)conservative prophecies about the end of the 'project of modernity' may have been as exaggerated as were those about the 'end of the social democratic century',[22] it was obvious that structural reforms were necessary in many fields. Here in the short run, the established politicians and parties could only lose. The catch-all parties which were considered to be part of the problem, began to lose votes from the mid-1970s on; volatility rose and the degree of cleavage anchoring decreased further. They also lost members (in Germany from the late 1970s on) and *militantes*, and many of the traditional linkages to allied intermediary organizations (labour unions, religious and church groups or liberal associations) began to weaken, as the membership of these organizations fell dramatically (Katz 1990; Scarrow 1994). The parties lost part of their clout on key issues, as well as a great deal of their potential for mobilization, and they faced new competition from social movements which gave voice to disenchantment with parties and more general anti-party sentiments. Party elites were increasingly portrayed as an autonomous, self-referential, and greedy 'political class', isolated institutionally and culturally from ordinary citizens. The new social movements, in contrast, were regarded by some as a viable alternative to parties, with weaker attachments, smaller size, less entrenchment, more diversity and openness, and greater ideological and programmatic flexibility. They were also seen as going beyond the traditional bounds of 'right' and 'left' by advancing a variety of 'single issues' (which contributed to fragmentation of the political agenda and weakened the interest-aggregation capacity of the party system), including those derived from new 'post-materialist' values and 'post-modern' lifestyles 'projects'.[23] In the end, these social movements have failed to live up to these expectations and emerge as a viable alternative.

Response and Outcomes

The outcome of the crisis so far has been mixed. On the one hand, programmes and ideologies have lost weight, while party identification, participation, and cleavage anchoring of electoral support have significantly declined, and electoral volatility has increased. On the other hand, the left/right cleavage in party systems remains significant, and the 'hard core' of the Western party systems has, on the whole, remained stable, with the only exception being Italy in 1993 (see Morlino 1995). In the aggregate, changes in most party systems appear to be manifestations of realignment rather than dealignment.[24] According to a comparative study of seventy-eight parties in eleven West European countries by Poguntke (2000), most parties have usually tried to compensate for what they have lost (the case of the classical mass and catch-all parties) or never gained (the case of new parties like the Greens or neopopulist right-wing parties) in membership, in proximity to collateral organizations, and in internal and external linkages, basically in two ways— either by establishing new, mixed short-term linkages, or by adopting new mechanisms (new campaign techniques, streamlined 'commercial' performance, appeal of a leader) in lieu of linkages.[25]

The potential for mobilization and the degree of representativeness of the parties has undoubtedly receded. The more active new social movements have, however, not been able to revolutionize the political systems. None of the established democratic systems in Europe has been fundamentally changed, not even the Italian. On the other hand, while the movements have not had a great impact (which is not surprising, given their fragmentation), they have mounted a challenge to the political parties which has had some positive and productive effects. By competing with them, particularly at the local and regional levels, they have forced parties to open up, to revise their priorities, to incorporate new issues into their programmes, and to adjust their traditional organizations and channels of participation.[26] In a number of cases this has led to a certain ideological revival ('parties matter again'), as well as to new intra-party cleavages and conflicts about priorities—features which are not normally found in the typical catch-all party. This mechanism has affected the Christian democratic, conservative and liberal parties, as well as the socialists and social democrats. The latter, in particular, in order to overcome their notorious 'electoral dilemma' of either losing traditional or new voters (if not both), have tried to establish a precarious balance between non-traditional reformist aspirations (like liberalizing and deregulating the economy) and an explicit attention to some traditional core issues (like improving educational, health, and welfare services) which continue to differentiate them from the conservatives.[27]

Broad coalition- and consensus-building within the party has again become an indispensable task of all political parties, particularly in light of the more urgent necessity to present a united party to the outside, both during and between the election campaigns. Most parties have had no choice but to respond to these challenges, address the deficits, and begin to reform and restructure their organizations and decision-making processes, though with different emphases (see Harmel *et al.* 1995). In the case of Germany and Austria this can be shown, in Italy it still remains to be seen. So finally another 'American' mechanism has become part of European politics: mobilized grass-roots efforts (and not just preventive adaptation engineered by elites) have brought about periodic reform of established structures and institutions before the structures and institutions break down completely.

The new movements, on the other hand, have also had to change. When they enter into political bargaining processes, they usually become less fundamentalist, more moderate, more 'political' and more institutionalized. Although they often resort to radical rhetoric, most of them have sought to exercise greater political influence and power by adapting to the mechanisms of party politics, becoming ordinary, though perhaps 'new style' parties. The most successful examples are the German Greens and the Italian *Leghe* (at least where in power), but we could also find similar processes of transformation from movements into parties in most of the Eastern and East–Central European countries in transition from communism. Revulsion towards the 'real socialist' regime parties, coupled with a defensive reaction against state repression, initially led the democratic opposition to organize as 'movements', in the form of unions (like Solidarnosc in Poland) or a broad 'civic forum' (as in Czechoslovakia). Over the long term, however, survival as significant political forces required them to transform themselves into political parties.[28]

This *force des choses* has also been due to the privileged role political parties have played in most transitions from authoritarian or communist rule, and in the consolidation of new democracies. Since democracy is based on free and fair elections, and the founding act of a new democracy usually is the first democratic election, it is not surprising that parties (which nominate candidates and conduct election campaigns) have acquired a structural advantage vis-à-vis labour unions, associations, and other kinds of interest groups. And given the virtual monopoly of parties over political action during the democratic transition and the first phases of democratic consolidation, they acquired sufficient power to enable them to continue as the predominant political actors over the long term. In Spain, for example, the

1977 *Pactos de la Moncloa* (which dealt primarily with economic and social issues) were not negotiated by entrepreneurs and unions, but by the political parties. In Portugal, where they began in a subordinate position due to the domination of the first stages of the transition by the revolutionary military, the democratic process soon developed a momentum of its own so that the military had to call for general elections in 1975 and gradually, if reluctantly, concede power to the parties and to parliament.[29]

The parties have been 'gatekeepers' of the new democracies, and in most cases they have also served as modernizers of the political and social systems. Their consolidation and the consolidation of the party systems have been beneficial to democracy, while unconsolidated and 'weak' party systems (as in Brazil) have usually been a liability also for democracy (Mainwaring 1999). It is interesting to note that in the more advanced new democracies (basically of Southern and East Central Europe), strong and 'moderate' party systems were established, and most parties, irrespective of their origins, have soon developed into modern catch-all parties, indicating the unrivalled attractiveness of the catch-all type. And the longer these countries have experienced democratic 'normalcy', the more their parties have exhibited signs of the crisis of the catch-all parties (see Morlino 1995; Diamandouros and Gunther 2001).

The 'Catch-All Party Plus': Agent of Enlarged Intermediation

The structural advantage of political parties in a democracy is, of course, not limited to the new democracies. It also exists in the older and traditional democracies because democracy is always about elections, and elections require, among other things, a territorial dimension of representation which is functionally satisfied by candidates provided by the parties. Thus, even in the recent crisis, the parties could not be replaced or done away with, and even catch-all parties have good prospects for survival if they reform, reorganize, and become responsive again, at least in the perception of the public. The functions they perform, however, have changed somewhat, in comparison to what they had been in the traditional and more monolithic *Parteienstaat* before the crisis: in a more decentralized set with more fragmented and still overlapping networks there are more actors in need of mediation by the parties and their elites. The parties have to mediate between the new social movements, citizens' organizations, public interest groups, in addition to old-type interests, pressure groups, and established constituencies, on the one hand, and the state agencies and institutions, the media, and corporatist networks, on the other. The 'political class' may no longer enjoy unchallenged access to the fruits of the *Parteienstaat* as a 'compensation' for what they have lost (Beyme 1993*b*) if they are not prepared to face the new and more complicated tasks of mediation, and hence act more professionally along the lines of a new service class.

Modern political parties at the beginning of the twenty-first century seem to have gone beyond Panebianco's (or Beyme's) electoral-professional functions to become professional agencies *and* loosely coupled networks of political intermediation. Indeed, professionalism has been strengthened in part because network servicing also requires a significant amount of professional competence in various fields. As indicated above, the trend clearly seems to go from catch-all party to 'catch-all party plus', and not to 'catch-all party minus', as a number of authors have suggested. A return to the earlier mass-integration party is impossible, because parties have retained the broader catch-all spectrum and intentions. As one of the parties' key tasks is mediation, nor would it be of use to confine the present and future parties to the functions of a 'new programme party' (Wolinetz, Chapter 6 below), a 'new politics party' (Poguntke 1987), or a 'new members' party' (Haungs 1994; Walter 1995). In contrast, the term 'modern cadre party' (Koole 1992, 1994) could underline the professional qualities and the key role of the elites if the term would not also suggest a nineteenth-century *déjà vu*. 'Network party' (Machnig 2000) might be a more open concept, but it has not yet been sufficiently specified. A more adequate conceptualization would cast parties as providers of 'linkages' (Lawson and Merkl 1988*a*), not only among elites, members, and voters (the classical variant), but also connecting individuals and groups, party and society, the media, collateral organizations, and government.

Along similar lines a tentative and fluid new type of great heuristic productivity for the analysis of present party change has been proposed by Katz and Mair (1995). The 'cartel party', in complete reversal of the liberal nineteenth-century mould, sees parties overwhelmingly as agents in the sphere of the state acting 'from above' in offering mechanisms and channels of participation and linkage to the citizens and to the groups of civil society. Although the type is capable of honouring the parties' service and broker functions, it tends to see the parties too exclusively as agencies of the state. It also neglects their catch-all character and the fact that the increased pressures exerted upon them by the groups and interests of civil society continually influence and modify the parties so that the stipulated 'cartel' character remains only a momentary and static impression in an ongoing process of party change. The authors of this concept seem to acknowledge that the challenge posed by a 'cartel party', the reactions it provokes, and the interactions it initiates may finally become much more important than the type itself. The cartel type may be even more fragile and 'vulnerable' than the catch-all type has ever been (see Wolinetz, in this volume), and it appears unlikely that it will dominate the next decades in the way the mass party and the catch-all party have previously. In their contribution to this volume, Katz and Mair have advanced their argument in making productive use of the analysis of the different relationships and linkages among three different levels of party: the party on the ground, the party in central office, and the party in public office. They see the 'classic' catch-all party as beset by conflict within the party in central office between the factions of the the party in public office and the party on the ground, and assume that in contemporary parties (which I refer to as 'catch-all plus') this struggle has been settled in favour of the party in public office, while the other two have been marginalized. Not all of these assumptions, however, are borne out by empirical evidence, particularly with regard to party finance, staff, and structural or temporal proximity to the government.[30] We might also find substantial evidence that the 'classic' patterns of conflict of the catch-all era still seem to be very much alive in contemporary parties, no matter how much they may have changed.

Towards re-equilibration

So what are the key characteristics of the performance of modified catch-all parties in and after the crisis? The principal tasks and functions of political parties, besides winning elections and providing patronage (the 'classics'), have been usually defined as follows: (1) defining policies, (2) articulation, aggregation, and representation of interests, (3) mobilization and political socialization of the citizens, and (4) recruitment of elites and the formation of governments.[31] In the light of recent changes it can be said that parties still have almost a monopoly in recruiting political elites and that their capacities to define policies have somehow recovered; at the same time, however, their mobilizational and representational functions seem to be challenged and in retreat. In addition, some new tasks or new aspects of old functions should be highlighted, including (1) the role of mediator or broker, (2) initiation of new efforts regarding control, restructuring, and reform of political institutions, including the parties themselves, and (3) their role as focuses of integration and identification, albeit perhaps in a more short-term, ad hoc manner than in the past.

One of the new characteristics of the modified catch-all parties is a greater degree of decentralization and 'loosely coupled anarchy' (*lose verkoppelte Anarchie*) (Lösche and Walter 1992). With the exception of Italy, however, this has not substantially affected the party systems. Loosening party discipline, expanding private television (a new quality!) and the manifold coalitions and folklore of a new localism have given more room than before to political mavericks and to the populist temptations of (allegedly) antiprofessional rebellions against professionalized politics. By and large, however, parliamentary systems (at least those under proportional representation electoral systems) have so far been able to contain these tendencies. These systems did not favour the rise of American-style political entrepreneurs, and many of the antiprofessional rebels later became professional politicians. Even if German media tycoon Leo Kirch or any charismatic showman had the political ambition of a Silvio Berlusconi, it is highly improbable that they would succeed without first being adopted by one of the major parties.[32]

While much distrust remained vis-à-vis the political class, and the problem of 'identity'—between the rulers and the ruled or between the state and civil society—remains 'unsolved', the changes in the catch-all parties have helped to restore some of their lost potential for responsiveness, and to broaden citizens' consent. More transparent and more flexible party structures, decentralization of decisions and information, more fragmented constituencies, moves towards greater responsiveness, and a more individualized, market-driven investigative journalism may also have slightly improved the capabilities of the system to control power and the political class. Indeed, in a number of European countries there have been significant ad hoc changes resulting from the activities of muck-raking journalists or populist mavericks, or brought about by the new social movements, by new alliances, or by rebellions within the less monolithic parties in a less oligopolistic system. And we must not forget that, despite the numerous tendencies towards more convergence of policies between the major parties, there still seems to be, in many sectors, a certain demand for political 'identities', for sentimental bonds, residual milieux, and for a political *Heimat* which can so far be satisfied by the many continuities still inherent in most parties and party organizations.

Though people no longer identify with the parties as much as they did previously, and though the parties can no longer claim to be as representative of the people as they were before, the rumours about the imminent demise of the catch-all parties and the *Parteienstaat* have been grossly exaggerated. In spite of their many losses and new acquisitions, both are still there, functioning on the whole along the same lines as before, even in Italy. The fall has been contained and limited. What we find is a modified and restructured *Parteienstaat* with modified and restructured catch-all parties. The crisis has so far not led to breakdown, but to re-equilibration.

A SECULAR CHANGE: LESS ORGANIZED POLITICS

The outcome of the recent crisis of the catch-all parties and of the *Parteienstaat* can be described as a move from more organized to less organized and differently organized politics—a move that reverses the century-long trend linking modernization to higher levels of party organization. Following the first two waves of political modernization through organization, the third has been a process of a more complex and more differentiated restructuring that has combined elements of continuity with those of discontinuity. Continuity we find in the ongoing commercialization and professionalization of politics, in the expansion of markets (both economic and political), in tendencies towards corporate agglomeration and corporatist intermediation, in the weight of state activities and intervention, and in the dependency of many social actors on the state, including the parties, when it comes to party financing and privileges. Elements of discontinuity can be found in the trends towards de-organization, deregulation, and decentralization, fragmentation, privatization, and 'decoupling'.

In the restructured *Parteienstaat* parties still matter, and they still form an oligopolistic cartel, but it is a more flexible if not a more diluted cartel because there is more competition. More actors are involved, and the tasks of coordination and mediation have become more multilateral and complex, while those of integration and identification have become more difficult. A trend towards 'loosely coupled anarchy' is apparent, and is associated with a tendency towards short-termism and what might be called 'ad-hockery'. With the fading of long-term orientations, programmes, and 'rooted' milieux, interests, political issues, and constituencies have become more fragmented, representation more personalized, and the establishment of standing structural loyalties, identifications, and alliances more difficult. Instead, we find ad hoc mobilization, ad hoc loyalties, identifications, and alliances, even ad hoc 'programmes' and policies. The primacy of the ad hoc mechanisms corresponds to some of the characteristics of the catch-all parties. This trend favours those parties that have traditionally been more ad hoc mobilizers—like the Spanish, Portuguese, or Greek socialists—rather than builders of structures like the German SPD or the social democrats in Scandinavia (Puhle 2001).

It is interesting to note that some features of what has been tentatively called 'post-modern' politics seem to bear a striking resemblance to those of 'pre-modern' politics, before the first wave of organizational modernization set in around the turn of the century. These features include less organization and machine politics, more personalized and often individualistic campaigns, more *ad hoc* mobilization, less electoral anchoring and more shifting votes, and less interest in identification and representation. In addition, elite structures are more fragmented, while sectoralized professional skills of individuals are in demand. Programmatic issues have returned, though in highly segmented and short-term variants, and so has a penchant to give a greater importance to the symbolic or bread-and-circuses functions of politics.

The recent crisis has often been interpreted as delegitimizing the catch-all parties and the *Parteienstaat*. This does not seem to imply a full-fledged crisis of legitimation. The catch-all parties and the basic mechanisms of the *Parteienstaat* have, on the whole, remained stable, and it has usually been possible to reorganize a sufficient amount of contingent consent in order to re-equilibrate the system, albeit often with different actors. Only parties that could no longer deliver (as in Italy in the early 1990s) or whose elites behaved in a self-destructive manner (such as the UCD in 1982—see Gunther and Hopkin, Chapter 8 below) were completely delegitimized and severely punished by voters. And even in such cases the crisis of the parties did not amount to a crisis of the democratic regime itself. At most it implied a restructuring of partial regimes, such as the party system. Indeed, it has been argued that the Spanish election of 1982, in which the governing party was completely destroyed and the party system reconstructed, made a positive contribution to the consolidation of democracy. In the two most dramatic cases of party crisis, Spain in 1982 and Italy in the early 1990s, what appears to have resulted is a process of realignment and re-equilibration.

Finally, it may be asked whether or not the crisis of the parties and the *Parteienstaat* has unfolded differently or had different long-term implications in the cases of early or late democratizers—for example, Germany and Italy, as opposed to Greece and Spain. It appears that, once the respective democracies have been consolidated, this distinction makes no significant difference. The characteristic opinion we have found in Southern Europe could have been voiced in any European democracy: people do not like the parties, but they know that they need them (see Morlino and Montero 1995).

NOTES

1. For our purpose political parties are defined as social organizations which present candidates for political elections and compete with one another for political power, whether or not they call themselves 'parties'.
2. The following considerations will primarily focus on a number of 'macro' theories about (or typologies of) political parties, i.e. theories which reflect on the *Gestalt* and the types of parties and party systems, on their interactions, and on their relationship with social groups, interests and the state. Theories of a more limited scope, referring to important sectors and functions of party activities, from the detailed interpretations of voting behaviour to the 'laws' of organizational sociology, cannot be dealt with here.
3. See Weber (1964 [1922]: 11–14 and 1063–80, 1971*a* [1918], 1971*b* [1919]); Ostrogorski (1964 [1902]); Duverger (1954).
4. See Downs (1957); Olson (1965); Inglehart (1979, 1990); Edelman (1974).
5. See e.g. Barnes *et al.* (1979); Budge and Farlie (1983); Dalton *et al.* (1984); Crewe and Denver (1985).
6. For the theoretical background of this distinction, see Strøm (1990*b*); Harmel and Janda (1994); Wolinetz, in this volume. For a comprehensive typology of political parties, see Gunther and Diamond (2001).
7. For classic statements regarding these questions, see Schattschneider (1942); also see Rose (1974*b*); Castles and Wildenmann (1986); Cansino (1995).
8. Ware (1987*a*) called these two party types 'elite-centered' parties and 'mass-membership' parties. Gunther and Diamond (2001) also referred to these as 'elite-based' and 'mass-based', but broke down the former category into 'traditional local notable' and 'clientelistic' party types, and the latter into socialist, nationalist, and religious mass-based parties.

9. Cf. Montero (1986); Font and Virós (1995); Kaase and Klingemann (1990); Eilfort (1994).
10. Rudolf Wildenmann (1989) considered this to be dangerous. Also see Wiesendahl (1992); Mintzel (1983); Mintzel and Oberreuter (1992).
11. Cf. Krockow and Lösche (1986); Starke (1993); Scheuch and Scheuch (1992).
12. For Panebianco (1988: 264 and 311), the 'electoral-professional party', in contrast to the older 'mass bureaucratic party' (which Neumann called the mass integration party), was clearly meant to be equivalent to Kirchheimer's catch-all party, and not its successor type.
13. Here we are referring to the democratic 'party state', not to party (semi-)dictatorships of any kind.
14. On the emergence of the mass integration party, see Neumann (1956), and Weber (1964, 1971b).
15. Here both terms will be used for the same phenomenon, as has been done by Kirchheimer and in much of the subsequent literature. Smith's (1989) suggestion to reserve the term 'people's party' for the more recent crisis-ridden and more vulnerable scaled-down version of the catch-all party, though it is interesting and legitimate, does not in my opinion appear to be categorically adequate.
16. See Kirchheimer (1966: 188–200; 1969); for further elaboration see Wolinetz (1979, 1991).
17. Among the few systematic comparative analyses published to date are Skidmore (1993); Schmitt-Beck (1998); Gunther and Mughan (2000). A major comparative research project on these themes is currently under way. Coordinated by R. Gunther, J. R. Montero, and H.-J. Puhle, the study of 'Political intermediation and democratic legitimacy in new democracies' includes comparative analysis of survey data and other information about the role of the media in election campaigns in thirteen countries on three continents.
18. The 'Gesetz über die politischen Parteien' dates from 1967, and has been changed many times. See *Bundesgesetzblatt* 1989: i. 327–36, and 1990: i. 2141–2.
19. There is a wide variation, however, ranging from 80% of all party funds in Finland, Italy in the late 1960s, and Spain in the 1980s, down to less than half in Britain, Denmark, and Germany. In addition to a notorious lack of transparency, these percentages are problematic due to unclear systems of revenue sharing between the various levels of party organization. For a comparative view, see Beyme (2000: 127–44); Katz and Mair (1992a); Pierre *et al.* (2000); Del Castillo (1985); and Landfried (1990).
20. Some aspects of this new constellation have been emphasized by Beyme (1993b), and by Katz and Mair's (1995) *cartel party* (which, for reasons discussed below, may not enjoy a stable future).
21. See Rose (1984); Castles (1982); Broder (1971).
22. Cf. Dahrendorf (1980); Przeworski and Sprague (1986). A more balanced assessment may be found in Merkel (1993).
23. On value change, see Inglehart (1979, 1990); Muller and Seligson (1994); Bürklin (1988). On the 'new' social movements, cf. Kitschelt (1989a); Dalton and Kuechler (1990); Poguntke (1993); Raschke (1993).
24. Cf. the findings in Daalder and Mair (1983); Bartolini and Mair (1984); Mair and Smith (1990). Doubts about the dealignment thesis are also voiced in Heidar (1994).

25. See also Beyme (2000). On the populist radical right, cf. Ignazi (1994) and Betz (1994); on the Greens, see n. 23.
26. Cf. Poguntke (2000); Mair *et al.* (1999); Niedermayer (1989).
27. For additional details, see Puhle (2001); Boix (1998*a*); Schmidt (1996). In the German SPD, a debate on the desirability of a more 'commercial' technocratic turn has recently led to open controversy: see Machnig (2000) and the comments in *Neue Gesellschaft/Frankfurter Hefte* (2001: 16–27). Blair's 'New Labour' and Schröder's 'Neue Mitte' may have disturbed this balance, at the expense of the traditional concerns of social democratic parties.
28. Cf. Evans and Whitefield (1996); Segert *et al.* (1997); Kitschelt (1992).
29. For more details, see Gunther *et al.* (1995); Linz and Stepan (1996); Merkel and Puhle (1999).
30. For more details, see Beyme (2000), Poguntke (2000), and the data in Katz and Mair (1992*b*).
31. This is basically the wording of the report of an official German advisory committee (*Bericht zur Neuordnung* 1983). Also see Beyme (1985); Steffani (1988); Gunther and Diamond (2001).
32. The exceptional case of Italy, where a localist protest movement turned halfway into party (the *Lega*) and an unprofessional and tendentially antipolitical maverick (Berlusconi) joined forces with the outcasts of the old system (*Alleanza*) to win a majority and reshape the party system, was due to a unique constellation of factors. These included a severe crisis of the eroded *Parteienstaat*, which coincided with the fading away of the Republic's broad antifascist founding consensus (which is different from the democratic consensus per se) and of the conspiracy scenarios of the cold war; see Morlino (1996, 1998).

4

Electoral and Party Competition: Analytical Dimensions and Empirical Problems

Stefano Bartolini

The use of the term 'competition' in the titles of papers, the discussion of the concept itself, and its measurement have grown in the political science literature since the Second World War. The terms 'electoral' and 'party competition' are utilized either as loose references to the entire cycle of electoral, parliamentary, and governmental politics, to particular election campaigns, party platforms and statements, or—in the context of the formal modelling of party strategies and voting choices—within the narrow limits of assumptions about actors' motives, preferences, and information. As a result of the varied and extensive use of this term, the concept remains vague and ambiguous.

The most fundamental source of this lack of precision and consistency in most uses of this term is that too much is borrowed from the economic theory of competition. For several reasons, this borrowing is excessive if not unwarranted. First, the assumed fundamental analogy, similarity, or resemblance between economic and political competition is erroneous. Competition in politics is altered by the degree of collusion that is inherent in the achievement of the exclusive good of public authority, and this difference is not one of degree. Moreover, like economists, political scientists tend to view competition as a uni-dimensional phenomenon—as a single property of which there can be 'more' or 'less', and whose upper limit is a model of 'perfect' competition.

As I will argue in this chapter, the conditions of competition in politics are manifold; they do not co-vary; and their maximization does not point to or reach 'perfection'. This is particularly true when we assess the conditions that need to be met in order for competition to produce, as an unintended by-product, 'social value'. As we shall see, the parallel maximization of these conditions is impossible. This calls into question analytical approaches that fundamentally assume that 'competition' is a one-dimensional concept, and that use techniques which make far too many simplifying assumptions about the real world of politics.

THE UNINTENDED 'SOCIAL VALUE' OF COMPETITION: SIMMEL, SCHUMPETER, AND DOWNS

From the early, almost implicit, appraisal of the beneficial effect of trade competition by Adam Smith, competition has achieved a generalized and explicit recognition as an adequate and valuable technique for the satisfaction of almost any need and the attainment of almost any value in almost any sphere of human activity. The exceptional value attributed to the parallel efforts by several parties to obtain the same prize is surprising when one considers the number of fields in which the principle of subordination of individual efforts to the collective goal is still prevalent and legitimized: private and public bureaucracies, productive processes, family circles and kinship groups. Yet, the 'ideological' trend nowadays prizes competition as the default and prevalent mode. Other principles or techniques of individuals' coordination are regarded as needing ad hoc justification and legitimation, and are reserved for fields where competition is regarded as unattainable or not yet attainable.

The social legitimacy of competition rests on one key point: competition among individuals over the same objective produces an unintended result that is advantageous to a 'third party'. Benefits gained from this unintended benefit can be either individualistic in nature or functionalist or systemic. In the first perspective, the benefits produced involve a collective welfare function which maximizes each individual's utility. In the second perspective, the advantage is the realization of some overall value which is positive from the systemic point of view. Georg Simmel (1955 [1908]) has analysed the sociological mechanism of this transformation of individual impulses into socially valuable results. From the formal point of view, competition rests on an individualistic principle—the refusal to subordinate individual interests to a uniform supra-individual or collective interest. Competition assumes that each competitor pursues his/her own self-interest, utilizes his/her energies in pursuit of such interests, and evaluates the results in terms of objective accomplishments. In the form of 'pure' competition, unlike other forms of conflictual interactions, the outcome of the pursuit of the prize is undetermined, and not in the hands of either adversary: 'each competitor by himself aims at the goal, . . . [and] proceeds as if there existed no adversary, but only the aim' (Simmel 1955: 58).

Competition presupposes, therefore, the existence of a common aim, of an objective value desired by all competing parties—be it profit, glory, scientific prestige, or power. The social legitimation of competition, however, rests on the production of social values beneficial to others as a by-product of the struggle between the contestants. From the point of view of the individual competitor, this ultimate objective (collective benefit) is neither wanted nor aimed at. As Simmel (1955: 59–60) points out, 'from the standpoint of the society, [competition] offers subjective motives as the means of producing objective social values: and from the standpoint of the competing parties, it uses the production of objective values as means for attaining subjective satisfaction.' Thus, from the collective point of view, competition is legitimized through its capacity to overcome, and indeed deny, the tension between subjective and collective goals. The latter are satisfied by the objective results of competition as opposed to the subjective goals of the competitors. Thus, even though it rests on the individualistic principle of non-subordination of these subjective goals, competition finds its legitimacy in the fulfilment of socially desirable ends. The relationship between competition and individualism is not complete without the legitimizing reference to these collective social interests. Seen in this light, individualistic competition is regarded as just as legitimate as other 'techniques' (involving coordination of individual efforts) for the attainment of collective goals or social values.

This conception of the valuable by-product of competition has entered into political theory later than in other fields. The objective prized by antagonistic individuals and groups in the political sphere is usually identified with political power (votes, offices, influence on policy). The socially valuable by-product of this antagonistic struggle for power is, however, less clearly defined. One such social value encountered in the literature is the assertion that competition produces as by-product democracy. I regard this argument as inadequate because political competition *presupposes* the existence of sets of norms and rules that offer at least a minimal regulatory framework, without which competition can degenerate into utter unregulated conflict. Thus, democracy, as a set of basic rights and of respected procedures, is a necessary precondition for political and electoral competition, rather than the other way round. Indeed, pluralism—which is a necessary condition of democracy—need not be 'competitive'. Other principles can and do regulate the interaction among a plurality of actors. Whether politico-electoral competition has a feedback effect in maintaining, defending, stabilizing, or otherwise improving the basic constitutional framework of democracy and/or its pluralism is another matter, but it does not change the logical priority of the latter with respect to the former.

With their influential works Joseph A. Schumpeter (1942) and Anthony Downs (1957) are the forerunners of the 'third-gaining-party axiom' of competition in the political realm. Schumpeter's innovation was to render irrelevant all motivations of political elites with the exception of their shared appetite for power. Once channelled within a 'social capsule' (Etzioni 1988: ch. 12) of norms and procedures defining appropriate and acceptable means, these appetites tend to produce social values that are of great interest for other groups and for society as a whole. There is no need to assume that parties engaged in the competitive struggle consciously aim at those social values. This notion redeemed the normative character of democracy by attributing to voters the role of selecting their rulers, while regarding as unnecessary the unrealistic levels of political competence, initiative, and altruism required by other theories of democracy that Schumpeter labelled 'classic'. It also facilitated the unambiguous distinction between democratic and non-democratic systems through the exclusivity of the popular sanction of government by elections. Finally, it helped to side-step the dilemma of 'classic theories' concerning the democracy–authority relationship, which required that a Leviathan, legitimized by a social contract, be free to operate for the common good.

Schumpeter established a close link between competition and democracy. Democracy was defined as 'government approved by people', and the democratic system was regarded as requiring formal rules set up for the exercise of a free, fair, and loyal electoral competition. The democratic method is only 'the institutional instrument to arrive at political decisions on the bases of which single individuals obtain the power to decide through a competition which has as object the popular vote' (Schumpeter 1942: 208). The procedures which constitute democracy are the constitutional aspect of politico-electoral competition; the 'social capsule' of competition. Schumpeter's procedural definition makes competition essential to democracy—indeed, as a defining characteristic of democracy. Yet he does not say much about competition itself. Nor does he formally define the socially desirable by-product of politico-electoral competition beyond the peaceful selection of the ruling elite, their submission at fixed intervals to the renewal of the mandate, and, in short, the institutionalization of the never-ending fight for power. He argues that, between the ideal case of perfect competition, which does not exist, and the real cases in which any electoral contestation of the ruling elite is prevented by force, a whole series of variations exists. Within this range, the democratic method of government fades by 'imperceptible steps' into the authoritarian method. However, he does not specify what makes for this variation (Schumpeter 1942: 210). Competition, therefore, is essentially conceived as electoral 'contestability'—that is, as openness of the electoral race to challengers. Schumpeter's explicit affirmation concerning the unintended 'social-value' by-product of politico-electoral competition is limited to the repeated selection process of the leadership and to its approval by the people.

Downs (1957: 19) builds on Schumpeter's insights, but pushes them further. Competition 'is a mechanism whereby political parties which are engaged in what Schumpeter called a "competitive struggle for the people's vote" are obliged to take account of the preference of the electors for one policy rather than another' (Barry 1970: 99). In this case, the unintended social value of competition is explicitly defined as 'responsiveness'. One does not need to assume that candidates and parties want to respond to voters' preferences—they are involuntarily forced to do so while pursuing their goals of power through maximizing the necessary vote. Thus, competition obliges elites to take into account the preferences of voters. Downs's (1957: 107) work is about how competition compels the transformation of each party's motives into the social value of each party's honesty, responsibility, and responsiveness to electors' desires.

This difference between Schumpeter and Downs is not a minor one. In Schumpeter, references to responsiveness are absent. As a sceptical European conservative, Schumpeter did not assume that voters know what they want and are able to evaluate whether their objectives have been achieved. Consequently, he did not dare to conclude that elites will give them what they prefer, and was not much concerned with the kind of policies that are offered. His *Capitalism, Socialism and Democracy* clearly separates the selection of rulers from the achievement of policy preferences:

> [we] make the deciding of issues by the electorate secondary to the election of the men who are to do the deciding. . . . [The voter's] choice does not flow from his initiative, but is being shaped, and the shaping is an essential part of the democratic process. . . . Voters confine themselves to accepting this bid in preference to others or refusing to accept it. (1942: 269 and 282)

In his text there is plenty of evidence to demonstrate Schumpeter's mistrust of any substantive link between what people want and what elites offer in exchange. With Downs, on the contrary, the concept of 'responsiveness' to the voter preferences becomes the essence of the unintended social value of electoral competition. Downs's conclusion is based on precise assumptions. His voter is a rational actor whose choice depends on the comparative evaluation of the advantages he/she expects from the governmental performance of different parties. He/she will offer his/her vote to the party that proposes that set of public policies which comparatively offer the highest return in terms of well-being as subjectively evaluated by the voter. Similarly, the parties/candidates offer to the electorate that set of policies that they perceive will maximize votes. What it is offered by parties/candidates and the basis on which the voters judge are not only relevant, but also essential to the achievement of the unintended social result of competition. Downs holds that through competition, procedural democracy transforms itself *ipso facto* into the only possible substantial democracy—a democracy which responds to voter preferences.

Schumpeter's goals could be achieved even with 'irrational', uninformed, or even foolish or random voters. For Downs, these kinds of voters do not force elites involuntarily to respond. Schumpeter's version of the competitive struggle for the vote is even compatible with a strong elitist vision whereby voter perceptions and preferences are shaped, informed, oriented, or otherwise manipulated by elite. Downs's version is not. Schumpeter emphasizes the periodic submission of elites to an otherwise unspecified voter judgement. Downs stresses the capacity of elites to respond readily and sympathetically to demands. Thus, government 'approved by' the people (Schumpeter) it is not to the same thing as government 'responsive to' the people (Downs).

THE CONDITIONS OF COMPETITION

The definition of the unintended social value achieved through the 'technique' of individual competition in politics is important.[1] Different 'social values' imply different conditions of attainment. If the value is the periodic accountability of governing elites, this can be guaranteed by procedural rules governing the holding of periodic elections and the possibility for several political actors to contest them. The only necessary condition to this end is *contestability*, the actual possibility for different political leaders and groups to contest free and fair elections. Contestability is a condition of competition but, at the same time, it is also a basic defining characteristic of democracy—the one which makes political pluralism possible. Contestability, therefore, is the point where democracy and competition overlap. There are, however, other conditions of democracy which are not necessary conditions of competition, as, for instance, equal or universal suffrage. At the same time, there are other conditions of competition which need not to be regarded as conditions of democracy.[2]

In brief, I will argue that there are three other necessary conditions of competition that must be considered if responsiveness is regarded as the social value to be attained through electoral competition. These can be identified working backward from responsiveness. What is the key to responsiveness in competitive races? Excluding as irrelevant individual motivations, the standard argument is that leaders in striving to keep or acquire power and office will be constantly worried about how voters are going to react to their actions. This worry is necessarily a function of the extent to which the leader is him/herself exposed to a reasonable threat of electoral sanction. Only if he/she will be worried about the reactions of voters will he/she be 'constantly piloted by the anticipation of those reactions' (Sartori 1977: 350). Responsiveness is achieved by introducing Friedrich's (1963) mechanism of anticipated reactions. It follows that a key condition of competition is the electoral *vulnerability* of incumbents.

In turn, what is the necessary condition of incumbents' vulnerability? The condition is that voters are willing to punish and reward; that is, they are able to modify their electoral choice. If they are not, incumbents are safe and vulnerability is unattainable. Full elasticity of the vote is not necessary, but some predisposition to electoral switch must be present if vulnerability is to be conceivable. I label this condition electoral *availability*.[3]

If responsiveness depends on vulnerability, and the latter requires voters' availability, what motivates the available voter to act for or against the incumbent government? This is the differentiation of the offer and the consequent perception of different potential outcomes. Whatever parties/candidates offer (programmes, policies, ideologies, images, etc.), it must be different and clearly 'spelt out' for the voters, in order to make vulnerability not just the chance outcome of random change in voting habits. The anticipated reactions of government and opposition parties (which are supposed to be the key to responsiveness) must relate to voters' responses to differentiated offers. The latter enable the voter to decide whether to change or not electoral preference, and also make intelligible to the elite the reactions of the voters. If products are not differentiated (or their difference is not perceived), voters can punish or reward, but no responsiveness will be achieved. Offers must therefore be decidable by voters in order to make the entire process intelligible to both voters and elite alike. I will call this condition the *decidability* of the offer.

The argument thus far has been the following. If we go beyond Schumpeter's minimal goal and admit that electoral competition is legitimized through its production of 'responsiveness' as a social value and as the yardstick for evaluating that competition, then the conditions necessary to this end are:

(1) electoral contestability,
(2) electoral availability,
(3) electoral decidability, and
(4) electoral vulnerability.

In the following sections, each of these conditions will be discussed in more detail.

Contestability

Contestability is a necessary condition of both democracy and competition. Conceptually, this overlap is ill starred. It generates a great deal of confusion, with the result that sometimes competition is equated with democracy and vice versa. In one of the few articles explicitly devoted to this topic, D'Alimonte (1989: 301–3) has argued the case for an orderly distinction between the two, insisting that 'democracy is a necessary but not a sufficient condition of competition', and that 'competition is neither a necessary nor a sufficient condition of democracy'. The logical corollary is that there can be democracy without competition, but not competition without democracy. Competition does not derive automatically from democracy, and democracy is not the product of competition. D'Alimonte (1989: 303) argues that the condition of freedom for parties to present candidates and programmes and the condition of freedom for electors to chose them 'identify democracy not with competition, but with an open politico-electoral market. In the latter, the freedom of access is guaranteed both on the demand side (the electors) and on the supply side (the parties).' However, if the politico-electoral market is open, it need not necessarily be competitive. The conditions of democracy are not the conditions of competition.

In other words, D'Alimonte separates democracy and competition, making contestability a property that defines an open electoral market (that is, democracy), not a competitive market (that is, competition). However, this line of thinking entails a significant drawback. Considering contestability as a property of democracy means that all democracies should present this feature. Hence, the possibility of regarding different democracies as having dissimilar degrees of contestability is curtailed. If democracies are open electoral markets, do they all have the same degree of openness? My answer is no. In the general concept of competition, I want to keep a dimension pointing to the openness of contestation of the electoral and political race. There are different political systems or circumstances whose democratic nature is undeniable, but which offer to new and old claimants very different opportunities for electoral contestation.

In addition, linking the condition of free entry with the idea of the market—and the frequent use of the term 'political' or 'electoral market'—is somewhat equivocal. If we take seriously the economic terminology, the market is defined as an institution for consummating transactions. A market best performs this function when every buyer who is willing to pay more than the minimum realized price for any commodity succeeds in buying the commodity, and every seller who is willing to sell at lower price than the minimum realized price succeeds in selling the commodity. In other words, a market exists when those who are willing to pay more acquire the appropriate good, and those who are willing to charge less find the appropriate buyer. A market is not defined by ease of entry, but by the 'obtainability' of transactions. In this sense, a political market condenses both what I call electoral contestability and electoral availability. It is questionable whether this concept is of any use in politics. Is it reasonable to derive from the market metaphor the notion that parties (sellers) will win when they offer the same policy package at lower prices (in the form of lower taxation)? If so, then irresponsible outbidding would be endemic. Conversely, is it reasonable to expect that voters who are intensely motivated by a particular policy will obtain it by 'paying more'—that is, by voting more than once?

A further shortcoming in the concept of the 'electoral market' is that market and competition are not only different things: they can have little to do with each other. A market can perform efficiently as an institution for consummating transactions and still be monopolistic or very non-competitive. On the other hand, the market can be highly imperfect in its performance and competitive at the same time (Stigler 1957: 6). When contestability is analysed in connection with political competition, the key operative issue is, how many actors do we need, or can we afford, to make competition lively and viable? The economic theory of competition, in more than a century of reflection,[4] has given no definite, straightforward answer to the question of how many firms are necessary to make a market competitive, and of what maximum share of the market control by one firm is compatible with competition (Stigler 1968: 181–2).

The solution offered is the definition of the conditions of 'perfect competition', refined over time. However, to say that there must be numerous traders on both sides of the market does not identify the minimal number necessary to define a competitive market. Moreover, the indicators usually utilized to evaluate empirically the degree of competition are extraordinarily ambiguous. Let us consider two examples. Concentration ratios are used, arguing that the lower the concentration the more competitive the market; but again the minimum concentration compatible with the definition of competition is not determined. Price homogeneity is often regarded as an indicator of competition (the more prices are homogeneous, the more perfect the competition); but the same indicator is often considered by the courts as a phenomenon more suggestive of collusion than of competition.

In conclusion, although economists tend to equate competition with openness of the market, they do not offer a useful solution to the problem of contestability in politics. The fact of the matter is that the question of entry is far more important in politics than in economics. It is somewhat paradoxical that economic metaphors are employed to conceptualize it. In politics, one can easily define in terms of contestability the point where competition ends and is replaced by something else. At the other end of the spectrum, we know that a high fragmentation of the offer is not likely to enhance 'perfect competition', but, rather, government instability or even political chaos. Authority being a public good, success in the competition offers authority not just over one's own supporters, but over all members of the polity. The indivisible nature of authority leads to strong pushes toward oligarchic tendencies and determines large economies of scale. Competition for private goods allows everyone to deal with the preferred partner, even though this partner is a very minor one. In politics, there is room for only a limited number of parties. New entries are immensely more difficult than in business. It is difficult to carve out a small niche in politics. Besides, small niches may be of very little use. Finally, oligarchic tendencies and economies of scale are also fostered by the protection against foreign or international competition that is typical, thus far, of political competition.

Our question should not be what is the 'perfect', but, rather, what is the 'viable' level of contestability? Several of the factors influencing the structure of opportunity to contest are institutional, like the electoral law, the requirements for the candidacy of individuals and lists, the threshold for access to public finance and media coverage, and the cost of campaigning in different circumstances. There are, however, several other factors that are not strictly institutional. It is therefore better (1) to keep contestability as an important dimension of competition (as will be clear later, the level of contestability impinges upon other conditions of competition); (2) to keep contestability clearly separate from electoral availability, avoiding the indiscriminate commingling of the two that is inherent in the 'open market' metaphor; (3) to consider contestability as a structure of political opportunity; and (4) to concentrate on the empirical factors which may impinge upon the variations in this structure of opportunities for new and old potential claimants.

Availability

In the Downsian approach, the rational orientation toward the policies offered by parties makes the voter a perfectly elastic consumer, who is, by definition, available to change partisan preference should a better offer be made to him.[5] For electoral competition it is essential that at least some segment of the electorate be available to such change. These available voters are the sought-after prize of the parallel efforts by competitors and the incentive for party competition, without whom it is unlikely that parties would be willing to engage in policy competition.

We do not have precise information about how large the available segment of the electorate must be in order to make an electoral contest competitive, or more competitive than another. The literature on electoral behaviour has accumulated a vast amount of material that indicates the extent to which individual voters and electorates are, in fact, little inclined to respond to changes of the offer of parties and elites with changes in party choice. Strong psychological identifications, resulting from organizational encapsulation, cultural bonds, and the like may anchor most voters, and make them unavailable for voting switches. Thus, the actual level of electoral availability in each given election or country is an empirical question which is of crucial importance for the study of electoral competition. Studies of electoral behaviour have probably not paid sufficient attention to the topic of electoral availability as indicator of the competitive nature of elections. We may simply assume that, *ceteris paribus*, the higher the level of potential availability, the higher the potential level for competition. However, the problem is complicated by the fact that the quantity of the available vote may be less important than its location.

At this juncture, it is important to underscore that the 'available voter'—defined as one who is willing to consider modifying his/her party choice— is not the same as the 'opinion voter', the 'informed voter', or, worse, the 'rational voter'. The 'available voter' is not necessarily informed about issues or programmes, but is sensitive to them.[6] Sensitivity entails neither high levels of information nor capacity of judgement; it simply refers to susceptibility to changes in electoral preferences in response to elements that relate to public debate or personal experience. What is certain, however, is that (1) strong party identifiers have a lower propensity to switch than sensitive voters; (2) voters' sensitivity is higher (*a*) the lower the number of cleavage lines activated or mobilized (segmentation), (*b*) the lower the organizational encapsulation of the electorate, and (*c*) the more diffuse the network of groups and the less interlocking is the link between specific political organizations (parties) and corporate groups outside the electoral domain; and (3) parties, if compelled, look for switchers irrespective of who they are.

Aggregate measures of electoral volatility (regarding both total system volatility and 'inter-bloc' volatility) have been constructed to characterize the volatility of different electorates at different points in time (Bartolini 1986a; Bartolini and Mair 1990: 20–37). It should be noted that these indices under-represent the true level of changes at the individual level since aggregation cancels out two-way flows between parties.[7] In addition, it is also noteworthy that actual shifts of electoral preferences (whether calculated on the basis of individual-level or aggregate data) underestimate the magnitude of potential availability, since they count only those within the 'available' sector who actually decide to change their electoral preferences, leaving aside potential switchers who do not. Thus, aggregate volatility underestimates individual voting shifts, and the latter underestimate actual electoral availability. None the less, aggregate volatility measures are extremely useful, and they are, by and large, the only thing that party leaders seem to consider when estimating the potential electoral availability in their system. They are also the only certain element that enables them to ascertain the electorate's reactions to their strategic choices and moves.

Eijk and Oppenhuis (1991) have suggested ways to operationalize electoral availability at the individual level that are very promising as they are conceptualized in close relation to the issue of electoral competition. They do not use the terms 'availability' or 'available electorate', but they pick up this dimension with survey data in which people are asked about their willingness to vote for parties other than the one they prefer. Respondents are then ranked according to their probability of voting for each of the parties in their party system. Voters range from those who are likely to vote for only one party, at one extreme, to those who are likely to vote for several different parties, at the other. This method makes it possible to distinguish between different electorates, as well as between different segments of the same electorate in terms of their electoral availability, although the authors (1991: 60–1) tend to dichotomize their result in terms of voters 'beyond' competition, as compared with those 'subject to intense competition'. Of great interest is their application of the data to individual parties, in which they compare the available vote for a party (those electors who declare it to be a possible choice) with the actual vote the party eventually receives at the polls. Eijk and Oppenhuis demonstrate that it is possible properly to conceptualize and empirically to compare inter-party and inter-system electoral availability, seen as a necessary condition of electoral competition.

Decidability

Even after taking into consideration electoral contestability and electoral availability, what happens if the parties do not want to compete? Are there conditions that push parties to limit or to avoid altogether the decidability of the products offered? Although most versions of the competitive theory of democracy—and, in particular, formal models of party competition— refer to the fact that parties offer programmes, policies, ideologies, images, issues, or whatever else, not much is said about the 'decidability' quality of these offers, which is necessary to guarantee, improve, maximize, or otherwise substantiate electoral competition. Is the quality of the offer so unimportant for electoral competition?

For party competition to produce leadership responsiveness, a necessary condition is the ability of voters to differentiate between what is being offered. The notion of choice is essential. In order to make a choice voters must perceive differences among parties/candidates in terms of emphasis, priority, or performance. Therefore, whatever the party offer, it must be (1) different from what other parties offer and (2) clearly perceived by voters. Policy or issue-position differentiation among parties and visibility and clarity of these differences for the voter are what I call decidability.

In formal models of voting choice, an important role is given to decidability. Both Downs (who refers to the net utility of the victory of the voter's preferred candidate: 1957: 38–40) and Riker and Ordeshook (who refer to the 'party differential': 1968, 1973) underline the importance of the perception by the voter that a victory by candidate X will make a difference for her or him. This obviously depends on the voter's product differentiation abilities. If products are undifferentiated, this term is zero, and the probability of affecting the outcome (which I will discuss in the next section as vulnerability) becomes irrelevant. Thus, party differentials count in theory, but are often little studied in formal models of competition, where they are reduced to party distances in a space either chosen as an example, or postulated, or drawn from some data set.

There are several reasons why little attention is paid to the decidability of the offer in theories of competition. First, the decidability of the offer is not regarded as essential, as the emphasis is on the competitive selection of political personnel. Second, the economic analysis from which political analogies are drawn does not attribute much importance to this aspect. Quite the contrary, in a perfect competition model, goods should be as homogeneous as possible. The third and more important reason is that the decidability of the offer is implicitly—not explicitly—postulated; that is, the differentiation of the products offered is assumed to result from other features of the competitive process.

Rational-choice theorists consider voter preferences as 'intrinsic'—that is, as 'exogenous to the process of party competition'.[8] Voters have preferences that are independent from the offers made by politicians and parties. Obviously this is a crucial assumption, as one could well imagine that voter preferences are shaped to a greater or lesser extent by the process of party competition and are in no way exogenous to it. Formal theorists, whether or not they discuss this issue, come to the conclusion that preferences are exogenous. The second assumption about voters' preferences is that they are stable during the process of competition itself. Combining the endogenous versus exogenous shaping of voters' preferences with their stability or volatility during the process of electoral competition, one can draw the scheme of Figure 4.1.

Clearly, a structure of preferences that is endogenously produced throughout the process of competition cannot be stable; therefore, Type III is impossible.[9] Type I is normally postulated by economic models of competition. By definition, the structure of preferences is exogenous, and, in the short run, such a structure is also stable; that is, it is not even affected by forces outside the competition process itself. Under these conditions the only thing parties/ candidates can do is acquire information about the stable and exogenously determined structure of preferences and try to adapt to it. They also need to engage in advertising campaigns, trying to inform the public of their stances. That is all. Party strategy is only an adaptive effort. Whatever complicating factors are added (activists' attitudes, organizational features, etc.) will only make the achievement of this predefined adaptation more or less easy and efficient.

Type II is a variation on this same theme. Keeping the exogenous formation of the structure of preferences, the simplification of the stable structure can be abandoned. Preferences can be modified even in the short term, but these modifications will be the result of factors external to party competition. These may take the form of cultural and value changes, social-structural modifications, or media coverage of events, etc. Whatever the sources of

Structure of voters' preferences assumed to be

		Exogenous to party competition	Endogenous to party competition
Structure of voters' preferences assumed to be	Stable	*Type I* Preference driven competition	*Type III* N.P.
	Changing	*Type II* Hetero-directed competition	*Type IV* Preference shaping competition

FIG. 4.1. *The structure of voters' preferences*

change, they are exogenous to the process of party competition. Even in this case, however, parties are just adaptive machines. They either can or cannot see the changes and the potential gains or losses associated with them, but they cannot influence them or affect the manner in which they are perceived by voters. Electoral competition is hetero-directed. In this static perspective, the decidability problem becomes marginal by definitional fiat. The parties' offers meet autonomously formed preferences. How can parties collude if their collusion does not modify the preferences of voters? How can they follow an alternative strategy of maximum decidability? Once preferences are made non-modifiable, the offer becomes nothing but a function of such preferences. Any other solution will only expose parties to totally unproductive risks. In this sense, I believe that the assumption of the exogenous nature of preferences implicitly contributes to the rendering irrelevant of the problem of the decidability of the offer.

The picture changes in Type IV: the structure of electoral preferences is not exogenous to party competition, but is influenced, if not determined, by it. Parties and politicians believe they can influence the preference of electors. This implies that they can do something other than merely adapt: they can get the electors on their side.[10] Adaptation to the structure of preferences and modification of the structure of preferences interact, begetting different mixes of adaptation and modification, as well as debates about the degree of adaptation and modification. The structure of electoral preferences changes, and these modifications depend to a certain extent on what parties and politicians offer. Party competition here is identified as the process through which parties and elite try to shape and modify to their advantage the structure of the electoral preferences. This is exactly the contrary of what is postulated by rational-choice theory. The way the electoral preferences are structured is not irrelevant to party competition, but is the object, essence, and core of party competition itself. It is in the context of a 'preference shaping' type of competition that decidability becomes crucial.

Constraints on Decidability

Once decidability is regarded as a necessary condition for competition, deliberate strategies of increasing offer-differentiation or of blurring actual party stands enter into empirical study. We must proceed from the recognition that political competition is built on a number of strong confining conditions of product differentiation. We can identify three processes of competition avoidance or restraint on the offer side:

(1) those situations in which the very interest or purpose of the group of suppliers necessitates a structure which strongly limits or even prohibits certain kinds of offers;

(2) those situations in which the interest and purpose of the suppliers are accessible to competitive practices and competition as such is not limited, but the means through which it is pursued are more or less restricted;

(3) those situations in which the interest and purpose of the suppliers are accessible to competitive practices, but competition is limited in its scope as a result of collusion which supersedes the competition itself.

The first case concerns the socio-political framework of a competition. The set of norms, social practices, and legal provisions that define the conditions of competition are normally protected from the basic principle of chance that operates in competition. The very interest and purpose of the group identify themes in which electoral competition, in terms of differentiated offers, is highly limited, as in the cases of symbols of national identity, unity, solidarity, and more generally sets of formal and informal constitutional rules.

The second case is that of the restriction of the means through which competition obtains. The principle that supersedes competition is often that of the mechanical equality of the parts. For instance, equality of competitive means is often invoked and aimed at by agreement on sharing equal access to television broadcasting, equal attention in written media, proportional access to public resources for electoral competition, or ceilings of the total amount of resources candidates and parties can invest in political advertising. Even the style of campaigning and political advertising may be the object of inter-individual (that is, voluntarily reached) or supra-individual (imposed by law or standards of morality) limitations.

The interesting question is whether the restriction of certain competitive means actually affects the substance of policy and issue competition. Certain restrictions do not limit competition, but, on the contrary, they enhance true competition by freeing it from unnecessary elements. Preventing the diversion of competition from diminishing the capacity of competitors, these restrictions can force competition to concentrate on the offer itself. It is therefore possible for competitors to establish agreements in a specific area of competition without weakening it in other areas. These inter-individual restrictions may grow to free competition from all those things that do not constitute competition, because in principle they can cancel each other out without effect. Just as shopkeepers can agree on fixed opening hours or sale periods, so political actors can agree on the muting or soft-pedalling of certain means and techniques of competition. Yet, one should not forget that the means of competition consist, in some cases, of advantages offered to other actors or the general public, which may suffer the consequences of excessive restrictions. These agreements can, in extreme cases, affect the very essence of competition—that is, bring about forms of collusion and cartellization that become plans for feeding the market according to a pre-established design.

The third form of restriction on competition is the most important in this context. What is actually restricted is the scope of the offer in fields that are, in principle, open to political competition. There are a number of forces and circumstances that are conducive to collusion and cartellization practices among political competitors. First of all, politics is inherently collusive as a consequence of the exclusiveness of authority. The high threshold for access to authority requires a high degree of concentration of the market. Indeed, much of the process of coalition formation (which is necessary in many democratic systems) entails, in essence, cartellization. In order to form electoral, parliamentary, or governmental coalitions, policy positions, issues, etc., are compromised, diluted, or totally muted so as to obtain the sought-after economy of scale. Coalition politics may indeed maximize other necessary conditions of competition, but unquestionably it brings about a restriction on the scope of competition on the offer side.

The multiplicity of the sites of party interaction is a second incentive to collusion. Contrary to economic competition, political competition takes place in different and yet inter-linked sites or arenas. Parties compete against each other electorally, but they then (as before) continue their interactions in other arenas including (but not restricted to) legislative-parliamentary and governmental domains. The same party may take different policy positions in these various arenas. Legislators group or regroup in different ways than they do at election time. The decidability of issues and policies may be voluntarily limited by the interplay of the electoral, legislative, and governmental party systems. Opportunities to boost the salience of issues exploitable in the electoral arena, and which may concern sizeable sectors of public opinion, may not be taken up or may be dampened because they would be damaging in other domains, such as in the process of bargaining over legislation. Conversely, the potential for fruitful legislative or governmental initiatives may be unrealized because of a party's reluctance to expose itself to subsequent electoral risks. In other words, the necessary interplay between electoral competition and legislative bargaining may lead to the downplaying of those issues regarded as favourable in one arena, but damaging in another.[11]

Finally, collusion and cartellization may be achieved through coordinated manipulation of issue saliency. Analytically, they can be classified as follows: (1) blurred and unclear party position or party policy on certain issues; (2) slow transformation of certain problems from clearly partisan to valence issue; and (3) transfer of certain issues from the domain of politically legitimized decision-making to arenas where different criteria of legitimation prevail. Unfortunately, an adequate discussion of these situations would require far more space than is available in this chapter, so I must limit the argument to a few points.

The transformation of divisive issues into valence issues is a process that weakens decidability. Position issues are 'those that involve advocacy of government actions from a set of alternatives over which a distribution of voter preferences is defined. And . . . valence issues [are] those that merely involve the linking of the parties with some condition that is positively or negatively valued by the electorate' (Stokes 1966: 170–3). Position issues are inherently divisive as they involve explicit choices 'for' or 'against'. Valence issues, on the contrary, entail only one value (positive or negative) that is shared by the vast majority, and they are essentially non-divisive.

Combining the more or less divisive nature of issues with the clarity of the party stance provides an interesting typology (Schneider 1980, 1974). The dimension of party choice, clear/non-clear, concerns whether the voter perceives a difference between the parties on a particular problem; it can be measured by the voter's ability to discriminate party positions and, consequently, voter shifts correlated with issue positions. The 'divisiveness' dimension distinguishes between position or valence issues. The two dimensions together refer to the decidability of the offer.

Since position issues are divisive by definition, the choice is offered. However, party positions can be blurred and unclear. For valence issues the question is more complex. A 'choice' in position terms is simply the anticipation that one solution is better than the other, and that, therefore, it makes sense to change or not to change. For valence issues, choice essentially refers to whether one party can do better than the other, which is defined as a matter of general and agreed concern. The choice of specific remedies and policies is less defined, being overshadowed by questions of 'competence'. As Schneider (1980: 82) puts it, 'the failure of choice would be evidenced by the widespread perception that no alternative government will work. The decision to vote one way or the other could mean little in terms of anticipated performance'.

For the decidability of the offer, divisive issues on which the party's stance is clear are by far the most decidable. Valence issues with a clear partisan orientation may still be decidable. That a valence issue is not divisive does not imply that it is not controversial. Its salience, to whom blame is attributed, whether voters perceive a difference between parties in terms of priorities and performance, makes for its more or less controversial and debatable nature. The level of decidability declines progressively when party stands are unclear, and it is at its lowest when, at the same time, issues are not divisive. If parties can shape preferences through competition, they will tend to do so by defining issues as more or less divisive and by making their stances more or less well defined—that is, by manipulating decidability.

Sheer removal of an issue from the agenda is a more complicated, but not infrequent solution. Issues and policy offers may be removed by 'constitutionalizing' them or by referring them to other domains of legitimation of decision-making. By 'constitutionalization', I mean the institutionalization of goals that therefore tend to be kept safely out of the policy domain regulated by parties. If the requirement of no public deficit (or of a maximum public deficit) or the prohibition of sending armed forces outside the national territory are constitutionalized, then the issue is to a large extent removed from public debate, and the need for parties and candidates to take clear stands is reduced correspondingly.

Alternatively, issues and policies can be transferred to domains where non-political legitimation principles exist. Issues may be predefined and left to the decisions of bodies where competence is the key resource: defending the value of the currency can be defined as an institutional goal and thus made the preserve of central bank authorities; controlling the political fairness of the mass media can be devolved to bodies and authorities on the basis of the same principle. Issues and policies may also be predefined and predecided by internationally accepted or imposed priorities and goals (EU decisions, IMF requirements, GATT agreements, etc.), which may be used by political parties as a defence against taking clear political stands on controversial questions. Finally, issues and policies can be left to the actors who control the resources for their implementation; to the market, or to forms of 'negotiated order' in which key economic actors agree to regulate macro-economic policies. Whether the principle invoked is efficiency, competence, or resource control, the actual result is an important muting of party differentials in key domains.

Of course there are barriers and obstacles to political cartellization and collusion. The first is imperfect knowledge of the consequences of rivalry and of the profit of collusion. When considering collusion, parties/candidates are uncertain as to the profit of this strategy as opposed to an adversarial competitive strategy. The second obstacle is the difficulty of determining the division of profits among colluders. Parties may be in disagreement and/or scared of the potential disagreement over how the advantages of collusion should be then distributed. In the first case, uncertainty concerns the unforeseen potential reactions of the voters. In the second case, uncertainty concerns the divisions of the advantages among the actors. In both cases, the result is unstable choices between more cooperative and more competitive relationships in the struggle for the vote.

This long list of potential sources of collusive behaviour on the part of political competitors is not meant to 'denounce' or otherwise 'fault' these practices, but simply to underline that their diffusion is a crucial empirical dimension in the study of the conditions of competitive politics (see Katz and Mair 1995). Laying too much emphasis on competition, we may easily forget that collusion is the essence of politics, that 'political classes' have much in common at stake to defend, that political elites can easily agree to share a value through the voluntarily equalization of effort rather than fighting for it, that competition on the offer side is not a natural outcome and requires special conditions in order to flourish. Continuous efforts are made to avoid it, and therefore continuous costs are met in order to preserve it. Paraphrasing

Gaetano Mosca's famous point about military rule, the real question it is not why parties sometimes collude, but why they do not do so all the time.

Vulnerability

In economic life and theory, the existence of a given product does not preclude the existence of a different one that can be chosen instead. Given the coercive nature of politics, if a policy is implemented, a different policy cannot be implemented at the same time. The products offered in a more or less decidable way to voters are mutually exclusive. There cannot be two agencies legislating and/or regulating on the same issue.

The exclusivity of policy and legislation rests on the exclusivity of government. There is a threshold for gaining the right to coerce. In economic life, a firm that sells 49 per cent of a product is not a failure. In politics it may well be. This basic difference is not often discussed in articles that focus on economic and political competition.[12] Vulnerability originates from and is meaningful only in relation to the exclusivity of political authority. For this condition of competition, no analogy with the market and economic competition seems possible.

It is not necessary to discuss this problem at length as a rich literature already exists. Vulnerability may be defined as the possibility for an incumbent government to be ousted and replaced or otherwise modified in its composition as a result of changes in voters' partisan preferences. In effect, vulnerability has two psychological effects: first, parties perceive the chance of gaining or losing the exclusive good of public authority; second, voters perceive an increase in the potential impact of their vote on the final outcome of governmental formation and/or renovation.

In the American context, there have been many post-war studies concerning this particular dimension of competition. The reference point of these studies was of course the American two-party system, where it was easier to collapse several conditions of competition into the single one of vulnerability. Therefore, vulnerability is regarded as being basically the same thing as competition, although the phenomenon was given different names, from 'closeness of the electoral outcome' to 'uncertainty of the electoral result'; from 'performance sensitivity' to 'decisiveness of elections for governmental turnover'; from 'changeability' to 'competitiveness' or 'systemic competition'.

The term *performance sensitivity* implies that the incumbent position is vulnerable as a result of the sensitivity of available voters to its performance when in government. This is to demand far too much. The basic difference between the other terms is that some of them tend to stress actual aspects of governmental turnover, while others tend to stress the potential turnover. Schlesinger (1955: 1122), for instance, links his concept of vulnerability to the number of elections won by each party and to the rapidity with which parties alternate in office. He argues that 'perhaps the rate of alternation is even more important in giving the participants a sense of competition than is the overall division of victories'. Similarly, the 'decisiveness' of elections for governmental outcome or 'changeability' stress the actual result of competition. Insisting on actual alternation means that, at every given moment, the perception of the vulnerability of government is the result of past experiences. The obvious critique is that vulnerability may be present without actual turnover taking place or vice versa.

Terms like *closeness* of electoral returns in terms of votes or seats (Ranney 1965), or *symmetry* of the distribution of votes and seats, or *uncertainty* of electoral outcome, refer to the psychological effect linked to the absence of safety, rather than the actual result. Closeness and uncertainty may not result in turnover, but may still have an impact on competition. Yet, without any prior information, how can the level of closeness or symmetry that would guarantee vulnerability be ascertained? What if close elections were repeated over time with the same governmental outcome?

Both the dimension of actual past record and present uncertainty have to be incorporated into the idea of vulnerability. Some element of the objective closeness of electoral returns must give rise to a sense of lack of safety for incumbents and a sense of opportunity for opponents, but, at the same time, this objective base cannot be defined without reference to some record of past experience. For this reason, among the great variety of measures of electoral vulnerability experienced in the context of the federal and state level, as well as for presidential, governors, and legislative elections in the United States,[13] I prefer the kind of measures which are expressed in the form of a ratio between some objective element of closeness of the race at a given moment and some objective element indicating the past competitive performance of the system.

Stern (1972; also see Meltz 1973) provides a useful measure involving the standard deviation of the vote for the majority party/candidate in a given territorial unit across several elections. If that vote minus two standard deviations is still over 50 per cent, then the government is regarded as safe. If that vote minus two standard deviations is below 50 per cent, but the same vote minus one standard deviation is above 50 per cent, then the contest is classified as marginal. If that vote minus one standard deviation falls below 50 per cent, than government is competitive. Stern's measure links the majoritarian advantage of the winning party to the past variability of this margin. If one were to replace the terms 'safe', 'marginal', and 'competitive' with the single dimension of the level of vulnerability, we go from a minimum vulnerability in the first case to the maximum in the latter.[14]

Vulnerability is a system property. It refers to the unit of the party system. It results from specific configurations of the number, the strength, and the alliance–opposition relationships among the units of the system without belonging to any of them. It presents important empirical links with other conditions of competition like contestability, availability, and decidability, but it is independent from all of them. Only two conditions can be regarded as necessary for the maximization of governmental vulnerability. The first is the visibility of the dividing line between government and opposition; the second, an average electoral availability along the incumbent/opposition line large enough to approach (or exceed) the winning margin of the incumbents.

In relation to the first condition, the visibility of the incumbents/opposition camps is decisively blurred in cases of greatly oversized majorities, truly minority government (to the extent that they rest on collusion with the opposition in Parliament), and frequent changes in government composition during the legislature. Truly minority government poses a special challenge to the concept of vulnerability. Minority governments are vulnerable by definition, as their survival rests on some sort of collusion with non-governmental parties. However, their high parliamentary vulnerability may result in their electoral invulnerability. Minority governments are relatively insensitive to electoral returns because their *raison d'être* is not electoral. At the same time we are not prepared to go so far as to say that the electoral process is irrelevant to them. We have to find some better argument than the 'non-applicable' one in this case.

As far as the second condition is concerned, it is often argued that what matters for vulnerability is more the 'decisive location' of the available electorate than its sheer quantity (although one can say that the higher the quantity, the greater the likelihood that a sufficient share of it will be located so as to contribute to vulnerability). The 'decisive location' of available voters is crucial only if a spatial representation of politics is given. Whether a spatial dimension of politics exists (in the electorate), the magnitude of this dimension, and how good an instrument it is for describing concrete historical situations remain empirical questions. Therefore, we cannot make the 'decisive location' a necessary condition. What matters is 'sufficient' incumbent/opposition electoral availability. Spatial location cannot be incorporated as a 'necessary' condition for vulnerability. As for the 'symmetry' (or closeness) of the vote/seats distribution, which is often listed as a necessary condition, I have already argued that it is not. It can, perhaps, be considered a facilitating one.

THE RELATIONSHIP AMONG THE
DIFFERENT DIMENSIONS OF COMPETITION

In Table 4.1, I have summarized my main points concerning the four dimensions of competition when it is regarded as a process leading to elite responsiveness to voters' preferences. The four conditions of *contestability versus closure, availability versus encapsulation, decidability versus collusion* and *vulnerability versus safety of tenure*, identify dimensions that can be maximized or minimized. First of all, if contestability is minimized, the process can go so far as to endanger pluralism, which is also, as I have said, a defining condition of democracy. Beyond the minimum necessary level of pluralism, contestability can vary, but a maximization of contestability is likely to bring about excessive fragmentation on the offer side. Second, when the forces of voter encapsulation are so strong as to lead to the extinction of electoral availability, then electoral transactions are also extinct. Whatever change is made to the political offer, it is unlikely that buyers will be found. On the other hand, the maximization of electoral availability points to a situation in which every

TABLE 4.1 *The dimensions of electoral competition: a summary*

Dimension Features	Contestability	Availability	Decidability	Vulnerability
Polar opposite	Closure	Encapsulation	Collusion; obfuscation	Safety of tenure/ inability to sanction or reward
It indicates	Openness of the market: supply side	Openness of the market: demand side	Party differentials	Expectations about the decisiveness of elections for the governmental outcome
Conditions	Low threshold for accession	Weakness of identifications	Clearness of party positions; divisive issues; no muting or deflection of issues	Visibility of the dividing line between government and opposition (decisive location of available voters)
Status	Necessary condition of pluralism	Necessary and non-sufficient condition for decidability and vulnerability [a]	Necessary condition for responsiveness [b]	Necessary condition of responsiveness [c]
Consequence of maximization	Excessive fragmentation	Electoral instability	Excessive polarization	'Permanent campaign' syndrome
Consequence of minimization	No exit options for voters	No incentive to product differentiation	No differentiation of the offer (political indifference and/or alienation)	No anticipated reactions of incumbents

[a] Contestability and availability are not sufficient conditions of decidability and vulnerability.
[b] Contestability, availability, and decidability are not sufficient conditions of vulnerability.
[c] Vulnerability alone is not a sufficient condition of responsiveness.

voter is likely to change his/her mind. The consequence would be exceptional volatility from election to election.

Third, when decidability is at a minimum, party positions on issues and policies are blurred and unclear, issues tend to slide from 'divisive' to 'valence' or to be simply muted and/or transferred to another domain of decision-making different from the electoral political channel. Consequences of collusive tendencies may include growing political dissatisfaction, voter defection, and even mass disenfranchisement. At the other extreme, a situation is defined in which the maximization of decidability brings about very high policy differentials and a very adversarial style of politics. This tendency can result in clear ideological polarization. Finally, safety of governmental tenure strongly undermines responsiveness. Yet, maximization of vulnerability has its owns drawbacks. In the extreme case it could bring about a 'permanent campaign' syndrome (Blumenthal 1982): frequent feedback on government popularity, on the relative salience of issue in the mass public, and on the preference of the public (even on issues not yet articulated by the opinion makers); more awareness by citizens of governmental actions, or possible actions and better chances to react more visibly to them; correspondingly, government's sense of being more exposed to political pressures from the general public; constant watching of opinion polls by politicians in order to evaluate the response of public opinion to policy options; politicians' belief in their capacity to immediately estimate the costs in terms of support for specific decisions (far greater than the capacity to appreciate the gains in support of the same decisions); and postponement of critical and divisive decisions by elected officials for fear of alienating potential supporters.

It follows that each dimension impinges on the other, not in a linear and additive manner, but in rather contradictory ways. High contestability may lead to high fragmentation. Intense minorities may find it preferable to enter the electoral race than to articulate their demands within more encompassing political parties, even if motivated by single issues or small-range concerns. This is likely to have a negative effect on the clear distinction between government and opposition, and therefore on vulnerability. High vulnerability may lead to low decidability and no differentiation of the political offer. 'Perfect' vulnerability is achieved when two parties (or coalitions) of equal size compete for a few median voters (in theory, just for the median voter). Unless the degree of contestability allows for credible third-party alternatives, party willingness to shape clear and alternative choices to voters is likely to be nil. In order to ensure decidability, one needs a certain amount of electoral availability that is not functional for vulnerability. At the same time, excessively volatile electorates, resulting from declining cultural and organizational ties, may bring about an issue- or policy-'balkanized' electorate with no dimensionality whatsoever.[15] A certain amount of voter identification and vote stability is therefore necessary to allow parties to plan the offer, to interpret the reaction of the electorate, and to reduce the risks of collusion resulting from their failing in this respect.

In my view, the most interesting interaction takes place between decidability and vulnerability. Decidability requires clear alternative choices: a clearcut policy or programmatic profile of candidates and parties; no muting of major and divisive issues; no transformation of divisive issues into valence issues. Vulnerability is increased by majoritarian electoral systems that avoid fragmentation and unitary executive institutions that allow for the clear attribution of political responsibility. It also rests on political conditions: no disagreement on fundamentals, such that system defence does not overshadow performance evaluation; a broad electoral coalition open to all sectors of the population; the absence of polarizing ideological issues; the bypassing of the historical divisions and the identities linked to them; and a strong orientation of the vote towards performance evaluation.

CONCLUDING REMARKS

To what extent are these two sets of conditions mutually compatible? Is it possible simultaneously to maximize decidability and vulnerability? Probably not. A vicious circle may exist in which increasing responsiveness implies the increasing credibility of sanctions for incumbents: the latter implies that increasing weight is given to median voter preferences by both governing and opposition parties, as well as decreasing differentiation of political offer, declining policy competition, declining decidability, and, finally, reduced responsiveness to preferences. Certainly, sensitive, far-from-median voters can exit, but the opportunity to have their preferences considered is linked to their chance of obtaining an alternative new party. Maximizing competition as vulnerability in the absence of easy exit options will result in the widening of what Matthews (1985: 12) calls the 'ideological gap' between governmental positions and sections of the electorate. The need to be 'competitive' at the governmental level may prevent parties from taking stands on controversial and divisive issues. In situations of high vulnerability, established parties may be unwilling to take the risk of identifying clearly with policies and issues, highlighting the cost to be shared by specific groups in exchange for broadly collective advantages whose electoral returns are uncertain. In these situations, there is a strong incentive to define issues in such a way that no opposing sides are identifiable, and to push parties to argue more about who is more competent or capable of assuring the achievement of consensual accepted principles, than about which principles should be embodied in policy. For these reasons, new parties emerge which concentrate on issues removed and transformed into 'valence' problems. Having no traditional constituency to defend, they can appeal across partisan lines. However, if new parties are needed to take partisan stands on new issues, then a decline in the vulnerability at the system level may result, so that what is gained in decidability is lost in vulnerability of incumbents.[16]

There may be too much pragmatism and incrementalism, as has been suggested, and the bringing of controversial issues before the public may be welcomed. The increasing sharpness of policy alternatives will provide voters with the opportunity to make choices between clear-cut policy sets.[17] But there might also be too little influence of voters on government and leadership selection, as others argue. Thus, we should welcome the bringing about of coalition formulas, of electoral institutions, of forms of government, of chief-executive selection procedures, which will provide the voter with a direct say in the selection of alternative government. If we call the first good 'to have a choice' and the second 'to have a say', we end up with a difficult predicament: choice without say or say without choice.

An empirical study of competition has no way to escape its contradictory multidimensionality. Stipulative decisions or assumptions can only avoid this. If the various conditions or dimensions of competition have complex relationships among themselves, this means that electoral or party competition cannot be conceived as a linear process going from zero or a minimum to a maximum, theoretically definable as 'perfect competition'. This appealing metaphor is not applicable in politics if we agree that the parallel maximization of all conditions of competition is not only impossible, but also detrimental. One cannot therefore speak of more or less competition, but rather of a different mix of contestability, availability, decidability, and vulnerability, without being able to incorporate them into the single dimension of competition.

The level of actual competition in any given setting is a moving point in a four-dimensional space where no equilibrium can be found, as the maximization of one dimension comes at the expense of the others. It is necessary to abandon the analysis of an optimized system and to concentrate on the study of which alternative decisions are available and valid in practice, to concentrate on configurations that pass the test of feasibility. And a different mix of the various dimensions can be evaluated only via choices motivated in each historical circumstance by the most needed values sought. We end up where we started: a search for answers concerning 'what form of competition' and 'how much competition' brings us back to the definition of the 'social value' that needs to be maximized in any given case.

Competition is not a defining characteristic of democracy, but a property of which there can be more or less. However, it is not a uni-dimensional phenomenon that can be studied 'under optimal conditions'. If competition has to produce social values for society as the unintended effects of political interaction, it must remain within relatively narrow boundaries. Those conditions that in an optimal-model perspective limit and constrain competition, at the same time sustain it and make it viable. The set of normative factors, of social bonds, and of legal and institutional provisions (Etzioni 1988) which shapes group loyalties and identifications, which determines a certain amount of collusive practices and which prevents an outright competitive logic to prevail, limiting both its scope and means, does not represent elements of 'imperfection', but *conditions of viability*. Obviously the factors which contain competition can be so powerful, encompassing, and tight that the restraint on competition can suppress it altogether. At the same time, these confining conditions can be so weak that they do not have the capacity to contain competition, whose effects in different domains of political life can be detrimental to the same beneficial effects competition is thought to produce. Political competition needs constraining–sustaining conditions as it is unlikely to be effective in a world of rational, maximizing, selfish, independent actors as much as it is in a world of communal closed groups.

NOTES

1. Other social values are regarded as by-products of competition. Many economists underline the 'elimination of unnecessary returns to party leaders and functionaries', seemingly defined in terms of spoils. See Stigler (1972).
2. On the conditions of democracy see Dahl (1971: 3). Note that he mentions the right to compete for electoral support, but he does not go so far as to include political competition as such.
3. This is the term used and discussed in Bartolini and Mair (1990).
4. The concept, although formulated much before, did not begin to receive explicit and systematic attention in the main stream of economics until the beginning of the 1870s; cf. Stigler (1957: 1).
5. Ideology is introduced in a second stage, to reduce the implicit huge information costs.
6. 'Sensitivity' normally is meant to refer to 'issue sensitivity'. Against this term several criticisms have been advanced; see for instance Campbell *et al.* (1964: 78), Robertson (1976: 13), and Sartori (1976: 330–3). In the context of this argument, my definition of the available voter does not make reference to the origins of this availability, to how the available voter makes up his mind, or to whether his/her position can be represented in spatial terms.
7. Individual-level volatility has also been studied through transition matrices of voting switches giving a more precise estimation of the amount of electors who actually change their mind from one election to the next; see Denver (1985). Unfortunately, these studies are not numerous and this kind of information is not collected routinely for all elections.
8. See Laver and Hunt (1992: 3). I will refer to this work that discusses and summarise the position of rational choice theory on the issue. Critical notes concerning the postulate of exogenous preferences are in Dunleavy and Ward (1981) and in Dunleavy (1991).

9. It can be conceived as an heuristic simplification. If the current structure of electoral preferences was shaped by past party activities, there are good reasons to believe that the future structures will be determined by current party activities. Even in presence of a stable short-term structure, one can work for the bringing about of a different one. A party may find itself cut off from chances of victory, given the existing structure of preferences of the electorate, but it is not necessarily compelled to adapt itself to this structure. Given that what it does may determine future changes in the voters' preferences, party competition is not only an adaptive effort.

10. In one short passage, Downs (1957: 140) states that 'though parties will move ideologically to adjust to the distribution, under some circumstances, they will also attempt to move voters toward their own location, then altering it [the distribution]'. The remark is not developed in the work, however, since it implies a revision of the whole model.

11. On the linkages between the different arenas of the party system see Laver (1989: 302–05).

12. An exception is Stigler (1972).

13. Dawson and Robinson (1963) stress this dimension of 'opportunity' rather than actual result. Also Elkins (1974) insists on opportunity and possibility rather than actual records.

14. I am currently working on incumbents' vulnerability using a measure that shares the same logic. For each given election, I consider the distance from the majority thresholds of each party/coalition/candidate. This distance is then related to the average aggregate volatility of previous elections along the incumbent versus non-incumbent dimension. For instance, a 10% margin over the 50% threshold does not give a reliable indication of the real or perceived vulnerability of the incumbent unless it is related to the average aggregate vote swing between incumbents and the opposition. If that average aggregate voting shift is 20%, then a 10% margin does not make for safety. If, on the contrary, it is only 2% then a 10% majority distance makes for low vulnerability. The same level of closeness of the votes between government and opposition makes government safe in a system with low electoral availability along the line which separates majority and opposition, and vulnerable in a system with high volatility.

15. On the declining partisanship and divisiveness of issues see Thomas (1975, 1980).

16. Some recent tendencies of electioneering (with their stress on candidate-centred campaigning, fund-raising, intensive radio and television campaigns, packaging of candidates by professional advisers, well prepared, media-controlled public appearances, parading before carefully screened audiences—up to the point of reducing appearances to chat-shows and 'infomericals') are the correlate of high leadership vulnerability, but they also tend to deprive the public, even the most informed part of it, of any real choice; see for instance Semetko *et al.* (1991), Butler and Ranney (1992), Field (1994), and more generally Gunther and Mughan (2000).

17. On this theme, the two reference works in the American context are Key (1966) for the idea that alternative coalitions leave the choice to rational electors on the basis of past performance; and Schattschneider (1960) for the sceptical and critical attitude about the electoral process leading to the exclusion of major issues, the avoidance of clear-cut policy-alternative, the non-representation of vast segment of the population, and consequent mass disenfranchisement.

Part II

Re-examining Party Organization and Party Models

5

The Ascendancy of the Party in Public Office:

Party Organizational Change in Twentieth-Century Democracies

Richard S. Katz and Peter Mair

This chapter is concerned with the development of party organizations in twentieth-century democracies, and deals specifically with the shifting balance of power between what we have earlier (Katz and Mair 1993) termed the three organizational 'faces' of party: the party on the ground, the party in central office, and the party in public office. We evaluate the changing balance among these three faces in the context of four models of party organization: the cadre (or elite) party, which was the dominant form of party organization prior to mass suffrage; the mass party, which emerged with, or in anticipation of and to militate for, mass suffrage, and which was widely regarded, particularly in Europe, as the 'normal' or 'ideal' form of party organization for most of the twentieth century; the catch-all party, development towards which was first commented upon in the literature in the 1960s (Kirchheimer 1966), and which has come to rival the mass party not only in prominence (which some have regarded as a bad thing), but also in the affections of many analysts, particularly in North America; and finally, what we have called the cartel party (Katz and Mair 1995; see also Koole 1996; Katz and Mair 1996), a new and emerging model of party organization which we believe to be increasingly evident among the established democracies in recent years. In tracing the shifting balance of power among the three faces and across the four models of party organization, we contend that the most recent stage of development has resulted in the ascendancy of the party in public office, and the concomitant 'relegation' or subordination of the other two faces. Moreover, while parties on the ground sometimes continue to flourish, we suggest that the ostensible empowerment of party memberships, or even their greater autonomy, may nevertheless be compatible with an increased privileging of the party in public office. Finally, we also briefly discuss both the sources and implications of party organizational change, suggesting an association between the most recent shifts in the internal balance of intra-party power, on the one hand, and the apparent growth in popular feelings of alienation from parties, on the other.

Although, as we shall argue, this general pattern of organizational development reflects a dynamic of stimulus and response, and so, in some ways, is a natural sequence, its actual form is largely specific to Western Europe, and even within Western Europe, it does not necessarily characterize the developmental trajectory of every specific party. Rather, each model represents one of a series of organizational 'inventions' which then becomes part of an available repertoire from which political actors may draw directly. Moreover, since many of the contextual factors (for example, the extent of enfranchisement, systems of mass communication, consensus regarding the desirability and necessity of the welfare state) that were among the stimuli to which earlier parties responded, and which conditioned their responses to other stimuli, were themselves temporally ordered and specific, it is not to be expected that this developmental sequence will be (have been) repeated elsewhere. None the less, these four party types both illustrate the problems that are generic to all parties and form the currently available body of experience on which the building of new parties is likely to be based, and so the relevance and utility of this treatment extend beyond its roots in the political history of Europe.

THREE MODELS OF PARTY ORGANIZATION

The Elite Party

Early parliaments in the liberal and proto-liberal states of Northern Europe were composed of representatives of local communities. Organization, to the extent that it existed at all, evolved on two levels. If there were division within the community (generally meaning if there were division within the local elite), there might be organization within an individual constituency to contest its seat(s).[1] To the extent that there were regular patterns of conflict within the Parliament, those who found themselves generally in agreement might organize to coordinate their efforts or demands. At the point when these two forms of proto-organization began to interact, with local competition for seats at least in part structured by the same divisions that structured cooperation and competition in the Parliament, and at least in part conducted for the purpose of altering the balance in Parliament, it becomes reasonable to talk about parties in something approaching the modern sense.

Given the highly restrictive suffrage of most pre-twentieth-century European elections, and the often even more restrictive requirements for parliamentary membership, Members of Parliament (and also, therefore, the members of the party in public office) of these elite parties generally were not simply representatives, but rather were themselves the leaders, or the direct agents of the leaders, of the communities nominally represented. Real local organization would only be necessary in the event of electoral challenge, and thus would be temporary in nature; to the extent that one could speak of an enduring party on the ground, it would be virtually indistinguishable from the personal network of friends and clients of the member or his principals (Ware 1987*b*: 120–1).

The second key feature of the liberal elite party, along with the high 'quality' and small number of the members of the party on the ground, is that the party on the ground and the party in public office were so intimately related as to be essentially indistinguishable. Moreover, where the party in public office and the party on the ground were not simply the same people, the connection between the two was focused at the constituency level. The essence of the elite party is a small core of individuals with independent and personal access to resources able to place either one of their number or their surrogate in Parliament as their representative (Duverger 1954: 62–7; Ostrogorski 1902: i).

This local focus leads to the third key feature of the elite party: the weakness, if not the literal absence, of the party in central office. This has several roots. Most importantly, because the members of the party in public office can rely either on their own resources or else on the resources of the individual members of the party on the ground, they have no dependence on central resources, and hence no need to defer to a central authority. While they may create some central office as an aid to coordinating their activities in Parliament, it will remain purely a service organization, completely subordinate to the party in public office. Further, so long as the primary functions of the state are administrative rather than directive (or so long as the members of the party in public office would prefer such a state), there is little need for reliable majorities, and hence little need for party discipline. Because the party on the ground in each constituency is fundamentally independent, these bodies as well have little need for a party in central office and no desire to subordinate themselves to any central authority. Additionally, the philosophical and social underpinnings of the elite party are incompatible with the idea that the local elite who comprise the party on the ground would be subordinated to such an authority. Another way of saying this is that the elite party is an agglomeration of local parties more than it is a single national organization (Beer 1982: ch. 2).

Even allowing for the continued prominence of a number of members who owed their seats to the patronage of some 'duke or lord or baronet' after the beginning of suffrage expansion, it is probably fair to say that the party in public office was the dominant face of the elite party, at least with regard to decisions taken in the Parliament. This is so for two reasons, both of which cast some doubt on the utility of talking about a dominant face at all. First, the party in public office tends to be the only group in the party that has either the need or the opportunity to make collective decisions; when one looks for the locus of party decision-making at the national level, there is nowhere else to look. Second, the individual members of the party in public office tend to appear unconstrained with regard to policy by the party on the ground, but this is largely the result of the indifference of party on the ground to most policy, coupled with the identity of the party in public office and the party on the ground.

The elite party model as just described reflects both the social and institutional structures of Northern Europe in the nineteenth century. Towards the end of the nineteenth century and into the twentieth, an alternative version of the elite party arose in Southern Europe. The resulting system, identified as *caciquismo* in Spain, or *trasformismo* in Italy, made a sham of electoral politics, relying more on centrally orchestrated corruption than on the local standing of parochial elites.[2] In organizational terms, however, the resulting parties were quite similar. The central organizers comprised the party in public office, which, even more than in Northern Europe, clearly dominated.

Distilling the organizational essence of the elite party model (a small party on the ground in each constituency able to provide its own resources, close and locally based ties between the individual members of the party in public office and their individual parties on the ground, a weak or entirely absent party in central office), however, suggests that parties quite similar to the European model might emerge elsewhere as well. Indeed, Duverger (1954) suggests that this is precisely what happened in the United States (see also Epstein 1967: ch. 5). There a local cadre of politicians (the caucus or machine) played the role of Europe's local notables while graft took the place of private fortunes in providing resources. Similarly, Hoskin (1995) suggests that the elite party model predominated in Colombia between the 1850s and 1930s (see also Kern 1973), while one might expect to find parties that closely fit the elite model emerging particularly in the more traditional areas of the new democracies of the late twentieth century.

The Mass Party

Even before suffrage expansion, some of the conditions that favoured the elite party in nineteenth-century Europe began to change. The expansion of the role of government (Fry 1979) and the development of notions of government responsibility to Parliament (Jennings 1969: 17–18) increased the value of reliable party cohesion within the party in public office. It also increased the national relevance of local elections, stimulating greater communication and coordination across the local parties on the ground. Coupled with a decline in the number and significance of 'pocket boroughs', this shifted the balance of power within European elite parties even more in favour of the party in public office over the party on the ground. But so long as active participation in electoral politics remained the preserve of a narrow stratum of society (or in cases such as the United States, in which voters could be mobilized through patronage or other personalistic ties), the divergence of class, interest, and personnel between the party in public office and the party on the ground that would be necessary before one could speak meaningfully of dominance remained minimal and the basic fusion of these two faces of party remained as well.

With the expansion of the electorate from thousands to hundreds of thousands, raw numbers became a valuable political resource, and at the same time more elaborate organization became a necessity. For those interests whose potential strength lay in numbers of supporters rather than in the 'quality' of their individual supporters, notably the working class and fundamentalist Protestants, the elite party model clearly was inappropriate. Archetypically, the parties that developed to represent and advance these groups initially had no party in public office, because they were excluded from electoral participation. Even if their core organizers included a few Members of Parliament elected through one of the 'bourgeois' parties, they perceived one primary task to be the formation of independent organizations that would mobilize their supporters, first to win the right to vote, and then to provide both the votes and the other resources required to win elections under the new conditions of mass suffrage.

Because these resources had to be amassed on the basis of many small contributions from ordinary people rather than coming from a few wealthy or powerful individuals, this effort required a substantial party on the ground. And because the demands of these groups involved fundamental changes in national policy, it also required organization and coordination across constituencies, that is to say, a substantial party in central office. Both of these requirements were heightened by the strategy of encapsulation, which required the maintenance of a panoply of ancillary organizations, and by the fusion of electoral mobilization with additional activities such as the provision of proto-welfare services (e.g. Roth 1963). The organizational form that evolved to meet these needs is the mass party.

Whether the party in central office was formed first for the purpose of creating a party on the ground or was formed as an umbrella for the political/electoral activities of previously existing organizations (for example, churches or trade unions) is less significant than the symbiotic relationship between the two. The party in central office provides support for the expansion of the party on the ground and central co-ordination for its activities, while the party on the ground provides the resources that are necessary for the existence and success of the party in central office. As in any symbiotic relationship, it is difficult to say whether the party in central office or the party on the ground will be dominant, or even what dominance would mean.

In the ideology and formal structure of the mass party, the party in central office is the agent of the party on the ground (Beer 1982: ch. 3). Its leading officials are elected at a party congress as the representatives of the mass membership. But having been elected by the members, and therefore occupying a position presumably subservient to the party on the ground, the leaders of the party in central office also have been given a mandate to manage the party, and presumably to make rules for and give directives to the party on the ground (McKenzie 1955). It is particularly in this nexus that questions about party democracy and the iron law of oligarchy are raised.

While the power relationship between the party in central office and the party on the ground is somewhat ambiguous, the fact that these two faces are separate is perfectly clear. The party in central office is staffed by full-time professionals; the party on the ground is overwhelmingly made up of part-time volunteers. People in the party in central office are paid to be members; people in the party on the ground generally must pay in order to be members. The party in central office and the party on the ground are likely to be motivated by different varieties of incentives, and to measure success by different standards (Panebianco 1988: 9–11, 24–5, 30–2). None the less, their relationship can be fundamentally harmonious. Even where the party in central office is clearly dominant, it claims to exercise this dominance in the name of the party on the ground, while to the degree that the party becomes a single national entity, dominance by the party on the ground can be exercised only through a strong party in central office.

The mass party model also clearly separates the party on the ground from the party in public office. No longer an informal caucus of a few individuals, the party on the ground grows to include hundreds, if not thousands, of members. The Member of Parliament can no longer be seen as simply one of the party elite taking/serving his turn, but rather Member of Parliament has become a distinct organizational role. Moreover, within the ideology of the mass party, the role of Member of Parliament, and hence the party in public office, is clearly to be subordinate to the membership organization. In the elite party, party organization is instrumental to the achievement of the goals of the individual members of the party in public office. In the mass party, the party in public office is instrumental to the achievement of the goals of the party organization. In this respect, the party in central office has another function, that of supervising and controlling the party in public office on behalf of the party on the ground.

The idea that Member of Parliament is a party role conflicts, however, with the previous idea that Member of Parliament is a public role. Even if the elite party did represent particular interests within society, it claimed to represent the interests of the nation as a whole, and the members of the party in public office claimed to be the leaders of the communities they represented taken as wholes.[3] (The latter claim is, of course, less true of the elite parties of *caciquismo* or *trasformismo*, where conflict is avoided by conceding that the role of MP is a 'private' one.) To the extent that this were true, the party and public roles of members of the party in public office could not be in conflict. The mass party, on the other hand, is explicitly the representative of only one segment of society. This, coupled with the idea that the member of the party in public office is in the first instance the agent of his or her party organization (whether the party on the ground or the party in central office as the agent of the party on the ground), sets up a potential conflict, which is only partially mitigated when the introduction of proportional representation allows the idea that each constituency is represented by its parliamentary delegation as a whole, rather than by each MP as an individual, partially to reconcile loyalty to party with loyalty to constituency. Each member of the party in public office has two groups to whom he or she is responsible (the party organization and the electorate as a whole); two sets of incentives and constraints (those stemming from the desire to maintain and enhance a position within the party and those stemming from the need to win elections); two sources of legitimacy (as the agent of the party and as the holder of a public mandate). Coupled with the difference in perspective between those in office, with both the responsibilities of power and direct evidence of the limitations of that power, and those in the party on the ground for whom the simple answers of ideology are not directly confronted with the hard realities of practical politics, this leads to the substantial possibility of conflict between the party in public office and the party in central office/party on the ground, and thus to the increased importance of the question of relative influence or power.

The mass party model is the first to involve a clear distinction among the three faces of party at the empirical level (distinct and separate organizational presences; made up of different types of people; different and potentially conflicting incentive structures) and not just at the theoretical/conceptual level. It implies a particular organizational form (local membership branches supplemented by ancillary organizations; a representative party congress electing a central party executive; etc.), but it also depends on a particular balance among the three faces. In the early days of the mass party model, and generally in the early days of any party organized in this fashion, the party in central office, whether acting independently or as the real agent of the party on the ground, is likely to be the dominant face, as required. It controls the resources. The party in public office will not have experienced either the demands or the rewards of control over the government. Particularly once the party in public office gains access to the resources of government, however, it is likely to assert greater independence, and thus to threaten the 'mass partyness' of the organization.

As with elite parties, there were significant differences in the evolution of mass parties in different parts of Europe, and these could have a substantial impact on this process. Where the powers of the *régime censitaire* were effective in managing elections and suppressing real competition (for example,

Italy and Spain), demands for effective participation were more likely to be met with suppression than with incorporation. One result tended to be the radicalization of the left, in particular with communist rather than social democratic parties predominating. Their organization tended to reflect their circumstances, with strong centralization in the party central office. While this increased the subordination of the party in public office to the central office, it also minimized the internal influence of the party on the ground. By contrast, where liberal regimes already tolerated trade unions before the effective extension of suffrage to the working class (for example, the United Kingdom), the unions often became the basis for party organization. One organizational consequence might be that corporate members (those who became 'members' of the party through their union membership), although numerically predominant, would be represented in party circles by their unions rather than as individuals. And while this too might result in a weaker (because less necessary) party on the ground vis-à-vis a party central office both paid for and controlled by the unions, it would also serve to weaken the legitimacy of the parliamentary party's claim on the loyalties of MPs, leading to a somewhat more independent party in public office.

The Catch-All Party

This alteration of the balance of power within an established mass party is one source of evolution towards the catch-all model of party organization. A second source is change in the structure of the societies in which the elite and mass parties arose (see also below). The elite party is the party of a securely dominant upper class; the mass party is the party of an excluded subculture. As the mass parties succeeded in achieving their political objectives of universal suffrage and the welfare state, both the class dominance that underlay the elite party and the subcultural exclusion that underlay the mass party were eroded.

From the perspective of the elite party, the problem for party leaders was to mobilize mass electoral support, and to secure provision of the greater resources required for electoral competition with mass electorates, without giving up the independence that they previously had enjoyed. In order to do this, they organized membership branches like those of the mass parties. This in turn required a party in central office to coordinate those newly organized and expanded parties on the ground. The end result was three clearly articulated faces, just as in the mass party. But where in the mass party the archetypical sequence was party in central office organizes parties on the ground in order ultimately to create a party in public office, in these cases the sequence was party in public office creates a party in central office in order to organize supporters in the form of parties on the ground. The intention may have been that the parties on the ground be no more than organized cheer leaders for the professional politicians in the party in public office, but once recruited, party members start to make demands, abetted by the principle first articulated as part of the ideology of the mass party that the party in public office should be responsible to the party's members. The result is that, although the party in public office may be the dominant face of the party, its dominance is constantly under challenge.

This challenge is furthered by changes in modern societies. Reduced working hours, increased, and increasingly standardized, education, the political eclipse of the traditional upper class, and indeed a general weakening of class divisions have made expectations of deference to party leaders more problematic. Rather than owing their positions as party leaders to their positions at the top of a general and natural social hierarchy, party leaders, like leaders in other areas of community life, increasingly have to justify their leadership positions with reference to their capacity to satisfy the needs of their followers, and the followers increasingly have the capacity and the inclination to define and articulate those needs for themselves.

The mass party tends to arrive at a similar result from the other direction (see also Svåsand 1994), that is, through the increased assertiveness of the party in public office rather than the increased assertiveness of the party on the ground. Once significant influence over government policy and entry into government office were perceived to be realistic possibilities, the leaders of mass parties (particularly those in the party in public office, but often those in the party in central office as well) tended increasingly to orient themselves toward the requirements of electoral victory, and increasingly to be constrained by the realities of governing. Whether this is properly seen as 'selling out' the party and its programme to self-interest, as was often charged by more doctrinaire leaders of the party on the ground, or a realistic settling for half or three-quarters of a loaf rather than none at all, is not important. The result from either perspective was to exacerbate tension between the party in public office and the party on the ground.

Again, these tendencies were furthered for both the old elite parties and the old mass parties by a variety of changes in society, many of which were the result of the success of the mass parties in pursuing their agenda of social provision in areas such as education and the gradual erosion of subcultural barriers. On one side, these made a strategy of encapsulation more difficult; social, occupational, and geographic mobility, the weakening of religious ties, the common denominator appeal of mass media, all helped blur the divisions between classes, religions, and regions. On the other, increased education, reduced working hours, the political eclipse of the upper class, and the gradual weakening of class divisions, made expectations of deference to party leaders more problematic. A further development of the later twentieth century is the organization of citizens into a panoply of independent interest groups. This is relevant to the internal workings of political parties because it provides the citizens with alternative channels of access to government, and party leaders with alternative (to their parties on the ground) access to resources, thus weakening the symbiotic relationship between the party in public office and the party on the ground.

In contrast to the elite party model, in which the party in public office is clearly dominant (albeit in part because the party in public office and party on the ground are fused), and the mass party model in which the party on the ground/party in central office nexus is clearly dominant, the essence of the catch-all party with regard to the relationships among the three internal faces of party is conflict. The place in which this conflict is played out is the party in central office. The question is whether the party in central office will be the agent of the party on the ground in controlling the party in public office, or rather the agent of the party in public office in organizing and directing their (compliant) supporters in the party on the ground. Concretely, is the real leader of the party the chairman/secretary of the central committee or the leader of the parliamentary party? Are inter-party negotiations over policy and government formation conducted by the party in central office or the party in public office? To what extent is membership of the party central committee controlled by or reserved for members of the party in public office? And how much control over the party programme is exercised by the party congress?

CONTEMPORARY PARTY ORGANIZATIONS

In contemporary party organizations, however, these conflicts seem to have been settled, in that what we now appear to witness is the ascendancy of the party in public office, which assumes a more or less undisputed position of privilege within the party organization. In other words, we suggest that the development of party organizations in Europe has gone beyond the catch-all period and has entered a new phase, in which parties become increasingly dominated by, as well as most clearly epitomized by, the party in public office. We also suggest that this new balance is evident almost regardless of how these modern party organizations might be more generally typified. In other words, even though we would argue that many of the factors which have facilitated the eventual primacy of the party in public office can also be associated with the emergence of what we define as the cartel party (Katz and Mair 1995), an emphasis on the privileging of the position of the party in public office with respect to the other faces of party organization is not in itself dependent on the validity or otherwise of a particular classification of party organizations. On the contrary, it is a development which can be seen more or less irrespective of whether modern party organizations might best be typified as cartel parties, as 'electoral-professional parties' (Panebianco 1988), or as 'modern cadre parties' (Koole 1994).

The first and most obvious symptom of this new pattern in the internal balance of power involves the distribution of financial resources within the party, and, in particular, the distribution of state subventions. Since the 1960s, when direct state subsidies to political parties were first introduced in a limited number of countries, the channelling of state aid to party organizations has become an almost universal practice in the contemporary European democracies. In most countries, these subventions were first allocated to the parliamentary fractions of the parties, and only later, if at all, was the practice extended to include direct subsidies to the central party organization itself. Even now, the lion's share of the available subsidy continues to go to the parliamentary party, and it is only in a minority of countries—examples include Austria, Finland, and Norway—that the greater proportion of the subvention has tended to be allocated to the central party organization 'outside' Parliament (see Katz and Mair 1992*b*). Precisely who within the party leadership decides how these sums are then allocated across items within the parties' budgets themselves is, of course, not easily known, and in this sense the existence of the subsidies as such may not seem a strong indication of the privileging of the party in public office. But the fact that the process of state subvention was often initially limited to the parliamentary fractions of the parties, that the fractions themselves often still continue to win the greater share of the total subsidy, and that it is in Parliament that the final decisions are taken as to the levels and types of subsidy to be made available, all suggest that the increasing availability of state aid is one of the key factors operating to the final advantage of those in control of public office.

The second symptom which follows immediately from this, being partly the consequences of the availability of state subsidies, is that by the end of the 1980s a clear shift had begun to take place within party organizations in terms of the allocation of party staffs. Such time-series data on party staffs as are available contain clear evidence of a common trend across countries and parties whereby the growth in the numbers of staff employed by the parliamentary parties, and hence by the party in public office, has significantly outstripped that in the numbers employed by the party headquarters.[4] Indeed, across all the countries for which comparable data are available over time, the average balance has shifted from somewhat more than 25 per cent of staff being employed within the parliamentary offices in earlier periods (usually in the 1960s or early 1970s) to slightly more than 50 per cent by the late 1980s. Although in some countries this shift is very substantial (from having no staff in the parliamentary offices to having more than two-thirds of all staff in the parliamentary offices in the cases of Denmark and Ireland), and in other countries almost negligible (from 62.7 per cent in the early 1980s in the Netherlands to just 66.6 per cent in the late 1980s), there is no single country which defies this general trend. Given that staff constitute a crucial organizational resource, these data also therefore confirm an increasing bias in favour of the party in public office.

The third symptom which is relevant here is one which we have already often highlighted elsewhere (see for instance Katz and Mair 1995; Mair 1997: 137–9), and that is that most substantial and/or enduring West European parties have recently enjoyed a period of office in national governments, and that most now orient themselves as a matter of course to the occupation of public office. In other words, there now remain few, if any, significant parties of opposition in the West European democracies; at most, there remain simply parties which, now and then, spend more or less limited periods outside government. Those that remain excluded from government office are those that occupy what is more or less the political fringe, a host of small parties which most usually represent either the extremes of left or right, or minority regionalist or environmental demands. The mainstream parties, on the other hand, now including a substantial number of Green parties, as well as even some of the representatives of the far right, have developed to a stage where they are now, or recently have been, holders of public office. This is a dramatic shift in contemporary party systems.

There are also two important aspects of this latter development which need to be underlined. First, as was emphasized above, the acquisition of a governing status is something which is now common to most of the established parties in Western Europe, and, being also something which has emerged through time, it therefore reflects a picture which is markedly different from that which could have been drawn even twenty-five years ago. Second, it is a development which will almost necessarily have impacted upon the internal balance of organizational forces within the parties concerned, since Panebianco (1988: 69) is certainly not alone in reminding us that 'the organizational characteristics of parties which are in opposition for a good part of their existence are different from those which stay in power for a long time'. Power—office—is itself an agent of socialization (e.g., Mughan *et al.* 1997). And much as the organizational style of parties has been influenced by the degree of commitment to and involvement in the parliamentary process, so too can it be expected to have adapted to the increasingly widespread incorporation into government. With time, then, and as governing becomes a standard experience and expectation for most mainstream parties, we can also anticipate that this will have led to the party in public office acquiring enhanced status, prestige, and autonomy. There occurs, in short, a process of 'parliamentarization' of parties (Koole 1994: 291–2), or even, in a more extreme version, a process of 'governmentalization' (Müller 1994: 73), a trend which inevitably risks relegating the importance of both the party on the ground and the party in central office.

Indeed, whatever happens about the party on the ground (see below), such evidence as does exist suggests that there is in fact less and less scope now available for any potential conflict of interests between the party in public office and the party in central office. In terms of the position of the parties' national executive committees, for example, as we have shown elsewhere (Katz and Mair 1993), the tendency has been to increase the degree of representation, and, presumably, the degree of influence, afforded to the party in public office. Parliamentarians and their leaders now tend to be accorded greater weight in these bodies than was the case in the 1960s and 1970s, and correspondingly less weight is now given to the otherwise non-office-holding representatives of the party on the ground. The trend, to be sure, is not universal, but it is nevertheless sufficiently common to imply that, more often than not, the party in public office now exerts greater control over the national executive than used to be the case.

In any case, and within the general scheme of things, the political position of the party in central office is now clearly less important than was the case during the primacy of the catch-all party and mass party. As noted above, the growth in organizational resources, as indicated by staff and money, has tended to be to the advantage of the parliamentary party. Moreover, the resources which remain within the central office appear to be increasingly devoted to the employment of contractual staff and consultants, and to the provision of outside expertise. In such a context, political accountability would appear to matter less than professional capacity, a development which might well imply the erosion of the independent political weight of the party central offices. It is interesting to note, for example, that while it often proves very difficult to identify the electoral impact, if any, of the development of new campaign techniques and technologies, what is clear is that they have helped to shift the weight of influence within party organizations from amateur democrats to the professional consultants who control these techniques (Bartels 1992: 261; see also Panebianco 1988: 231–2). More specifically, the gradual replacement of general party bureaucrats by professional specialists may act to 'depoliticize' the party organization and will almost certainly help to create the conditions within which the leadership, in public office, can win more autonomy, not least because the activities of these new professionals are almost always more directed (externally) at winning support within the electorate at large rather than (internally) at the organization and maintenance of the party on the ground.

This also underlines a further important shift in the general orientation of modern party organizations. As television and the mass media more generally have emerged as the key channel of communication between party leaders and voters, offering the benefits of a direct linkage in place of what previously had been mediated by organizational cadres and activists, party campaigning has become more centralized and 'nationalized', with the core of the parties' messages now emanating directly from a single national source. A specifically local input has therefore become less and less relevant to the national campaign,[5] implying that the parties also need to devote less and less effort to the organization and mobilization of the party on the ground. Resources become devoted instead to selling the party message to the electorate at large, and this can result not only in a changed—and more professionalized—role for the party central office, but also in the eventual erosion of the division of responsibilities between the party apparatus in central office and that in public office. Indeed, as parties become more externally oriented, the roles of the professionals serving the party in central office and of those serving the party in public office become almost inseparable, with both responding in the main to the demands of the party leadership in Parliament and in government.

MARGINALIZING THE PARTY ON THE GROUND?

All of this might well lead to the hypothesis that, with few exceptions, the modern mainstream parties have now been transformed simply into parties in public office, and that the other faces of the party are withering away. Hence it is not simply the party in central office that may have been eclipsed, subordinated, or marginalized by these most recent developments, but also the party on the ground, with contemporary party organizations becoming effectively indistinguishable from their parliamentary and governmental leaderships. The leaders become the party; the party becomes the leaders. One obvious symptom of this change is, of course, the sheer *physical* withering of the party on the ground (for some recent evidence, see Mair and Biezen 2001). Among thirteen long-established democracies in Western Europe, for example, party membership as a percentage of the national electorate has fallen from an average of almost 10 per cent in 1980 to less than 6 per cent at the end of the 1990s, a decline which, to varying degrees, is characteristic of *each* of these thirteen long-established democracies. Nor is this physical withering of the party on the ground simply a function of the expansion of electorates, such that, as was the case in the 1970s and 1980s, falling membership ratios might be attributed to the failure of the party organizations to keep pace with the growing numbers of enfranchised voters. On the contrary: in each of the long-established democracies there has also been a fall in the absolute number of party members being recorded, a fall which is sometimes very substantial. Indeed, with the exception of Germany, where the parties now count a host of new members within the former East German *Länder*, each long-established democracy in Western Europe has seen raw membership levels decline by at least 25 per cent with respect to the levels claimed in 1980. The evidence of organizational decline in this respect is unequivocal.

At the same time, however, and seeming to defy the hypothesis, there is also widespread evidence to suggest that party memberships are, in fact, being increasingly empowered. Thus different parties in an increasing number of polities have now begun to open up decision-making procedures, as well as candidate- and leadership-selection processes, to the 'ordinary' party member, often by means of postal ballots. Rather than witnessing the withering away of the *power* of the party on the ground, therefore, what we see is the apparent democratization of internal party life, with the ordinary members beginning to win access to rights which formerly were jealously preserved by the party elites and activists.

On the face of it, of course, and despite the potential privileging of the party in public office, there appear to be a number of reasons why modern party leaderships should be unwilling to allow the power and even the sheer size of the party on the ground to evaporate.[6] Despite the growth in state subventions, for example, members continue to offer a valuable resource to parties in terms of both money and (campaigning) time. Members also offer themselves, as it were, constituting a reservoir of 'warm bodies' which can be used by the party to maintain a presence in local councils, advisory boards, and elective agencies, and through which the party can both exert influence and avail itself of feedback (see Sundberg 1994). In this sense, members continue to provide an important linkage mechanism through which the party can remain in contact with the world outside Parliament. That said, however, it is important to recognize that even these imputed benefits are substitutable or even dispensable. Thus, the share of party income which is derived from the membership can eventually be replaced by increased public subsidies, provided that the other parties in the system are willing to cooperate in the necessary legislation and decision-making. Moreover, and as noted above, it is also evident that the contribution of the membership to election campaigning is proving less and less necessary, as the campaigns themselves become increasingly controlled by and executed from the centre. And while the provision of 'warm bodies' may well be non-substitutable, it is nevertheless eventually dispensable, and it is perfectly possible to conceive of what might be seen as 'first-order' parties, which develop in such a way that they pay little or no attention to building a penetrative strategy on the ground, preferring to focus instead on a primarily 'national' presence.[7]

If parties continue to feel the need to foster a presence on the ground, therefore, it is probably due largely to the legacy of the past and to the inheritance of earlier models. Party organizations do not begin *ex novo*, but are inherited by party leaders, and although these leaders can attempt to effect major reforms and innovations within the organizations they inherit, there are nevertheless clear limits to the capacity for change. In other words, if a party already enjoys a presence on the ground, then it is unlikely that this can be easily amputated. Membership may not be valued very highly, but a membership-oriented tradition cannot easily be dismissed. In addition, and as part of this legacy of the past, membership may also imbue the party leadership with a sense of legitimacy. In Sweden, for example, 'the parties seem to want to maintain the *image* of a mass party, with a positive membership development being taken as proof that the party is perceived as a viable channel for political representation' (Pierre and Widfeldt 1994: 342). And a similar imperative clearly underlined the major membership drive undertaken by the British Labour Party following the election of Tony Blair as the new party leader. Conversely, in the case of new parties, and most especially new parties in new democracies, it is unlikely that a party on the ground will be assiduously cultivated (Kopecký 1995; Mair 1997: ch. 8; Biezen 1998). Other things being equal, the emphasis on maintaining a party on the ground, and, indeed, the sheer existence of a substantial party membership, is therefore most likely to characterize parties which have progressed through a long history of organizational development, in which the legacy of the mass party model continues to weigh upon contemporary conceptions of organizational style and legitimacy. For most of the long established parties in Western Europe, then, it is simply the case that the party in public office cannot avoid the presence of a party on the ground: however troublesome to the leadership it might prove to be, a mass membership is part of the party tradition.

Given this legacy, how then can the primacy of the party in public office be successfully asserted? At one level, the answer is for the leadership to marginalize the party on the ground, and even to let it wither away; whether consciously planned or not, for example, this certainly appears to reflect the recent experiences of the mainstream parties in Denmark and the Netherlands. At the same time, however, and as noted above, any such strategy risks costing the party leadership more in terms of declining legitimacy than it might benefit them in terms of increasing their freedom of manœuvre. The preferred strategy, therefore, might be one which ostensibly enhances the position of the party on the ground, thereby making membership seem all the more attractive to potential supporters, while at the same time limiting the potential for a real challenge from below.

There are two possible ways in which this preferred strategy might be developed, both of which are already evident in a number of contemporary party organizations (see also Mair 1994: 16–18). In the first place, the ostensible power of the party on the ground can be, and has been, enhanced through internal party democratization, in which, as noted above, the ordinary member acquires a formal voice in the selection of candidates and party leaders, as well as in the approval of policies and programmes, and in which the mass membership becomes, in effect, a mass (party) electorate. This certainly represents an empowerment of the membership. At the same time, however, it also serves to erode the position of the party activists and the *organized* party on the ground, in that voice now no longer depends on militancy or organization. This is a particularly significant development, since it was precisely from within the more militant stratum of the party on the ground that the party in public office has always proved most vulnerable to criticism. By enfranchising the ordinary members, often by means of postal ballots, the party leadership therefore effectively undermines the position of its more militant critics, and does so in the name—and practice—of internal party democracy. Almost by definition, the often disorganized and atomized mass membership of the party, entry to which now demands fewer and fewer prerequisites,[8] is likely to prove more deferential to the party leadership, and more willing to endorse its proposals. It is in this sense that the empowerment of the party on the ground remains compatible with, and may actually serve as a strategy for, the privileging of the party in public office.

The second approach is perhaps less evidently manipulative, and simply involves promoting a more effective 'division of labour' between the party in public office, on the one hand, and the party on the ground, on the other, in which the linkage between the two levels is more or less restricted to the local selection of candidates for election to national offices. In other words, and reflecting the tendencies initially noted in the American case by Eldersveld (1964), party organizations may increasingly adopt a stratarchic form, in which different and mutually autonomous levels coexist with one another, and in which there is a minimum of authoritative control, whether from the bottom–up or from the top–down. 'Local parties', reflecting the party on the ground, then work primarily at the local level, enjoying almost exclusive control over the policies, programmes, and strategies to be pursued within their own territorial limits. The national party, on the other hand, which is dominated by the party in (national) public office, is also free to develop its own policies, programmes, and strategies, unhindered by the demands and preoccupations of the party on the ground. The party on the ground may of course flourish in this stratarchic setting, but, in the end, it remains on the ground, being linked to the party in public office only through its control of that party's composition.

PARTY ORGANIZATIONAL CHANGE: SOURCES AND IMPLICATIONS

There is, of course, no 'single' party organizational form; on the contrary, what we witness today, as in earlier generations, are variations on quite a wide variety of different themes (Koole 1996; Katz and Mair 1996). Nor is there an 'ideal' party organizational form; rather, organizations develop in an often idiosyncratic way, being influenced not only by the specific social and economic contexts in which they operate, but also by the prevailing institutional structures, as well as their own histories. Commonalities can nevertheless be established. Despite evident national peculiarities, for example, the fact that participation in political decision-making was formerly restricted to a small class of privileged social actors has proved sufficiently determining to allow us to draw cross-national generalizations about the character of the once dominant elite party. In a similar vein, the impact of mass democratization has also proved sufficiently powerful as to facilitate generalizations about the emergence and character of the mass party. And while the spread and relevance of the catch-all party continues to be debated, it is none the less clear that many parties did begin to shift towards a new mode of operation in the 1960s, in which there emerged substantial sources of conflict between the party in public office and the party on the ground.

It has been our contention in this chapter that even this most recent stage of development has now been superseded through the emergence of yet a new *modus operandi* in which the primacy of the party in public office is increasingly being established. To be sure, as noted above, the patterns which we identify are not always necessarily true, or not always necessarily true to the same extent, in all parties. Indeed, none of the specific patterns which can be discerned in the variety of party organizational forms has ever been wholly realized. What is certainly true, however, is that as party organizations adapt to the demands of contemporary democracies, they tend increasingly to revolve around the needs and incentives of the party in public office. And while the reasons for this change are myriad, with the immediate source being usually found in the internal politics of the party, the ultimate source can often be traced back to the environment in which the party operates. Although, other things being equal, it is possible that an equilibrium might emerge over time among the various faces and actors making up a party, changes external to party inevitably will upset this steady-state balance. Sometimes these environmental changes bring new pressures and challenges; other times they represent new opportunities. In each case, however, they alter the distribution of resources or incentives within the party and therefore the pattern of interactions within it.

The environmental changes that have received the most scholarly attention undoubtedly have been those relating to the electoral system. Indeed, the very existence of modern political parties with both their bureaucratic and their mass membership organizations usually is attributed directly to expansion of the suffrage, with the pace and timing (particularly relative to industrialization) of enfranchisement taken to explain many of the differences among parties (Lipset and Rokkan 1967*b*). As noted above, the party bureaucracy was made necessary by the need to organize and communicate with electorates numbering in the hundreds of thousands rather than the hundreds and the mass organization furthered the encapsulation of the party's electorate as well as the pooling of financial and other resources. And, of course, to be 'necessary' is just another way of saying that one is in control of a 'zone of organizational uncertainty', and therefore powerful. Other changes in electoral laws, such as modifications of the electoral formula (including changes in electoral thresholds or district magnitude) or (dis)allowing an intra-party preference vote may also lead to changes in the internal life of parties, as well as to changes in the balance among parties (Katz 1980: 31–2). Even more directly, parties may have some or all of their organizational structure 'imposed' by statute, a constraint which becomes increasingly relevant as the provision of public subsidies is accompanied by the introduction of laws on parties.

Parties must also adapt to changes in the availability of, and need for, various resources. The evolution of media of mass communication provides one prominent example. The development of a party press allowed party organizers to communicate with their followers and potential supporters regardless of the cultural or political biases of the publishers of 'independent' newspapers. The party press naturally enhanced the importance of its publishers, primarily party bureaucrats, at whatever level of centralization the press was organized. It also required a well-articulated organization in order to disseminate and subsidize publications. It thus strengthened the bureaucratic and mass membership faces of the party vis-à-vis the party as government. The rise to central importance of broadcasting, especially television, has had just the opposite result, however. As noted above, television allows central party leaders, particularly those in public office to whom broadcasting time generally is allocated and who are seen as being the most personally 'newsworthy', to communicate directly with the public, both within and without the party, without the intervention of, or need for, a party organization per se. On the other hand, these new possibilities for direct communication also create a need for new varieties and levels of professional expertise.

Provision of public subsidy to political parties represents another obvious example of how changes in the availability of resources can alter the balance of forces within a party. Before public subsidy, many parties were financially dependent almost exclusively on voluntary contributions, either from their members or from business or other organizations hoping to buy influence or access. Loss of such support could have a devastating effect both on the party in office and on the party bureaucracy, and this made them dependent on those contributing to their campaign expenses and salaries. State subsidy reduces party dependence not only on outside contributors (as it was overtly intended to do), but also on the party's own grass-roots members. And again, to the extent that the membership organization is less valuable to other aspects of the party, the status and influence of those who hold office in the membership organization declines.

A variety of secular changes in the political environment also have the potential to force, or have forced, party adaptation. The traditional mass party of integration was based on a highly structured social system in which the relevant cleavages, be they class, religion, ethnic grouping, or whatever, were sharply drawn and unlikely to be bridged. When a party built a network of ancillary organizations and attempted to encapsulate its supporters, it was basically reflecting a pre-existing social reality. The 'freezing of political cleavages' was based on a more general freezing of social cleavages. The 'thawing' of these cleavages, spurred by such trends as increased and more meritocratic higher education and the homogenization of culture through mass media and mass consumption, thus undermine the traditional bases of mass organization. For example, the relative decline of social solidarity as the glue of the membership organization may make ideological purity relatively more important, and thus lead to strengthened demands for such purity from its leaders. The resulting constraints may be interpreted as making the membership organization relatively more costly to the governing organization, and thus as leading to attempts to secure alternative access to the resources the members provide.

This general social change has been accompanied by two more directly political changes. On the one hand, increased levels of education have only been one contributing factor to generally higher levels of political competence in the mass public. Better informed, more articulate, with more leisure time, voters become less dependent on party organizations for their connection to the political world. They also become less willing to accept the relatively passive role that the traditional mass party has given to its rank-and-file supporters (e.g. Barnes, Kaase *et al.* 1979). As the troops refuse blindly to follow, the influence in the party of leaders whose position rests on their command of these troops naturally declines. On the other hand, increased civic competence coupled with weakening social ties and increased use of general rather than party channels of communication mean that many of the processes that previously would have instilled a strong sense of party (or more general subcultural) identification have weakened. But since party identification not only provides a cushion of support that allows a party to survive temporary setbacks, but also is the basis for solidaristic rewards of membership, this too may alter the balance of forces within parties.

Although this discussion suggests how party change may be driven by the need to adapt to the environment, at least three qualifications to the simple dichotomy of external stimulus and internal response are necessary. First, some of the stimuli to change are internally generated, and once a party begins to adapt, it sets in motion forces that can have a ripple effect throughout the organization. Second, and perhaps more importantly, many of the 'external' stimuli discussed above are the result of party actions. For example, it is the parties in government that have voted themselves public subsidies, access to mass media, or (less directly, through the welfare state) longer lived and better informed electorates. Finally, to complete the circle, the environment also responds to changes made by the parties, and thus one explanation for the decline in party identification, for example, is the decision of the parties to reach out beyond their traditional social bases, and in other ways to distance themselves from both identifiers and members. In many cases then, rather than simple stimulus followed by single response, or cause followed by consequence, there develops instead a self-reinforcing process, which, we argue, is now leading parties throughout the contemporary democracies to a position in which the party in public office is now firmly in the ascendant.

Even though we have suggested that this shift in the internal balance of power can be identified almost regardless of how party organizations more generally may be typified, we would also contend that the drift towards the primacy of the party in public office is nevertheless facilitated by precisely the same factors which we associate with the emergence of the 'cartel party' and with the absorption of parties into the state (Katz and Mair 1995). More specifically, the increasing reliance of parties on state subsidies, a process which facilitates the growing primacy of the party in public office, clearly draws these parties into an ever closer involvement with the state. The increasingly widespread participation of parties in government, a development which has helped to privilege the party in public office, is also central to the cartelization process. Furthermore, the movement towards cartelization is also likely to be enhanced as parties in public office are encouraged to acquire substantially more autonomy than was available to them under the old mass party model, and even under the catch-all model. Finally, albeit more indirectly, as politics itself increasingly assumes the status of a career, and as the substantive and ideological differences between competing political leaderships wane away (through either a voluntary or an enforced consensus), the leaderships themselves appear to assume an increased commonality of purpose, with each leadership seeming to find it easier or more appropriate to come to terms with its direct counterpart than with its own following on the ground. To paraphrase Michels, it now appears that there is increasingly *less* in common between two party members, one of whom holds public office, than there is between two public office-holders, each of whom comes from a separate party. Thus, while the position of the party in public office might well be in the ascendant in any one of the varieties of contemporary party organizations which have been identified and theorized about in the modern literature on parties, nevertheless such privileges are clearly a sine qua non of the emergence and consolidation of the cartel party.

CONCLUSION

While the scope of this present chapter is too limited to permit an exploration of the full implications of these changes, three brief points can be noted by way of a conclusion. In the first place, it seems to us appropriate to trace an association between the increased ascendancy of the party in public office, and the hypothesized cartelization of parties, on the one hand, and the apparent growth in recent years in popular feelings of alienation from, or even mistrust in, mainstream politics and parties, on the other (see Poguntke and Scarrow 1996*a*; Daalder 1992 and Chapter 2 above; and Torcal, Gunther, and Montero, Chapter 10 below). As party leaderships become more autonomous from their own following, and as they become increasingly busy with themselves and their own world, it is almost inevitable that they will be seen as being more remote. This in itself is problematic enough. But when this remoteness is also accompanied by a perceived failure to perform (even though such failure may well derive from constraints, both national and international, that are beyond the specific control of party), it can then develop into a sense of alienation and mistrust, in which the political leaderships are not only seen to be distant from the voter, but also to be self-serving.

Second, and following from this, it is evident from recent experiences in both Europe and the United States that there now exists a potential catchment area that can be exploited by so-called 'anti-party parties', often of the extreme right, which seek to combine an appeal to those alienated by the established parties with an appeal to more xenophobic, racist, and essentially anti-democratic sentiments (e.g. Mudde 1996). In other words, by lumping together all of the established parties as a 'bloc' to be opposed by the neglected citizen, these new extremist parties often attempt to translate a particular opposition to what we see as the cartelization of parties into a more generalized assault on the party system as a whole, and possibly even into an assault on democratic values as such. And while, with few exceptions, the appeal of such parties remains relatively marginal, it is here that we can see a genuine problem of legitimacy in contemporary democracies beginning to emerge.

Third, as indicated above, and as we have argued at greater length elsewhere (Katz and Mair 1995; Mair 1997: ch. 6), it is important to recognize that much of what is problematic here has been the result of decisions and actions which have been carried out by the parties themselves. In other words, in privileging the party in public office, the parties have risked being seen as privileging themselves, and, whether directly or indirectly, to have been using state resources in order to strengthen their own position in terms of subsidies, staffing, patronage, and status. As their position on the ground has weakened, parties have helped to ensure their own survival as organizations by more or less invading the state, and, in so doing, they may well have sowed the seeds for their own crisis of popular legitimacy. With the ascendancy of the party in public office, in short, parties in contemporary democracies, which often appear to be less relevant, now lay themselves open to the charge of being also more privileged.

NOTES

1. See Neale (1949); Hirst (1975); Namier (1970).
2. See Linz (1967: 202–5); Malefakis (1995: 54); Ware (1987: 123).
3. For an analogous interpretation of the role of MP from an earlier period in the history of Northern Europe, see the letter from A. Henly MP to his constituents quoted by Sedgwick (1970: 126).
4. These data are reported in detail in Katz and Mair (1992*a*).
5. There are exceptions, of course, most notably in those systems where the peculiarities of the electoral system (e.g. STV in Ireland, or preferential voting within a list system) may leave sufficient room for the national competition between parties to be supplemented by local competition between individual candidates *within* parties, and where local branches of a particular party can serve as the competing intraparty campaign organizations of the rival local candidates. See Katz (1980); Mair (1987: 126–7).
6. See Scarrow (1994); Katz (1990); Mair (1994: 13–18).
7. One possible example of such a 'first-order' party is perhaps Forza Italia (Morlino 1996: 16–17), although this new party also appears to echo many of the features of the earlier elite party. The term 'first-order' party is adapted from the distinction between types of elections which was drawn by Reif and Schmitt (1980).
8. Although many parties used to stipulate a variety of conditions and obligations which had to be met before membership could be acquired, this practice no longer really pertains, and it is now often possible to acquire membership simply by affiliating to the party at national level and by paying the subscription by credit transfer, or even by signing up through the internet.

6

Beyond the Catch-All Party: Approaches to the Study of Parties and Party Organization in Contemporary Democracies

Steven B. Wolinetz

Imagine two different kinds of political party. One is a skeletal organization, intermittently active. Constituency associations exist throughout the country, but most of the time the party outside of Parliament is barely visible. However, this changes dramatically when an election has been called. Then, the party turns into a well-oiled machine, distributing literature, organizing rallies, and getting voters to the polls on election day. This flurry of activity ceases as soon as the last ballot has been counted. The only other time that the party organization is visible is when nominations or the party leadership are at stake. Candidate organizations recruit members to elect delegates to nominating meetings and for a few weeks the party is more like an arena for competition than a cohesive machine. But new members drop away almost as soon as they are enlisted and, except for a small office staff, the party outside of Parliament returns to its dormant state.

The second party operates at several different levels, and possesses not only a national office, but regional and local organizations. Local sections hold regular meetings. There is a detailed party programme, drafted by the central office and parliamentary caucus staff, debated vociferously by party members and adopted by a party congress. The party outside Parliament is active not only during election campaigns but also in between. However, the party organizes only a small percentage of its voters as members and many of these rarely attend meetings. Election campaigns are run by a small team, in and around the leader and the central office, and most members rarely do more than attend an occasional rally or display a party poster in their front windows.

The first party corresponds to one of the two large Canadian national parties (Liberals, and in better times, Progressive Conservatives) and would typically be termed a *cadre party*, or perhaps an *elite-centred party*. The second is modelled on the Dutch Labour Party (PvdA) but also resembles the Christian Democrats (CDA) or Liberals (VVD). The organizational form is that of a *mass party* but, as Ruud Koole (1992, 1994) has pointed out, the level of activity is reminiscent of a cadre party.

The existence of these two different kinds of parties, as well as a plethora of others, points to a problem in the parties literature: parties exist in a variety of different forms, but we have few effective ways of classifying them. Some of the schema which we use to classify political parties are nearly a half-century old. Age is not necessarily a disadvantage (it should facilitate comparison), but the claim that substantial changes have occurred in the ways in which parties are organized or approach voters has been a persistent theme in the literature. Moreover, new parties have been established in some previously frozen party systems. Some, such as Silvio Berlusconi's Forza Italia, built on the basis of a ownership of TV networks, their advertising arm, and a successful soccer team, are very different from the parties which they seek to replace. Categories devised to characterize parties in one time or place may not be suitable to differentiate them in another.

Of course, these schemata are not our only tools. Political scientists have devised new types to cope with change. Kirchheimer's (1966) *catch-all party* entered our vocabulary in the 1960s. More recently, Panebianco (1988) has proposed *the electoral-professional party*, a variant more precisely defined in organizational terms, Poguntke (1987, 1993) the *new politics party*, Katz and Mair (1995) the *cartel party,* and more recently, Hopkin and Paolucci (1999), the *business firm* party. However, this practice has advantages and disadvantages. A profusion of categories can confuse as well as clarify. Even if proponents carefully specify their categories, definitions are often stretched as others use them. The catch-all party has become a generic description of present-day parties, but its characteristics are not always well-defined. Even if they were, there is another problem: these types focus primarily on Western Europe. But transitions to democracy have greatly increased the number of parties which might be included in comparative studies. Categories devised primarily to compare Western European parties—most of which developed and continue to operate in parliamentary systems—may not be suitable for comparing parties in mixed parliamentary-presidential systems or presidential systems.

There are good reasons for re-examining existing classifications and seeing if others can be developed. However, reworking categories is a complex process, requiring further research and interaction between theory and data. This is a preliminary effort, focusing primarily on parties in established liberal democracies. The first half of this chapter examines the adequacy of existing categories in light of the literature. The second considers ways in which contemporary parties might be compared.

CATEGORIES AND CONCEPTS IN THE
COMPARATIVE LITERATURE

That students of political parties have problems classifying them may seem surprising. The comparative study of political parties is nearly one hundred years old. We know a good deal about a wide range of political parties, and have little trouble locating many on left–right spectra. There are also well-known classifications, such as Duverger's (1954) distinction between *cadre* and *mass* political parties, or Neumann's (1956) distinction between *parties of individual representation* and *parties of democratic (mass) integration*. However, students of political parties have typically worked as much *around* as *with* classificatory schemes, employing them where they are useful, and ignoring or omitting them when they are not. This has been possible both because of the ways in which the comparative literature has developed and the ways in which research has proceeded. Several facets of this are worth exploring.

First, the comparative study of political parties has been primarily a West European venture in which the other parties which researchers knew most about—those in the United States—were sufficiently different for them to be walled off into a separate literature. Only occasional efforts have been made to include Canadian, Australian, or New Zealand parties in the discussion (see, for example, Epstein 1967) or to engage in broader comparison (see, for instance, Gunther and Diamond 2001). Attempts such as Janda (1980) to collect or analyse data on parties in very different settings are unusual. The Western European emphasis has had a number of consequences. One is that political scientists could work within a well-defined subset of relatively comparable cases. Another is that specialists did not have to preoccupy themselves with alternate classifications or dimensions on which parties might be arrayed: most Western European parties could be located on left–right spectra or linked to well-known ideological families to which they belonged.

Second, until recently, more attention has been paid to party systems than parties, their organization, or the ways in which they should be classified. To be sure, studies of individual parties often considered internal politics and organization, but the systematic study of party organization is a relatively recent phenomenon. Parties were often treated as single actors in which the complexities of party structure and internal party life played no role (Daalder 1983). It is only recently that political scientists have begun to pay more attention to parties as organizations. Major studies are under way, and we are learning more about how parties are organized (see Katz and Mair 1992*a*, 1994), as well as ways in which different facets of party organization might be distinguished (Katz and Mair 1993). However, these have not yet produced any new classification of parties.

Third, students of parties have shown a persistent fascination with change. This is reflected in older debates on whether an end of ideology had occurred, the galvanizing effects which Kirchheimer's catch-all thesis had, arguments about the decline of political parties (see Daalder 1992, and Chapter 2 above), concern about the possible thawing of frozen party alignments, and arguments about the evolution of party organization. The debate between Epstein (1967) and Duverger (1954) on the evolution of party organization—whether the mass party ('contagion from the left') was the wave of the future, as Duverger had asserted, or whether more capital-intensive approaches ('contagion from the right') would be the norm—is a notable example. Fascination with change has skewed analytical capacities: we are better equipped to characterize the ways in which certain parties have changed or evolved than to compare differences and similarities among parties existing coterminously. Nor have parties across the spectrum been systematically studied. We typically pay more attention to parties of the left than parties of the right. However, any deficiencies which this might cause are mitigated by the assumption that parties are converging: it is frequently presumed that parties competing in the same systems, responding to the same financial and electoral regimes and the same technological imperatives, are becoming more and more alike.

Let us examine the classifications we use in light of these comments. Aside from types, such as Poguntke's (1993) new politics party, mooted to characterize particular subsets of parties, there are two distinct clusters in the literature. One is a set of distinctions descended from Duverger's *Political Parties*, the other a typology building on Neumann (1956) in the conclusion of an edited volume on *Modern Political Parties*. The first builds on Duverger's distinction between cadre and mass parties, sometimes expressed as elite-centred versus mass membership parties (Ware 1987*a*). The second extends Neumann's original distinction between parties of individual representation and parties of democratic integration into a broader longitudinal typology: here, the first addition was Kirchheimer's (1966) claim that parties of mass integration were transforming themselves into catch-all parties. The most recent renovation has been from Katz and Mair (1995). Reconstructing the typology based on parties' relationship with the state, they posit transition from elite parties (Duverger's cadre party, Neumann's party of individual representation) to mass parties, catch-all parties, and a new type, cartel parties, so dependent on state subsidies that they have become part of the state.

Duverger and Neumann treated the same parties in different ways. Duverger (1954) hoped to prepare the way for an eventual general theory of political parties by examining and synthesizing what was known about the parties of his time; he differentiated among cadre, mass, communist (cell) and fascist (militia) parties, each with their own distinctive organizational structure, class basis, and needs. In contrast, Neumann (1956) distinguished among parties of individual representation, parties of democratic integration, and parties of total integration. Because they take account of the same liberal democratic and anti-democratic parties existing in pre- and post-war Europe, the two schema are similar. The principal difference is that Neumann emphasizes parties' functions while Duverger concentrates on their organizational features and tries to relate differences in party organization to party origins, class bases, and organizational needs. Nevertheless, the two schema have suffered different fates: Duverger's scheme has been reduced to two categories (the cell and militia types are no longer relevant), detached from its original theoretical underpinning, collapsed to one or two dimensions (membership, organizational articulation, and complexity), and survives largely as a descriptive categorization. In contrast, Neumann's distinction, stripped of its totalitarian category, has provided the basis for the extended longitudinal typology described above.

CADRE VERSUS MASS PARTIES

The distinction between cadre and mass parties derives from Duverger's *Political Parties* (1954), and before that from Max Weber's comments on the growing professionalization of party politics. Cadre parties are loosely structured, elite-centred, parties with minimal organization outside of the legislature, while mass parties have highly developed organizations which aspire to enlist a large percentage of their voters as party members. Rooted in the literature, the distinction is well understood and readily measurable by examining the ratio of party members to voters and comparing the extent and activity of extra-parliamentary organization.

Duverger's distinction was originally part of a broader theory about party origins, organizational forms, the class bases of parties, and organizational needs, parts of which have now been discarded. The loose informal organization of the cadre party, based on closed caucuses of prominent individuals, was sufficient to raise funds, mobilize resources, and ensure the representation of the middle and upper classes. In contrast, members of the working class, outside the political system, had to organize intensively in order to raise funds and mobilize their principal resource, numbers. Duverger regarded the mass party (based on sections and branches) as a more modern or superior form of organization to loosely organized cadre parties (based on closed caucuses of locally prominent individuals), and argued that mass parties would predominate over archaic cadre parties. These suppositions, however, are now more widely accepted as a theory of how Western European parties developed than as a statement of their present situation.

Duverger's distinction survives, detached from its original theoretical origins. We typically use the term cadre party to describe both loosely organized parties and parties without large memberships. Whether this provides a measure sufficiently refined to distinguish among contemporary political parties is open to question. The cadre parties which Duverger studied were clearly different from mass parties on the left. The latter were intensely organized and well-articulated structures, while the former barely existed outside the caucus. Parties today are rarely as loosely organized or poorly articulated as the Third and Fourth Republic parties which served as Duverger's prototype for the cadre party. Parties of the right and centre in France, for example, have been supplanted by the better organized Gaullists, now the Rally for the Republic (RPR), and the Union of Democrats for France (UDF), an umbrella organization of several smaller clubs. The component parties of the latter, such as the Parti Republicain, fit the cadre type, but the RPR poses greater difficulties: the RPR organizes a large membership, but without the participation which we would normally expect in a mass party (Criddle 1987). As such, it is neither a cadre party nor a mass party. Nor is the Parti Socialiste (PS) a typical mass party. When it was organized in 1971, the PS employed a factional structure to incorporate divergent clubs and tendencies on the non-communist left. Factions have persisted, though not necessarily with the active participation which characterized the 1970s (Sferza, Chapter 7 below). Moreover, the proportion of voters who were members has never been high.

French parties are not the only source of difficulty. Recent research has shown that most political parties, for legal or other reasons, have some kind of formal organization and a membership base, large or small.[1] If many former cadre parties have well-defined organizational structures, and former mass parties have difficulty in enrolling as large a proportion of their supporters as members as they once did (Katz and Mair 1992a), then the distinction between cadre and mass parties becomes blurred. Koole (1992, 1994) has argued that Dutch political parties should be considered *modern cadre parties* because the percentage of their supporters whom they enlist as members is small, and the parties are primarily vehicles for active members. Koole (1994: 299) lists the characteristics of the modern cadre party as:

(1) predominance of the professional leadership groups (especially the parliamentary party), but with a high degree of accountability to the lower strata in the party;

(2) a low member/voter ratio, although members remain important as a source of finance, as a means of recruiting candidates for political office and as the bodies who are required simply to maintain the party in working order;

(3) a strong and broad-ranging orientation toward voters, but with a strategy which is neither catch-all, on the one hand, nor focusing on a *classe gardée* on the other;

(4) the maintenance of the structure of a mass party (with vertical organizational ties), not only to maintain a specific image, but also to guarantee a certain degree of internal democracy; and

(5) the reliance for financial resources on a combination of both public subsidies and the fees and donations of members.

This is useful in differentiating contemporary Dutch parties from earlier cadre or mass parties, but raises questions about how we should classify other parties which also differ from nineteenth- or early twentieth-century cadre parties. Canadian parties, for example, differ considerably from contemporary Dutch parties: both national and provincial parties have highly disciplined and invariably cohesive caucuses, dominated in government and (most of the time) opposition by their leaders. However, extra-parliamentary organization is minimal and virtually invisible except when an election has been called or is anticipated, or a leadership convention is under way. The principal parties have no fixed membership, and anyone can join up to the actual selection of candidates or delegates. Until recently, leaders were selected by special party convention rather than the caucus as in the Westminster model. However, several provincial parties have adopted balloting systems which allow anyone who declares themselves an adherent of the party to vote by telephone or at special polling places.

Lack of permanent mass organization does not present problems. When elections are called, parties—particularly if they are likely to gain a majority—can count on a bevy of workers to canvass potential voters, distribute literature, or drive voters to the polls. Once the election is over, this organization disintegrates as rapidly as it emerged, leaving elected officers and skeletal staffs to mop up, report on finances, enforce party rules, and, if possible, maintain an office. In contrast, the parliamentary caucus and their staff are active whether they are in government or in opposition. Typically, the leader and caucus are the only visible manifestation of the party between elections.

Intermittently active, the Canadian parties might also be characterized as modern cadre parties, but they are clearly different from the Dutch parties described above. Ironically, members and prospective members of Canadian parties are more involved in nomination processes and leadership selection than their counterparts in the Dutch parties. However, lines of accountability are more confused than these populistic elements suggest. Policy conventions are infrequent and inconsequential. Leaders declare party policy during election campaigns, but do not necessarily feel bound by manifestos once elected. In office, the leader is usually unassailable. Promises may be kept or ignored. Although party members may secure leadership reviews at specified intervals, once selected party leaders are in charge. However, leaders' survival depend on maintaining the support of caucuses which did not select them. Challenges usually occur when parties are in opposition; if they do not resign of their own accord, leaders are more likely to be dumped by legislative caucuses or factions within the party than by decisions of party members.[2]

Difficulties in distinguishing among cadre and modern cadre parties and other types are not confined to the Canadian case. Fitting in American parties is equally difficult. The extent of state and local organization varies considerably (Mayhew 1986), and national parties are little more than frameworks for internal competition. The national committees, once described as committees without power (Cotter and Hennessy 1964), have become more involved in House and Senate election campaigns, but are still not the only actors in the field: candidates, particularly incumbents, rely heavily on their own organizations, and Political Action Committees (PACs) rival the national committees as fundraisers. Even so, the Republican National Committee, which pioneered greater national party involvement, is sometimes described as a super-PAC. To further complicate matters, primary elections deprive party leaders of control over nominations. Parties provide candidates with labels or banners under which competition takes place, but do not monopolize or even perform many of the functions attributed to them in the literature. American parties are frameworks for candidate-centred factional competition and are best described as cadre parties. However, they are different not only from Duverger's classical cadre parties, but also the 'modern' Canadian and Dutch variants described earlier.

Contemporary French parties present further problems. Although the French Socialist Party shares many characteristics of the *modern cadre party* (Sferza, Chapter 7 below), its internal factionalism is not specified among Koole's (1994) criteria. However, even if we were to consider this a special case, or subsume factionalism under a different scheme, we still need to know whether other contemporary parties should be classified under the same rubric. Parties of the right and centre in France fit some of Koole's criteria, but are far more centred on their leaders. Jacques Chirac's RPR, for example, has the form of a mass organization, but has neither of the elements of accountability or internal democracy which Koole specifies. Embracing three smaller parties in an umbrella-like structure, the Union of Democrats for France (UDF) defies easy classification. So do parties created largely as personal vehicles, such as Berlusconi's Forza Italia. Although we might want to classify many of these as cadre parties, if we are to test hypotheses, or classify likes with likes, we need to be able to specify different variants of this type.

Ware (1987a) has tried to deal with this problem by refining Duverger's distinction, and distinguishing between *elite-centred* and *mass membership* parties. Elite-centred parties, such as the British Conservatives or the Gaullists, can have large memberships, but their core characteristic is domination by a relatively small group at the centre. In contrast, membership-based political parties are ones in which members are more than a workforce and have some voice or ownership in the party. Thus, it is not size of membership which makes a difference, but rather the degree to which they are expected to participate. Both large and small parties—for example, Greens and other parties

on the left—could be membership-based. We can take Ware's distinction
either as a restatement of Duverger—which is how he puts it (see Ware 1987*a*:
5–12)—or as the addition of a second dimension, extent of membership
involvement, to the primary dimension, size of active membership. This provides a basis for a four-cell table, distinguishing older or 'classic' forms of
cadre and mass parties, and their more modern equivalents, Koole's modern
cadre party, and leader-centred parties with large memberships (Table 6.1).
This could provide also a basis for further classification, but we need to know
where the cut-off points are, how to classify parties, and what difference this
makes.[3]

This two-dimensional classification is an improvement over the standard distinction between cadre and mass parties. Arraying parties on two dimensions
enables us to distinguish among 'classic' cadre parties (the UDF in France,
Canadian parties, the Republicans and Democrats in the United States),
Koole's 'modern' cadre party, 'leader-centred' cadre parties, and 'classical'
mass parties. Nevertheless, problems remain: party memberships have been
declining throughout Europe both in absolute numbers and as a percentage of
parties' electorates (Mair and Biezen, 2001). Although variation in the proportion of voters who are party members persists, the decline in the 1990s, evident
in most the European countries, suggests that there will be very few parties with
large memberships and that most cases will crowd into upper cells of the table.
Alternatively, we may have to rethink what we mean by party membership. As
it is, the parties in the upper left-hand cell, dubbed 'classic' cadre parties,
include disparate kinds of parties: American and Canadian parties, segments of
the public active either in primary elections or nominating meetings, are very

TABLE 6.1. *Cadre vs. mass party distinction: a revised version*

No. of members	Extent of members involvement	
	Low	High
Low	'Classic' cadre party *Examples*: UDF (France) Liberals (Canada) Progressive Conservatives (Canada) Republicans (US) Democrats (US)	Modern cadre party *Examples:* PvdA, CDA, VVD (Netherlands) Labour (UK) SPD, CDU (Germany) PS (France)
High	Leader-centred party *Examples:* RPR (France) Conservatives (UK)	Mass party *Examples:* SAP (Sweden) PDS/PCI (Italy)

Source: Adapted from Ware (1987*a*: 5–12).

different than French parties, such as Giscard's Republicans. Difficulties such as these might be resolved by adding an 'intermittently active' or medium category to the horizontal dimension (levels of political activity), but the classificatory scheme would still be largely descriptive. Nor do we have any theory explaining why different parties might have emerged as 'classic', 'modern', or 'leader-centred' cadre parties.

It is useful to consider what the cadre versus mass distinction, and Ware's reworking of it, does and does not measure. The distinction originated as a summary description of what were once very major differences in organizational forms, styles, and approaches to the electorate. What has survived is largely a measure of the size of membership and a very approximate estimate about the extent of organization. Both are important, but neither encompasses all that we might want to know about party structure or organization. Not included are the complexity of party organization (for example, the degree to which the party is organized on different levels), the presence or absence of multiple centres of power, factional or coalitional structure, relationship to other organizations, or the ways in which parties assemble resources, conduct election campaigns, or present themselves to the public. Any of these could provide a basis for differentiating political parties.

PARTIES OF MASS INTEGRATION, CATCH-ALL PARTIES, AND BEYOND

In contrast to Duverger's (1954) distinction, Neumann's typology has provided the basis for an extended historical typology. We have already seen how Kirchheimer (1966) and more recently Katz and Mair (1995) have built on Neumann (1956) and, to a certain extent, Duverger. At a minimum, the distinction between elite, mass, catch-all, and cartel parties provides a useful device for examining the ways in which certain kinds of parties may have changed. Whether it provides any help in distinguishing among contemporary parties is open to question. We can examine the matter by considering Kirchheimer's argument, Panebianco's restatement, and the latest addition, the cartel party.

Kirchheimer's (1966) argued that a major transformation of Western European parties and party systems was under way: parties of mass integration were transforming themselves into ideologically bland catch-all parties. Bowing to the law of the political market, parties were abandoning previous efforts at the 'the intellectual and moral encadrement of the masses', downplaying or abandoning ideology, bidding for the support of interest groups, emphasizing the qualities of their leaders, and seeking support wherever it could be found. Although not all parties would follow this course, Kirchheimer claimed that the success of one catch-all party would force other parties to imitate it, producing a transformation of Western European party systems.

Although doubts can be raised about the extent of transformation and its impact on party systems (Wolinetz 1979, 1991), the catch-all thesis has become a metaphor for describing changes in political parties and the ways in which they approach the electorate. Used to distinguish contemporary parties from former parties of mass integration, the catch-all party is an effective device. Used to distinguish among contemporary political parties, the catch-all party is as blunt an instrument as Kirchheimer feared it would be a vehicle of representation. Kirchheimer died before he could complete his essay and was not trying to build a typology, but rather characterize changes which he saw occurring in many but not all parties. The catch-all party is imperfectly operationalized (Dittrich 1983), and its characterization is exaggerated and incomplete (Smith 1989); in some respects, we have a better idea of what it is not—a party of mass integration—than what it is. Depending on how Kirchheimer is interpreted, the catch-all party can be translated as a highly opportunistic vote-seeking party, a leader-centred party, a party tied to interest groups, or all of the above. Whether or not it retains a mass membership or how such a party might differ from parties in the United States or Canada is uncertain. Nor are we sure whether the term describes a strategy or orientation (Wolinetz 1979), or an organizational form in which members have been marginalized and campaign professionals have assumed a more dominant role,[4] or some combination of these. Kirchheimer argued that not all parties would be forced to undergo this transformation; some might remain as mass parties, defending the interests of a particular group or class. However, not all parties were originally mass parties or parties of mass integration. Although such parties might be labelled cadre parties, we not only need schema for classifying them, but also some way of taking account of other changes which may have occurred.

Panebianco's Respecification

Panebianco (1988) tries to resolve ambiguities in the specification of the catch-all party by translating Kirchheimer's characterization into organizational terms. The crucial transformation becomes a change from the *mass-bureaucratic party* to an *electoral-professional party*. Both are defined as ideal-types. The mass-bureaucratic party, equivalent to Duverger's mass party or Neumann's party of mass integration, is characterized by the central role of a representative or elected bureaucracy, emphases on membership, collegial internal leadership, financing through interest groups, and stress on ideology. In contrast, the electoral-professional party is characterized by the centrality of professionals, its electoral orientation and weak vertical ties to its membership, the prominent role of elected representatives, financing

TABLE 6.2. *Panebianco's distinction between mass-bureaucratic and electoral-professional parties*

Mass-bureaucratic parties	Electoral-professional parties
Central role of the bureaucracy (political-administrative tasks)	Central role of the professionals (specialized tasks)
Membership party, strong vertical organizational ties, appeal to the 'electorate of belonging'	Electoral party, weak vertical ties, appeal to the 'opinion electorate'
Pre-eminence of internal leaders, collegial leadership	Pre-eminence of the public representatives, personalized leadership
Financing through membership and collateral activities (party cooperatives, trade unions, etc.)	Financing through interest groups and public funds
Stress on ideology, central role of believers within the organization	Stress on issues and leadership, central role of careerists and representatives within the organization

Source: In Panebianco (1988: 264).

through organized interests or government subsidies, and its stress on issues and interests rather than ideology.

By defining ideal types and laying out specific dimensions, Panebianco provides a basis for arraying parties on each and considering the extent, if any, to which they fit either type. This is an important step, but it is insufficiently developed to permit full comparison of contemporary parties. Throughout his book, Panebianco emphasizes the importance of party origin and develops a number of different genetic types, which he argues will follow different paths of development. However, his suppositions about change, injected in the final chapter, take little account of the genetic types—government parties, opposition parties, charismatic parties, such as the French Gaullists—developed in the earlier chapters of the book. This is surprising. Although Panebianco does argue that rates of change and the extent of transformation will vary, his final chapter does not consider the possibility that parties might change in ways which would produce either significantly distinct types or, failing that, different variants of the electoral-professional party. Instead, like Kirchheimer, and many others, he assumes that homogenizing trends are under way. This is particularly striking in light of his emphasis on the distinctiveness of party types. It is not clear, for example, why parties which started out as charismatic parties, such as the RPR in France, should end up as electoral-professional parties rather than as a more distinct leader-centred type. The same could be said of parties of the extreme right such as the Front National in France or the Danish or Norwegian Progress Parties: although it is conceivable that such parties might evolve into mainstream parties dominated by electoral-professionals, it is equally possible that they might either continue as leader-centred parties. Nor is it clear how Panebianco would treat the National Liberals (FPÖ) in Austria, which has been transformed by Jörg Haider from a small cadre party to a larger charismatic vehicle. As Ware (1996: 104) points out, Panebianco does not consider the very different ways in which parties might adapt to the pressures of electoral competition.[5] Instead, it is presumed that parties, whatever their genetic origins and initial differences, will succumb to the temptation to become an electoral-professional party.

The Cartel Party

The latest extension to Neumann's typology is Katz and Mair's (1995) addition of the *cartel party*. The cartel party is a new type, defined by its relation to the state. Competing for votes on the basis of their leaders and the effectiveness of their policies, catch-all parties find themselves increasingly vulnerable to the vagaries of the electorates who have detached themselves from previous political moorings (Mair 1997: ch. 2). Unable to rely on the loyalty of members, who have become more distant, parties allot themselves larger and larger subventions and become dependent on state subsidies for their support. In contrast to more entrepreneurially oriented catch-all parties, cartel parties appeal to an even broader or more diffuse electorate, engage primarily in capital-intensive campaigns, emphasize their managerial skills and efficiency, are loosely organized, and remote from their members, who are barely distinct from non-members. Even more important, rather than competing in order to win and bidding for support wherever it can be found, cartel parties are content to ensure their access to the state by sharing power with others. In Katz and Mair's view, cartel parties have ceased to operate as brokers between civil society and the state (the *modus operandi* of catch-all parties) and have instead become agents of the state.

Katz and Mair's assertions are interesting but problematic. The central argument is that state support has changed the overall orientation and direction of political parties. However, other than noting that almost all parties have at one time or another governed or joined coalitions, they give very little evidence of ways in which parties' behaviour may have changed because of increased state support. Nevertheless, it is easy to acknowledge that certain parties have been more anxious to govern than to win elections. More important for our purposes is that the catch-all party has been redefined in a less exaggerated or stereotypical fashion than Kirchheimer did (see Katz and Mair 1995: table 1), and that a number of dimensions have been specified on which parties might be classified. Although some are characteristics of the time period (such as the proportion of the electorate enfranchised or the dispersion of politically relevant resources), others (such as nature of party work, sources of revenue, relations between members and leaders, and the role of members) can be used to differentiate parties.

Even though Katz and Mair have been quite explicit in their specification of each party type, there are difficulties in using either the cartel type alone or the typology as whole as a way of differentiating contemporary political parties. The typology posits a broad transformation from elite and mass parties to catch-all and now cartel parties. Taken as such, it is useful in distinguishing contemporary parties from their predecessors. Less certain is whether all or even most parties have now become catch-all or cartel parties, existing coterminously, or have evolved into cartel parties. Katz and Mair argue that the cartel party is not the end point of party development, but rather that its style is likely to generate its own response in the form of anti-party sentiment and parties capable of mobilizing it. This makes room for anti-establishment parties, such as Poguntke's (1993) new politics party, as well as extreme right populist parties, but leaves open the question of whether all established parties have become so alike that there is no point in distinguishing among them.

Thus far, our analysis has done more to demonstrate the limitations of existing schemata than to develop new bases of classification. This is a problem which we will consider in the next section.

NEW BASES FOR CLASSIFICATION? VOTE-SEEKING, OFFICE-SEEKING, AND POLICY-SEEKING PARTIES

Criticizing existing schemata is easier than developing new ones. In this section, I will consider directions which students of political parties might follow if they are to develop more meaningful classificatory schemes. The discussion is meant to be more heuristic than definitive. Ultimately, classificatory schemata derive from research and application. If they are to be useful, such schemata must not only distinguish among different types of political parties, but do so in ways which reflect questions we are interested in. The latter implies that there is no one universally valid scheme, but rather that the utility of a schema depends in part on what we want to know and that a classification useful for one purpose may not be useful for another. The scheme mooted below distinguishes among *vote-seeking, policy-seeking*, and *office-seeking* political parties. In this section, I will argue that such a distinction is useful both because it reflects facets of parties' or factions' behaviour and preferences, and can also be related to party structure and organization.

In the literature on coalition formation, distinctions among policy-seeking, vote-seeking, and office-seeking parties have been introduced to account for coalitions not readily explained by previous models (Strøm 1990a). A policy-seeking party is one which gives primary emphasis to pursuit of policy goals, a vote-seeking party is one whose principal aim is to maximize votes and win elections, while an office-seeking party is primarily interested in securing the benefits of office—getting its leaders into government, enjoying access to patronage, etc.—even if this means sharing power with others or pursuing strategies which fail to maximize its share of the vote. Although in practice no party will be exclusively policy-seeking, vote-seeking, or office-seeking, the scheme pinpoints orientations which can be related to other characteristics of parties and the social, economic, geographical, and institutional environments in which they operate. This scheme also provides us with categories which are widely applicable and not tied to any one geographic area or subset of parties.

The distinction between policy-seeking, vote-seeking, and office-seeking parties is borrowed from Strøm's (1990b) analyses of the circumstances under which parties enter or support minority governments. Although they have been used by Harmel and Janda (1994) to analyse party change, these categories are more common in formal modeling and theories of coalition formation and have only recently been used in empirical research.[6] Each orientation is a separate dimension on which parties can either be high or low. However, the dimensions are neither mutually exclusive nor entirely independent of each other. Although parties in electoral competition must pursue votes in order to win office and carry out programmes, parties giving higher priority to one orientation will typically be lower on at least one of the other two. Following Strøm, we can array the three foci or orientations as points of a triangle and plot parties according to the relative priority which they give to each (Figure 6.1).[7] Parties emphasizing policy-seeking would be located in the lower left-hand corner, parties emphasizing office-seeking at the lower right, and parties which emphasize vote-seeking at the peak. If a party were equally disposed toward all three orientations, it would be plotted at the centre of the triangle.

The Policy-Seeking Party

The policy-seeking party corresponds to a civics book image of what many people think that parties should be like in a liberal democracy. Policy-seeking parties are issue-oriented and, quite simply, give priority to their policies. They vary widely. Included in this rubric are not only parties with well-defined programmes and/or well-articulated ideologies, but also single-issue and protest parties. Policies may either be logically constrained or a loosely connected agglomeration of demands. Policy-seeking parties run the gamut from former parties of mass integration (as long as these had clearly defined ideological or policy goals) and some of their modern descendants to parties articulating green or environmental issues. If they have well-defined goals, new-right parties can be included as well; like their counterparts on the left, they seek to *redefine* the political agenda in order to bring about changes in a

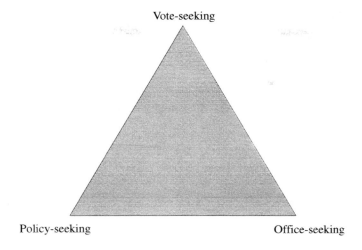

FIG. 6.1. *Primary emphases or orientations of political parties*

number of areas. The main characteristic would be that the party more often than not gave greater priority to articulation or defence of its policies than to either the maximization of votes or securing office. We would expect such a party to have an active though not necessarily large membership interested in some or all of its goals. Examples would include most Northern European social democratic parties, many liberal and some Christian democratic parties, as well as green, left-libertarian, and some new-right parties.

The Vote-Seeking Party

A vote-seeking party is different from a policy-seeking party. Here, the primary emphasis is on winning elections: policies and positions are not locked in. Instead, they are regularly manipulated in order to maximize support. Such a party would be a classic Downsian party. If it were operating either in a heterogeneous society, and/or under a winner-take-all system of elections, a vote-seeking party would probably have a coalitional structure, broad enough to embrace different social groups and give the party a chance of winning a majority. In a multi-party system, the equivalent would be a catch-all or electoral-professional party, trying to maximize support from a broad, through not necessarily all-inclusive portion of the electorate.

A vote-seeking party should be organized to win office at all or almost all levels (local, regional or provincial, national) in which elections take place, but is likely to maintain only the minimum degree of organization required to recruit and select candidates and get them elected. In the past this might have required a labour-intensive campaign organization. Today, such a party might rely on private or government funds to finance capital-intensive campaigns run by campaign professionals and marketing agencies. An organized membership, if there was one, would be kept at arm's length: although members might have voice on the selection of candidates, they would have little say on party policy. All in all, we might expect a thinly staffed organization, made up primarily of party professionals, candidates, and would-be candidates, but capable of adding volunteers when and if they were needed to conduct election campaigns. Levels of activity would vary considerably, rising when nominations were being made or elections contested and falling sharply if they were not.

Examples of vote-seeking parties include the intermittently active Canadian parties, whose policy commitments can vary from election to election, depending on the predilections of the leader; American parties, because of their skeletal organization and lack of fixed programmatic content (parties are largely electoral vehicles into which specific content is poured depending on the outcome of nomination contests); leader-centred parties such as the Gaullists in France, with no fixed ideological orientation (the RPR under Chirac has taken very different positions in successive presidential elections); and classical catch-all parties such as the German Christian Democratic Union. In addition, because they benefit from assembling broad coalitions in order to compete for a single indivisible office, parties in presidential systems might be tempted to take this form.

The Office-Seeking Party

The office-seeking party is the third type. Here, the primary emphasis is on securing government office, even if it is at the expense of policy goals or maximizing votes. Office-seeking parties seek either to hold power alone, or more realistically (in the context of the systems in which they operate) to share power with others—either for the purposes of survival (one implication of the cartel party model), or to act as a stabilizer or balance within the system or, more likely, to gain access to patronage. An office-seeking party should avoid policy commitments which might make it undesirable as a coalition partner and eschew electoral strategies, such as attacking prospective partners too fiercely, which would make coalitions impossible. The aim—defined in the context of a well-established party system—would be to win enough votes to ensure inclusion in coalitions.

Office-seeking parties can exist in different forms. One would be a party, large or small, built atop patron–client networks, whose operation required it to maintain a continuous flow of benefits. Another might be a small party in a multi-party system, anxious to be included in coalitions for the prestige that this might entail. Like its counterparts, an office-seeking party is likely to be organized to contest elections at different levels of government. However, such a party is unlikely to attract or retain political activists whose primary concern is policy. Instead, its principal participants are likely to be office-holders or office-seekers. The larger the party is, the more likely it is to be divided into factions competing for the resources which the party can command. Examples of office-seeking parties include parties participating regularly in coalitions in consociational systems or governing coalitions in one-party dominant systems. Examples of the former include the Christian Historical Union (CHU) in the Netherlands—one of the parties which merged to form the Christian Democratic Appeal (CDA)—and the mainstream Belgian political parties, all of which are generally more concerned with being in office than pursuing any particular policy agenda. Examples of the latter include the smaller parties in the pre-1993 Italian party system, such as the Liberals (PLI), or the Republicans (PRI), or on a larger scale, the former Christian Democrats (DC) or Socialists (PSI). Ensuring a continuing flow of benefits, large and small, became these parties' *raison d'être*; for many elements in these parties, winning elections or controlling office was a means to maintaining position. Ironically, the Italian Christian Democrats did this by sharing power with others in centre-left or five-party coalitions (*pentapartito*), but ultimately lost power when the system of which they were architects became untenable.

The utility of such a scheme depends on our ability to find indicators for key terms or orientations and the degree to which we can use these to pose and test hypotheses about what difference this makes. We will consider the difficulty of operationalization below, and then show how these distinctions could be used to test hypotheses about the extent to which trends toward homogenization, widely assumed in the literature, have actually taken place.

Problems of Operationalization

The three categories discussed previously are polar types, to which parties in electoral competition are unlikely to conform completely. Although it is conceivable that a policy-seeking party might compete in elections solely to put forward its positions, most policy-seeking parties are interested in winning sufficient votes to win seats in the legislature. Similarly, vote-seeking parties often put forward policies in order to win office, and office-seeking parties must seek votes in order to gain access to the state. Moreover, parties may be divided internally, with different factions or tendencies pursuing different objectives. In practice, most parties will display elements of at least two of the three orientations. Nevertheless, once a party is well-established and its practices and modes of operation are institutionalized, differences in emphases and priorities should be visible. In policy-seeking parties, programmatic concerns should be apparent in the ways in which the party determines its positions, contests elections, and behaves in office. Operational measures might include the proportion of time devoted to policy discussion at party congresses, the emphases placed on policy during election campaigns, and the attention given to policy by elected representatives. Other indicators might include the presence or absence of party research bureaux or other infrastructure (for example, policy committees) for the development and articulation of policy, or party members' views about what they think their party ought to be doing. We would expect a policy-seeking party to exhibit considerable preoccupation with policy on most of the above indicators.

Vote-seeking parties should score differently than policy- or office-seeking parties. Here the central preoccupation is maximizing votes. Although such a party would typically have policies, these might change frequently, with the party maintaining only the minimum degree of Downsian consistency needed to avoid alienating supporters or followers. In election campaigns, the emphasis will be on techniques designed to win votes rather than on specific policies, which will change from election to election. As Kirchheimer suggested, devices employed may involve bidding for the support of specific interests, emphasizing leaders, or otherwise packaging the party so that it will maximize votes. The devices available to parties have broadened considerably since Kirchheimer wrote in 1966: these now include media spots, negative advertising, telemarketing, and continuous polling to monitor the effects of different strategies.

Because vote-seeking parties may also emphasize policies from time to time, measuring such an orientation is difficult, but not impossible. Nevertheless, preoccupation with policy should either be minimal or else confined to the party leadership or the party in government—that is, compartmentalized. In the former instance, open policy discussions would be *pro forma* or perfunctory (perhaps be confined to exultatory speeches), while in the latter instance, policy would be manipulated in order to maximize support. In the case of a vote-seeking party, we would expect considerable emphasis on maximizing support, even at the expense of consistency. In extreme cases, this might be indicated by frequent and sharp reversals of policy positions, de-emphasizing or blurring positions, and aggressive pursuit of votes. However, vote-seeking should not be measured solely by campaign tactics. How strategy is determined and what is taken into account are also important.

Office-seeking is the most difficult of the three orientations to operationalize. All parties contesting elections could be considered office-seeking, but we know that the goals and purposes of seeking elective office can vary: some parties want to win the seats or offices being contested, while others hope either to bring forward a point of view or lay the groundwork for future victories. An office-seeking party should be more preoccupied with gaining

TABLE 6.3. *Policy-, vote-, and office-seeking parties: operational measures*

Possible indicators	Parties		
	Policy-seeking	Vote-seeking	Office-seeking
Internal policy debate % of time spent at party meetings	High	Low	Low
character of debate	Intense, protracted, issue-focused	*Pro forma*, diffuse, unfocused	*Pro forma*, diffuse, unfocused
extent and level of involvement	Extensive; most levels of party involved	Confined to leadership or policy committee; compartmentalized	Confined to leadership or policy committee; compartmentalized
Consistency of policy positions assumed	High	Medium to low, prone to change depending on leader's directions, electoral opportunity structure	Medium to low
Election campaigns prominence of policy	High	Varies	Low
determination of strategy	Follows from policies	Policies developed to fit strategy, maximize votes	Varies, preference for low-risk strategies
use of new electoral techniques	Low to medium	High	Low to medium
Infrastructure to support policies (e.g research bureaux, think-tanks, affiliated organizations)	Present	Either minimal or at disposal of leaders, office-holders	Either minimal or at disposal of leaders, office-holders

office—either seats in Parliament or portfolios in government—than maximizing votes or putting forward policies. Indicators might include resorting to low-risk strategies (in effect satisficing), the orientation of leaders and hangers-on, or parties' use of patronage. Regular or continuous participation in government would *not* be an adequate indicator of an office-seeking party because vote-seeking or policy-seeking parties might also be frequent participants in government.

Operationalizing each of these orientations is difficult. Any assessment of party orientations must be based either on repetitive behaviour or attitudes which can be tapped and replicated using similar research instruments. This assumes that orientations and behaviour are (*a*) relatively stable and (*b*) rooted in party structures and practices. However, the orientation and direction of some parties may very well be an area of dispute, changing whenever new leaders assume power or different factions gain control. Ultimately, the extent to which the orientation of parties changes over time must be the subject of empirical research. Nevertheless, unless the party's formal and informal structures are weakly institutionalized—for example if the party is little more than a vehicle for individual leaders (Ross Perot's Reform Party, Berlusconi's Forza Italia) or a framework for factional conflict (in some respects, American parties)—we should not expect sudden or frequent changes in party orientation or direction. On the contrary, as anyone who has been involved in processes of internal reform can attest, attempts to bring about changes usually meet resistance, and entrenched habits and practices are likely to continue.

Numerous examples illustrate the slowness with which parties change. The cases of the British Labour and Conservative Parties are instructive: prior to the 1970s, both combined elements of vote-seeking and policy-seeking. In the 1970s and early 1980s, Labour and Conservatives not only departed from the post-war consensus on the desirability of a welfare state and a managed economy, but also became more overtly policy-oriented. Under pressure from militant factions on its left, Labour assumed hard-left positions which cost it support in the 1980s. However, neither the shift to the left nor Labour's eventual return to the political centre took place without considerable internal strife. Throughout the post-war period, Labour had been divided between its left and right wings, but despite the split, the right or social democratic wing dominated the leadership and controlled key party bodies, such as the Annual Conference, the National Executive Committee, and the Parliamentary Labour Party (PLP). In the 1970s, economic decline and disputes over European Community membership shifted the balance towards the left, who were making concerted efforts to gain control of constituency associations. Internal disagreements intensified throughout the decade, but changes in party positions and orientations did not occur until 1980. Labour was defeated by Margaret Thatcher's Conservatives in 1979. James Callaghan resigned the leadership and had been replaced by Michael Foot, a long-time adherent of the left At a special party meeting in 1980, the left won mandatory reselection of MPs and the election of the party leader by an electoral college of MPs, trade unions, and constituency associations rather than the Parliamentary Labour Party. This provoked the exit of part of the right and the formation of the Social Democratic Party. Labour emerged from the process positioned further to the left and far more policy-oriented than it had been before.

The road back to the political centre was no easier. Changes begun by Neil Kinnock in 1983 and continued under John Smith—who sought to move the party 'one heave further'—were only completed when Tony Blair assumed the leadership after Smith's death in 1994. After four successive election defeats, Labour was anxious to return to power. Under Blair, Labour abandoned clause IV of the party constitution (Labour's long-standing commitment to public ownership of the mean of production), and marketed itself as 'The New Labour Party'. *New Labour* is a vote-seeking party. Former left-wingers, such as Tony Benn, remain, but their radical impulses have been brought under control.

The Conservatives' shift to the right was less tortuous: shifts tentatively initiated by Edward Heath became more permanent when Margaret Thatcher ousted him in 1975. However, despite Thatcher's deep convictions, the party's shift to the right was not immediate. Thatcher's first Cabinets included centrists such as Sir William Whitelaw. Only when she had consolidated her hold on the party were 'wets' marginalized within the party. Like Labour in the 1980s, Conservatives became more overtly policy-oriented. However, commitment to Thatcher's new-right agenda did not keep the Conservatives from governing. Although their popular vote never climbed above 42–3 per cent, the Conservatives won parliamentary majorities in successive elections. Only in 1997 did internal divisions and competition from the newly recast Labour Party consign them to the opposition. In both the Labour and Conservative Parties, the need to keep the party together and the weight of existing organization and practices prohibited rapid changes in orientation or style. The same was true of processes of programmatic renewal in the Dutch Labour Party (PvdA) in the 1980s and early 1990s (Wolinetz 1993).

The 'stickiness' of programmatic change in policy-seeking parties contrasts sharply with the experience of American and Canadian parties in which selection of a new leader or candidate can result in substantial changes in posture. However, the underlying orientation of vote-seeking parties is not nearly as malleable as the positions which such parties assume. In the United States, the occasional nomination of candidates with policy positions outside the 'mainstream'—a Barry Goldwater or George McGovern—typically results in electoral defeat and reversion to middle positions the next time around. In Canada, the travails of the Progressive Conservative Party (PCs) in the 1990s are equally telling: before 1993, the PCs had a parliamentary majority. However, reactions against former Prime Minister Brian Mulroney and competition from both the Bloc Quebecois and the Reform Party reduced the PCs to two seats in the 1993 general election. Defeat forced the PCs to regroup and reorganize. Efforts were made to make the party more policy-oriented. However, supporters were more enthusiastic about having policies than specifying what they should be. Ultimately, party positions for the 1997 parliamentary election were determined by the party leader, Jean Charest. Despite his own leanings, Charest took the party to the right on economic issues in order to compete with the Reform Party. Charest won twenty seats and restored his party to official party status in the Canadian House of Commons. Ironically, though, most of the MPs elected with him were well to the left of official party positions on most issues. The election over, Charest indicated that, although the platform was binding, party positions could evolve over time. In this instance, the vote-seeking orientation was relatively fixed despite the rapidity with which policy changes could be executed. Nevertheless, there seem to be limits to vote-seeking without consideration of policy. Although badly hurt by competition from the Reform Party, and the exit of its right wing and western support, Progressive Conservatives have persistently refused attempts by the Reform Party and its successor, the Canadian Alliance, to unite the right.[8] One reason for this is that few Progressive Conservatives regard themselves as part of the right. The parties orientation has typically been centrist, if not red Tory, a Canadian equivalent of one-nation ('wet') conservatism in Britain.

These examples suggest that changes in the underlying orientation of parties is infrequent. In most instances, the modes and mores—the internal political culture—of a party inhibit rapid change in party orientation. However, this does not mean that fundamental changes cannot occur because a leader or faction insists on them or because crises or galvanizing events encourage change. In practice, both leadership and circumstances play a role: successive defeats made the British Labour Party more prepared for Tony Blair's reconstruction. In the Netherlands, years in opposition made the Dutch Labour Party (PvdA) more open to change. Nor are processes preparing parties for change necessarily confined to the electoral arena. In Spain, democratization and electoral opportunity facilitated the remaking of the Spanish Socialist Party (PSOE) in the late 1970s.

The foregoing analysis suggests that party orientations—whether a party is policy-seeking, vote-seeking, or office-seeking, or more likely some combination of two or more of these—are durable features of political parties and unlikely to change without consistent and durable efforts by an individual or group to re-make or re-orient the party. Systematically operationalizing such orientations will be difficult but possible. However, classifying parties as policy-seeking, vote-seeking, or office-seeking is not an end in itself. Although having one more classification might be useful for taxonomic purposes, the real value of any classificatory scheme depends on its utility in developing and testing propositions about either the circumstances under which certain phenomena (in this case, types of political parties) are likely to exist or, alternatively, what difference they make. Earlier, we argued that classifications such as Duverger's distinction between cadre and mass parties had lost their utility not only because they failed to classify adequately, but also because they had become detached from their theoretical origins. If classificatory schemes, whether those suggested above, or others which might be developed, are to be useful, connecting them to theories and propositions about parties is essential. Developing new theory is beyond the scope of this chapter, but suggesting the ways in which such classifications might be used is not. In the section which follows, we will examine the ways in which distinguishing among policy-seeking, vote-seeking, and office-seeking might be used to refine our suppositions about the ways in which Western European systems have changed and to compare parties in different historical or geographic contexts.

PATTERNS OF CHANGE IN WESTERN EUROPEAN PARTIES

Let us return to our earlier discussion. There, I had argued that the categories used to characterize change in Western European political parties were imprecise and posited a uni-directional pattern of change: all or most significant parties according to Kirchheimer or Panebianco were becoming catch-all or electoral-professional parties; all or almost all are now cartel parties according to Katz and Mair. One limitation of this mode of analysis was that it made little allowance for alternate models for contemporary political parties. Parties, it has been argued, were unable to sustain former modes of operation as parties of mass integration or elite-centred parties. However, the only variations posited in the ways in which they might change were differences in the speed of transformation.

Using the more general dimensions of policy-seeking, vote-seeking, and office-seeking, it is possible to posit different patterns of transformation. The vote-seeking party corresponds to a catch-all or electoral-professional party, while the cartel party is one variant of an office-seeking party. Let us suppose that the *programmatic party* is a variant of a policy-seeking party and consider the possibility that at least some parties might emerge as programmatic parties, either because they never made the transformation to catch-all or cartel parties, or alternatively because programmatic emphases were a plausible response to the competitive environment in which they found themselves. To do this it is useful to return to arguments about catch-all parties and problems which they face.

The starting-point of our analysis is that contemporary parties are organizations under stress. Sources of this stress have been discussed in the literature. Parties which were once accustomed to the regular support of 'electorates of belonging' find that both the relative size and loyalty of these electorates have shrunk, and electronic media deny parties control over the political agenda. In addition, parties find it increasingly difficult to offer selective incentives which would help them to attract and retain members; interest groups and single-issue movements are able to offer more direct channels of influence and action (Panebianco 1988; Pizzorno 1981). Parties can respond to these problems in different ways. The dominant supposition, particularly for former parties of mass integration, is transformation towards a new form, the catch-all party, or as reformulated by Panebianco, the electoral-professional party. The changes have been mentioned earlier, but it is useful to restate them here: orientation towards 'opinion electorates' rather than electorates of belonging; emphasis on issues or personalities rather than ideology; campaign professionals supersede both members and representative bureaucrats; increased reliance on interest groups or government for financial support, and in general terms the transformation of parties which previously emphasized representative or 'expressive functions' and often defended well-defined policies into opportunistic, vote-seeking parties, distant from their supporters. (Kirchheimer 1966; Panebianco 1988)

Kirchheimer viewed the catch-all party as a highly successful electoral machine, sufficiently adept at winning votes that it would force its competitors to adopt similar ploys. We have since come to see it differently. Panebianco (1988), Smith (1989), and Mair (1997: ch. 2) characterize the catch-all party as a highly vulnerable entity: without a large electorate of belonging, the catch-all party has no secure bases of support. Voters who support it in one election can desert it in another. However, this is only part of the problem. Catch-all parties have largely abandoned the expressive or emotively representative functions of parties for a politics of brokerage and governing. In doing so, they leave opportunities open to others—protest or alternative politics parties, new social movements—who are better able to mobilize discontent or provide the solidarity incentives which electoral-professional parties are unable to supply. Reflecting this, Katz and Mair (1995) posited a further transformation, into cartel parties which use their control of the state to protect themselves from the vagaries of the electorate.

Cartel parties are equally vulnerable. Close to, if not a part of the state, cartel parties are responsible not only for the successes of state policy, but also shortcomings and failures—numerous in a period of shrinking resources. Although ostensibly insulated from voters' wrath by state subsidies and their ability to join coalitions, cartel parties are nevertheless exposed to competition from parties freer to take more purely oppositional stances. These include new politics parties, new-right protest parties, and occasionally, parties in the centre, such as Democrats '66, less complicit in government policy. Although the victories of such parties may be temporary, the threat of losses can generate internal pressures which force parties to modify their strategies.

The vulnerability of both catch-all and cartel parties has considerable significance for our analysis. Susceptible to some losses whether they emphasize representative and expressive functions, or bid for as wide an electorate as possible, or assume responsibility for public policy, parties may find themselves pulled in conflicting directions. Challenged by new competition, parties might respond by re-emphasizing policy and programmes in order to reaffirm support of key groups, *or* by emphasizing their leader and adopting more sophisticated campaign techniques, *or* by ensuring further access to patronage or state subsidies. Depending on where the party started out from, we have a shift towards one of the three orientations discussed earlier: policy-seeking, vote-seeking, or office-seeking.

Each can be plotted on the triangle in Figure 6.1 according to the ways in which they deflect, resolve, or fail to resolve these pressures (see Figure 6.2). Toward the lower left corner are programmatic and other policy-seeking parties. In the upper corner are parties whose primary emphasis is winning elections and holding office alone. Included would be catch-all or electoral professional parties, as well as parties in many adversarial systems. In the lower right corner we would find classical patronage-oriented parties, whose principal *raison d'être* was to gain office in order to win personal benefit, as well as more recent converts (for example, Blondel's party patrimonial, Chapter 9 below), and cartel parties which have shied away from all-out competition.

What determines a party's positioning? Our point of departure was that parties were under stress and pulled in conflicting directions. But some parties are more subject to these stresses and strains than others. Parties operating in systems in which there is little expectation that they fulfil expressive roles or articulate programmes—for example, the mainstream Canadian parties until recently—may feel very little pull to move towards the lower left-hand corner. The same may be true of parties without large memberships or in which leadership is insulated from members' pressures. Nevertheless, many

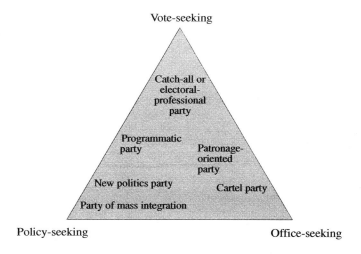

FIG. 6.2. *Vote-seeking, policy-seeking, and office-seeking political parties*

parties do try to enrol members. Even if they are not enlisted as troops in modern election campaigns, parties can use members to demonstrate that they have support, to maintain a presence in society, or to establish a base from which future candidates can be recruited (Scarrow 1994, 1996). However, enrolling members has a cost. As I have posited, electorates of belonging have shrunk, and parties may have difficulty enlisting members solely on the basis of solidarity. Selective incentives, such as the prospect of office, may be sufficient to attract some individuals, but in order to enrol a larger membership, parties may have to offer members a voice on programmes and policies. However, the more they do this, the more difficult it may be for parties to evolve as purely vote-seeking (for example, catch-all party or electoral-professional party) or office-seeking parties (for example, cartel party). Under such circumstances, programmes may serve as a glue— or perhaps more accurately as a set of elastic bands, of varying strengths— which hold the party together. De-emphasizing or scrapping programmes or policies in order to win more votes may cause some of these bands to break. So too could sacrificing policies in order to join or maintain coalitions. Rather than sacrificing members or risking a split, parties may choose to emphasize programmes rather than either maximizing votes or opportunities to govern.

Emphasizing programmes, of course, is not the only way in which politicians can reconcile conflicting pressures. Alternate solutions might be to disengage members, reducing them to the largely demonstrative cheerleading roles envisaged by Katz and Mair (1992c) as a characteristic of the catch-all party, or to convert the party into a party of office-holders. The latter is said to be characteristic of many Southern European socialist parties, which have largely abandoned ideological commitments. Alternatively, the orientation of a party may be a source of internal contention, as was the case in both the Dutch Labour Party (PvdA) and the British Labour Party in the 1970s and 1980s. The fact that many social democratic parties in the 1980s were engaged in processes of programmatic review and programmatic renewal (Paterson and Gillespie 1993) suggests at a minimum that programmes are important for party leaders and party activists. However, this may be a point of contention within parties.

Using the distinction between policy-seeking, vote-seeking, and office-seeking parties introduces an element of play into discussions about transformation and change in Western European parties. Rather than assuming one homogenizing trend which all or most parties follow, we have argued that parties can respond differently to the pressures said to lead to the emergence of catch-all and more recently cartel parties. How parties respond will depend in large measure on their internal characteristics, the competitive environment in which they operate, and decisions which their leaders and followers make.

CONCLUDING REMARKS

I have argued that existing classifications for political parties are inadequate and suggested ways in which alternate classifications might be developed. These include classifying parties according to membership size and activity, or distinguishing parties according to whether they are policy-seeking, vote-seeking, or office-seeking. I have also argued against assuming that parties undergo uniform or uni-directional patterns of change and have stated that some (but not all) Western European parties may have transformed themselves into programmatic parties rather than catch-all or cartel parties. Our analysis has been tentative and preliminary, designed to break through two different log-jams. One was to escape the uni-directional or homogenizing thrust of models of change prevalent in the Western European parties literature. The other was to suggest ways in which a broader cross-national study of political parties might be facilitated. Throughout the discussion, I have mentioned many dimensions of analysis (for example, facets of party structure) which might be also be considered. However, no variables or categories are sacrosanct. Ultimately, the variables and dimensions pursued and the typologies and frameworks which we use must depend on the questions posed. The principal point is that we need to rethink our categories and classifications in light of a broader terrain of research and that now is a good time to do it (see also Gunther and Diamond 2001).

Schemata such as the one which I have suggested (classifying parties as policy-seeking, vote-seeking, or office-seeking) facilitate drawing comparisons among parties in different parts of the world. Transitions to democracy in other parts of the world mean that we can no longer confine the comparative analysis to Western Europe, with occasional forays into North America. A broader comparative study of political parties, the circumstances in which they operate, and what difference they make, requires us to consider parties in a much wider range of systems and contexts. However, extant categories provide us with little purchase for such a study. A brief look at parties in Latin America demonstrates the point. A history of coups and periods of authoritarian rule has meant that Latin Americanists have not devoted much attention to political parties (Mainwaring and Scully 1995). When they have, they have typically argued that mass parties are rare and that *personalismo* is the norm. If forced to do so, we would probably classify most Latin American parties as cadre parties. Unfortunately, this would tell us very little either about what kind of cadre parties were the norm, how they varied, or why cadre parties were the dominant form of party organization. As it stands now, we lack not only data, but also categories around which it could be collected. This makes hypothesis-testing and theory-building impossible. Latin American specialists might argue that *personalismo* reflected prevailing cultural norms. That may indeed be the case, but it would still be useful to know whether certain kinds of parties—loosely organized vote-seeking parties, structures which were more typically networks than tightly organized entities—were more typical in presidential systems, in which the desire to capture a single indivisible office brought divergent groups together (forgetting principles and policies in the process). In a different vein, we know that in some parts of the world patron–client relationships have either substituted for political parties, or have been built up within them. Unfortunately, although we know something about the circumstances under which *clientelismo* is likely to occur, we know very little about the circumstances under which the distribution of patronage will become the dominant activity of political parties.

Some political scientists may be sceptical about moving beyond the comfortable nexus of Western European parties, fearing that all that will be discovered is that parties elsewhere are different. This has all too often been the result of European-American comparisons or those few studies which have ventured into other parts of the world (e.g. Lawson 1980). Nevertheless, the European cases are not as homogeneous as we sometimes make them out to be—there are important differences between Southern and Northern European systems, and between parties in the British isles and the continent. And transitions to democracy and the spread of competitive politics to countries in other parts of the world provide us with an unprecedented opportunity to study the emergence of parties and party systems in settings very different from late nineteenth- and early twentieth-century Europe. Although comparing individual parties which have developed in radically different settings may not be useful, there is a good deal to be learnt from considering the circumstances under which different types of parties emerge and survive. For example, we may find that certain party systems sustain a variety of different types or orientations, while in others vote-seeking or office-seeking were predominant. This, for example, has been the case in the Canadian party system despite the sustained presence of a policy-seeking party, the New Democratic Party, to the left of the larger established parties. The prevalence of one type might reflect competitive dynamics, cultural factors, institutions, the electoral system, or simply the kinds of parties which got entrenched first. Other facets which might be considered are party structure and organization, age of party organizations, the availability and uses of patronage, and the characteristics of the society or economy. Whatever the case, we would be better positioned to develop and test hypotheses than we are now.[9]

NOTES

1. See e.g. Beyme (1985); Ware (1987*a*); Katz and Mair (1994); Scarrow (1994, 1996).
2. See Perlin (1988); Carty (1988); Carty *et al.* (1992: 10–16); Courtney (1995).

3. Unfortunately, Ware does not elaborate on any of these points in either his 1987*b* volume or his 1996 book. The latter, intended primarily as a text book, pays greater attention to the debate between Duverger and Epstein than to the merits and demerits of Duverger's classification (Ware 1996: 95ff.).
4. Panebianco (1988); Mair (1997: ch. 2); Katz and Mair (1994, 1995).
5. Ware (1996: 102–4) argues also that Panebianco's classifications are 'overtheorized' and based on too narrow a range of cases. Although Panebianco is widely cited, there have been surprisingly few books or articles written on the basis of his work. This may reflect the difficulty of applying his classifications.
6. Müller and Strøm (1999*a*) is a notable exception.
7. My usage is somewhat different than Strøm's (1990*a*). Strøm's primary concern is to build an integrated model of party behaviour which can explain outcomes (the formation of minority governments) not readily explained by existing models, and for that he uses the literature on coalition formation and spatial models of party positioning to deduce the organizational forms from which such behaviour might flow. In contrast, I have drawn on traits of actual parties to elaborate the characteristics of each type or orientation.
8. The Canadian Alliance (formally the Canadian Reform Conservative Alliance) was the product of such efforts. Frustrated by Reform's inability to win seats outside the Canadian west (i.e. in Ontario and the provinces to east), Reform Party leader Preston Manning pressed for the unification of the right. Although rejected by most Progressive Conservatives, Reform's efforts resulted in the reconstitution of the party as the Canadian Alliance (or Alliance).
9. One example of this is Harmel and Janda (1994). The authors use Strøm's (1990*b*) schema, augmented by a fourth category, the democracy-seeking party, to develop propositions under which parties, pursuing different goals, are likely to embrace or avoid major changes.

7

Party Organization and Party Performance: The Case of the French Socialist Party

Serenella Sferza

Much of the literature on parties centres on decline and failure. Since the appearance of mass parties, observers have suggested that parties should be best seen as a by-product of tradition, rather than modernity; lamented their inability to perform their alleged functions; and questioned the viability of party-based forms of representation. The virtual absence of political parties from most influential theories of interest representation in the 1970s and 1980s is a telling sign of how widespread the belief in the irrelevance of parties had become.[1] The alleged advent of 'post-materialism' raised further doubts about the viability of established parties in advanced industrial societies (Inglehart 1990).

Recently, however, the decline hypothesis has come under attack on both empirical and theoretical grounds. As Hans Daalder shows in Chapter 2, this literature has strong normative undertones, and it collapses different and not necessarily complementary explanations for decline. Most important, it is now apparent that the crisis of parties had gone further in the literature than in reality (Webb 1995). Commonly used indicators of decline, such as increased voter volatility, have been seriously contested, while party failure is both elusive and rare (Bartolini and Mair 1990; but see Gunther and Hopkin, Chapter 8 below). As remarked by Rose and Mackie (1988), parties are composite organizations with multiple purposes—ranging from organizational self-preservation to the pursuit of power and the realization of policy preferences. Since the relative ranking of these purposes shifts depending on external challenges and intra-party politics, there is no uncontroversial yardstick for failure, short of full bankrupcy and disappearance. Even when this happens, the failing of a party may spell success for another one. Further, as indicated by the unexpected success of the European left, even established parties which are viewed as obsolete may be revitalized. At the same time, the functional equivalents, be they interest groups, social movements, or state bureaucracies, which were expected to displace parties have failed to do so.

The decline of the decline hypothesis, and the renewed interest in parties it has spurred, have exposed major shortcomings in dominant views of party development. As analysts have shifted their attention from crisis to party change and revitalization, they have found that the unexpected recovery of their subjects has undermined their analytical tools. Nor is additional investment in dominant approaches likely to resolve this impasse. First, most of them are fairly old. Some of the distinctions on which these models were built are no longer relevant, at least in advanced industrial countries, such as the distinction between parties of notables and class-mass parties, or between section- and cell-based parties. Further, they have already produced all the generalizations they could generate, leaving analysts to wonder about the many exceptions which they cannot explain (Lawson 1980). Second, some of the most influential views of party development are too committed to the decline hypothesis to survive its apparent demise. Catch-allism, which most political scientists saw as the 'one best' party type in advanced societies, for example, is an instrument of both adaptation and weakness by almost all measures of performance, such as membership, voter loyalty, programmatic capacity, control over policy agendas, and the selection of political personnel (Kirchheimer 1966). From this developmental perspective, the electoral success of parties hinges on their marginalization as instruments of interest representation, policy-making, and governance. Third, most approaches to political parties offer an externalist view of party development. Whether these approaches emphasize socio-structural or institutional determinants of party trajectory, or both, they cast political parties as passive takers of their environment.[2] As political scientists have become more aware of the plasticity of both interests and rules, this view of parties is markedly at odds with the considerable leeway we attribute to other political actors and organizations.

Whatever the solution to this impasse may be, it clearly requires looking at party development not only from 'without', but also from 'within', in ways that capture the two-ways link between intra-party politics and resources and inter-party competition. While the approach to parties qua organizations is one of the oldest in political science, recent versions have expanded its scope to include a much wider range of organizational variables, and have broken with the determinism of older studies.[3] Kitschelt (1994), in particular, has recast party organization as the byproduct not only of necessity, but also of choice, and as a major cause of variations in party performance and strategy. This perspective brings back not only intra-party politics as a crucial political arena, but also parties as central political actors. Whether it can lead to a new model of party development, however, remains to be seen.

This chapter explores this possibility by applying the emerging 'new' organizational approach to the trajectory of the French Socialist Party (SFIO, the Section Française de l'Internationale Ouvrière, until 1971, PS afterwards). In the 1970s, the French Socialist Party staged a spectacular

renaissance which, within a decade, transformed it from a historical under-
achiever into a major winner, and brought it from near extinction to power
amidst hopes that it would 'change life'.[4] Since then, policy and moral failures
have dissipated much of this popular enthusiasm, and shrunk the PS's audience. By the mid-1980s, the PS was losing ground, and when, after a series of
ups and downs, the Socialists went down to major defeat at the legislative
election of 1993, and lost the presidential election of 1995, many commenta-
tors doubted its recovery. The left's victory at the 1997 elections, the popularity of the current Socialist-led government, and the weak challenge posed
by new politics formations, however, suggest that much of the capital the PS
accumulated in the previous decade remains in place.

This chapter provides an internalist account of the PS's jagged trajectory.
The party's renaissance and its retrenchment, I argue, were largely fuelled by
the shift from a territorial to a factional mode of organization introduced
at the party's refounding Epinay Congress. In the 1970s, factionalism was a
major source of dynamism and growth because it fit with the strategic
challenges facing the party. The comparative advantages of factionalism,
however, were highly contingent. In the changed context of the 1980s, factionalism prevented the PS from adjusting to the new environment in ways
that might have better preserved its recent gains. By the mid-1990s, factionalism had become such a handicap that the Socialists' regained popularity
partly stems from their ability to curb it.

A major argument of this chapter is that environment-driven explanations
of party performance are largely meaningless unless complemented by internalist ones which account for what a party makes of a given opportunity
structure, or how it manages to reshape it to its own advantage. At the same
time, I argue, the advantages of a specific organizational form are unlikely to
consolidate into a 'one best' format.[5] This is partly because of changes in the
environment, and the internal dynamic of organizational forms, and partly
because parties do not actually conform to a single organizational form.

The chapter unfolds in four parts. First, I summarize my criticisms of
externalist approaches to party development. The inherent ambiguity of
institutional and social environments create substantial blindspots which
can be dissipated only by looking at party specific resources. Second, I
analyse the trajectory of the PS over the last three decades in terms of first
the match, and then the mismatch, between party organization and the
environment. Third, I look at regional variations within this national pattern. By focusing on two different cases I nuance and deepen my analysis
of the comparative advantages of organizational formats, and show the
limitations of unitary models of party organization. Last, I discuss the
resilience of factionalism and draw the implications of this case for the study
of political parties.

A 'PARTY WHOSE TIME HAD COME'?

Externalist analyses of party performances come in a sociological and an institutional version: while the former (e.g. Przeworski and Sprague 1986) emphasizes underlying socio-economic and demographic changes, the latter (e.g. Sartori 1976) focuses on electoral regimes and the formal properties of party systems. Standard accounts of the PS's renaissance draw on both. The rapid modernization of French society since the late 1950s, as manifested in the dramatic increase in the educated, white-collar, and urban sectors of the population and in the pronounced process of secularization that took place in this period, is said to have created a 'natural' constituency for a culturally liberal and socially reformist party like the PS. In a similar vein, the simultaneously polarizing and centripetal logic of the Fifth Republic is said to have endowed the PS with a large positional rent by virtue of its centre-left location on the political spectrum. Together, these developments, so the argument goes, made the Socialists' success practically inevitable. As the standard text on the French Socialist Party puts it, the PS was 'a party whose time had come' (Bell and Criddle 1984).

These accounts show how external developments created an opportunity structure which worked to the advantage of a party *like* the PS. By failing to explain *how* the PS managed to be such a party, however, they leave out the most interesting part of the story, and the one which determined the way in which it ended. Consider the rapid modernization of French society. Developments associated with this modernization can hardly be said to have dictated the radical strategy chosen by the PS, or its success once chosen. It is precisely these sorts of changes that are routinely invoked to account for the triumph, in other comparably developed societies, of catch-allism— a form of party organization and strategy that stands in marked contrast to the radicalization and increased activism of the PS throughout the 1970s. Further, although the mobilization of 'new politics' actors and themes in the early 1970s eventually provided the Socialists with a catalyst for revitalization, the PS's prospects for tapping these sources of renewal were anything but certain. In its initial stages, the mobilization spurred by May 1968 was intensely anti-political, reflecting a profound disillusionment with the prospect of change through political means, and an even deeper distrust for traditional political formations (Berger 1979). The transformation of the energies unleashed by '68 into an ideological and militant reservoir for the PS, therefore, has to be explained.

Similarly, a closer look at the systemic logic of the Fifth Republic reveals that it was much more open-ended than it is generally assumed. Received wisdom attributes the PS's success to the polarizing and centripetal drives that benefit the moderate components of each bloc. The PS, however, did more than occupy a pre-existing space with a set rate of return. Before the left could

tap the system's centripetal drive, the Socialists had to displace the
Communist Party as the dominant left's formation, a highly resource-
intensive task which rested on their ability to convince the Communist electorate of their left credentials and intents. To grow 'vertically' within the
pre-existing left bloc, the PS had to radicalize its programme and alliance
strategy in ways that promised to exacerbate the system's polarizing drive.
This, however, did not augur well for the Socialists' capacity to expand 'hor-
izontally' outside of the traditionally left bloc by attracting moderate voters,
whose support was necessary for the left's victory, but who were hostile to the
PCF and the statist tradition it stood for. To be sure, the presidential election
smoothed the conflict between these alternative growth strategies. Still, the
Socialists' credibility and effectiveness in pursuing both was a direct by-
product of their ideological and organizational repertoire.[6]

Far from steering the PS into a clear direction, the societal and institutional
contexts of Fifth Republic pulled the PS in opposite directions, any one of
which alone would have been insufficient for success and which, taken
together, amounted to a recipe for incoherence and paralysis. If the rapid
expansion of the 'new' middle class and the centripetal drive of presidential
elections seemed to call for a catch-all strategy, the polarization of the party
system, the conditions of intra-left competition, and the extraordinarily high
level of mobilization called for the militant and programmatic approach associated with class-mass parties. The Socialists' response to these conflicting
environmental pulls was highly distinctive: shunning the catch-all approach,
they went 'backwards' in a sense, not to the class-mass stage—which never
really applied to the SFIO—but to elements of their ideological and organizational legacy (see Sferza 1999). Whereas both ingredients were critical to
the Socialists' renewal, this chapter focuses on how their organizational
make-up helped them to meet apparently incompatible demands by combining features associated with class-mass, catch-all, and framework parties.

THE SHIFTING ADVANTAGES OF ORGANIZATIONAL FORMS: FACTIONALISM VERSUS TERRITORIALISM

The shift from a territorial format to a primarily factional one (through the
adoption of proportional representation of ideological currents) was the
major organizational reform adopted by the new PS at the Congress of
Epinay in 1971. Spurred by the need to keep together the heterogeneous coalition headed by François Mitterrand that took control of the party at the
Epinay Congress, this shift deeply affected the party's culture, its functioning,
and its growth potential.

The main hypothesis I wish to explore is that ideological factionalism affords
key advantages over territorialism during periods of high social mobilization

and intense intra-bloc competition.[7] Territorial models of party organization are patterned to reflect local, electoral and administrative concerns, and they are likely to favour issues and forms of recruitment and mobilization that 'fit' with existing electoral alliances and power structures. For these reasons, especially in highly centralized systems, they tend to discourage programmatic innovations and leadership renewal. Hence, territorial formats would appear suited to the conservation of resources and party reproduction at times of low mobilization. By contrast, factional structures that rest on vertically integrated units which compete on ideological grounds are less bounded by immediate electoral concerns, more sensitive to shifts in the ideological climate, and better equipped to dialogue with social movements and collective actors. In addition, by allowing distinct political projects and organizational networks to coexist, factionalism may enable parties to differentiate their political 'offer' without diluting their programmatic appeal (Gaxie 1985). For these reasons, factionalism may open new avenues of growth and encourage ideological and leadership innovation, especially when high mobilization provides factions with a wide pool of ideas and activists they can tap.

The relative advantages of specific forms of party organization, however, are not constant across institutional, social, and political contexts. Factionalism, in particular, is better suited to opposition than power, and, once in place, it does not easily change in the absence of major systemic or societal pressures. Factionalism, hence, is a double-edged format: while it can be extremely conducive to renewal, it can also be dysfunctional and a source of sclerosis. This is precisely how it worked in the case of the PS.

The 1970s: Factionalism as an Asset

In the highly mobilized 1970s, factionalism was a major source of symbiosis between the PS and its environment. As factions eclipsed territorial federations as the main *loci* of activism, socialization, political debate, and party governance, they promoted an ideological and institutional dynamic which was conducive to militant and electoral growth. In particular, factional pluralism and inter-factional competition were a major factor of party extroversion and a powerful instrument of party-building. They lent credibility to the PS's effort to represent both traditional left demands, ranging from nationalizations to a more labour-inclusive system, and 'new politics' ones, like *autogestion* and gender issues, and they helped the party gain proximity to a variety of new political actors, while reasserting its closeness to labour. As a result, the PS became both a more catch-all, and a more militant, party.

Most important, factionalism enabled the PS to combine 'horizontal' growth, by which I refer to the widening of the Socialists' audience beyond the left's traditional partisan and sociological borders to newly mobilized or previously hostile groups, and 'vertical' growth, by which I refer to the deepening of their support among the left's core audience. It is important to note that horizontal growth is not synonymous with catch-allism. During periods marked by the emergence of new collective actors and demands, in particular, potential supporters may have strong ideological preferences and identities that make them impervious to a catch-allist appeal. In this case, horizontal growth hinges upon a party's capacity to develop programmatic affinities with these groups and ways of integrating them into pre-existing partisan structures, thereby leading to what I term 'thick' horizontal growth (see Sferza 1988). As mentioned above, reconciling what are usually alternative types of growth was essential to the PS's renaissance. In the following subsections I discuss the contribution of factionalism to key aspects of this process.

Ideological revitalization

In the early 1970s, factionalism was primarily an ideological phenomenon. The PS's major factions embodied different stances on all the major issues that had long been a matter of contention within the French left. The faction associated with Michel Rocard closely identified with the participatory ethos of 1968, and adhered to a society-centred view of political and economic transformation which would empower workers and citizens and bring about change through the practice of *autogestion*. In keeping with this view, the Rocardians intended to build a 'framework' party that would link a wide array of groups and associations, and they sought to emancipate the left from the ideological and organizational hegemony of the PCF which they saw as inherently authoritarian and hence conservative. The faction identified with François Mitterrand, by contrast, combined more conformist views, rooted in the Republican tradition of the French left, with its emphasis on statism and *laïcité*, with a unitary left strategy, one in which the alliance with the PCF was both instrumental to the Socialists' electoral expansion and justified by their shared historical legacy. Even in this faction, however, traditional concerns for justice and equality were broadened and expanded to encompass new groups and issues, such as women's rights (see Jenson and Subileau 1995). The third principal faction, the CERES (the Centre d'Études et Recherches Socialistes), stood for an original synthesis of old and new demands, combining statism and mass participation, openness to modernist technocratic themes and attachment to Republican values, with a strong commitment to party-building. Extremely critical of the transformative potential of the left as long as it was divided, the CERES sought to transform the PS into a class-mass party with solid working-class support, and to promote its fusion with a reformed Communist Party.

The rules of intra-party representation added to the ideological and competitive character of these factions. Making participation in the party's leading bodies dependent upon the support mustered by Congressional motions encouraged ideological confrontation and the growth of permanent factional networks, two features that stimulated ideological innovations and served as an optimal conductor for the energies unleashed by 1968. Since no faction gained hegemony until 1981, party congresses became major arenas for programmatic confrontations and political and leadership choices. What is more, factions sought to strengthen their position by reaching out to new members and ideas. In their competitive drive to gain proximity to collective actors and to impart political coherence, albeit as parts of competing strategies, to the demands of a wide variety of groups, from regionalist and women's groups to Catholic unionists and secular associations, they built multiple bridges between the party and mobilized sectors of society (Panebianco 1988). Recruitment was all the more successful since the raised stakes and vitality of intra-party politics gave left activists a strong reason for joining the PS.

Recruitment

The original contribution of factionalism to the PS's growth was that it acted both as a 'widener' and a 'deepener' of the Socialists' appeal. On the one hand, the coexistence of different discourses and projects allowed the PS to diversify its offer and stretch its coverage of the political spectrum, thereby achieving the electoral effectiveness usually associated with catch-allism. With each faction catering to a distinct audience, the party as a whole succeeded in giving expression to a variety of currents which had developed outside of mainstream party politics and whose appeal extended well beyond the left, while at the same time renewing long-standing commitments to the traditional goals and audiences of the French left. Some factions, like the Mitterrandists, Mauroyists, and, in part, the CERES, emphasized ideas and policies such as *laïcité* and nationalization, which had long been part of the left's historical repertoire. They were especially effective as instruments of vertical growth, competing with the PCF for the support of those occupational and cultural collectivities such as civil servants, public school teachers, secular 'red' peasants, and sectors of the working class that comprised the left's core support base. By contrast, the Rocardians, but also the early CERES, incorporated into the Socialists' symbols, discourse, and programmes a wide array of demands, ranging from *autogestion* to decentralization, which had gained popularity after May 1968 (Subileau 1987). Hence, they were especially effective as instruments of horizontal growth: they (especially CERES and the Rocardians) attracted to the PS newly mobilized groups that had no prior ties to the left, such as peasants in Western France, progressive Catholics, regionalists, and middle and upper level cadres; promoted the rapprochement between what was still a largely anti-clerical party with weak links to organized labour and the CFDT—a previously Catholic Union which had led the most symbolic struggles of the early 1970s; and presided over the party's expansion into France's most conservative regions.

On the other hand, factionalism enabled the PS to eschew the ideological and militant demobilization which is usually associated with horizontal growth. By compartmentalizing its audience into separate factional networks, with distinct political discourses and leaders, the PS could assert a militant and programmatic stance in spite of its eclecticism. Throughout the 1970s, factions created separate microcosms with distinct paths of recruitment, activism, and political career. By publishing their own reviews or bulletins, organizing conferences and summer schools, promoting political tourism, housing their members in distinct hotels at party congresses, and discouraging cross-factional fraternization, factions created high levels of factional identification and insulation among party members. This compartmentalization recreated within factions the political coherence which might have been lacking at the global party level. As a result, factionalism not only contributed to the diversification of the PS's ideological and sociological appeal, but it also provided an antidote to the ideological blandness and the decline of militancy which this diversification usually entails (Pizzorno 1966).

In the highly mobilized and polarized 1970s, the role of factionalism as a deepener of the PS's appeal was essential to party growth. At that time, the PS was starved of the ideological and militant resources that would allow it to displace the PCF as the dominant component of the left. The collective actors which controlled these resources, like the CFDT, however, were unlikely to respond to the individualistic appeal and weak message associated with catch-allism. Steeped in the anti-politics ethos of 1968, these actors put a high premium on ideological consistency and direct political participation and distrusted parties as inherently bureaucratic and opportunistic. Factions helped bridge the ideological and institutional gap between these groups and movements and the PS in a variety of ways.

First of all, factionalism offered potential recruits an extensive menu of choice and a strategy of 'qualified entry'. By joining a faction, activists selectively embraced those elements of party ideology and programme, like *autogestion* or extensive nationalization, which they shared, while neglecting, or even combating, those with which they disagreed. As a former CFDT official put it, 'one joined the CERES, not the PS' (in Lewis 1993). This option made membership in the PS congruent with a broad range of prior beliefs and militant practices. Second, factionalism seemed an antidote against the stifling of debate and participation associated with large organizations. By channelling participation into smaller ideologically defined subunits, each of which had its own channel of socialization and chain of command, factions multiplied the symbolic and, in part, the selective incentives that sustain activism (Olson 1965), thus replicating within the PS the energizing dynamic that tends to develop in small and cohesive groups. Third, the PS's acceptance of factions, especially when seen against the monolithism of the PCF, was interpreted as a guarantee of internal pluralism, leading newcomers to believe they could reconcile their prior ideological commitments and solidarities with party membership.[8] For all these reasons, factions facilitated the recruitment of key groups of activists who brought to the PS extremely valuable skills and societal linkages with the labour movement and other less traditional movements.

Leadership renewal

In addition to helping the PS incorporate new ideas and activists, factions helped it shed old ones. In light of the wide discredit the SFIO had earned, the latter task was as crucial as the first one, and the decentralized structure the PS had inherited made it a difficult one as well. This power structure, centred on local notables who pursued a variety of alliance strategies tailored to their special needs, was bound to produce strong pockets of resistance to the innovations endorsed by the PS in 1971, and, in particular, to its nationwide alliance with the PCF. By creating direct links between the national and local levels that cut across geographic locales, factionalism recast intra-party lines of loyalty and solidarity. Since in most federations factional loyalties were stronger than geographic-based ones, this format provided national leaders with a chain of command that bypassed territorial structures, and was quite effective in overcoming parochialism. In addition, factionalism also promoted a style of party politics which changed the criteria for access to leadership, and accelerated the renovation of party personnel.

As ideological and political-programmatic considerations informed by factional solidarities and rivalries took precedence over territorial loyalties, technical expertise, personal notoriety, and seniority gave way to more explicitly political criteria of leadership selection. At the same time, by casting competition among leaders in ideological terms, factionalism also gave these conflicts political dignity, thereby limiting their negative impact on the PS's morale and image. Furthermore, the existence of multiple factional networks encouraged the spreading of political vocations and increased the supply of new leaders, thereby making the selection process more competitive. Many territorially based party leaders and power brokers who remained outside the symbolic discourse set by the factional axes of conflict were disarmed. In their place, new types of leaders came to the fore: ideologues bred by the factional system, and militants whose activist background entitled them to speak on behalf of mobilized societal actors. In this way, renewal at the rank-and-file level quickly extended to the party's intermediate level, enhancing the PS's association with social struggles and lending credibility to its radical rhetoric.

Party governance

Throughout the 1970s, factions effectively compartmentalized their followers within distinct micro-parties. In so doing, they played a role similar to that of vertically integrated 'pillars' in consociational societies, helping the PS not only to host multiple political projects and audiences, but also to contain the conflicts engendered by this diversity (Hanley 1986). In particular, by organizing recruits on the basis of explicit political projects, factions softened the clash between historically opposed sociological and religious identities at a time in which the inflow of both Catholics and Marxists in the party made such conflict inevitable. Most notably, the fact that the two most politically opposed factions, the CERES and the Rocardians, recruited heavily among Catholics lessened the salience of the religious cleavage as a raw source of intra-party conflict.

Factionalism in the Changed Context of the 1980s and 1990s

As the political and social circumstances that attended the birth of the new PS changed, however, factions degenerated into a source of paralysis and dysfunction. To be sure, the faction-induced mismatch between the PS and its environment was not the only cause of a decline which began in the mid-1980s and culminated in the 1993 debacle. The shift from opposition to government was bound to be taxing for a party which had promised to 'change life'. Access to power in an international conjuncture that was highly unfavourable to the left's expansionary programmes, and a variety of political errors, moral and policy failures, contributed heavily to the disarray of, and disillusionment with, French Socialists. Yet, just as the favourable environment of the 1970s is not a sufficient cause of the PS's success, so the difficult environment of the 1980s does not fully account for its decline. Some of the drawbacks of factionalism which became apparent in the mid-1980s, for example, had already surfaced, as indicated by the stagnation of membership, before the Socialists' victory.[9] In addition, factionalism was itself a factor of governmental performance, in the sense that it contributed to some of the most damaging aspects of the left's governmental experience. Public opinion data confirm that the Socialists' problems did not all come from their governmental role: the public image of the PS was at times worse than that of the governments it led. In 1990, a time of intense factionalism, even Socialist activists were more satisfied with their government than with their party (*Libération*, 14 March 1990).

Four developments, stemming from changes in the external environment and from the dynamic of factionalism itself, affected the returns of factionalism. First of all, mobilization declined sharply in the 1980s. This depleted the reservoir of ideas and activists on which factionalism had fed, and devalued many of the societal linkages factions had built. Second, the reduction of the Socialist–Communist alliance to a purely electoral pact, the retreat of Socialist-led governments from many of their more controversial and radical commitments, and the emergence of new issues, like immigration, the environment, and European integration which were outside factional alignments, undermined the factions' programmatic *raisons d'être* (Cameron 1996). Third, once in office, the PS could not longer profit from the ambiguity created by partly overlapping and partly contradictory factional projects. Fourth, the triumph of 1981 consolidated the Mitterrandists' hegemony over the party, and gave them extensive access to governmental resources. These developments altered the logic of inter-factional rivalry from a competitive and extroverted one into a collusive and introverted one, contributing to the PS's transformation from a programmatic into a 'patrimonial' party (see Blondel Chapter 9 below).

Factionalism as a Liability

Once established, factions replicated within the PS the freezing of cleavages and alignments which parties strive to maintain in political systems. The centrality of factional affiliation for access to governmental and party posts contributed to their entrenchment.[10] As factions clung to ideological framework which the narrowing of policy options and the decline of mobilization had rendered obsolete, and which seemed especially unwarranted in light of the transformation of factions into instruments of power acquisition and maintenance, the PS lost touch with the concerns and issues facing the left and labour movement. After having lent the PS ideological and programmatic credibility, factions became associated in the public mind with the most Byzantine and opaque aspects of intra-party politics. Even among the Socialists' core audience, factionalism turned from a magnet to a deterrent. Many sympathizers who intended to join the PS were discouraged by the realization that effective participation in its activities hinged upon their joining a faction as well. By the late 1980s, relations among factions were so bad that, where multiple sections existed, factional criteria had displaced geographical ones in determining which one members would join (Philippe and Hubscher 1991).

As it became clear that no faction or coalition of factions could challenge the Mitterrandists' hegemony, moreover, party leaders, irrespectively of their factional affiliation, came to value the preservation of existing local and national equilibria over the uncertain benefits of recruitment and growth. In many federations and sections where inter-factional power equilibria were vulnerable to marginal shifts in membership, the addition of new members of undeclared factional allegiance seemed a source of destabilization and a risk which was not worth taking. This negative attitude towards recruitment was so widespread that the party's leadership even coined a new label, 'Malthusianism', to disparage it. Since the party also experienced serious losses among those groups which best symbolized the horizontal growth of the 1970s, and which were particularly disgusted by the discovery that factional politics meant 'power politics as usual', membership declined throughout the 1980s. This haemorrhage was especially pronounced in federations where intense factional rivalries had corroded territorially based forms of partisan sociability and participation.

Major problems emerged also with respect to party governance. As personal ambitions and loyalties displaced ideological convictions and factions lost much of their cohesion, national leaders became unable to enforce the inter-factional deals through which they had governed the party since 1971. In 1986, the breakdown at the local level of the agreement which apportioned among factions the expected shrinkage of the party's parliamentary group was a clear sign of the factions' reduced effectiveness as vertical chains of command (Sawicki 1986). Since, as noted above, factions also bequeathed to the party a 'surplus' of leaders armed with distinct networks of support and a confrontational practice of intra-party democracy, this resulted in bitter local infighting and the appearance of rival Socialist slates. The implosion of factions was particularly destabilizing since the PS had always handled party matters through factional channels, and hence lacked explicit and routinized procedures for settling conflict. In this context, conflict spread from issues to procedures, and challenged the legitimacy of party deliberations. The extreme instability of the party's leadership—the PS has had six First Secretaries since 1986—and the vibrant protests raised, in all but two cases, by the modalities of this turnover, exemplify this state of affairs.[11] Moreover, as conflict became more personalized, it also proved more difficult to mediate. This was nicely illustrated by the 1990 Rennes Congress, where the PS failed to agree on a common platform in spite of the fact that the contributions presented by the factions were virtually identical. This public display of intense rivalries and ambitions dealt a major blow to the PS's public image and internal morale.

VARIATIONS WITHIN ONE MODEL OR PLURALITY OF MODELS

Thus far I have discussed how the introduction of factionalism helped the PS benefit from the political and social context of the 1970s, but hurt its adaptation to a changed context in the following decade. I hope to have shown that much can be learnt by relating the PS's performance to its organizational format. This national perspective, however, only partially captures the nature of the PS, and oversimplifies the relationship between organizational and environmental variables. In the period under discussion, the PS was experiencing two partly contradictory developments. On the one hand, organizational and programmatic reforms had rendered the party's functioning and electoral performance more similar across locales. As we saw, the shift to a factional format was a major source of 'nationalization' of party life, the standardization of alliances was another, and horizontal growth partly redressed the imbalance between strong and weak federations, with all but one electing at least one deputy. On the other hand, internal reforms mixed with pre-existing local traditions and leadership styles in different ways, producing a less noticeable trend toward intra-party diversity (Sadoun 1989). Far from being negligible, these regional variations resulted in distinct modes of party functioning and vulnerability to environmental changes.

Factionalism and Territorialism at the Subnational Level

The interaction between factionalism and territorialism could generate three major configurations: factions could eclipse federal structures; territorial structures could resist factional inroads; or a hybrid pattern based on the interpenetration of factionalism and territorialism could emerge. Which outcome prevailed was not accidental, but the by-product of structural factors and the strategy of local leaders. In general, the permeability of territorialism was inversely related to the strength of the SFIO's implantation (see Hanley 1986). In *départements* where the SFIO controlled substantial electoral resources and posts, local leaders were reluctant to jeopardize this capital and well positioned to co-opt factional challengers. Since these tended to be 'red' *départements* with strong intra-left competition, Socialists also feared that factional conflict would play in the hands of the PCF. The fact that these federations followed a predominantly vertical growth also meant that they were internally diversified and, by the same token, less prone to factionalism. Resistance to factionalism was strongest where the transition from the SFIO to the PS had been negotiated by a dominant notable (Gaston Defferre) who subsequently used his local and national clout to fend off factional competition and reforms. By contrast, factionalism tended to prevail in *départements* which were 'white' (and hence conducive to horizontal growth), had experienced the mobilizations of the 1970s, and lacked a dominant notable. While these structural factors deeply affected the confrontation between factionalism and territorialism, significant variations among similar *départements* show that local leaders could also tilt the balance one way or another. In some cases, the locally cooperative and inclusive behaviour of factional leaders resulted in a hybrid organizational format which blended territorial and factional structures.

The next two subsections take a closer look at two Socialist federations which exemplify opposite growth trajectories and organizational outcomes. The Ille-et-Vilaine federation replicated in magnified form the PS's faction-driven dynamic. By contrast, the Pas-de-Calais developed an original synthesis between territorialism and factionalism. In the 1970s, the Ille-et-Vilaine federation symbolized the dynamism of the new PS, while its stagnating Pas-de-Calais counterpart seemed untouched by the shift from the SFIO to the PS. By the end of the 1980s, however, the relative standing of the two federations had been reversed: while the Ille-et-Vilaine stagnated, the Pas-de-Calais had become one of the PS's few bright points (see Sferza

1988; Sawicki 1986, 1997). The party congresses hosted by these federations in the 1990s illustrate this state of affairs: whereas the Rennes Congress was unanimously viewed as the most disastrous one in the PS's history, the one held in Liévin was hailed as an unexpected success.

The Factional Model: The Ille-et-Vilaine Federation

Brittany, once a missionary land for the left, is the region where the PS won its greatest electoral gains. The SFIO's weak implantation, the relatively low threat posed by the PCF, the presence of a vital Catholic subculture, and the region's involvement in some of the most visible social, cultural, and environmental struggles in the 1970s meant that the Breton PS was built primarily through a process of horizontal growth. Here, to a greater extent than at the national level, the PS grew by incorporating themes and activists previously extraneous to the left, and taking its distance from the religious cleavage. This is best exemplified by the profile of Socialist Breton leaders in the 1970s: breaking with the right's *notabiliaire* tradition and with the left's *laique* mould, they were mostly young and unknown but for their involvement in a dense associational and militant network, and their itineraries bridged the religious divide of Breton politics. In Ille-et-Vilaine, for example, the PS's largest sections were headed by Catholics, a teacher in a private school and a small farmer. These Socialist candidates no longer campaigned for the abolition of private schools, but for a wider range of issues, from the maintenance of schools in small rural communes to the economic, cultural, and political empowerment of Brittany. As these unconventional Socialists reached across the religious divide to socially progressive Catholics, they sometimes won spectacular victories. Organizational growth followed suit: between 1973 and 1979, the Breton PS expanded from 800 to 6,500 members (Philippe and Hubscher 1991).

In the near absence of pre-existing party structures and influential leaders, factions met with very little resistance. Moreover, the availability of a wide pool of activists and themes which did not belong to the mainstream left benefited the most innovative factions, the CERES and the Rocardians (Hanley 1986). Far from being simple receptacles for members, ideas, and leaders, these factions played a constitutive role in seeking out and forming activists, and they shaped the local political context by countering the localism that the regionalist mobilizations of the 1970s might have produced. The Rocardians, with their capacity to link Breton concerns for decentralization and cultural specificities to a global vision of bottom–up transformation through *auto-gestion*, are a case in point. By the same token, factions gave an edge to the most 'political' among potential leaders, who could articulate local and national concerns. Due to the lack of territorially based apparatuses that could arbitrate conflicts and enforce apprenticeship requirements, moreover, factions became the primary instruments of party governance and leadership allocation.

The Ille-et-Vilaine federation well exemplifies this regional pattern. Here, it was the CERES which propelled party renewal. *Laïque* leaders opposed to the union of the left were expelled, sections which clung to centrist alliances were dissolved, and new ones were created which testified to the party's cultural and sociological opening. Many of the new members were peasants, Catholics, and newly urbanized white- and blue-collar workers with no previous ties to the left. In some sections, like Rédon, not a single member had belonged to the SFIO; in others, like Fougères, working-class members, affiliated to Catholic organizations like the CFDT (Confederation Democratique du Travail) and the JOC (Jeunesse Ouvrière Catholique), provided most of the recruits (Sferza 1988). The new members who joined via the CERES, and later on the Rocardian faction, linked the PS with a variety of mobilized groups, from peasants to neighbourhood, Third Worldist associations, and Catholic workers. Many of these new members privileged political principles over electoral success, as exemplified by the designation of a young unknown CERES representative, Edmond Hervé, as the leader of the party's list at the Rennes municipal elections of 1971 and 1977. On both occasions, Hervé was preferred on ideological grounds to a much more widely known and experienced leader, who, even in the eyes of Hervé's supporters, stood a much better chance of winning this highly visible race. When Hervé became mayor of Rennes in 1977, after a campaign that spurred unprecedented grass-roots mobilization and swelled the ranks of the party, his victory was seen as a vindication of the CERES's aggressive strategy of party-building, and a major sign of party renewal.

The hopes and expectations raised by this success, however, were short-lived. The municipal campaign of 1977, the one episode which is fondly remembered by current and past party members, marked the high point of the PS's renewal in the *département*. Some of the difficulties experienced by the Ille-et-Vilaine PS were rooted in regional specificities, and were shared by all Breton federations. The conquest of local and national office diverted the energies of most capable leaders from party-building when its foundations were still weak. In Ille-et-Vilaine, this was notably the case of Hervé. Moreover, the shift from opposition to power undermined the PS's symbiosis with regional and social movements. In part, this was the inevitable result of the PS's transformation from a magnet for cultural and political contestation into a target of protest. In part, however, this was the paradoxical by-product of the PS's responsiveness to the demands of these movements. By offering new points of entry and leverage, the left's decentralizing reforms and the cooperative stance of Socialist elected officials also reduced the dependence of regional and local actors on party-specific resources.

Some of the problems encountered by the Ille-et-Vilaine PS, however, were *département*-specific, and stemmed from unfettered factionalism and the behaviour of local leaders. Here, the party's past weakness and recent growth meant that the creation of territorial structures of arbitration and socialization hinged upon the emergence of a hegemonic leader, or the adoption of cooperative and inclusive behaviour by territorial leaders. Neither condition obtained in Ille-et-Vilaine. When the CERES, the federation's dominant faction, traded *autogestion* for an increasingly statist approach, many of its local supporters left the faction. Instead of coming to an understanding with the federation's Rocardian minority, however, past and current CERES leaders continued to cooperate in combating the Rocardians, while engaging in a competitive effort to reposition themselves closer to the nationally dominant Mitterrandist faction. In a region where all the principal Socialist leaders belonged to the more peripheral CERES and Rocardian factions, this was a strategy that promised handsome returns. However, since the PS's ideologically charged climate prevented open migrations across factions, it also translated in a politics of *trasformismo*, based on personal and cross-factional alliances resting on procedural tricks and ad hoc conversions.

The manipulation of factional allegiances for personal goals emptied factions of their ideological legitimacy, poisoned interpersonal relations within the federation, embittered the Rocardian minority, encouraged a highly conspiratorial mode of party politics which made intra-party conflicts more pervasive and hermetic, and excluded the rank and file. As a result, the Ille-et-Vilaine PS experienced the drawbacks of factionalism earlier and in a more extreme form than the party at the aggregate level. Here, where factionalism had produced both excess leadership and a void of arbitral powers or accepted criteria that could harness it, the presence of competing leaders quickly became a source of paralysis and introversion. Since the small size of the federation and the narrow advantage of the dominant coalition over the Rocardians meant that relatively few new members could swing control of the federation from one camp to the other, majority leaders were extremely wary of recruitment, and the Ille-et-Vilaine federation became a perfect illustration of the Malthusianism lamented by Socialist leaders. By the early 1980s, the PS was practically absent from the local political scene and had reverted to a pattern of vertical recruitment. The federation organized virtually no public meetings and had no sustained contacts with outside groups, recruitment efforts were limited to the co-optation of 'safe' individuals, and important organizational and militant resources had been purposefully squandered. In some cases, prominent sympathizers were discouraged from joining; in others, valuable cadres who belonged to the 'wrong' factions were deliberately wasted in posts for which they had no skills. Membership declined steeply, with losses being most pronounced among groups less fit to survive, or most unwilling to stomach, the federation's Florentine politics. Catholic peasants, representatives of associations, CFDT unionists, and workers left the party or were confined to peripheral sections, and the federation fell back onto the *laïque* milieu, with public school teachers and principals providing an estimated 80 per cent of its section secretaries. The federal youth branch was now actively recommending that its members join Force Ouvrière, a union that especially in Brittany represents the mixture of *laïcité*, narrow social basis, and conservatism which had marginalized the old SFIO. Whatever broader societal linkages the PS maintained, they were increasingly the doing, and by the same token the personal capital, of isolated activists and leaders.

Faction-induced retrenchment, in fact, encouraged the disengagement of Socialist elected officials from party life, thereby contributing to the very *notabilism* the CERES and the Rocardians had sought to combat. In a *département* where the left remained minoritarian, Socialists who had won, or hoped to win, electoral office reacted to the growing introversion of the Federation by extricating themselves from party life and developing their own networks of support. In one case, this resulted in the creation of a parallel quasi-party, several hundreds strong, which had no ties with, nor paid dues to, the party's much smaller local section. In Rennes, where the PS owed its municipal victories to the support of numerous diverse groupings, contacts with associations were maintained nearly exclusively through municipal channels, and relations between the federation and the Socialist administration were poor. Hervé had barred the party from even the small privileges, such as access to photocopying machines and to the municipal bulletin, that in most French municipalities are considered a basic right of the governing party, whereas federal leaders could hardly wait until the end of the 1983 municipal campaign to remove Hervé's posters from the party's headquarters.

Reformed Territorialism: The Pas-de-Calais Federation

The Pas-de-Calais federation followed an altogether different path, one which combined territorialism and factionalism in a mutually beneficial way. The resilience of territorialism had several causes. First, here the PS was grafted onto a strong pre-existing Socialist tradition with a large, if not very active, working-class following. This implantation offered career opportunities whose preservation called for the revitalization of the federation's existing capital, rather than its overhaul. Second, the left had long dominated politics in the *département*. Here, the smallness of the centrist reservoir forced the Socialists into a path of vertical growth at the PCF's expense. Moreover, first-hand familiarity with a very aggressive and orthodox Communist federation had demystified the PCF in the eyes of local Socialists: even members of the CERES, the faction most committed to the union of the left, doubted its reforming impact on their Communist partner. Third, the Pas-de-Calais had been relatively untouched by the social and cultural upheaval of the 1970s: its economy was dominated by a declining and heavily state-funded coal industry, and, accordingly, the left's imagery and symbols privileged classic themes linked to the miners' struggles. Here, tight intra-left competition had induced progressive Catholics to join the Socialists before the CFDT and other Catholic organizations embraced *autogestion* and other radical themes, and hence on a more individual basis and with a less distinct political identity than in other regions like Brittany. For all of these reasons, the Pas-de-Calais was a relatively infertile terrain for factionalism.

Yet, differently from what happened in other *départements* where similar conditions applied and where territorialism survived virtually unchanged, in the Pas-de-Calais the territorial model was modified through the selective assimilation of innovations elsewhere associated with factionalism. In this way, the federation preserved territorial solidarities while benefiting from the revitalization spurred by factionalism. As a result, the Pas-de-Calais PS thrived throughout the 1980s, whereas most old Socialist strongholds experienced a decline as steep, or even steeper, than that of the PS at the aggregate level (Philippe and Hubscher 1991). To account for this outcome we have to turn to non-structural factors, such as the strategies of local leaders and party craft.

Ironically, the cross-fertilization between territorialism and factionalism stemmed largely from opposition to party renewal. Having sided against Mitterrand at Epinay, the Pas-de-Calais lacked leaders who could negotiate the transition to the new PS. This opened a window of opportunity for a young but disparate group of activists who wanted to bring the federation into line with the PS's new orientation and leadership, and who were induced to join forces by the old guard's stiff resistance. Their strategy was two-pronged. On the one hand, they sought to contain the spill-over of factional conflict into *département*-wide politics by downplaying their links with national factions. In spite of their different factional affiliations, the renovators closed ranks behind Daniel Percheron—a Mitterrandist—and continued to cooperate even after they took control of the federation. Even with factional infighting in the PS at its highest, the Pas-de-Calais maintained a unitary secretariat in which all factions were represented. To preserve this unitary mode of governance, innovations adopted by the party or sponsored by individual factions were sifted and reinterpreted through territorial concerns. On the other hand, the Pas-de-Calais renovators sought to curb the influence of local notables by simultaneously strengthening the party at its base through the recruitment and education of new members, and at its top by greatly expanding the logistic, propaganda, and ideological capacities of the federal leadership. In this way, the renovators altered both the federation's territorial power structure and the national dynamic of factionalism in mutually beneficial ways.

This is best exemplified by the success of the Pas-de-Calais federation in renewing its links to the working class. While this was a major goal of the new PS nationwide, efforts to establish the party's presence at the workplace became entangled with, and bogged down by, bitter inter-factional struggles on the form this intervention should take, and for control over the newly established enterprise sector. The CERES, the faction which had worked hardest to bring the PS to the workplace, wanted the party to create fully autonomous factory sections. Other factions, however, viewed the enterprise sector as a Trojan horse for the CERES and boycotted it altogether, or, alternatively, favoured the creation of factory groups whose members would remain under the jurisdiction of territorial sections. In keeping with their strategy, the Pas-de-Calais renovators took the path which was most compatible with the federation's power structure, and chose, CERES included, to create factory groups. At the same time, the federal leadership went out of its way to give these groups visibility and resources. In the end, the factory sector, which nationally fell victim to factional struggles, locally produced respectable results: by the early 1980s, the Pas-de-Calais had the least conflict-ridden and the strongest enterprise sector of the whole PS.

Inter-factional cooperation in a highly factionalized party, however, carried a price. In a party which was deeply split between supporters of state and society centred views of Socialism, for example, the Pas-de-Calais search for a synthesis produced an outstanding aberration, known as *Guesdisme auto-gestionnaire*. Coined by Daniel Percheron, the Pas-de-Calais federal secretary, this formula associates what are in fact two radically opposed terms in the iconography of the French left, and would have been rejected as blasphemous in any other context. Its acceptance in the Pas-de-Calais testifies to the extent in which factions had actually been disarmed, and to the willingness of their leaders to forego participation or be ridiculed in national party politics in order to pursue their territorial strategy.

Initially, this strategy hardly seemed to pay off. Throughout the 1970s, the Pas-de-Calais federation stagnated in terms of members and voters, and was marginalized in the PS's faction-based power system. In the longer period, however, as shown by the example of the enterprise sector, this reformed territorialism outperformed both the factional and unreformed territorial alternatives. First, it made possible an effective allocation of leadership resources, with the federation managing the career and the promotion of its cadres, even moving its most dynamic candidates from one newly acquired district to a still unconquered one. This strategy gave the PS a decisive edge in its long-standing war of position against the PCF: its effectiveness can be appreciated by contrasting the success of the Pas-de-Calais Socialists in capturing nearly all Communist-controlled municipalities with the total failure to do so of their counterparts in the neighboring Nord (Giblin 1984). Second, reformed territorialism increased the federation's capacity for self-governance. Percheron repeatedly used referenda in order to curb the local notables' opposition to controlled renewal and to insulate the federation from decisions taken by the party's national leadership.[12] Third, territorial governance enhanced the federation's pressure power *vis-à-vis* Socialist governments, as shown by its ability to win important state aid for the *département*'s depressed economy, such as its efforts to block the planned demolition of several mining towns, to alter the trajectory of the new supertrain (the TGV), to build two new universities in the *département*, and to provide job retraining for its largely unskilled workforce. Fourth, territorialism kept alive a type of participation centred on sociability and local solidarities which was somewhat shielded from the vagaries of national politics. When the ideological excitement of the 1970s subsided, the federation was more successful in retaining its members than its factionalized counterparts. By the end of the 1980, the Pas-de-Calais had become a standing example of the comparative advantages of territorialism, and an authoritative spokesman for internal party reform through the curbing of factions. In the end, however, reformed territorialism could not withstand disintegrating national and local tendencies: by the mid-1990s, Percheron was discredited by the numerous turnabouts he had effected, and local, personal, and factional rivalries had come to the fore of politics within the *département*.

CONCLUSION

In this chapter I have argued that the recent trajectory of French Socialism can be best understood by focusing on party-specific ideological and organizational resources. In particular, I have emphasized the impact of factionalism on the PS's performance. In a highly mobilized context characterized by high intra-bloc competition, I have argued, factionalism is more conducive to party renewal and horizontal growth than territorialism. In the case of the PS, it was precisely those federations which most closely conformed to the factional model that grew most in terms of voters and members throughout the 1970s.

These advantages, however, were short-lived. The example of the PS suggests that factions do not age well, and adapt poorly to environmental changes. Once the conditions which preside over the formation of factions subside, or factionalism ceases to be competitive, this format is likely to degenerate into a vehicle for acute personal rivalries, party introversion, and sclerosis. If not counterbalanced by territorialism in the longer run, factionalism has a high potential to turn into an instrument of party disfunctionality. In the case of the PS, factionalism proved unsuited to consolidating the growth it had made possible and directly contributed to the squandering of party resources. It is significant, in this regard, that throughout the 1980s federations where factionalism had been kept at bay by a strong territorial leadership, or where factional leaders had adopted conciliatory choices, managed to contain, or at least to delay, the drop in members and votes that the PS experienced in these years.[13]

Socialist leaders were not blind to these developments, and some sought to curb the damage of factionalism. As would-be reformers were to discover, however, factionalism, once established, is extremely sticky. This is due to its nature, and to party-specific and environmental factors. First, factionalism, in addition to providing important benefits for key groups in the party, is supported by normative arguments. As a politically motivated format, resting on the notion that internal party democracy should meet the same standards that obtain in the broader political system, factionalism cannot be easily defeated on efficiency grounds. Second, factionalism is a genetic component of French Socialism, which is deeply rooted in its repertoire and historically transmitted political culture. Indeed, the SFIO, itself, was created in 1906 out of a merger among different parties which maintained their distinctiveness long after their fusion; in the 1970s, most factions sought legitimation by claiming a close filiation with the SFIO's founders (Noland 1956; Bergounioux and Grunberg 1992; and Roucaute 1983). Decades of intra-left competition, during which Socialists flaunted their internal pluralism as proof of their commitment to democracy and used it to criticize the PCF, and the close link between the reintroduction of factionalism and the PS's renaissance, lent this format additional legitimacy. The factional structure, thus, was literally woven into the party's constitution and identity. In addition, territorialism itself was transformed and co-opted by two decades of factional dominance. As factions lost some of their ideological ethos, territorial leaders learned to manipulate inter-factional rivalries to their own advantage, and used their factional affiliation as a bargaining chip in their dealings with key national leaders. The interlocking between an ossifying factional format and a de-energizing territorial one produced a hybrid system with a low potential for reform.

Third, institutional arrangements, both at the systemic and at the party level, also contributed to the entrenchment of factionalism. An important systemic feature that affects the viability of factionalism is the relationship between party and government. In the case of ideologically based factions, pressures against factionalism appear strongest in regimes where the identification between party and government is greatest. This is because factionalism requires a broad ideological space, whereas party-based government encourages intra-party uniformity and consensus. In Britain, for example, the constraints of 'party government' are such that, even when in opposition, parties mimic the format they would assume when in government (Kogan and Kogan 1982). This, together with close ties to the trade unions, has been a major obstacle to the viability of factionalism in the Labour Party. In France, where even majority parties play a relatively marginal role vis-à-vis the executive, the faction-inhibiting impact of office is rather limited, especially on faction-prone parties like the PS. Such impact, moreover, is offset by the usefulness of factions as informal channels of presidential influence, and as launching pads for would-be presidential candidates. In the case of the PS, the

faction-enhancing impact of systemic institutions is compounded by an internal make-up in which powerful intermediate structures, the federations, provide factions with stable bases of existence (Panebianco 1988).

Last, but not least, the decline of social and ideological mobilization in the
1980s meant that none of the movements which emerged in this period had
the strength to break the hold of existing factions, either by inducing them to
update their agendas or by launching new ones. The 1980s witnessed several
attempts to transcend the old factional cleavages, the formation of the so-
called *transcourants*, the flourishing of less formal political clubs loosely
linked to the PS, and the efforts of some factions to capture social movements
like the BEURS (second generation immigrant youth), the students, and the
ecologists. Instead of revitalizing the PS, these attempts undermined and split
the movements they targeted (like in the case of *S.O.S. Racisme*) and encouraged the flight of socialist activists into outside groups (like in the case of the
Greens). In this context, the PS's factional structure changed through the
implosion of old factions, rather than through renewal. Factionalism, in sum,
was too embedded in the ideological and power structures of the PS to be easily displaced from within the party, and systemic and social pressures were
too weak to impose the disappearance or the realignment of factions from
without.

Thus, it was not until the unexpected emergence of Lionel Jospin as the
party's new leader in the aftermath of his excellent performance at the 1995
presidential election that factionalism began to lose its grip over party politics. Indeed, Jospin's appeal was itself partly due to his withdrawal from factional activities. After Jospin became prime minister in 1997, the PS
confirmed this new course by electing a secretary, François Hollande, who, as
a founder of the *transcourants*, had long stood against factionalism, and by
arriving at this decision through clear and uncontroversial procedures.
Significantly, the 1997 Brest Congress which ratified this choice became
known as the 'Peace Congress'. At a broader level, prolonged *cohabitation*
also narrowed the systemic incentives to factionalism by strengthening the
parliamentary component of the French political system vis-à-vis its presidential component.

This analysis of the PS has mixed implications for the study of political parties. On the one hand, it suggests that parties have a higher potential for
renewal than it is usually acknowledged and that they can get new mileage
and life out of their ideological and organizational repertoires. In the case of
the PS, factionalism helped the party to revitalize its old roots, and to derive
new life from its association with new issues and groups. The type of growth
afforded by this format, moreover, had a lasting impact on the French left: it
contributed to the marginalization of the PCF, and it also enabled the PS to
steal the thunder from 'new politics' groups and movements, thereby consolidating the hegemony of established party formations over the French left.

On the other hand, the example of the PS also suggests that the quest for the 'one best format' is largely an illusory one. Whereas different organizational formats carry distinct comparative advantages, these advantages are highly contingent, and parties have limited access to these formats and little capacity also to shift across them as their returns change over time. At the same time, parties rarely conform to a single format. Rather, they encompass traits drawn from more than one model which combine in different ways in different historical periods and locales. Far from being minor nuances, these intra-party variations in adaptive strategies and organizational formats variations are important sources of flexibility and rigidity that affect organizational dynamics and party development. Approaches to party development which ignore their existence and impose a false coherence on party forms may be detrimental to our understanding of parties. Overall, we should be more optimistic about party adaptation and renewal than model (re)building.

NOTES

1. See e.g. the works of Philippe Schmitter, Theda Skocpol, and Claus Offe, and the extensive debate on corporatism, statism, and social movements they have spurred.
2. Even approaches which emphasize party institutionalization as a key factor of cleavage formation and reproduction have little to say on political parties as such and on how they affect the representation and intensity of cleavages. This ultimately results in the reification of cleavages. See Lipset and Rokkan (1967*a*); Bartolini and Mair (1990).
3. The 'classics' include Ostrogorski (1964 [1902]), Michels (1962 [1911]), and Duverger (1954), and the 'innovators' are Panebianco (1988) and, especially, Kitschelt (1989*a*, 1994).
4. In 1969, the Socialist presidential candidate attracted less than 5% of the vote. In 1981, shortly after François Mitterrand's presidential victory, the PS won 37.5% of the vote and the majority of seats. Although their electoral audience shrank from the mid-1980s onwards, the Socialists remained in power almost uninterruptedly until 1993, when they fell below 20% of the vote. In 1995, the Socialists lost the presidency, but their candidate, Lionel Jospin, did better than expected, and after the 1997 legislative election, the PS won back power as the dominant component of a 'plural' left government which included the *Verts* and the PCF.
5. While there is an abundant literature on factional dynamics within specific parties, there has been little attempt to reflect in a systematic way about the consequences of factional formats. Exceptions include Sartori (1976); Panebianco (1988); Hanley (1986); Bergounioux and Grunberg (1992); Hine (1982).
6. Standard accounts of the PS do not totally ignore party-specific resources, but they usually identify such resources with leadership traits, notably Mitterrand's political astuteness and clairvoyant reading of the environment.

7. To be sure, this dichotomy does not cover the full range of possible configurations. Since almost all parties contain a certain amount of factionalism and, as long as parties contest elections, factions never fully replace territorial units, it downplays similarities across formats while ignoring critical differences within formats, such as those between ideology and patronage-centred factionalism and between centralized and decentralized territorial formats. Still, it does capture different institutional logics of party organization.

8. This was the case with the CFDT union confederation, whose most politicized unions affiliated informally to the PS through particular factions.

9. Party membership grew from about 70,000 in 1970 to 180,000 in 1978, peaked briefly at 213,000 in 1982, and declined to about 170,000 by the end of the decade (see Philippe and Hubscher 1991). By 1994, membership in the PS had dropped below the highly symbolic threshold of 100,000.

10. As a result of their monopoly over party and governmental position, the French press commonly referred to the factions' leaders as 'the elephants'.

11. Pierre Mauroy, Laurent Fabius, Michel Rocard, Henri Emmanuelli, Lionel Jospin, and François Hollande. In all but the last two instances, disgruntled factions denounced the outcome as the result of a coup.

12. In 1986, when the shift to proportional representation condemned the federation to a major downsizing of its parliamentary delegation, the Pas-de-Calais was the only department which rejected the quota-by-currents system nationally endorsed by the PS to allocate the expected losses among factions by asking its members to rank the various candidates. Confronted with a unique case of internal democracy, albeit one which was heavily shaped by the way in which the federal leadership had organized the referendum, local losers and national factions alike could find no grounds for complaining.

13. Even in federations where factions gained only a marginal foothold, the existence of a factional rivalry and dynamic at the national level provided innovative leaders with a leverage over old notables and helped breeding new life into territorial structures.

8

A Crisis of Institutionalization:
The Collapse of the UCD in Spain

Richard Gunther and Jonathan Hopkin

> I believe that we gave to the world an example of how to complete an
> important political transition. But we also gave a negative example of
> how a party in power can commit suicide.
>
> (Excerpt from an interview with a former UCD president)

Political parties are such a fundamental part of democratic political life that
they take on an appearance of stability and solidity which is rarely questioned. Therefore when a political party collapses, political scientists are usually taken by surprise; for instance, few predicted the recent disappearance of
the Italian Democrazia Cristiana and Partito Socialista Italiano. In this context, the remarkable collapse in 1982 of Spain's governing party, the Unión
de Centro Democrático (UCD), long regarded as an exception to the rule of
party stability, may provide some clues as to the causes of recent cases of
party crisis.

The catastrophic defeat of the UCD in the 1982 general election was primarily the result of a reaction by the electorate against the highly visible internal struggles and schisms which beset the party during the preceding two
years (see Gunther 1986a). In many respects, it represented a *voto de castigo*
('punishment vote') by an electorate which had become fed up with squabbles
that had even reached the point (in the attempted military coup on 23
February 1981) of threatening the survival of the new democratic regime
itself. In Western Europe, the only comparable historical precedent for this
kind of party collapse was that of the Liberal Party of Great Britain following the First World War—and by no means was its electoral decline as pre-
cipitous as that of the UCD in 1982.[1]

The purpose of this chapter is to explore the origins of these destructive
intra-party conflicts. Several different explanations of this phenomenon have
been set forth by scholars and journalists,[2] as well as by UCD leaders themselves in publications and in the course of extensive post-election interviews.[3]

The UCD was regarded as having been overburdened with major political and economic problems—such as terrorism and the economic crisis, not to mention the task of creating a new constitutional order. Organizational defects of varying kinds have been cited as major causes of party disunity. The ideological heterogeneity of the party was regarded by some as an inevitable source of conflict whenever important policy decisions had to be made. A highly critical press worked to magnify initial divisions among the UCD's leadership, and, in combination with harsh attacks mounted by rival parties, ultimately discredited the UCD in the eyes of the electorate. A shift to the right by the Catholic Church under Pope John Paul II and his new nuncio in Madrid has been cited as a cause of increased intra-party tensions over religious issues. Abandonment of the UCD by the business community transferred important resources to the rival Alianza Popular and appeared to present some centrist politicians with incentives to defect to the right. And ineffectual leadership of the UCD by the technocratic Leopoldo Calvo Sotelo (who was widely regarded as uninterested and unskilled in dealing with intra-party matters) permitted the process of decomposition to accelerate during the party's final year of existence.

All of these explanations are credible, and we will argue that they all may have contributed in varying degrees to the progressive disintegration of the UCD. But the most important of the explanatory factors to emerge from interviews with the principal protagonists in these struggles is that the UCD was insufficiently 'institutionalized' at the elite level.[4] The concept of 'institutionalization' is multifaceted, difficult to operationalize, and sometimes conducive to tautological argument. Certain aspects of the concept pertain to organizational structures, their degree of complexity and adaptability, and the extent of their development and penetration. In general terms, the organizational capabilities and extent of mass-level penetration of the UCD were not deficient. As we shall argue later in this chapter, the UCD had established highly effective campaign organizations throughout the country and an impressive infrastructural presence in the newly established municipal governments, and had attracted a base of dues-paying members which exceeded that of the PSOE.

The UCD's problems of low institutionalization were to be found, instead, among the highest-ranking party leaders in Madrid. Specifically, too few of them valued the UCD as a legitimate institution in the abstract, and too many of them were unwilling to compromise their conflictual programmatic objectives or sacrifice their factional or personal ambitions in the interest of the party as a collectivity. In other published studies, Gunther (1992; see also Gunther and Blough 1981; Gunther *et al.* 1986) has argued that a shared abstract commitment played a crucial role in the transition to democracy: a commitment to the ultimate objective of establishing a stable democratic regime, in combination with historical memories of the consequences of the absence of democratic stability (that is, the Civil War and the establishment of the authoritarian Franquist regime), helped to induce the regime-founding party leaders to interact with each other in a non-rancorous (often amiable) manner, to make concessions on historically divisive issues, and to establish consensual support for the new regime through the adoption of quasi-consociational procedures. In contrast, in-depth interviews with high-ranking UCD elites revealed a striking lack of commitment by several important leaders to the party as an institution. In short, the UCD never took on an institutional life of its own which transcended the loyalties and ambitions within some of its factions. That process of identification with the party as an abstract entity, however, was well under way by 1982, and clearly affected the behaviour of many other UCD leaders. And at the provincial level, it was quite far advanced. But among high-ranking party leaders in Madrid, it was not sufficiently developed to stabilize intra-party relations and forestall the disintegration which preceded the 1982 general election.

One critical facet of this lack of institutionalization was a lack of consensus concerning the model of party in accord with which the UCD should develop and govern itself. Three different models of party coexisted uneasily among important sectors of the party elite. Adolfo Suárez and Rafael Arias Salgado (the two principal authors of the party's official development strategy) were proponents of the 'catch-all' model. Certain other UCD leaders, however (and in particular, certain party barons and those of the so-called Plataforma Moderada), conceived of a party more along the lines of what Huneeus (1985, borrowing very loosely from Lijphart 1968*a*) called a 'consociational' party, or what we have referred to as the 'holding-company' model of political party (Gunther *et al.* 1986). A third party model—which shall be referred to as the 'factional model'—was not explicitly advanced by UCD elites in the course of in-depth interviews, but analysis of their behaviour and public statements and a more critical interpretation of some of their interview statements suggest that perceptions and calculations based upon the logic of this model may have substantially affected their behaviour at certain crucial periods. Differences over these models directly led the contending sets of elites into conflicts over electoral tactics, long-term development strategies, the nature of relations with secondary associations in Spanish society, and, most importantly, the internal governance of the party.

Unlike in fully institutionalized parties, there was no consensual understanding among UCD elites over decision-making procedures, norms of behaviour, and basic organizational structures. In the absence of common agreement over the basic nature of the party, it was not possible to adopt practices employed elsewhere to regulate conflict and stabilize intra-party relations. In other faction-ridden parties, such as the Japanese Liberal-Democratic Party (LDP) and the French Parti Socialiste (PS, see Chapter 7 above), explicit acknowledgement of internal divisions has made it possible to institutionalize factions and, consequently (as will be argued below), to lessen the level of tension among the various groups. Similarly, in 'institutionalized' parties with a unitary structure, either acknowledgement of the legitimate authority of the party's executive or the threat of disciplinary action can contribute to the satisfactory regulation or suppression of intra-party conflict (see Duverger 1954: 47–50). Instead, the UCD precariously straddled different and in some respects incompatible party models, and never did establish a consensus over organizational structures and behavioural norms.

In part, this was because elites of all factions found themselves progressively constrained by decisions they (and others) had made in the past. Decisions made at previous stages in the transition to democracy may have made sense in the context of these earlier periods, but with the passage of time and changes in the political environment, they ultimately proved to be sources of intra-party conflict. The ideological heterogeneity and factional diversity of the UCD may have been unavoidable in May 1977, but five years later it had become clear that factional conflicts were destroying the party.

It must also be borne in mind that Spanish party leaders following the death of Franco were faced simultaneously with several different tasks: they had to build party organizations, sometimes from the ground up; they had to formulate successful electoral strategies; and they were faced with the enormous responsibility of negotiating with traditionally hostile opponents over the founding of a new regime. As we shall see, in several respects the tasks of *party-building, vote maximization,* and *democratic consolidation* are incompatible with one another, such that steps taken in one of these spheres of activity had decidedly negative side effects in another.

The sharpest of these incompatibilities was between party-building and the tasks of constructing and consolidating the new democracy. The highly successful 'Spanish model' of democratization stressed moderation, inter-party concessions and compromise, and strict intra-party discipline. The decision-making procedures and behavioural norms associated with the so-called 'politics of consensus' helped to depolarize the political atmosphere during critical stages of the transition, to regulate satisfactorily or resolve historically divisive issues, and to secure a broad consensus in support of the new constitutional order from parties ranging from the post-Franquist Alianza Popular, on the right, to the Communist Party, on the left. But those same norms and practices created dissatisfaction within parties and a sense of alienation or betrayal on the part of their respective electoral clienteles. And they explicitly entailed an abandonment of provocative partisan rhetoric (which can be so useful in mobilizing partisan supporters and attracting a solid core of militants to the party's organization) and a rigid defence of the interests of particular social groups (which can be useful in establishing a stable core of supportive secondary associations and segments of the electorate). Seen from this perspective, the failure of the UCD can be regarded as the price that was paid for engineering the successful transition to, and consolidation of, a new Spanish democracy.

The tasks of party-building and winning elections are not entirely compatible either. As we shall argue, the institutionalization and consolidation of a party can be facilitated by the articulation of a clear and consistent ideology (which party militants usually find appealing), and by the forging of clear representational, if not institutional, bonds with specific interests and organized groups. Moreover, the loyalty of party activists may depend on consistency in adhering to core ideological principles. The converse of this proposition is even more powerful: party militants may feel betrayed and alienated if their ideological commitments are abandoned or cynically manipulated by party leaders. Similarly, the reliable and continuous defence of the interests of supportive clienteles may be their price for support over the long term. 'Catch-all' vote mobilization strategies (which have become overwhelmingly dominant within modern democracies), however, can be undermined by identification with a particular ideology or association with a specific set of interests or organized groups. Hence, in so far as the UCD's leaders embraced catch-all electoral strategies (which enabled them to win the first two democratic elections), they alienated important sectors of the party and the social groups which with they were allied.

All four of Spain's nationwide parties faced these same dilemmas, and they all experienced major crises during the period between 1978 and 1982 (Linz and Montero 2001). The other three parties, however, survived and flourished (in the cases of Alianza Popolar and the Socialist Party), or, at least, recovered over the long term (the Communist Party). A key difference between the UCD, on the one hand, and the PSOE and PCE, on the other, in their respective efforts to regulate or resolve internal conflicts was that the existence of an institutionalized party structure—in the case of the Socialist Party, dating back over one hundred years. The same could not be said of the UCD. Without the same reservoir of legitimate institutional authority, the UCD was unable to bear the burdens placed upon it.

The ideological differences present within the PSOE prior to the Extraordinary Congress of 1979 were at least as great as those dividing UCD leaders from one another: coexisting within the same party were Marxists, devoted to eliminating private ownership of the means of production, and social democrats, some of whom, following the Socialist victory of 1982, would adopt economic policies which were much more restrictive than those formulated by any UCD government. Similarly, other major parties have been as faction-ridden (the Japanese LDP and the Italian DC, for example) and ideologically heterogeneous (for instance, the British Conservative and Labour Parties) as was UCD, and yet they survived intact for long periods. But the ideological and organizational features of the UCD, in combination with its lack of institutionalization, led to a more devastating outcome.

Given the centrality of institutionalization in our analysis, and the complexities surrounding its application to empirical research, we begin with a definition and general discussion of this concept.

THE CONCEPT OF INSTITUTIONALIZATION

The classic formulations of the concept establish that institutionalization is the process by which an organization, from being a means to an end, becomes an end in itself. For Selznick (1957: 21–2), 'Organizations are technical instruments, designed as means to definite goals. They are judged on engineering premises; they are expendable. Institutions, whether conceived as groups or practices, may be partly engineered, but they also have a 'natural' dimension . . . They are less readily expendable.' Organizations are created for specific purposes and have value to the extent that they are efficient instruments for achieving those purposes. Institutions, on the other hand, have value in and of themselves, as Huntington (1968: 12) has maintained: 'Institutions are stable, valued, recurring patterns of behavior. . . . Institutionalization is the process by which organizations and procedures acquire value and stability.' To institutionalize, therefore, is 'to *infuse with value* beyond the technical requirements of the task in hand' (Selznick 1957: 17). The organization is valued both internally, by its members, and externally, by the community (or parts of it) in which it exists. The practical consequence of this is that such an organization is likely to survive situations of crisis because of the support of people and groups who are committed to it.

The institutionalization of a political party therefore implies that it begins to be valued in its own right, rather than as an instrument for the achievement of some specific political objective(s). For Huntington (1968: 410), the level of institutionalization of a party is reflected in 'the extent to which political activists and power-seekers identify with the party and the extent to which they simply view the party as a means to other ends'. Political institutions act as a brake on egotistical and individualistic behaviour, by articulating common interests and needs. It is these kinds of common interests which encourage political actors to sacrifice short-term private advantage for the sake of the long-term health of the institutionalized party.

In short, institutionalization involves stable, long-term commitments to a party as a 'legitimate institution in the abstract'. The more a party member identifies with the party, the less likely he or she is to withdraw from participation, even though the party may fail to provide concrete benefits of any kind. But institutionalization requires time, and all parties must survive an initial period of vulnerability to organizational shocks. The conceptual framework presented here, inspired particularly by Hirschman's (1970) work on 'exit, voice and loyalty', aims at providing the means to explain how a party can achieve the necessary stability of commitments to survive early threats and for the process of institutionalization to begin.

Political parties can begin to institutionalize when a situation of stable cooperation is created among the key actors and groups who control the most important resources for the organization's functioning (Panebianco 1988). These actors make their resources available in return for some kind of incentive provided by the party: purposive incentives in the form of policy decisions, solidary incentives emerging from the social interaction and recognition inherent in party membership, or selective incentives such as public office (Clark and Wilson 1961). When incentives are scarce, elites may withdraw from participation, threatening the party's functioning. Recognition of the value of cooperation—the awareness that these incentives are made available by collective action with the other party members—discourages exit from (and encourages loyalty to) the party, and contributes to the party's survival into maturity.

The maintenance of a given framework of cooperation is, in part, a function of its political and social context. The extent to which members are likely to tolerate the frustrations of remaining in a party whose performance dissatisfies them depends in part on the existence of other possibilities of collective action—'exit options' (Hirschman 1970: 80)—for the achievement of their objectives. For party members, exit options are generally other parties whose objectives are similar enough to offer some prospect of adequate incentives. If a dissatisfied participant has limited exit options, he/she is much more likely to bargain with the party than leave it. The chances of a party surviving its early vulnerability are therefore conditioned to some extent by the nature of the political environment in which it acts, and the degree to which it can acquire a 'monopoly position' in the political 'market', encouraging a sense of loyalty among party members (Hirschman 1970: 55–75; Panebianco 1988: 31).

So the availability of exit options to party members provides them with a degree of autonomy with regard to the organization, making disloyalty possible. The more autonomy elite members or subgroups have, the less dependent they are on the rest of the party for the achievement of their objectives, and the greater their bargaining power—in Hirschman's terms, the greater the effectiveness of 'voice'. Voice precedes exit, giving the organization a chance to rectify its poor performance (Hirschman 1970: 82–4). The form this bargaining or voice takes becomes fundamental in determining the maintenance of participation and the continued provision of resources by the most powerful party members. Key participants' willingness to have recourse to voice rather than exit is a function of the potential for real influence over the process of formulation of party objectives. Certainly this influence can take different forms, and Hirschman's conceptualization of voice has been criticized for its imprecision (Barry 1975). For the purposes of this study, it seems useful to distinguish between voice as formal organizational influence (that is, a recognized role in party decision-making), and a 'noisier' version of voice as internal protest against the party leadership. In any case, the success of voice and the extent to which exit can be postponed depend on the way in which the party's decision-making processes are structured.

Following Hirschman (1970: 74), it can be taken that, for each political party, there is an 'optimal mix' of exit and voice options, whereby the opportunities for voice will be sufficient to prevent the withdrawal of elites in the event of their being unhappy with the party's output. The extent to which that optimal mix is achieved is dependent on the organizational structures a party adopts, and the ability of those structures to adapt to reflect changes in the party's internal coherence and external environment. This is where the importance of party models comes in (as will be explained below).

Interacting with a party's organizational structure and the particular model upon which it is based is the nature of its relationship with its social base. The stability and commitment of an organization's social base is a fundamental element of institutionalization, and the 'selection of a social base' is of considerable importance (Selznick 1957: 104). For political parties, this involves, primarily, the establishment of a stable supply of electoral support sufficient to provide the means to distribute incentives to party members. This electoral support, at least before party identification begins to emerge, requires the distribution of some kind of concrete benefit—generally policy positions which defend the perceived interests of the electors. Any reasonably large party has a heterogeneous electorate, which naturally implies varied responses to the party's output. Voters with feasible alternative choices are potentially more unstable, and the extent to which a party chooses a strategy likely to satisfy exit-prone or captive electors is an important decision influencing its ability to institutionalize.

The choice a party makes depends on the extent to which it decides to maximize short-term electoral support from marginal voters, or consolidate the long-term support of its 'core constituency'. This corresponds to Kitschelt's (1989a: 48–61) distinction between two types of party strategy: the logic of electoral competition and the logic of constituency representation. Organizational consolidation is facilitated by emphasizing the latter, and can be undermined by an 'unprincipled' pursuit of the former, as some scholars have suggested (Blondel 1978). Such a strategy may be untenable, however, if ignoring exit-prone voters within a competitive context set by a majoritarian electoral law would threaten to marginalize the party from real parliamentary and governmental influence.

Party development strategies are further complicated by the existence of other organizations involved in the political process. Most major parties have some kind of relationship with interest groups or other socially important organizations in their 'hunting domain', such as trade unions, on the left, and employers' organizations or religious associations, on the right. In some cases, where the external organization controls resources indispensable to the party's functioning, this places the party in a subordinate role (Panebianco 1988: 51–6). The relationship of dependency thus created can undermine the party's institutionalization: not only does it imply a lack of institutional autonomy, but if the party fails to distribute sufficient benefits to sponsor organizations, they may withdraw key resources, threatening the party's survival.

The problem of external sponsors or secondary organizations presents parties with a dilemma. Such organizations can make an important contribution to 'solidifying' a party's core electorate, as well as providing other kinds of support. However, these relationships inevitably affect the party's internal bargaining process, as the external organization de facto becomes part of its dominant coalition, and its demands must be taken into account when party strategy is decided (Panebianco 1988: 55–6). This creates the potential for conflict among the demands of key party members, the external sponsor, and possibly also sectors of the electorate. A sponsor organization may have a jaundiced view of the real nature of the party's social base, or simply expect the party to provide it with selective benefits. As stated above, this may conflict with the party's desire to maximize votes. Channelling benefits to the core constituency may deny marginal voters the incentives that might have attracted them to the party; and organized groups falling within the core constituency may serve as 'negative reference groups' for marginal voters, repelling them from the party. Party institutionalization therefore requires that these relationships reinforce a stable bargaining process among the various participants, rather than introducing elements of instability.

These considerations suggest that a party's choice of organizational model can have important implications for its political output, and for the policy payoffs provided to party members in return for their participation. The party's relationship with external groups can determine which sectors of the electorate it appeals to, with direct consequences for policy and strategy. Similarly, the extent to which structured opportunities for voice are available can have a dramatic effect on the loyalty of party members (especially elites) with exit options. Party models become much more than abstract questions of organizational forms: they can determine the extent to which different groups of party members are willing to subordinate their individual interests to the collective authority of the organization.

The theoretical tools outlined here provide a framework through which to examine why the UCD failed to institutionalize. The rest of this study will use this framework to examine the party's development and propose an explanation for its collapse. In order to examine the origins of this collapse, and in order to gain some appreciation of the historical or dimension of the UCD's development, let us begin with a brief and highly selective survey of the origins of the UCD.

THE CREATION OF THE UCD: FACTIONS, INCOMPATIBILITIES,
AND THE TRANSITION TO DEMOCRACY

> The UCD completed its historical mission—a mission which deserves our
> respect. It is a party which achieved a political reform with hardly any
> conflict in the streets. It is a party which secured a constitution of con-
> sensus and compromise. It is a party which helped us to modernize. But
> [a centrist party] would make no sense now.
>
> (Excerpt from an interview with a former UCD minister)

It has often been argued that the UCD was strictly a party for the transition
to democracy. It may have been desirable for that transition to be led by a
moderate centrist party, some have claimed, but once the transition was completed the UCD had no role to perform and centrism became an outmoded
and artificial stance (see e.g. Martín Villa 1984: 74). In most regards, we reject
the 'historical determinism' inherent in such arguments and much of the
rationale which underlies its application to Spain in 1982. In some respects,
however, the problems of the UCD can only be understood as products of the
particular circumstances of that transition which surrounded the formation
of the party. Some of the characteristics of the UCD which ultimately proved
to be so troublesome—particularly the party's heterogeneity of ideology and
personnel—were consciously grafted onto the emerging party in order to
meet certain prerequisites for a successful political reform. Other undesirable
party attributes—such as the presence of factions among the party's highest-
level leaders—were unintended, but were perhaps unavoidable under the circumstances of Spanish politics during the critical formative period of 1976–7.

Following ratification of the Law for Political Reform in the December
1976 referendum, Adolfo Suárez was without any doubt the most popular
political leader in Spain.[5] In the immediate aftermath of that electoral victory,
he toyed with the idea of founding a political party under his personal leadership, a party more ideologically homogeneous and progressive than the
UCD which ultimately emerged in June 1977. Suárez was discouraged from
launching a partisan venture of his own at that time, however. He was perceived by some as too ambitious, and forming a party at that time could have
undermined the chances for success of the transition itself.[6] Thus it was necessary to delay.

During the following six months, a plethora of political parties emerged to
clog the centre of the political spectrum (see Gunther *et al.* 1986: 92–6; Duelo
1977). By the time Suárez was able to relaunch his partisan venture, in the late
spring of 1977, it was obvious that at least some of those groups, particularly
those which had banded together to form the Centro Democrático, would
have to be enlisted as coalition partners: the new electoral law would severely
punish partisan fragmentation, to the extent that the presence on the ballot of
too many contenders for the same political space could lead all of them to

electoral defeat. To corrupt Hirschman's terminology, this incentive to cooperate promoted 'entry' into a collective project, and made the UCD's creation possible.

But there were additional reasons why Suárez was induced to collaborate with other parties. His basic strategy for the transition to a new democratic regime dictated that the reform process be guided by a broad centrist party. By May 1977, such an enterprise could not ignore the coalition of groups which had joined forces to form the Centro Democrático. Implementation of Suárez's strategy for the transition was dependent upon collaboration with several of those 'moderate opposition' groups (Tusell 1985) for other reasons as well. Given his Franquist political origins and the fact that he came to office through procedures set down by General Franco himself—not through democratic processes—Suárez's legitimacy and his capacity to negotiate successfully with key political forces were limited by widespread mistrust and apprehension. In his view (as explained in a 1983 interview), an alliance with 'these *partiditos*, which were very small but which had international contacts, could contribute a certain international acceptance and a certain credibility' to his leadership of the transition.

At the same time, the Christian democratic, social democratic, and liberal parties which made up the Centro Democrático coalition could benefit from the kinds of assets that Suárez would offer. They were all very small and almost totally lacking in financial and organizational resources. None of these *taxi parties* (so called because the entire membership of such a party could ride in one single taxi) was even minimally capable of fielding candidates or undertaking an adequate election campaign in a significant number of provinces. Suárez, however, headed the government and could count on the support of many local officials. As the incumbent government leader, he had little difficulty in raising funds. And his enormous popularity among Spanish voters was an electoral asset of great importance.

For these reasons, Suárez (through his close collaborator Leopoldo Calvo Sotelo) negotiated with the Centro Democrático leaders the formation of the Unión de Centro Democrático on the very eve of the 1977 elections. By design, this party would be ideologically heterogeneous: its leaders included social democrats of the centre-left, Christian democrats of the centre-right and right, liberals advocating free-market economics and liberal social values, as well as others with more eclectic ideological predispositions. But the new coalition also included individuals whose origins could be found in the political institutions of the old regime, including the National Movement and its system of corporatist labour syndicates. Thus, in addition to programmatic or ideological differences which divided leaders of the UCD, the political origins of various party leaders constituted a cleavage within the party's elite, and hindered the distribution of solidary incentives, one of the most effective mechanisms for encouraging organizational loyalty.

Why were the so-called 'independents' infused into the new party's leadership? One reason is that their ties to extensive associational or personalistic networks throughout the country helped to offset the infrastructural deficiencies of the original Centro Democrático parties (Jáuregui and Soriano 1980). When asked why he chose to include them within the UCD coalition, one key participant in this process responded: 'We were aware of the connections which they had at the local level—at that time those who counted at the local level were mayors appointed under the former regime.' Given the party organizational vacuum within which the first democratic election in over four decades was conducted, these assets had an appreciable impact on the UCD's electoral fortunes. A more important reason for the inclusion of the 'independents' within the UCD's elite was set forth in a 1983 interview with a founder of the UCD: 'They were persons with government experience . . . [They were recruited because of] their efficacy, their capacity to govern, their capacity to take a seat in a ministerial department and begin to act, without having to pass through a period of apprenticeship.' Moreover, the inclusion of 'independents' within the UCD coalition helped to bridge the gap in Spanish society between collaborators and supporters of the Franquist regime, on the one hand, and its opponents, on the other. Although interview data suggest this was not the explicit intention of Suárez's circle, the inclusion within the governing party of persons with ties to the old regime helped to legitimize the new regime. In addition, for those voters with lingering sympathies towards the Franquist regime, as well as those fearful of abrupt political change in general, their inclusion provided a modicum of comforting continuity, thereby broadening the electoral appeal of the UCD.

The vague, eclectic ideological stance of the UCD was electorally useful. The eclecticism of the UCD's 'ideology' enabled it to appeal to different segments or political families within the politically informed strata of the Spanish electorate, at the same time that its vagueness fit well with the vague, inchoate political preferences of most voters. In ideological terms, as well as with respect to its electoral strategies, the UCD emerged from the first democratic election as the catch-all party *par excellence*. As will be seen later, this had important implications for the way the party was to develop.

The nature of UCD's origins hindered institutionalization in two fundamental ways. First, by aiming its appeal at a broad and varied sector of the Spanish electorate, the UCD failed to establish a core electoral constituency among which it could encourage a sentiment of collective identity linked to support for the party. Perhaps more importantly, by integrating a similarly broad spectrum of ideological positions and political background within the party elite, the UCD effectively denied itself the opportunity to institutionalize solidary commitment mechanisms among its most powerful members. The supposed incompatibility between ex-*franquistas* and former 'tolerated' opponents of the regime has, we feel, been exaggerated; there is little doubt, however, that this perceived divide restricted the distribution of solidary incentives.

Second, the political exchange which gave rise to the UCD was essentially favourable to Suárez and his 'independent' supporters. The dominant position of the leader, both in electoral and practical political terms, was critical for the creation of a highly centralized party, which would leave Suárez sufficient room for manœuvre to negotiate a constitutional settlement through inter-party consensus. The restrictions this placed on the exercise of 'voice' within the party were the source of subsequent controversies over party organization. The policy of consensus was therefore contentious, not only for its global political consequences, but also for the concentration of party power around the leadership that it implied.

THE COST OF CONSENSUS

The most important task facing the UCD government which took office in the aftermath of the 1977 election was to preside over a constituent process which would, it was hoped, lead to widespread support for a new democratic regime. The success of this constituent process must be regarded, in retrospect, as a considerable achievement. While past Spanish constitutions had lacked support from important sectors of Spanish society, the Constitution of 1978 was acceptable to all major political parties (except Basque nationalist parties) and was endorsed by huge majorities (except in the Basque Country) in the December referendum. It also dealt with traditionally explosive issues (such as the role of the monarchy, relations between Church and state, and dismantling of the hypercentralized state) in a manner regarded as satisfactory by all significant political forces (except for some Basque nationalist groups).

In addition to the constitutional consensus, the new regime benefited from the manner in which inter-party agreement was secured concerning other important pieces of legislation during this 'era of consensus' (1977–9). An example of this is the manner in which the economic crisis was addressed by the first UCD government. The broad, inter-party negotiations (which included the Communist Party) that culminated in the Pacts of Moncloa in 1977 not only helped to stabilize the labour market and establish a consensus in support of continued social and political reforms, but they also helped to co-opt once excluded opposition groups into the processes of governance of the new democratic regime. Similarly, negotiations in 1979 with the Basque Nationalist Party (PNV) and Convergència Democràtica de Catalunya (CDC) over Statutes of Autonomy for the Basque and Catalan regions represented important manifestations of the 'politics of consensus', and contributed greatly to acceptance of the regime by important sets of political actors. Indeed, a former UCD secretary general claimed that 'it is very difficult to conceive of a stable democracy in Spain without the integration into the political regime of Basque and Catalan nationalists'.

To a considerable degree, these successes can be attributed to compromises made by political leaders acting in accord with quasi-consociational rules of the game. Apart from certain structural features (including private negotiations among representatives of all politically significant groups), the most important characteristic of consociational politics is the explicit abandonment of majoritarian or winner-take-all principles of partisan interaction. Accordingly, the key participants in these successful negotiations defined their goals not as the maximization of the interests of their respective clienteles, but rather as the creation of a legitimate and stable regime within which their respective supporters' interests would merely be 'satisficed' (to use Herbert Simon's term).[7]

The behaviour of UCD representatives in these talks greatly facilitated their satisfactory outcome. But the stands taken by the party in the course of negotiations over the Constitution, passage of Autonomy Statutes for the Basque Country and Catalunya, the fiscal reform of 1977 and subsequent fiscal policies, as well as bills legalizing divorce and regulating educational institutions, activated the latent tensions among the party's component political families. These tensions took two forms. First, many elite members of UCD with backgrounds in the 'tolerated' opposition to Franco were disappointed that what they saw as their important contribution to UCD's success was not rewarded with dominant influence over the party's political line. While figures such as Miguel Herrero de Miñón and Óscar Alzaga took part in the formal constituent process, the bulk of the responsibility for negotiating constitutional agreements remained in the hands of Suárez's entourage (particularly Fernando Abril and Rafael Arias Salgado). The limits this imposed on the distribution of participatory opportunities to the ex-Centro Democrático elites were a source of discontent.

The effects of consensus on the availability of 'voice' as formal decision-making influence were far-reaching. Suárez, encouraged by his close adviser Arias Salgado, sought to counterbalance the UCD's heterogeneous parliamentary elite by developing the party's extra-parliamentary organization. The clear intention behind this strategy was to reinforce the leadership's control over the party by establishing a grass-roots membership united behind Suárez's charismatic image, and indifferent to the doctrinal conflicts between Christian democratic, liberal, and social democratic parliamentarians. The membership drive was combined with a formal organization which placed decision-making power firmly in the hands of the party president. This 'presidentialization' of the UCD, unsurprisingly, met with deep suspicion among the parliamentary elite, although the unifying purpose of a democratic constitution kept internal dissent to a minimum. In the long term this party model, with the restrictions it placed on the factional expression of voice, was a key factor in the UCD's collapse. By denying the most conservative factions the formal decision-making powers to which they aspired, the presidential model pushed them towards 'noisier' kinds of voice, which were very damaging to the party's pivotal governing role and to its electoral performance. In the short term, however, it was a necessary part of the politics of consensus, as it provided Suárez with sufficient freedom of manœuvre to reach agreement with opposition groups on key passages of the Constitution. In this sense, the UCD's policy-makers may be regarded as having sacrificed party unity in the interests of establishing a legitimate democratic regime. More generally, the intra-party struggles which were exacerbated by these compromises may be seen as negative side effects of consociational or quasi-consociational elite interactions.

A second and related source of internal tension was the practical impossibility for the UCD of mobilizing and representing a concrete electoral constituency while taking on the role of maintaining consensus between rival political forces. As one key protagonist in these processes explained in a 1981 interview, the party was obliged to practise 'the politics of state,' which prevailed over the interests of the party, and this implied an abandonment of representational ties' to important sectors of Spanish society, as well as the sacrifice of their particularistic demands as concessions necessary for securing inter-party compromise agreements. Several *críticos* within the liberal and, especially, the Christian democratic families of the UCD expressed also considerable anger (the 'noisy' form of voice) over some of these compromises, and regarded them as a 'betrayal' of the party's electorate. Singled out for particular attention were the fiscal reforms enacted in 1977, changes in the text of the divorce law in 1981, and the Ley de Autonomía Universitaria (LAU), which were regarded by one prominent *crítico* as part of a pattern of 'constantly making concessions to pressures from the PSOE.' This led many previously supportive groups (including the CEOE, Confederación Española de Organizaciones Empresariales, the country's 'peak' business organization) to abandon the UCD and shift their financial and political support to rival parties. In so far as conservative *críticos* regarded concessions on economic and Church-related issues as unnecessary, and preferred a different approach to the writing of basic constitutional documents—while Suárez and his collaborators argued that these were essential contributions to the establishment of a stable and legitimate new regime—it can be argued that the progressive disintegration of the governing party was one of the long-term costs of 'the politics of consensus' (see Chamorro 1981: 104–8).

From a different perspective, however, and somewhat paradoxically, the special requirements of the transition to democracy may have helped to hold the UCD together over the short term. Indeed, agreement over the achievement of democracy through *ruptura pactada* gave the UCD a unifying goal which made convergence in a unitary party possible in 1977. As described by a former UCD minister, the UCD was 'an omnibus party, within which there was perhaps one adhesive element—that was to undertake a political transition in a manner different from the *ruptura* model favored initially by the Socialist party, and from the *continuista* manner favored by the AP in 1977.' In order to secure this higher objective of regime transformation, party leaders were more willing to cooperate with one another than they would be after the transition had been completed. 'The tension inherent in the transition experiment', claimed a Suárez collaborator, 'made each one of the leaders of the various factions accept secondary positions. As long as they were collaborating on that principal objective—the transition—they were capable of overcoming their uneasiness and their particular personal and group interests.' Once that objective had been secured, however,

they began to position themselves in advance of the new phase. They sought to gain their shares of power and positions of advantage, so that they could hold and enjoy the fruits of power. [The UCD] was converted into a kind of underworld, within which everyone was engaging in tricks and deceit, one minister against another, one group against another. There was then a brazen struggle for power.

The rapid change in the political environment after 1979 made the institutionalization of the Suárez/Arias Salgado organizational order very difficult to achieve, as it had been justified in terms of the demands of inter-party consensus. The end of consensus provided the *críticos* with an opportunity to propose a redefinition of the UCD's organizational needs, forcing Suárez to concede them greater formal voice within the party.

The end of 'the politics of consensus' contributed to the disintegration of the UCD in another way as well. The *ad hoc, ad seriatim* process through which the Spanish state was decentralized—through a series of bilateral negotiations between UCD government officials and representatives of the various regions—was leading regional politicians to progressively raise the level of their demands and expectations, at least in part to avoid the impression that (compared to the Basque Country and Catalonia) there were being relegated to the status of 'second-class citizens'. Many UCD and PSOE leaders were beginning to fear that this process was getting out of control. Accordingly, leaders of the two parties reached a secret agreement that would slow the accelerating momentum of this decentralization process, beginning with the granting of autonomy to Galicia, followed by Andalucía. In the face of an intra-party rebellion by regionalists in Galicia, however, the PSOE abandoned that agreement, isolating the UCD as the only signficant proponent of the 'slow route' to regional autonomy for all regions except the Basque Country and Catalonia. This tactical shift by the PSOE had enormously damaging consequences for Suárez and the UCD. During the pre-referendum campaign in Andalucía, the PSOE attacked the UCD for its alleged opposition to the autonomist aspirations of Andalucía, and, more generally, for working to perpetuate the hyper-centralized Franquist state. The UCD's embarrassing defeat in the Andaluz autonomy referendum was followed by setbacks in the Basque and Catalan regional elections, in the course of which nationalist party candidates were quick to pick up on the PSOE's accusations of alleged UCD hostility to the concept of regional autonomy. As we will argue later, these election setbacks directly contributed to the downfall of Suárez.

While the destructive fight over Gallego and Andaluz autonomy cannot be regarded as a cost of the 'politics of consensus' (indeed, it was the result of the absence of inter-party consensus), it was somewhat similar in so far as an unpopular policy, set forth on the basis of concerns for the stability of the political system as a whole, inflicted substantial damage on the UCD as a partisan institution. In short, it was another cost of the transition to democracy.

THE MODEL OF THE PARTY: CATCH-ALL, FACTIONAL, OR HOLDING-COMPANY?

A major source of disruptive conflict within the UCD elite was the lack of consensus over the model of party according to which the UCD should develop. This lack of consensus undermined institutionalization in two ways. First of all, different models had different implications for the development of the party's ideology and social base, thus compounding basic doctrinal disagreements. Second, the failure to agree on an organizational model delegitimized the party's decision-making structures, undermining the constructive exercise of voice by discontented party minorities. The concept of 'party model' which we will set forth is multifaceted: conflicts which arose over the proper model for the UCD involved differences in emphasis among three of the most important functions of parties (electoral, representational, and secondary-elite recruitment), over determination of the clienteles which the UCD should serve, over electoral strategies and tactics, over the structure of party organization and its decision-making procedures, over the nature of the party's ties to secondary organizations, and over the distribution of patronage. Extensive elite interviews, as well as a survey of the literature on the collapse of the UCD, both indicate that different conceptions of the preferred party model were significant sources of internal conflict within the UCD.

The models we shall set forth are 'ideal-types'. Two of them (the 'catch-all' and 'factional' models) are derived from the existing comparative literature on political parties; but they are set forth and operationalized here with greater precision than is normally found in that literature. In addition, interviews with Spanish party leaders suggested that incompatibilities among these models could only be explored in light of 'ideal-type' conceptions which

are broader in scope than the initial formulations of these concepts.
Specifically, it became clear that the varying degrees of emphasis given to one
or the other of the basic functions of parties—electoral (as is given greatest
prominence in the catch-all model), the representation of interests (the
'holding-company' model), or the dispensing of patronage and recruitment of
secondary elites (the 'factional' model)—had important implications for several other features of the party. Thus, for example, our conception of the
'catch-all party' is one which deals not only with the nature of the electoral
clienteles of the party and the electoral strategies adopted to attract support
from those social groups; it also elaborates upon the implications of these
electoral objectives for the organizational characteristics of the party itself.
This model, therefore, is somewhat more elaborate than the original
Kirchheimer formulation.

At the time when the initial UCD coalition was formed, there was little concern for establishing consensus among the founding elites over a proper
model for the party. As one of the key decision-makers in this process
explained in a 1983 interview,

We had no model in mind; neither did we have time to organize ourselves in accord
with a model. It was necessary to improvise everything. The day I met for the first time
with the heads of those embryonic parties, I told them, 'In order to win the elections,
we need two things above all—electoral lists and money.'

He frankly admitted that the process of drawing up lists of UCD candidates
for the 1977 election 'was a complete improvisation'. The extreme haste with
which the UCD was created (due to the short period of time before the election was to be held) simply precluded full discussion and analysis of what
kind of party would eventually emerge. Thus, individual party leaders joined
the coalition without being fully aware of what kind of association they were
entering into.

Following the election victory of 1977, however, it was necessary to address
these issues. The first decision which had to be made was whether a single
political party would be created, or whether the UCD would continue to exist
as a coalition of parties. And if a single party were brought into existence,
would it have a unitary or a federal structure? The majority of the party's
leaders opted for creation of a unitary party, and demanded that the separate
organizational structures of the founding *partiditos* be abolished. Even
though this was successfully accomplished before the end of 1977, it was not
enthusiastically endorsed by all the relevant party leaders. Thus, the subsequent processes of developing the organizational structure, programmatic
commitments, and electoral strategies of the party were complicated by the
fact that the very act of founding a single party was itself controversial. This
absence of consensus impeded development of feelings of loyalty to the UCD
as an institution in the abstract, and as a result, as one UCD leader lamented,

'the passage of time has demonstrated that that political document had no validity, and inside of the UCD there continued to exist factions of Christian democrats, liberals, social democrats, etc.' Those individuals who had been presidents or secretaries general of the component parties exchanged their formal positions as leaders of independent organizations for informal roles as the new party's barons.

The next major phase in the party-building process began with creation of a Political Council and an interim executive committee in September 1977, and with the appointment of Rafael Arias Salgado as the party's first secretary general in May 1978. Both the executive committee and the Political Council were heterogeneous, and included representatives of the diverse 'political families' which had merged to form the UCD. Thus, the Political Council, in particular, was reflective of the lack of full consensus over the proper 'model' for the UCD. Arias Salgado and Suárez, however, were committed to development of the UCD along the lines of one particular party model—what Kirchheimer (1966) first called the 'catch-all' party, and what Kaste and Raschke (1977) have later called the *Volkspartei*.

The party model which we shall refer to as 'catch-all' is obviously very well known. It is that of an electoral organization whose overriding (or only) objective is the maximization of votes. Given this overriding purpose, catch-all parties in societies in which the distribution of public opinion (on a left–right continuum) is, and is believed to be, unimodal and centrist will strive to appear to be moderate in their policy preferences and modes of behaviour. If such parties draft formal ideological statements, they will tend to be vague, moderate, and eclectic. Lacking an explicit ideology, such parties may emphasize the attractive personal attributes of their most prominent candidates, and the nomination of party candidates in general will be largely determined by the electoral resources at their disposal, rather than by other criteria, such as years of experience in the party organization or, more generally, 'seniority' in politics. Finally, the party's campaigns will strive to attract votes from a wide variety of social groups, and will not emphasize ideological claims to represent the particularistic interests of any specific class or set of social groups.

In the case of the UCD, this implied several strategic and organizational features. As Spain's most popular political leader, by far, the leadership role of Suárez should be highlighted as much as possible. This was compatible with the 'presidential' structure of party organization favoured by Suárez, although such an organizational structure was not absolutely essential in terms of compliance with the 'catch-all' model. Secondly, the ideology of the party was vague and eclectic. This was not only a central feature of the catch-all model, but it was perhaps inevitable, given the varying ideological stands of the liberal, Christian democratic, social democratic, and 'independent' parties which merged to found the UCD (see UCD 1978: 149). A third implication of this model for the UCD was its lack of specific ties to secondary organizations, and its lesser concern for representing the particularistic interests of electoral clienteles than for advancing the interests of Spanish society as a whole during the course of the transition. Several of these features of the party came under attack from important UCD leaders.

The dominant position of Suárez was resented by many of the barons of the UCD—that is, the former leaders of the original founding parties. Conflict between Suárez and many of the barons was particularly intense between March 1979 (when the government formed by Suárez excluded most of the barons of the party for the first time) and September 1980 (when Suárez was forced to reincorporate many of them within a new government). To some extent, this animosity had its origins in the very process which had given birth to the party. Since the UCD had been created through the merger of formerly independent parties, the leaders of those groups regarded themselves as co-equal founders of the UCD, regardless of how small and politically insignificant their respective organizations had been. Given the barons' self-perceptions as political equals, they fought vigorously against Suárez's efforts to increase the power of the presidency of the party, and demanded a shift to a more collegial or collective form of party leadership.

The barons were only able to act against Suárez because the process of 'presidentialization' of UCD from 1978 had been slow to eradicate coalitional practices in party decision-making. Despite the formal creation of a unitary party, the informal 'baronial' structure of the party's leadership remained. The perpetuation of this 'baronial' structure was the product of several different factors. Most importantly, an informal pattern of proportional representation within the party's governing bodies quickly developed. 'In spite of the fact that party members were not ascribed to any faction', explained a former UCD minister in a 1983 interview, 'at the top of the party there existed a distribution by quotas, as if it were a corporation in which each stockholder had a seat on the governing board'. This proportionality in the distribution of government posts and positions on electoral lists can be seen in Table 8.1. UCD voters' self-identifications with the three relevant political families (as measured by survey data) are presented in the first column. In the second column is a breakdown of the party origins of UCD candidates for the Congress of Deputies. The third column breaks down the UCD delegation in the 1977 Congress of Deputies by party of origin, the fourth lists UCD Deputies in the 1979 Parliament by political family, and the fifth column displays similar data for the UCD executive committee in 1978. The remaining columns break down UCD governments between 1977 and 1980 along these lines. As can be seen in these data, only the absence of liberals from the May 1980 government violated the principle of proportionality to any significant degree.

Associated with this proportionality was a struggle over party and government posts, which will be analysed later in this chapter. As one former minister

TABLE 8.1. *Proportional representation of political families with UCD, 1977–1980 (%)*

Political families	UCD voters 1978	Candidates for the Congress 1977	Deputies 1977	Deputies 1979	Executive Committee 1978	Members of Council of Ministers			
						1977	1979	May 1980	Sept. 1980
Social democrats	16	6	12	17	14	11	26	22	23
Christian democrats	20	11	14	13	23	21	13	17	9*
Liberals	5	15	13	15	14	11	9	–	5
Popular Party	–	16	19	NA	17	5	9	13	14
Other/none	59	52	42	55	32	52	43	48	49

Sources: For UCD voters and candidates for Congress of Deputies in 1977, Linz *et al.* (1981: 477 and 464); for UCD deputies in 1977, EDC (1977: 30); for UCD deputies in 1979, Chamorro (1981: 79); for the UCD executive committee and the government ministers, Huneeus (1985: 219 and 205).

*In actual fact, 14% of the ministers in the Sept. 1980 Cabinet were Christian democrats; because of the inclusion of the Partido Popular as a category, the actual representation of Christian democrats and liberals within these bodies is greater than one would conclude on the basis of the above table.

bluntly described it, 'the UCD functioned as a federation of families which sought benefits for their members'. What had begun (perhaps inevitably) as an effort to give representation to each of the significant political families which joined forces to create the new party evolved into a jealous competition among factions over prestigious government positions. This struggle over the dispensation of patronage, in turn, heightened the awareness of factional differences and reinforced factional loyalties and animosities.

In light of the ideological incompatibilities among those factions, it was perhaps inevitable that the party so hastily formed on the eve of the 1977 election would to some extent employ factional or coalition methods of distributing decision-making power. This was reflected in the party's doctrinal development too. The heterogeneity of the party's ideological precepts was maintained at the first UCD congress in 1978. What emerged from that meeting was 'not a synthesis, but rather', as described by a party leader, 'an accumulation of ideologies' (see Gunther *et al.* 1986: 104–7). In the absence of an overriding ideological closeness between the UCD subgroups, taking the 'presidentialization' of the party to its logical conclusion would have been deeply divisive. In view of this, Suárez took a pragmatic approach, combining formal centralization of power around the presidency with informal bargaining with the natural barons of the party.

For their part, several of these barons appear to have favoured development of the UCD along the lines of what may be called a 'factional party'.[8] In sharp contrast with the unitary and presidential structure favoured by Suárez, they supported a collegial form of party leadership in which each of the factions would enjoy considerable autonomy and institutional recognition. 'Factional parties' (such as those in Japan and 'First Republic' Italy) place greater stress on the elite-recruitment function of political parties than on the purely electoral (vote-maximizing) objectives of the catch-all party. Accordingly, the advancement of secondary figures to positions of greater prominence should be under the control of the leadership of each respective faction, rather than under a central party office or single leader, and the criteria for promotion of secondary elites would place greater emphasis on service and loyalty to faction leaders than on the electoral appeal of the individual in question. Distribution of patronage and representation in the governing councils of the party, moreover, are to be determined in strict proportion to the strength of the various factions within the base of party militants (in the Italian case) or within the parliamentary group (as in the Japanese LDP). Finally, long-term control of the party apparatus by a single leader is rejected in favour of regular turnover in key leadership positions.

Considerable tension arose over inconsistencies between moves by Suárez and his collaborators to develop the UCD along the lines of a catch-all party with a presidential leadership structure, and demands by party barons that the rights and privileges of the various factions be respected. A former minister pointed out that, among the UCD elite, 'there were two conceptions of a party. One conception was that of a confederation of groups, a bit like the Italian DC—a confederation of organized factions. And then there were those who wanted to make a unitary party out of what was not a unitary party. There was a conflict between these two conceptions.'

A small minority of UCD elites interviewed (most of them within the conservative and predominantly Christian democratic Plataforma Moderada) advanced a third model. We have referred to this as a 'holding-company' model, while Huneeus (1985) calls it 'consociational'. It conceives of the party as an organized alliance among elites who represent distinctly different sectors of society. Policy decisions should be made through negotiations among these representative elites. In the case of the UCD, policy lines would be established through negotiations among representatives of the Christian democratic, liberal, social democratic, and 'independent' political families. An assumption basic to this conception of the party is that these 'political families' represent clearly distinguishable sectors of the society as a whole, and that those sectors acknowledge the representational role played by the relevant party elites.

This model is distinct in some respects from the factional model. While both the factional and holding-company models would favour collegial forms of decision-making and considerable factional autonomy from central party control, the holding-company model requires that the 'representative' elites be closely linked to secondary organizations in society, and not merely serve as leaders of intra-party factions, however institutionalized those factions may be. The holding-company model placed greater emphasis than the factional model on the selection and mobilization of a social base as a prerequisite for institutionalization. In actual practice, elements of both models may be found within a single party. Within the Italian Christian Democratic party, for example, were factions which were closely tied to organized interest groups, such as various groups within the Catholic Action organization, the Christian Democratic trade union (the CISL), the agricultural organization Coltivatori Diretti, and some business groups; other DC factions were more personalistic or organized in support of a particular ideological position (Belloni 1978: 79–84). The collapse of the DC in the mid-1990s after almost fifty years in government power suggests that this party model is not always successful in building institutional strength.

Differences between the holding-company and catch-all models, however, are sharper, and appear to have given rise to much more conflict within the UCD. In contrast with the catch-all party, the holding-company model places greater stress upon representation and defence of the interests of allied social groups than on mere electoral objectives. Ever since Michels (1961 [1911]), students of modern political parties have pointed to the tensions inherent in trying to maximize votes, on the one hand, and representing the interests of electoral clienteles, on the other. The holding-company model clearly emphasizes the representational function, while the catch-all model places greater stress upon the electoral. In addition, the holding-company model requires that the autonomy of the 'representative' elites (or faction leaders) be respected, while the catch-all party would subordinate the rights and privileges of secondary party elites if that were necessary to advance the electoral interests of the party. Finally, the two models differ with regard to the nature of relationships between the party and various secondary organizations. Proponents of the catch-all model would argue that it is electorally undesirable to closely link the party to specific interest groups, while the holding-company model is based upon the notion that such ties are not only central to the performance of the representation function, but are electorally useful as well. Instead of relying solely upon the party's own organized electoral efforts, its campaign activities would be augmented through mobilization of the allied secondary organizations. Among those groups most frequently mentioned as potential allies in this regard were professional, business. and agricultural associations, the *cuerpos* (corps) of public employees, and especially religious and quasi-religious groups, such as parent–teachers' organizations.

Proponents of the holding-company model attacked Suárez for policies which allegedly 'betrayed' the interests of the UCD's electoral clienteles, such as through enactment of the 1977 tax reform, legalization of divorce, and enactment of the statute regulating universities (the LAU). They also criticized the electoral and organizational development strategies of Suárez and Arias Salgado, particularly for not establishing close, if not institutionalized ties to organized social groups. Supporters of the Suárez/Arias Salgado strategy dismissed these criticisms: such ties 'were never rejected', claimed a former secretary general. 'Nobody refused to enter into contact with the real forces in society, or even to serve as a channel for their representation.' They believed, however, that explicit organizational links between the party and interest groups could reduce the attractiveness of the UCD by giving it a narrow, sectarian image. Formal ties to religious institutions, for example, could alienate non-religious voters from the UCD. Such overt links to particularistic interests, moreover, might unduly constrain its ability, as the governing party, to shift positions on various issues or to enter into compromises with other political groups. In this respect, a rigid defence of the interests of electoral clienteles could have impeded the compromises central to the 'politics of consensus', and perhaps undermined the prospects for a successful consolidation of the new democratic regime. If the UCD had been closely associated with big business organizations, to cite another example, the obligation to articulate or defend business interests could have substantially undermined the party's manœuvrability on economic issues. Again, Suárez's model of party development was in part inspired by the higher interest of the political stability of the new democratic regime. Moreover, he was also aware that it could put at risk the future of the party itself, by provoking electoral failure and condemning the party to opposition. As a former secretary general said, 'what we would not do is convert the UCD into the party which represents the most conservative interests of the Catholic Church, or the most reactionary sectors of the Spanish business class. With that representation one could not win elections.' Such a strategy, they believed, would not fit with the social characteristics of the new Spain, which had become much more secularized than it had been previously, and within which the Catholic Church itself did not favour close ties to any particular political party.

Although many of the conflicts which broke out among UCD leaders were rooted in incompatible preferences for party models, during Suárez's period of leadership they found their most common behavioural expression in simpler terms: proponents of both the factional and holding-company models joined forces to demand an increase in 'internal democracy' (that is, a shift towards a more collective form of party leadership) as a reaction against what they regarded as Suárez's efforts to create a personalist and internally authoritarian party. They argued that collective leadership or some kind of federal structure would make it possible to respect the real diversity which existed within the party elite, and would help to minimize internal conflict.[9]

An examination of survey data and case studies of comparable parties in other democracies gives some indication why proponents of differing models and organizational structures for the UCD were unwilling to make concessions to their opponents in the interest of reaching some common understanding. Simply put, arguments can be made against each of the alternatives which faced the UCD in the particular context of Spain after the 1979 election. The stalemate over the proper model of the party was a major obstacle to the generation of elite loyalties to the organization, and hence to its institutionalization.

The case against the 'holding-company' or 'consociational' model is the most clear-cut. Consociationalism requires a clear division of society into separate groups, as well as the institutionalization of those cleavages. In the case of contemporary Spain (with the exception of those regions with distinct languages and cultures), the requisite social divisions either did not exist or were substantially declining in salience. The Christian democrats who were the strongest proponents of this model conceived of their clientele as a sizeable bloc of religious believers who constituted a distinct political family. Our survey data reveal that, while most UCD voters were practising Catholics, this religious practice was by no means equivalent to a clear identification with the Christian democratic political family. These data show that 22 per cent of those respondents who claimed to have voted for the UCD in 1979 regarded themselves as 'very good Catholics', and another 33 per cent considered themselves to be 'practising Catholics'. But other survey data suggest that

Gunther and Hopkin

religiosity in Spain was not clearly reflected in a subcultural identification, nor was it institutionalized to the same degree as in other Western European countries, such as Italy (Huneeus 1985: 176–7). A poll conducted by DATA in 1978 showed that only 12 per cent of those who were 'very good Catholics' also regarded themselves as 'Christian democrats' (*democristianos*) (Linz *et al.* 1981: 296). Only 8 per cent of our 1979 survey respondents (and just 12 per cent of UCD voters) were members of a religious organization. Perhaps more importantly, from the standpoint of development of the party's electorate over the long term, the percentage of the Spanish electorate who regarded themselves as Christian Democrats was relatively small to begin with, and it declined substantially after 1977.

The degree of organization of and conscious identification with other social groups in Spain was even lower. Only 3 per cent of UCD voters (4 per cent of the electorate as a whole) were members of professional organizations or *colegios profesionales*—two of the clienteles targeted by the proponent of the 'holding-company' model quoted extensively above. Overall, by 1978 only 23 per cent of the Spanish electorate—and only 41 per cent of UCD voters—identified themselves with any of the three political families on which a UCD development strategy of that kind would be based. Moreover, the instability of these survey responses over time (as can be seen in Table 8.2) suggest that such identifications with political families were not deeply rooted.[10] Coupled with the low levels of organizational affiliation of the Spanish electorate in general, this clearly suggests that Spanish society was by no means compartmentalized (or, in Lijphart's [1968a] terms, 'pillarized'), as the consociational model requires.

TABLE 8.2. *Identification with political families by the Spanish electorate, 1975–1993 (%)*

Political families	1975	1977	1978	1982	1989	1993
Supporters of Franco regime	15	12	8	4	3	3
Falangists	4	2	—	1	—	—
Conservatives	—	4	6	10	8	9
Liberals	3	4	4	5	6	7
Christian democrats	14	16	8	7	4	4
Social democrats	6	13	11	10	6	5
Socialists	5	15	28	30	23	25
Communists	1	2	9	4	4	4
Revolutionaries	—	1	4	2	1	1
Others	2	1	3	4	—	10
None/don't know/ no answer	50	30	19	23	45	32

Sources: For 1975, 1977, and 1978, Linz *et al.* (1981: 14, 162, and 296); for 1982, 1989, and 1993, Montero (1994: 86).

Nor could the parties which merged to form the UCD claim legitimacy as valid spokesmen for the interests of the relevant sectors of society. Given the very short periods of time in which they existed prior to formation of the UCD (in most cases, only a few months) and their shallow or non-existent penetration into Spanish society, none of the faction leaders could expect deference to their leadership claims from their respective clienteles, which the consociational or holding-company model requires. A public opinion poll taken in March 1977, for example, indicated that less than 10 per cent of Spanish voters could name even one of the centrist parties which later merged to form the UCD, and that less than 20 per cent of the electorate could identify José María de Areilza, the most prominent of the Centro Democrático leaders (Huneeus 1985: 159). Even several years later, the most visible of those who claimed to speak on behalf of important sectors of Spanish society were largely unknown to the general public.[11] In light of these data, the holding-company or 'consociational' model seems ill-suited for contemporary Spain. And some of these data also undercut the potential viability of the factional model. Not only were the putative faction leaders largely invisible to the general public, but they also lacked elite-level recognition of their alleged leadership positions. Both in the sense of lacking geographical bases of support and in having no control over secondary elite recruitment, factions were totally uninstitutionalized. And leadership of even the most formally organized faction, the Plataforma Moderada, was shifting and unstable (as the struggle between Herrero de Miñón and Alzaga in late 1981 and early 1982 clearly demonstrated).

The broader question of whether a unitary/presidential versus more collective or factional forms of leadership would be most appropriate for a heterogeneous party like the UCD is not so clear-cut, and immediately leads to a dilemma for party-builders. On the one hand, adoption of a collegial decision-making structure within a party created through a process of fusion could artificially perpetuate divisions and factionalism within the organization. Indeed, the basic thrust of both federalism and the 'factional model' is to institutionalize permanently those initial divisions. Many of the most faction-ridden parties found in other democracies (such as the LDP and the Japan Socialist Party, the DC and the Italian Socialist Party, and the Israeli Labor Party) had been created through processes of fusion, followed by institutionalization of the initial divisions. On the other hand, forced unification of formerly independent parties can breed resentment and (depending upon the powers and perceived motivations of the party president) fear among other faction leaders.[12] This could induce them to join forces to topple or curtail the authority of the party leader (as the UCD barons did in the second half of 1980).

In some respects, fully factional or federal party structures may help to reduce tensions within heterogeneous parties: they can give faction leaders a sense of security, which was absent among leaders of the UCD. In a highly

unified party, the ability of a single individual to control the nomination of
party candidates heightens the stakes in the struggle for control over the party
apparatus. Faction leaders and political opponents have a powerful incentive
to topple the party leader or defect to rival parties, if they regard that course
of action as the only means of advancement, or if they believe that they are on
the verge of being purged from the parliamentary lists. Both factional and
federal party structures help to reduce such fears, and thereby stabilize intra-
party relations. As Fukui (1978: 61) describes the recruitment of secondary
elites in the Japanese LDP,

each faction develops a waiting list of candidates for appointment, based on seniority
in terms of both Diet membership and affiliation with the faction or its leader . . . So
long as this principle of rewarding seniority is consistently adhered to, every member
of a sufficiently large faction can expect eventually to rise to the top of the waiting list
and to be appointed to a desirable party or government post, which will in turn guarantee his success in future Diet elections. Because of this, the system looks eminently
fair and reasonable to most LDP politicians.

Similarly, the security of secondary elites is heightened in federal parties as a
result of the relative autonomy of each subunit in the nomination of candidates
for office. Not only was this sense of security lacking in the UCD, but the expul-
sion of the barons from the government following the 1979 election (not to
mention Suárez's drastic proposal for party reform in 1982, which will be discussed below) greatly undermined confidence in their own futures within the
party. This directly increased the stakes and the intensity of their conflict with
Suárez.

Unfortunately for party-building engineers, the converse of this proposition
is not necessarily true. There is no guarantee that adoption of a federal structure or increased factional autonomy can prevent the breakup of heterogeneous partisan groups. Even a cursory examination of the development of
the Spanish party system reveals that parties with a federal structure are no
more inherently stable than unitary parties. Alianza Popular, for example, had
a completely federal structure prior to 1978, with some of its component parties having the same degree of autonomy (from the Partido Unido de Alianza
Popular) as was advocated by some of the *críticos* within the UCD, and yet the
AP federation disintegrated in 1978 (García Guereta 2001). In the end, six of
the 'Magnificent Seven' who had founded the federation abandoned it.
Immediately thereafter, AP entered into the Coalición Democrática according
to a formula that did not involve fusion of the component parties into a unitary party. This coalition also soon broke down following the departure of the
top leaders of one of the allied 'parties'. Finally, the 1986 collapse of Coalición
Popular—a coalition with AP forged by many of the same individuals (such as
Alzaga and José Luis Álvarez) who had advocated such a structure for the
UCD—casts doubt upon the credibility of assertions that a looser organizational structure would have saved the UCD.[13] An examination of the history

of the UCD itself reveals further evidence which suggests that a federal structure would most likely have failed to prevent the disintegration of the party. The Catalan branch of the party, Centristes de Catalunya, was a federation linking the regional branch of the UCD to the Christian democratic Unió Democràtica de Catalunya and the liberal Unió del Centre de Catalunya. This experiment was even more short-lived than other regional branches of the UCD.

Suaristas rejected proposals for a more collegial or decentralized structure of party leadership on other grounds as well: they believed that more cumbersome decision-making procedures and a relaxation of party discipline (which would have resulted from such a change) might have undercut efforts to complete the transition successfully and consolidate the new democratic regime. One of the central elements of quasi-consociational conflict resolution procedures (such as those over the Constitution, the Basque and Catalan autonomy statutes, and the Pacts of Moncloa) is deference to party leaders who possess full authority to make binding agreements on behalf of their respective clienteles.[14] One can easily imagine how these crucial constituent negotiations might have been impeded if UCD representatives in those talks had been denied the authority to make binding decisions, necessitating instead full deliberations within the UCD Political Council. Studies of factional parties in other countries suggest that the institutionalization of factions may help to moderate intra-party tensions, but that it also undermines the decisiveness and rationality of decision-making (see Fukui 1978: 64–8; Belloni 1978: 74).

A unitary party structure which emphasizes the prominent leadership role of a single individual, however, poses a different kind of dilemma: it may preclude or hinder resolution of the inevitable problem of succession. This may be a particularly explosive issue if other party elites question the motives of their leader, and believe that he is interested only in creating a party solely for the purpose of advancing his own political fortunes. Several elite respondents expressed such concerns. They regarded the dominant position of Suárez as undemocratic, excessively personalistic, and disturbingly reminiscent of the former regime.

The prominent position of Suárez as linchpin of the UCD's electoral strategy was functional for the party as long as he remained popular with the electorate (which he was between 1977 and 1980). But leadership of a predominantly electoral catch-all party can be quite precarious. If the leadership claim of the party head is based only on his or her electoral appeal, then support for the party leader is dependent upon continued electoral success. And if an election or two is lost, the authority of the party leader may be called into question, as it was in light of what one former minister described as the UCD's gathering momentum of defeat, triggered first by UCD's embarrassment in the Andaluz autonomy referendum, followed by setbacks in the

Basque and Catalan regional elections and two by-elections. This greatly undermined support for Suárez both among party elites and the electorate. Public opinion poll data collected at regular intervals since 1976 do, indeed, reveal that the electoral appeal of Suárez had declined substantially by mid-1980. Three months after first taking office, the performance of Suárez was approved by 58 per cent of those polled. His popularity peaked, at 79 per cent, in April 1977, following the success of the Law for Political Reform and legalization of the Communist Party. During most of 1979 (when the UCD won a near-majority of the seats in the Congress of Deputies), Suárez's approval ratings ranged between 39 per cent and 45 per cent. But in 1980, in the aftermath of the Andaluz, Basque, and Catalan setbacks and parliamentary debate over a Socialist-sponsored *moción de censura* in the Congress, it dropped precipitously, reaching 24 per cent by July 1980. At the time of his resignation in January 1981 it stood at 26 per cent (with a disapproval rating of 59 per cent).[15]

Suárez's decline was a serious blow to efforts to consolidate UCD, however. The creation of the party around the unifying objective of democratic reform had been made possible by the dominant position Suárez enjoyed in the initial phase of the transition process. The logic of the presidential structures set in place in 1978 and the process of organizational penetration through which the party's provincial structure was established both presupposed the existence of a strong leadership figure capable of imposing compromise when agreement was not reached by negotiation. Given the fundamental differences over party models between factions, the weakening of the unitary model inherent in Suárez's decline was an enormous blow to the process of institutionalization. Policy disagreement, the loss of leadership authority, and lack of legitimacy of the party's organizational rules, combined to create fierce internal conflict.

INTERNAL CONFLICT AND EXTERNAL OPPORTUNITIES:
RATIONAL EXITS?

It was argued earlier that the political context in which the first democratic elections took place encouraged cooperation, rather than competition, among the various groups on the centre-right of the ideological spectrum. 'Entry' into the UCD became the most effective means for centre-right *taxiparties* to achieve parliamentary representation; 'exit' (in this case, staying out, rather than entering) implied political oblivion, as the Christian Democrats who stood alone at the 1977 elections discovered to their cost. The UCD was in a strong electoral position, while the alternative options, in particular the formally Marxist PSOE and the neo-Franquist AP, were unfeasible coalition partners for most of the UCD component groups.

After 1979, this situation began to change. The close cooperation between UCD and PSOE in 1977–8 came to an end, and Suárez came under heavy and electorally damaging attack from the Socialists. The UCD's rapid fall in popularity revealed the fragility of its electoral base, and the loss of the support of the non-identifying centre electors whose votes Suárez had obtained in the 1977–9 period (Maravall and Santamaría 1986). The UCD as an electoral machine no longer held the same attraction for ambitious faction leaders. At the same time, the behaviour of rival parties threatened UCD's position as the only valid option for the electorally crucial centre vote. The PSOE, after a period of crisis, removed all traces of Marxism from its ideology and began to appeal to centrist voters, and to elite members of the UCD associated with the social democratic faction. AP, after two crushing electoral defeats, made strenuous efforts to present itself as a moderate party of the centre-right, and sought contacts with UCD conservatives. This threatened the UCD's monopoly of the political centre which, as one interviewee explained, was a fundamental source of party cohesion: 'The UCD . . . occupied the center space, defined more by what it was not than by what it was.' For disillusioned UCD faction leaders, unhappy at the party's electoral prospects, the option of 'exit' became possible.

These changes were compounded by pressures from interest groups such as the bishops' conference, which was moving away from the political neutrality it had adopted at the beginning of the transition, and, in particular, the CEOE. In the course of the transition the increasingly representative and well-organized business organization acquired a political weight it had lacked at the time of UCD's foundation. By 1981 1,250,000 firms were affiliated, representing 80 per cent of employment in Spain, and business elites were an important part of the UCD's electorate: in 1979, 65 per cent of chief executives, and 58 per cent of CEOE association leaders voted for the party (Martínez 1993: 127). On this basis, the CEOE (somewhat extravagantly) presented itself as the voice of the UCD social base. But in spite of this, Suárez marked his distance from the CEOE leadership and representatives of the big banks, often refusing to receive them, or making them wait months for a meeting. In response to being denied 'voice' within the party structure, the business sector's criticisms took on a less constructive tone. The CEOE and especially the banks were not only unhappy with UCD's economic policy, but also with the fact that their significant financial contributions to the 1977 and 1979 election campaigns were not rewarded with any particularly favourable treatment from UCD governments. When the UCD no longer seemed capable of defeating the Socialists, conservative business interests began to push the UCD towards an alliance with Fraga's AP, to create a so-called *mayoría natural* ('natural majority'). The aim was to create a unified conservative party anchored to the right as a vehicle for the defence of business and financial interests. This implied the effective destruction of UCD as a flexible 'catch-all' party of the centre.

The intervention of business sectors in the internal affairs of UCD was encouraged by the conservative factions. The CEOE's belligerence provided an ideal opportunity for factional members to overcome their dependency on Suárez and create a new political subject. Key anti-Suárez dissidents supported the *mayoría natural* strategy; in particular, Herrero de Miñón—elected parliamentary spokesman against the leadership's instructions—and Alzaga were outspoken in their advocacy of a parliamentary pact with AP to anchor the UCD to the right (see Herrero de Miñón 1982). The emergence of these exit options had a particularly destabilizing effect on the UCD as a result of the ultimately destructive intentions of some faction leaders. Rather than using the implicit threat of exit as a bargaining counter, some UCD elite members seemed determined to make use of their exit options as part of a broader political strategy to polarize the Spanish party system.

These considerations led several conservative UCD leaders to adopt unreasonably intransigent positions in conflicts over the government's policies regarding such matters as secondary and university education, as well as to criticize harshly the government's allegedly left-wing economic policy; they were part of their efforts to push the party into a conservative alliance backed by the Church and business interests. Moreover such behaviour was not limited to the right of UCD; the position adopted by Francisco Fernández Ordóñez on divorce was a provocation to the more Catholic sectors of UCD, and may have amounted to retaliation for the hard-line attitude of the right over Catholic private education. But it was also an expression of the increasing autonomy of the Social Democrat faction, due to Fernández Ordóñez's well-known contacts with the PSOE leadership. The fact that the former had the exit option of passing over to the now more or less social democratic PSOE, leaving UCD with an even narrower majority, afforded him significant 'blackmail potential' in his dealings with the party leadership.

This view of ideological conflict as a pretext for overhauling the party system is supported by examination of the circumstances surrounding the defections from UCD of a number of key elite actors in the period 1981–2. The first to depart with a portion of an ideological faction in tow was Fernández Ordóñez, in November 1981. He founded a social democratic Partido de Acción Democrática (PAD), arguing that the UCD had shifted too far to the right. But this assertion was firmly rebutted by another prominent social democrat (one of many who remained loyal to the UCD), who pointed out in a 1983 interview that, 'analyzing decision by decision, analyzing the economic policies of the government, there was no shift to the right. And proof of that is that today the economic policy of the PSOE government is a policy of basic continuity with that undertaken by UCD governments.' Nor can one argue convincingly that the social policies of the UCD shifted to the right prior to the departure of Fernández Ordóñez: he had, after all, just won his battle in favour of a more liberal divorce law. It is true that the constant interferences from right-wing interest groups suggest that the Social Democrats' future within UCD was by no means assured. However, the timing of his departure lends credibility to accusations by other party leaders that he used his stands on the divorce law, the Estatuto de Centros Docentes, and the fiscal reform of 1977 at least in part as a means of gaining entry into the PSOE on favourable terms (including his appointment as Minister of Foreign Affairs in the mid-1980s). Overall, the defection of the PAD can be explained largely in terms of the appearance of an attractive exit option—the Socialist leadership had been encouraging Fernández Ordóñez to leave the UCD ever since it was created.

The next major defections ostensibly justified on ideological grounds were from the right, specifically, the departure of the UCD's former floor leader, Herrero de Miñón, to the ranks of Alianza Popular, and the subsequent (20 July 1982) formation of a conservative Christian democratic party, the Partido Demócrata Popular, under the leadership of Alzaga. The most frequent and persuasive interpretation of the evolution of the UCD after November 1981 is that the departure of Fernández Ordóñez and his sixteen supporters in the Congress and Senate disrupted the precarious balance among the UCD's political families, and shifted the party's centre of gravity somewhat to the Christian democratic right. This did not affect the composition of the government formed shortly thereafter (largely because key *críticos* refused government posts): Calvo Sotelo's second government remained broadly representative of all political families, and included a number of social democrats. But it did substantially affect control of the party apparatus itself. Social democrat Rafael Calvo Ortega was replaced as secretary general by the Christian democrat Íñigo Cavero, and the conservative Calvo Sotelo replaced Agustín Rodríguez Sahagún as party president. Cavero's party secretariat was dominated by a coalition of Christian democrats and liberals. This change in control of the party apparatus was decisive in Suárez's ultimate decision to quit the UCD, since, in his view, it shifted the party to the right and violated a personal understanding with his successor as prime minister, Calvo Sotelo. None the less, this ideological reorientation of the party was insufficient to induce either Herrero de Miñón or Alzaga to remain in the party. Thus, highly visible leaders of the party's right wing bolted from the UCD at the same time as the party was shifting perceptibly to the right. Again, this constitutes prima-facie support for claims by other UCD leaders that these defections were motivated less by ideological considerations than by considerations of personal interest (specifically, expectations that chances for career advancement were better in other parties than within the crumbling remains of the UCD).[16] However, in contrast to Fernández Ordóñez's group, these defectors were markedly unsuccessful in gaining access to political power outside UCD, and ultimately became junior coalition partners of Fraga's AP—hardly an improvement on the political influence they enjoyed in UCD. Again, this departure can be explained in terms of the appearance of an exit option. Fraga's overtures to this group, and the support offered by external allies in the episcopal conference and business sectors, created an option for exit which, while not as attractive as Fernández Ordóñez's transfer to the PSOE, did create an alternative to political life in the UCD.

The final and most disastrous defection was that of Suárez himself. On 29 July 1982 he announced that he was quitting the UCD, and creating a populist, centre-left Centro Democrático y Social (CDS). Ideological justifications were set forth by several respondents who had been early defectors to the CDS. The conservative image and policy preferences of Calvo Sotelo were regarded by them as representing an abandonment of the original centrist stance of the UCD. In addition, *suaristas* argued that a shift to the right would be electorally unsound: Manuel Fraga had firmly established his position as the leading Spanish conservative, and efforts to attract votes from the right would be fruitless. Finally, *suaristas* argued that a serious mistake had been made at the birth of the UCD by including within its parliamentary elite individuals who were insufficiently progressive: many of them would fit better within Alianza Popular, they believed, and their presence within the UCD had given rise to intra-party conflict and instability.

These arguments standing alone, however, are not entirely persuasive. Several of Suárez's most bitter enemies on the right had already left the UCD: Herrero de Miñón had crossed the aisles to join the AP delegation in the Congress well in advance of Suárez's defection, and Alzaga and several of his Plataforma Moderada followers announced formation of their own conservative Christian democratic party nine days prior to Suárez's announcement. In addition, these ideological justifications are inconsistent with Suárez's own proposal that Christian democrat Landelino Lavilla stand as the UCD's candidate for President of Government in the next elections. A fuller and more adequate interpretation of this final and most devastating schism suggests different reasons for Suárez's departure.

On 4 July 1982, Suárez, Lavilla, and Calvo Sotelo entered into private negotiations over the future of the party. In those talks, Suárez proposed that Calvo Sotelo step aside as leader of the party and the government. Calvo Sotelo would be replaced as President of the Government by Lavilla, according to these plans, while Suárez himself would regain control of the party apparatus. The baronial nature of the party's leadership would be eradicated, and a more electorally appealing progressive-centrist stance would be reflected in the nomination of UCD candidates for public office. Authority to nominate candidates, moreover, would be much more decisively concentrated in the hands of the party president, in part, so that a future UCD delegation in the Cortes would be more unified and dependable. As described by a participant in these talks, the basic thrust of Suárez's proposal was to 'reconstruct the party from its very roots, appealing to the base of the party, and eliminating the existing leadership—putting them in the refrigerator for a while'. The keystone of this strategy was that Suárez's control over the nomination of candidates would be greatly strengthened: 'the electoral lists will be drawn up by Adolfo Suárez', explained a Suárez collaborator; he 'will create more homogeneous lists of the progressive center'.

These proposals were clearly incompatible with conceptions of the UCD held by other leaders (not to mention their respective career ambitions). They clashed directly with the ideological heterogeneity of the party's elite, and they were inconsistent with the collegial leadership practices preferred by the party's barons. Suárez's plan also revived suspicions and hostility regarding what some believed to be his intention to convert the UCD into personal political machine. As one of the participants in these negotiations claimed,

Suárez wanted us to hand over the party to him, and hand it over to a dictatorial regime—with the collegial organs of the party, the executive, the Political Council all dissolved; that we would give full powers to him; that he would personally have powers that the statutes give to the executive and the Political Council; and that he could do, and undo, without being accountable to anyone until the following elections.

In the aftermath of these negotiations, Calvo Sotelo announced his intention to not seek re-election as President of the Government, relinquishing that honour in favour of Lavilla. But that was the only segment of Suárez's plan which was realized. His demand for control of the party apparatus was firmly rejected. Believing that the UCD was inherently flawed at the top level of its organization and that only drastic surgery would ever make it possible for the UCD to develop as a institution with a stable delegation in the Cortes, Suárez quit the party which he had founded and led during these eventful years. This event, occurring less than three months before the next parliamentary election, was a serious blow to the party's chances of survival. As Figure 8.1 reveals, public support for the UCD declined sharply in direct response to these elite-level policy disputes and defections, particularly that of Suárez himself.[17] The failure of Suárez's new invention to make a significant impact on the Spanish political map makes his departure the least coherent of all. Although Suárez did not have many options to exit from UCD, he still chose not to attempt to reform UCD from within by exercising 'voice'. Moreover, even in the other cases of defection where coherent exit options did exist, it is difficult to interpret this behaviour as a rational pursuit of political influence: only in the case of Fernández Ordóñez did defection from UCD bring real political dividends.

So ideological heterogeneity and the changes in the party's political environment which opened up exit options to discontented participants do not provide a complete explanation of the party's collapse. Problems in the distribution of solidary incentives and incentives of ideological identity cannot explain the party's calamitous collapse in 1982, since there is little evidence to

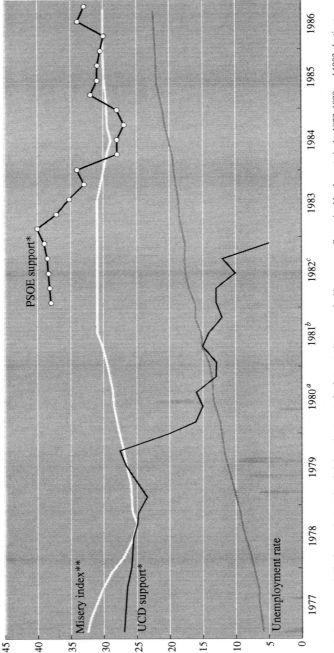

FIG. 8.1. *Intra-Party clashes, economic conditions, and support for the UCD and POES as incumbent parties, 1977–1986*

* *Party support* is % of respondents stating their intention to vote for that party, interspersed with votes actually received by the party in the 1977, 1979, and 1982 elections (as % of total electoral census). The source is CIS (1986).
** *Misery index* is the sum of the unemployment rate and the rate of inflation in consumer prices.
a In 1980, Andaluz referendum; Vote of censure; meeting at the 'Casa de la Pradera'; pre-Congress struggles.
b In 1981, Suárez resigns; Divorce Bill; 'Plataforma Moderada'; Fernández Ordóñez quits.
c In 1982, Herrero quits, Suárez quits.

suggest that ideological divisions could not have been overcome as they have been in other similar cases. The rapid change in the political environment after 1979, which brought UCD factions the option of exit, can take us closer to a realistic interpretation of the party's collapse. However such an interpretation is weakened by the 'irrational' nature of the exit of UCD leaders from the party. The subsequent development of the Spanish party system has shown that, in nearly all cases, defection from UCD did not bring obvious benefits. What must be explained is why UCD politicians were so quick to choose exit from the party, instead of seeking to reform it from within. This outcome is paradoxical, since the exit option was largely unbeneficial to those who elected to exercise it. In our view, the key to explaining this paradox lies instead in the divergences between the different models of party advocated by the various UCD factions, and the obstacles this presented to the party's institutionalization.

CONCLUSION

Several observers, even some protagonists in this drama, have claimed that 'the UCD never existed as a political party'. In some respects, this is simply not true. By the time of the 1979 general election the party had established branches throughout the country which were fully adequate for conducting large-scale election campaigns and other activities designed to create a stable base of support. By 1981 it had attracted a nominal membership base of 144,000 affiliates, placing it ahead of the PSOE and second only to the PCE in terms of affiliation (Montero 1981: 44). While UCD militants at the grassroots level were, on the whole, less active participants than their Socialist or Communist counterparts, they were also less troublesome. And interviews conducted in 1983 with former provincial leaders indicated that the overwhelming majority of them remained loyal to the party until the bitter end. Even more impressively, the UCD had deeply penetrated into the interstices of local politics by electing nearly 30,000 municipal councilors and 3,000 mayors. It is reasonable to argue, however, that among many prominent leaders of the party at the national level the UCD did not exist as a legitimate institution in its own right. Indeed, it is this lack of legitimacy of the party as an institution which emerges from elite interviews as the most fundamental cause of the breakdown of the UCD. The party simply did not survive long enough to develop the institutional authority which might have enabled it to survive the intra-party struggles described above. In the words of a former secretary general, there was 'insufficient time for the party to have jelled as a solid organization'.

This chapter has attempted to explain the UCD's failure to survive and undergo a process of institutionalization. The dispute over what kind of party

UCD should be impeded any serious attempt to build links with the electorate, and deprived the party of the commitment of a secure social base. But this cannot simply be regarded as short-sightedness on the part of the UCD elite; senior party leaders, most notably Suárez himself, deliberately postponed the process of building social commitments in order to maintain UCD's room for manœuvre in the inter-party bargaining characteristic of the Spanish transition to democracy. From this point of view, the UCD's institutional weakness was part of the price paid to preserve democracy.

But the UCD's failure to process internal disagreement through recognized channels for conflict resolution prevented it from overcoming this weakness. The lack of consensus over the model of party made each policy disagreement potentially disastrous, as competing factions used ideological differences as part of a wider conflict over party organization. Suárez's initially dominant position, and the centralizing logic encouraged by the electoral law, suggested a unitary party based on strong leadership, and this formulation was clearly the source of UCD's early successes. However, the unwillingness of the *taxiparties* and their leaders to defer to Suárez's authority threatened party cohesion. With Suárez's electoral and political decline after 1979, the unitary party rested on increasingly fragile foundations.

But the alternative party models proposed by the barons, and in particular by the conservative *críticos*, were deeply flawed, and implied possibly unsustainable electoral and political costs were the party to adopt them. To destroy an effective political machine such as UCD, in favour of an organization representative of the narrow interests of the Catholic heartlands and the financial elite, was political suicide and key UCD leaders—in particular those closest to Suárez—were well aware of this. But the pressures from both inside and outside the party to move in this direction became irresistible. This stalemate made coexistence increasingly difficult, and hindered the functioning of the party's organizational structures and the exercise of 'voice' by dissatisfied participants. The differences over party models were therefore both a source of conflict and an obstacle to their resolution. The emergence of exit options, as UCD's political rivals enticed key elite members in defecting, set in motion a process of disintegration which made an effective electoral campaign impossible.

The key conclusion to be drawn from this analysis is that institutionalization requires the existence of internal consensus over organizational rules and structures as much as over policies. Decision-making processes must be recognized as legitimate by elites in political organizations if the damaging outcome of exit is to be avoided. There is little parties can do to prevent the emergence of exit options in the form of alternative political formations or interest groups. If exit is to be avoided, elites must have the option of voice through organizational rules accepted by all participants. Voice provides a safety valve which cushions parties from the worst consequences of internal unrest. However, voice may require taking on board unrealistic or unreasonable proposals from discontented party elites. The UCD was the victim of a disjunction between the party's internal cohesion and the strategies required for its political effectiveness, which left the party leadership with a choice between bowing to unreasonable demands and risking the explosion of intense internal conflict.

NOTES

1. The Liberal Party's share of the vote declined from 45% in the last pre-war election, in 1910, to 30% in 1918, to 18% in 1924.
2. See Huneeus (1985); Chamorro (1981); De Esteban and López Guerra (1982); Muñoz Alonso (1984); Santamaría (1984); Wert (1984); Figuero (1981); Oneto (1981); Navalón and Guerrero (1987); Jáuregui (1987).
3. Over twenty-eight hours of in-depth interviews with eight of the highest ranking UCD leaders and a handful of former provincial-level officials were conducted by Richard Gunther between June 1983 and May 1984, and fifteen hours of interviews were conducted by Jonathan Hopkin in 1992/3. These interviews included representatives of all of the party's major 'political families', but slightly over-represented the Christian democratic and *suarista* factions. Published accounts by political figures include Meliá (1981); Martín Villa (1984); Ysart (1984); Attard (1983); Calvo-Sotelo (1990); Herrero de Miñón (1993).
4. This chapter is a greatly abbreviated version of our separate analyses of the collapse of the UCD published elsewhere; see Gunther (1986*b*); Hopkin (1999).
5. At that time, 74% of the Spanish electorate approved of the performance of Adolfo Suárez. See *Cambio 16* (8 June 1981), 27.
6. Ysart (1984: 154) corroborates this interpretation, which had been set forth in a confidential 'deep background' segment of an interview with a prominent former UCD leader. (A pledge of confidentiality to the respondent precludes publication of additional details.)
7. For a more extensive analysis of the 'politics of consensus', see Gunther (1992).
8. This party model is derived from descriptions of the LDP set forth by Fukui (1978), and of the DC by Belloni (1978) and Sartori (1976: ch. 4).
9. This rationale was frequently encountered in elite interviews, and is set forth in Martín Villa (1984: 74).
10. Ideally, panel data would be used to test this proposition. In the absence of panel data, however, cross-sectional survey data will have to suffice. Given the huge size and the high reliability of these survey data, these prima-facie conclusions appear to rest on safe ground.
11. In 1983, a Centro de Investigaciones Sociológicas (CIS) poll indicated that about 60% of the Spanish electorate knew so little about Óscar Alzaga (who had defected from the UCD a year earlier to form his own party, the Christian democratic Partido Demócrata Popular) that they could not even evaluate him using a 'feeling thermometer'. In contrast, less than 10% of respondents had difficulty in evaluating the major party leaders, such as Suárez, González, Fraga, or Carrillo.

12. Ysart (1984: 153) argues that this was, indeed, the case. He claims that the clumsy manner in which Leopoldo Calvo Sotelo presented the founding document of the UCD coalition to the other party leaders made them regard it 'not as a pact, but rather as an imposition. They never ceased to feel humiliated, and day after day extracted a price for their submission.'

13. For examples of extreme tensions between the PDP and the AP, even at the time of founding the coalition, see Muñoz Alonso (1984: 38), and Wert (1982: 68–9); a thorough anlysis in García Guereta (2001: ch. 2). The ultimate breakup of this coalition had drastic consequences for leaders of both of the relevant parties: both Manuel Fraga and Óscar Alzaga were forced into early retirement as a result of this destructive conflict.

14. See Lijphart (1968*a*: 139–77); Gunther and Blough (1981); Gunther (1992).

15. While these data offer convincing evidence that approval of Suárez as President of the Government had eroded appreciably, they should not be construed as evidence that, by January 1981, the UCD had ceased to be a viable electoral vehicle. A poll conducted by the magazine *Cambio 16* in Jan. 1981 revealed that 28% of voters were still willing to vote for it if elections were held at that time (which compares with 34% for the PSOE and only 7% for Coalición Democrática).

16. Claims were made in the course of interviews with former UCD leaders that Herrero de Miñón quit the party not on ideological grounds, but, instead, because he was about to be dismissed by President Calvo Sotelo as the party's floor leader in the Congress of Deputies.

17. Between Nov. 1980 and July 1982, the percentage of respondents in CIS polls stating their intentions to support the UCD had remained quite constant, fluctuating within a narrow band between 12 and 15%. But following the fragmentation of the UCD in July 1982, support fell by just over half: from 12% in July, to 7% in Sept., to 5% in Oct. (Maravall and Santamaría 1986: 107; CIS 1984).

Part III

Revisiting Party Linkages and
Attitudes toward Parties

9

Party Government, Patronage, and Party Decline in Western Europe

Jean Blondel

The 1990s will be remembered as years during which liberal democracy emerged triumphant; they may also be remembered as years during which serious questions were raised about the future of the main instruments of liberal democracy, the political parties, in many, if not in all Western European countries. Several older parties suffered serious electoral setbacks; a few even disappeared. Yet there were few signs that a challenge was seriously coming from new phoenixes: on the whole, the protest parties on the right and centre and the Greens on the centre and left have obtained a place, but one which has remained modest. The old guard may be shaken, but not because it is being replaced by other, more dynamic elements. Almost nowhere is there a realignment: what is occurring is an erosion of the weight of the traditional parties and of some of the grip of these parties on society.

The phenomenon of the decline of parties in Western Europe has long exercised observers. Indeed, parties have been said to be in decline almost from the moment they became established. However, since the 1970s at least, empirical analysis seemed to provide evidence for the view that slow, but long-term changes were affecting parties and party systems. These changes were leading, not merely to the emergence of new parties, but also to increased abstention and to greater 'independence' of the electorate vis-à-vis the established parties, as well as to a drop, indeed in some cases a substantial drop, in party membership. Although the incidence of these developments is not uniform across Western Europe, some movements along these lines have taken place almost everywhere: they have naturally been linked to the societal changes of the second half of the twentieth century which have eroded the traditional political cleavages on which Western European parties and party systems had been built, and in particular the class cleavage and the religious cleavage.[1]

As these long-term changes were slowly reducing the 'weight' of Western European parties, a further shock came from a different quarter, a shock which was orchestrated by the media. Many established parties started to be under attack because of dubious practices in which they were said—and at times found—to be engaged, practices ranging from the distribution of favours to outright corruption. The Italian party system was to be the most notorious sufferer: several of its key components collapsed under accusations of illegal behaviour. But cases of 'sleaze' and of 'shady' deals were also substantiated elsewhere in Western Europe to a greater or lesser extent, notably in Spain, Belgium, France, and even Britain.[2]

If, as electoral results of the late 1980s and of the 1990s seem to suggest for a number of countries, the occurrence (and uncovering) of illegal or semi-legal practices contributes, alongside long-term societal changes, to the decline in support for established parties in Western Europe, two questions need to be answered. First, why should such practices have taken place among many parties of the area in the last decades of the twentieth century? Are we really witnessing a new phenomenon or is it simply that greater 'transparency' has been achieved in Western European politics? Greater transparency is not the only explanatory factor: while there have always been 'shady deals' involving parties, there is also evidence that they have become more widespread. In Italy, for instance, corruption has been shown to have increased during the 1970s and the 1980s (Della Porta and Vannucci 1995); there also appears to have been a greater incidence of 'sleaze' in Spain, France, or Britain during the same period, the much larger costs needed to cover party expenditure, especially in the context of election campaigns, often being given as a reason for the inevitability of these deals. Thus the recent increase in these practices needs to be accounted for. A second question arises, however. Since there are substantial variations across parties and across countries in the incidence of shady deals, what can be the cause of these variations? 'Sleaze' seems to have taken place on a substantial scale in Belgium, Spain, France, or Britain, but not in Scandinavia or the Netherlands. And lack of transparency surely cannot be invoked, Scandinavian countries and the Netherlands being among the most open societies of Western Europe.

THE RELATIONSHIP BETWEEN PARTY, STATE, AND GOVERNMENT, AND THE CONCEPT OF PARTY GOVERNMENT

Scandals and 'shady deals' involving parties occur first and foremost because these parties or some of their members are able to exploit public bodies. Since these practices vary across parties and across countries, it seems natural to turn to an examination of the nature of the relationships between party and state in Western Europe, and to look in particular at what is classically referred to as 'party government'. Shady deals and corrupt practices take place only if parties can extract such advantages from the state as 'jobs for the boys' or contracts for businessmen willing (and obliged) to give funds to parties. These parties can be said to 'invade' or even to 'take over' the state. Conversely, practices of this kind will not or will scarcely occur when the distance between party and state remains substantial. This suggests that illegal or semi-legal practices involving parties are less likely to take place where barriers exist, so to speak, to such an invasion of the state: this may be because party personnel and state personnel are truly separate at the top and lower down the hierarchy of the public service, for instance if the principle of neutrality of public servants is strictly maintained. Party and state are then at arm's length.

In liberal democracies, however, there is necessarily a limit to such an arms-length posture: the policies implemented by public servants cannot be expected to originate and indeed must not originate from these public servants, but from politicians, that is to say from party politicians. This is so especially in parliamentary systems, since, in these systems, more than in many others, governments are composed mainly of the members of the elites of those parties which win the elections. On becoming ministers, the members of these party elites are expected to give orders to the public servants, however neutral these may be; the neutrality of public servants is said to help alternation between parties to take place smoothly. If there are to be shady deals or instances of corruption, this has therefore to occur with the complicity and help of governments using their power to dominate the public servants and force through illegal or semi-legal advantages to the parties supporting these governments (and indeed in some cases to other parties as well).

Thus increases in illegal or semi-legal practices in some Western European countries raises the question of why relationships between party, government, and state should have changed during the 1970s and 1980s. This means also investigating why governments should have been readier (or more able) in some countries than in others to affect adversely the arms-length position of the civil service.

The 'invasion' of the state by parties is often referred to as *partitocracy*. In such a case there is what seems to be an unhealthy symbiosis between those who represent (the party or parties) and those who rule (government and public service). The expression 'partitocracy' has been used principally to describe practices taking place in Belgium, Austria, and (pre-1992) Italy; it is rarely used in the context of other countries. However, while shady deals do not seem to have occurred widely, as we noted, in Scandinavia, the Netherlands, or even Germany, they have spread apparently beyond the 'partitocratic' countries. They have taken place on a substantial scale in France, a country in which parties have been typically regarded as weak, in which civil servants are reputed to be very strong, and in which governments, rather than the parties, have been in control of public life, even though these governments have been composed (but not exclusively) of members of party elites. Nor do British parties 'dominate' society, as is the case in Belgium or Austria. In Spain, the Socialist Party gave for a while the impression of being in control of wide sectors of the society, but this control remained relatively limited: party membership has always been small.[3]

There seem therefore to be at least two kinds of party–government relationships within which illegal practices involving parties have been substantial and have apparently increased. There is thus both a need to examine what 'partitocracy' has meant in the countries in which it has taken place to discover how far it may have facilitated shady deals, and a need to investigate why illegal or semi-legal practices occurred in some countries which were not partitocratic while they did not occur in others. However, we must first look at what party government consists of, at its forms and at its characteristics, as only when this is done will it become possible to assess whether, and if so in what circumstances, party government may be in part responsible for party decline in Western Europe.

THE NATURE AND FORMS OF PARTY GOVERNMENT, AND THE QUESTION OF PATRONAGE

Party government is still understudied. It refers to the 'insertion' of parties— of some of the parties, those which choose to support the government—in governmental life, but the nature of this insertion needs to be clarified. First, party government is not a straightforward given: it is not all or nothing. As Katz (1986: 44) points out, 'party government is also a multidimensional concept'. Thus a particular system may closely approximate the ideal-type in one respect but not in another. He thus comes to consider an essential aspect of the relationship between governments and the 'government parties' (the parties supporting the government), namely that this relationship can vary and indeed does vary markedly. He therefore suggests that one should look for different 'types' of party government and proposes the notions, inherently incremental, of 'partyness of government' and of 'party governmentness'. Party government is diverse: the nature of the relationship between the two sides—government and 'supporting parties'—and the forms which this relationship takes differ from country to country and vary in each country over time, though diversity over space is probably larger than variations over time, at least so long as there is no major change in the political institutions of a country.

As there are both cross-country and within-country variations, the nature of the relationship between the two sides and the forms which this relationship can take must be made clear.[4] The *nature of the relationship* must be examined because it seems to be assumed that the 'insertion' of parties in government necessarily means a kind of 'invasion' of parties in government. In reality, the intensity of the involvement—the closeness between the government and the parties which support it—can vary markedly. Moreover, it is far from being necessarily the case that supporting parties always invade governments: the movement can be in the opposite direction, as governments may well invade parties. There are many ways in which this can occur, from the outright creation of a party or the major restructuring of an existing party by a government leader—a development which occurs frequently in the Third World but is not unknown in Western Europe—to a host of types of influence exercised by government ministers on the parties to which they belong.

The *forms* which party government takes need equally to be carefully monitored. In particular, while party government is typically examined by reference to policy-making and to appointments, the role of patronage is often forgotten, even in elaborate definitions such as that of Katz (1986: 43), who states that three conditions have to be fulfilled for a government to deserve the title, so to speak, of 'party government'. These are, first, that all major governmental decisions must be taken by people chosen in elections conducted along party lines, or by individuals appointed by and responsible to such people; second, that policy must be decided within the governing party, when there is a 'monocolour' government, or by negotiation among parties when there is a coalition; and, third, that the 'highest officials (e.g., cabinet ministers and especially the prime minister) must be selected within their parties and be responsible to the people through their parties'. While the last two of these characteristics are precise, the first ('major governmental decisions') remains somewhat vague, although a distinction between 'major' and 'minor' decisions can probably be made in practice. What is truly missing is any reference to patronage.

THE RELATIONSHIP BETWEEN GOVERNMENTS AND SUPPORTING PARTIES: FROM AUTONOMY TO INTERDEPENDENCE, AND FROM PARTY-DEPENDENT GOVERNMENTS TO GOVERNMENT-DEPENDENT PARTIES

Even in parliamentary systems, let alone in other types of systems, not all governments are so dominated by parties that the overall arrangement can be described as partitocratic. To begin with, the ties between governments and supporting parties may not be very close; there may even be aspects in which or moments during which the two sides are autonomous from each other. Admittedly, at the limit, if there is no relationship at all between the two sides, there is no party government: the government exists and acts without paying attention to parties. Such a state of affairs is no longer found in Western

Europe, but it occurred frequently in the nineteenth century in constitutional monarchies of a bureaucratic character, such as the Austro-Hungarian or the German empires. What can still be found in Western Europe and indeed in liberal democracies in general are traces of autonomy. There is probably more scope for governmental autonomy in separation of powers systems, such as the United States, than in parliamentary systems, since parliamentary systems link the executive to the legislature and the parties are the key chains in this link. Yet there are variations, traditions and institutions being diverse: the government has always been more distant from the Parliament in the Netherlands than in Belgium, for instance; the government has also in many countries tended to enjoy a substantial degree of autonomy in the conduct of foreign affairs.

Moreover, when and to the extent that a government is not autonomous from the party or parties which support it, there is a relationship of interdependence; but that interdependence does not take place in one direction only. The concept of party government appears to suggest that influence goes from parties to governments, an extreme case of this type of flow being partitocracy. Yet influence does not always flow that way; nor is it even certain that it flows that way in the majority of cases. There are for example many instances in which governments put pressure on supporting parties to agree to policies. Government influence may go even further: the leader may have created or markedly expanded the party and he or she may therefore be able to exercise major pressure on all party decisions. In such cases, instead of the government being dependent on the supporting party, it is the supporting party which is dependent on the government. It follows, first, that, as influence can take place in both directions, there may well be close links between governments and supporting parties but no partitocracy. Second, in the same country and at the same time, there may well be instances of governmental influence on supporting parties as well as instances of influence of supporting parties on governments. At the limit, both types of influence may be so evenly balanced that they cancel each other out.

Overall, government-supporting party relationships have therefore to be analysed by reference to two dimensions. They vary, first, according to the extent to which government and supporting party or parties are *autonomous from each other*. This is a dimension because the government is more or less autonomous, as we noted: there may be autonomy in some fields and dependence in others, for instance. Where there is *interdependence* between governments and supporting parties, the relationships vary, second, from what can be regarded as total subjection or dependence of the government on the supporting party or parties, at one extreme, to, at the other extreme, total submission or dependence of the supporting party or parties on the government, with a potentially infinite number of intermediate positions. Strictly speaking, the two dimensions are related in that interdependence occurs only where parties and governments are not autonomous. But, as there may be autonomy in some respects and not in others, it is right to refer to a two-dimensional space to define the nature of government–party relationships in individual countries at various moments in time. In practice, the relationships are located within a triangle (Figure 9.1). The bottom side of this triangle constitutes the 'direction of influence' axis while the other two sides join each other at the autonomy end of the 'autonomy-interdependence' axis and at the middle point with respect to the 'direction of influence' dimension.

FORMS OF PARTY-GOVERNMENT RELATIONSHIPS IN PARTY GOVERNMENT: POLICIES, APPOINTMENTS, AND PATRONAGE

Party government is obviously concerned with the development of policies; it is also obviously concerned with a variety of appointments. The part played by appointments in party government is likely to be particularly large in parliamentary systems because of the close relationship between parliament and government, though, in other systems, too, appointments are one of the ways in which parties and governments relate to each other.

Little needs to be said about the fact that *policies* are one of the forms which link governments to supporting parties. It suffices to note that these links can

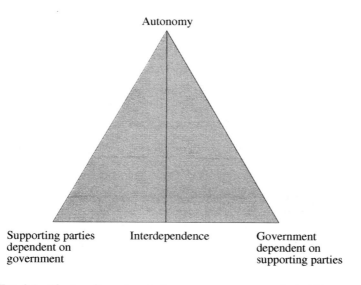

FIG. 9.1. *The two dimensions in the government–party relationships*

be more or less close as governments may or may not follow the policies which the supporting parties had previously adopted and may or may not consult parties in the context of policies which they are in the process of adopting. Almost certainly, the government line will be closer to that of the supporting party or parties—at the limit, 'dependent' on the supporting party or parties on some matters and less dependent on others, on which it might be 'autonomous' or on which it might impose its will on the supporting party or parties.

The role of *appointments* in relating governments to supporting parties stems, to begin with, from the fact that most and in many cases all cabinet positions are filled by members of the top group of the supporting party or parties; in many cases, too, in coalitions, the allocation is made by the leadership of the relevant party rather than by the head of the government. This is one of the ways in which parties hope to control cabinets. Indeed, this form of relationship is typically regarded as crucial in parliamentary systems as it is felt to be the main way in which parties can ensure that their proposals are implemented. Moreover, the relationship of dependence may be the converse one: members of the government may interfere in appointments taking place at the top of supporting parties in order to ensure that these parties accept the policies which the government proposes. The relationship between supporting parties and governments with respect to appointments can thus be as complex and as varied as the relationship between supporting parties and governments with respect to policies.

These two sets of relationships must be viewed as taking place on two distinct planes, although there are connections between them. The influence exercised on appointments to the government by the supporting parties (and, reciprocally, the influence exercised by the government on appointments to the supporting parties) may take place independently from policies. It may be exercised merely in order to achieve power, for instance. Moreover, even if appointments are made with a view to ensuring that certain policies are carried out, there is only a hope, not a certainty, that the policies will indeed be approved. In practice, problems often arise, especially as time passes: ministers may well gradually become more independent from their party as they acquire prestige and popularity; supporting parties may well increasingly criticize governmental positions. Finally, there is dissociation between the plane of policies and that of appointments when a party supports a government without entering it: such a party must be able to obtain policy advantages in return for its lack of participation (see e.g. Strøm 1984, 1990*a*). The extent to which government–party relationships are close or distant from each other on the plane of appointments thus both varies markedly and varies independently from the extent to which the relationships are close or distant from each other with respect to policies.

There is a third plane on which government-supporting party relationships take place, the plane of *patronage*. The existence of this plane is less often recognized, in part probably because the very idea of patronage being part of the definition of party government seems unappealing: patronage is assumed to be at best para-legal and probably always somewhat immoral. Yet it exists and it takes many forms, even though it is not equally widespread everywhere and even though it is not regarded everywhere as being equally acceptable.

Patronage is concerned with the distribution of favours to individuals in exchange for political advantages accruing—or being expected to accrue—to those who give the favours. The provider of the favours may be the government or it may be the party: whether coming from the government or from the party, the favour constitutes patronage if the advantage gained by the recipient involves the public sector directly or indirectly. Thus the favour may be an honour, a job or position, a contract, an advantage given to a particular district, such as a road or a hospital: in all these cases the government has to be involved (though this may be the local or provincial government and not the central government) as the favour could not be provided unless a decision was made by the government to give the favour.

It is obviously difficult to classify favours and even more to rank them in terms of the *extent* to which they are illegal, 'immoral', or 'corrupt'. At one extreme, some occur everywhere: a government cannot operate without having to put pressure occasionally on parties and to distribute in this context certain advantages. At the other extreme, practices involving the granting of vast sums of money in exchange for favours occur in a few cases only: whether the character of party government and the form which it takes facilitate the occurrence of such practices must be investigated. Between these two extremes, the distribution of honours, jobs, positions, and other advantages to ensure the loyalty of members of various groups of party supporters appears to be relatively widespread, although it does not take place universally, at least on extended scale: here, too, whether the character and forms of party government account for these variations must be examined.

Not merely the extent of patronage distribution, but the *source* of the distribution—party, government, or perhaps both—varies from country to country. Patronage may result either from party or from government initiatives, although, given the fact that these favours involve the public sector, they have to be formally granted by or in the name of the government and take place only if the government concurs, at any rate passively. The character of party government plays a prominent part in the origin of favours. Where the supporting party or parties truly 'invade' the government and dominate its decisions, they control the nature, extent, and distribution of patronage; where the government dominates the supporting parties, it controls the nature, extent, and distribution of patronage; in some cases, both act together. The distinction between supporting party dependence on government and government dependence on supporting parties thus applies to patronage as well as to policy-making and to appointments.

The overall character of government-supporting party relationships—whether they are relatively autonomous or fully interdependent, and, if so, whether they tend towards party dominance, towards government dominance, or are intermediate—is determined by the way in which these relationships take place on all three planes of policies, appointments, and patronage. Thus appointments may render certain kinds of policies more likely and/or facilitate the distribution of patronage: these situations constitute cases of *reinforcement* of one form of relationship by the other. On the other hand, appointments may benefit one 'side' while policies benefit the other, or patronage is allowed by one 'side' because the other would not concur to certain policies otherwise: these situations constitute cases of *compensation* of one form of relationship by the other. Finally, there are cases in which the relationship is 'incomplete' if one of the forms of the relationship does not occur or occurs only on a very small scale. There are naturally always appointments, but policies may be few or trivial, and patronage may be non-existent or be very limited in scope. A comprehensive analysis of the nature of party government has therefore to take into account the extent to which the forms and the character of government-supporting party relationships are affected by reinforcement or compensation and whether these relationships take place on two planes only or on all three planes.

PATRONAGE AND THE TYPES OF PARTY GOVERNMENT RELATIONSHIPS

Three broad types of party government relationships exist in parliamentary systems. In his classical books on *Democracies* and *Patterns of Democracy*, Lijphart (1984, 1999) draws a fundamental distinction between two broad types of parliamentary systems, those which are based on the 'Westminster' model and are majoritarian, and those which are based on coalitions and are consensual. While this distinction is crucial, it needs to be made two-dimensional in order to account for the full panoply of parliamentary systems, especially those of Scandinavia, alongside those of Britain and of the continental countries. One dimension is constituted by the size of the parliamentary support, which ranges from minority and small majority, including small coalitions, to 'oversized' coalitions. The other dimension relates to the spirit in which the decision-making process occurs, especially between the government 'side', on the one hand, and the opposition and 'civil society', on the other: this leads to a distinction between an 'adversarial' and a 'consensual' or 'conciliatory' type of political life (Blondel and Cotta 2000).

These two sets of distinctions help to account for variations in the nature of party government and in particular for the part played by patronage in parliamentary systems. These variations may occur across countries. They may even occur to an extent within a country: there may be more or less autonomy, more or less dependence of the government on the supporting parties, or more or less dependence of the supporting parties on the government, within the same government as time passes, between different governments when a different party or different parties come to power, especially when a coalition replaces a single-party government, and, above all, if the party system comes to change in the country. However, in the Western European context at least, given the fact that the institutional framework and the 'established' parties tend to remain broadly the same for decades, within-country variations are appreciably more limited than between-country variations. It seems therefore justified to concentrate on the variations in the nature of party government across countries.

Moreover, as was pointed out earlier, governments are rarely autonomous from the supporting parties in parliamentary systems. Cases of autonomous governments tend to occur essentially in transitional periods or in emergencies: a 'technical' government is then appointed, typically for a short period only. The French semi-presidential system is not different from other parliamentary systems in this respect: the executive of the Fifth Republic is not autonomous from the supporting parties, whatever its founder, Charles de Gaulle, may have originally wanted. In Western Europe, therefore, one can find at most traces of autonomy with respect to policies, appointments, or patronage: by and large, interdependence is the rule.

On the other hand, government-supporting party relationships differ appreciably from each other in terms of the character which this interdependence takes, as there may be marked dependence of the government on the supporting parties, marked dependence of the supporting parties on the government, as well as any number of intermediate positions. This means that, at a minimum, three broad situations must be taken into account. One of these is constituted by the cases in which parties are relatively dependent on the government; a second situation corresponds to the cases in which the supporting party or parties predominate; and the third, to the cases in which governments and supporting parties are in conditions of mutual or reciprocal interdependence.

Outside Western Europe, the most extreme situations of the first type are to be found in those countries where a charismatic leader has set up a party entirely devoted to and entirely dependent on that leader. In Western Europe, the clearest examples, naturally not as extreme, are provided by British Conservative governments. Conservative prime ministers and cabinets exercise considerable influence on the life and decisions of the party supporting them, an influence which is accepted, indeed perhaps demanded, by the rank and file and even the middle-level leadership of the party: if there is dominance, it is requested dominance. Admittedly, immediately after an election victory following a period of opposition, there is for a while a kind of 'fusion' between the leadership of the party and that of the government, but this fusion soon gives way to government dominance. A somewhat similar situation occurs in the British Labour Party: party influence is rather larger, but Labour governments have always (successfully) insisted on their right to play the major part in shaping policy. Outside Britain, this group includes the polities referred to by Lijphart (1984: 1–20; 1999: 9–21) as being of the *'Westminster-type' majoritarian* character, which are based on a sharp distinction between a government party or coalition and an opposition party or coalition. France and Spain belong to this group, although the dominance of the government is stronger and less 'naturally' accepted; Germany is close to this situation but, possibly because of its federal structure, it shares also some of the characteristics of the intermediate group.

Second, situations near the other corner of the triangle and in which supporting parties dominate were traditionally occupied outside Western Europe by the former Communist states, as these constituted cases where party leadership, rather than governmental leadership, dictated policy and as the former appointed the latter (and indeed appointed, through the *nomenklatura* system, members of the public service well below the governmental level). This system was also a case of 'fusion', but of a 'fusion' exercised to the benefit of the party rather than to the benefit of the government or, to use the Communist terminology, of the 'state apparatus'. The partitocratic Western European countries have somewhat similar characteristics: parties, not governments, are at the centre of the political process, although, of course, the political process takes place in these countries in a pluralistic and liberal democratic framework. This model characterizes, in the main, Belgium, Austria, and pre-1992 Italy, although, in the Austrian case, during part of the Kreisky governments of the 1970–83 period, because these governments were single-party social democratic and the chancellor was a towering figure, government dependence on the supporting party was markedly reduced. In general, in these countries, the relationship between the main parties tends to be along the lines of the other model of parliamentary systems proposed by Lijphart (1984, 1999), but it would seem more realistic to describe that relationship as consociational rather than as consensual.

Finally, polities in which there is reciprocal dependence differ primarily from those belonging to the other two groups because the character of politics in these countries tends to be *conciliatory* or *consensual*, rather than conflictual or 'adversarial'. On the other hand, these polities do not differ from the others because they happen to be ruled by a large coalition rather than by a single party or a small coalition. Scandinavian countries are often ruled by single-party governments, many of which have a minority character, while Finland and the Netherlands are ruled by coalitions; the size of the government majority also varies. The key difference comes from the fact that the relationship between government, opposition, and 'civil society', and by way of consequence between government and supporting parties, is less conflict-ual. Whether the governments of these countries are closer to the Westminster model (as in Sweden, Norway, and to an extent Denmark) or are based on the consociational model (as in Finland or the Netherlands), they all share a political culture based on conciliation. This characteristic has important con-sequences for the way in which governments and supporting parties relate to each other, and it renders these countries rather similar from the point of view of the nature of party government.

In the countries in which politics is conciliatory, government and support-ing parties are almost in equilibrium. More than in partitocratic countries, supporting parties accept that the role of government is to govern, perhaps because the state has kept some of its traditional distance from all political parties, supporting or not. Conversely and more than in Westminster-type majoritarian countries, the government accepts that parties play a legitimate part in the determination of the agenda of politics and therefore takes into account, indeed takes care to examine carefully, not just what supporting par-ties had adopted in the past but what they continue to propose. The climate of discussion and negotiation between the two sides is more egalitarian than in either of the other two groups of Western European parliamentary polities, as, in Westminster-type polities, the government tends to dominate the policy process, while in partitocratic polities, the supporting parties determine the agenda and decide on thorny issues.

Differences in Patronage and Party Government

The characteristics of party government in Western Europe differ markedly depending on whether supporting parties dominate, whether governments dominate, or an equilibrium exists between government and supporting par-ties. The nature of the parliamentary system is affected by these differences: the forms which party government takes are therefore likely to vary as a result. In particular, the extent and characteristics of patronage are also likely to be affected.

In partitocratic systems, the supporting parties endeavour to benefit from all three aspects of government-supporting party relationships (policy-making, appointments, and patronage). Patronage is widespread and widely distributed: it is in effect institutionalized. In these systems, it plays an important part in relating party leadership to rank and file, as they are based on 'consociational' coalitions, in which no party can implement fully its pro-gramme and in which, therefore, party members and even some of the lead-ers experience frustration, especially those party leaders who are not involved in the compromises which have to be struck when a governmental coalition is built. The role of patronage is therefore to reduce this frustration by distributing widely jobs among the party faithful, most of these jobs being of a relatively low grade. The party leadership also ensures in the process that many party members and supporters continue to support 'their' party, whatever its policies, as these members and supporters would lose benefits if the party was defeated. The mechanism of allocation underlines the prominent part played by the supporting parties: those who do the allocation are party officials placed alongside ministers in the government. Ministers ratify the decisions, but the real decision power rests with these officials who ensure that the patronage distribution takes the form which the party approves of, on the basis of an overall pattern of allocation agreed to previously and sometimes many years previously among party leaders. While the extent to which patronage occurs may vary somewhat, the fact that it is institutionalized means that it is both large and permanent: this was the case in Belgium, Austria, and pre-1992 Italy, although in Italy an increase did also occur in the 1980s as a new form of patronage, more akin to that which developed in some Westminster-type parliamentary systems, began to emerge.

In Westminster-type majoritarian systems, patronage has traditionally been low, though not non-existent. Ministers are appointed from among the leaders of the supporting parties to implement the election programmes of these parties. So long as this is the case, there is only a limited need for the government to distribute patronage to secure or maintain the loyalty of party members. The only party members likely to be restive are those members of the party elite and especially those Members of Parliament who have not been given government posts and may experience some frustration as a result. Favours are therefore likely to be targeted at these key individuals and in particular at influentials in the parliamentary party/ies and in the party/ies in the country, these favours tending to be in the nature of honours or of positions in the public or even private sectors. Favours are also sometimes targeted at a specific purpose, for instance when the parliamentary majority is very small or a difficult vote is to be taken at a party congress or in one of the important party committees. Unlike the favours distributed in partitocratic systems, those which are distributed in Westminster majoritarian systems are initiated by the government and contribute to reinforce the dependence of the party on the government. If, as has been the case in the 1980s, illegal and semi-legal practices have become widespread in some countries belonging to that group, new circumstances have had to occur to account for such a change.

In conciliatory systems, patronage is even less developed. The relationship between party leaders, members, and electors is based on traditionally strong bonds of loyalty which do not need to be boosted by material incentives and benefits, even if there is no highly developed party programme or if the government is based on a coalition in which each participant has had to limit its demands. Moreover, there is no need to combat the frustrations of parliamentarians or of party leaders not in the government by distributing honours or positions. The relationship between the government, on the one hand, and supporting parties, on the other, is based on discussion and negociation: this gives those who are not part of the government opportunities to participate in decision-making. Such a situation is due in part to the historical conditions in which parliamentary government developed in these countries. In Denmark, Sweden, and the Netherlands, the power of the monarch gave strength to the state. Popular participation did grow, but it was channelled essentially through Parliament, in a first phase at least: a kind of de facto separation of powers emerged as a result. In the Netherlands, in contrast with Belgium, the arms-length relationship between government and Parliament inherited from the constitutional monarchy continued to characterize the country up to the end of the nineteenth century; in Sweden, the distinction between the small ministries close to the government and the larger boards administering services also led to a sharp distinction between a party area and a state area. Patronage was therefore neither necessary nor really possible.

Where has Patronage Increased?

We can now return to the case of those countries in which, as a result of new circumstances, patronage grew appreciably in the 1980s. The countries concerned were principally France and Spain, both of which are Westminster-type majoritarian systems, and, among the partitocratic countries, Italy. In the French and Spanish cases, two elements combined. On the one hand, Socialist Parties, previously rather weak, achieved major electoral successes without having developed truly strong roots in the country: they needed to develop these roots as, on the other hand, difficulties arose at the policy level. In the French case, the Socialist programme of 1981 was overambitious and could not realistically be implemented; U-turns had to take place. In the Spanish case, the socialist programme of 1982 was less ambitious, but changes and even U-turns had also to be made. After a relatively short period, partly out of realism, partly as a result of a kind of fatigue on the part of the government, policy was modified and the reforming element markedly reduced. What had been a 'party-programmatic' phase of governmental action was coming to an end.

Yet, while the governments of these two countries reappraised what they wished to achieve, they did not want to abandon power. Nor did the electors force them to do so, as the Socialist government was returned to power in Spain for over a decade and it came back to power in France in 1988 after an interruption of only two years. The basis of the 'contract' between the government and the supporting party was markedly altered, however: the programme was no longer the basis of this contract. Yet a bond had to be found if the relationship between government and supporting party was not to be difficult, even acrimonious. Patronage was to constitute a key element in this new bond. It was to provide a kind of compensation for party-based programmatic action: the party received the patronage and even controlled in part its distribution (a case of government dependence on supporting parties) while (at least much) policy-making was henceforth to take place on the basis of governmental initiative (a case of dependence of supporting parties on the government). In doing so, the government was moving from its early party-programmatic phase to a 'party-patrimonial' phase in which patronage had acquired a place which it did not previously occupy.

The trade-offs on which the relationship between government and supporting party were based could be achieved in the French case because the membership size of the supporting Socialist Party had remained small and because many influential party members, especially at the local level, were more concerned to maintain their influence in their district than to fight with the leadership about national policies. Thus the government could develop its own policies, provided members locally received the favours they were anxious to obtain. The situation was rather analogous in Spain, though the movement was slower, as the reformist zeal of the Socialist Party had not been as pronounced as it had been in the French case. Interestingly, in contrast, in Britain, where the two main parties had been well-established for decades, the extent to which illegal party practices took place remained limited, even during a very large part of the long period of Conservative rule of the 1980s and 1990s, although, towards the end of that period, 'patrimonialism' began to spread at a time when the belief in the programmatic action of the Conservative government started to wane.

The Italian case was different in its origins, but the effect on patronage was similar. The emergence of a new form of patrimonialism stemmed from the ambition of the Socialist Party leader, Bettino Craxi, to abandon gradually the partitocratic formula and to challenge the dominance of both the Christian Democrat Party and the Communist Party: this was to be done by 'surpassing' the latter in order to be in a position to oppose the former, in a manner analogous to what had occurred in France and Spain when the Socialist Party became dominant during the same period. To achieve this goal, however, the Italian Socialist Party needed the support of a substantial proportion of the managerial and professional classes, especially in order to build its strength at the local level; and it needed money to have a large infrastructure across the country. These requirements could be fulfilled only by means of a 'party-patrimonial' system through which funds would be extracted from businesses to finance the expansion of the party.

Patronage therefore increased markedly in two types of situations. It increased where programmatic rule was abandoned because circumstances rendered programmes inadequate or a degree of 'fatigue' came to be combined with a fall in the enthusiasm for the 'cause' at a time when party–government relationships had to be kept relatively smooth and free of major conflict. Patronage also increased where a party attempted to move away from traditional partitocratic arrangements in the direction of a more adversarial, Westminster-type system.

Meanwhile, in the countries in which politics was based on conciliation, patronage did not increase, as parties were strong and were associated to policy changes which governments initiated from time to time when events forced them to modify the original course of action: in Sweden in the 1990s, for instance, the marked change in economic and financial policy took place on the basis of a broad agreement. Thus, while Westminster-type governments are often regarded in a highly positive manner because they are said to be able to provide the people (occasionally at least) with a say in the policy-making process and because they are viewed as capable of acting decisively, there is a price to pay when the aim of the action is an overambitious programme which turns out to be difficult to implement. The temptation to avoid paying the price by means of favours, bribes, and corruption is difficult to resist, especially when the supporting parties are rather weak, as, in such a case, these parties can be more easily dominated by the government.

PATRONAGE AND PARTY DECLINE: IS THERE A RELATIONSHIP?

Patronage thus plays a different part, and a part which has changed more or less in the three broad types of party government which we have identified in Western Europe. How far the existence of the increase in patronage has contributed to party decline is more problematic, given that the extent of party decline itself is also problematic. Moreover, if that decline is measured by a battery of indicators among which the most important are lower membership, higher abstention, greater volatility, and greater success of new parties eating into the electorate of the established ones, while some decline has taken place everywhere and has taken place to a varying degree, it has *not* occurred more markedly in the countries in which patronage has figured prominently.[5] Scandinavian parties have taken their toll, while Belgian parties, in the 1980s at least, have had a limited decline. Thus the only truly clear case is that of Italy where patronage does appear to have led directly to the collapse of the party system which existed up to the early 1990s. Yet, not only is this example unique in Western Europe, but the collapse of the Italian party system has to be viewed in the context of the changes which were beginning to occur and which the Italian Socialist Party, in particular, was attempting to achieve.

Moreover, despite the massive criticisms levelled at parties in some quarters of the media, where governments and supporting parties are occasionally presented as riddled with scandals and corruption, these supporting parties have not collapsed nor even seem to have been permanently weakened except in

Italy. In the only two other Western European countries in which cases of major party collapse occurred, France and Spain, the collapse of a party did occur in one occasion, but this was appreciably earlier and for reasons which has nothing to do with patronage, let alone 'scandals'. The French Christian democrat party (MRP) disappeared in the 1960s as a result of having been marginalized by the Gaullist party on the right and centre of the political spectrum when the Fifth Republic was established; and the collapse of the Spanish Union of the Democratic Centre (UCD) in the early 1980s was mainly due to the lack of institutionalization of that party, which was a complex federation of a number of political groupings uneasily brought together during the first phase of the new democracy under the strong, but somewhat unsure leadership of Adolfo Suárez (see Gunther and Hopkin, Chapter 8 above).

In order to come at least to some conclusion about the relationship between patronage and party decline, the specific evolution of the party system in both partitocratic and Westminster-type polities has to be examined on a country-by-country basis. To begin with, in the partitocratic countries, while the Italian case is a clear case of decline, that of Belgium is not, and Austria appears to be in an intermediate position. In Austria, there have indeed been profound and seemingly long-lasting changes in the party system since the middle of the 1980s. The old two-party system which characterized politics in the country between the late 1940s and the 1980s has ceased to exist, at least one of the two main traditional parties having experienced a major decline. Meanwhile, the Freedom Party's success can be attributed in part to discontent with patronage as well as to the absence of real choice under the old system. On the other hand, in Belgium, no such movement has occurred: the traditional parties have resisted remarkably (as the Liberal Democratic Party was also to do in Japan) despite the many scandals with which one of them at least had been associated. The traditional parties have maintained a firm hold on the electorate. Even movements from one of the main parties to another have not been particularly large in the 1980s and 1990s: greater volatility had been experienced earlier, at a time when the question of patronage was not being raised. As a matter of fact, the less-established parties have been those which suffered most since the 1980s, including the moderate nationalist Flemish party, the VUB, whose electorate dwindled in the 1990s in the light of the growth of the more virulent Vlaams Blok. Thus traditional parties have weathered the storm in Belgium, at the very moment when the collapse of the Italian party system suggested that other party systems would follow suit.

The conclusions which can be drawn in relation to the Westminster-type majoritarian political systems are not entirely clear-cut either. If Greece is added to Spain, France, and, to an extent, Britain, it would appear that the greater occurrence of 'sleaze', illicit favours, or outright corruption in these countries had not resulted in a permanent decline of the traditional parties but had primarily the effect of rendering more rapid the alternation from one of the major parties (or groups of parties) to the other. Admittedly, in France, the radical right National Front grew during the period and thus modified to an extent the landscape of politics; but some of its electorate came from among disaffected Communist voters whose numbers declined markedly during the same period. Thus there has been no realignment in France, admittedly in part because the electoral system made such a realignment more difficult to occur. What did take place was principally alternation between right and left in 1986, 1988, 1993, and again in 1997, when, somewhat surprisingly, the Socialist Party recovered most of the ground it had lost at its massive 1993 defeat, a defeat which had in part been due to scandals affecting that party. Meanwhile, the setbacks of the Socialist Parties in Greece in 1989–90 and in Spain in 1996 for similar reasons were relatively limited, indeed markedly more limited than the defeats of the French Socialists in 1993 and of the French and British Conservatives in 1997. While accusations of 'sleaze' and indeed proven cases of illegal practices seem therefore to have affected government parties in Westminster-type majoritarian countries to an extent, the effect is either not very marked or, when large, not seemingly durable.

Thus, the effect of the growth of patronage in partitocracies and in Westminster-type majoritarian polities is complex. It may not be permanent, and it is not uniformly spread. However, to examine more fully what this effect might be, we must go one step further and consider patronage in the context of the other aspects of government-supporting party relationships and in particular of policy-making.

THE APPARENTLY DIFFERENT EFFECT OF PATRONAGE IN PARTITOCRATIC AND IN WESTMINSTER-TYPE MAJORITARIAN POLITIES

The Partitocratic Polities

In the three Western European polities in which the partitocratic system prevailed since the Second World War (Belgium, Austria, and Italy), patronage had existed for so long and had become so much part of political and social life that it seemed to have been, not just accepted, but even viewed as normal. Favours distributed by parties and by ministers on behalf of parties have covered so many aspects of public life and reached such a large proportion of the population that this *normalcy* of patronage could scarcely be questioned without also questioning the whole of the political arrangements. Thus the system could be stable: scandals which exploded occasionally did not affect its overall economy.

Why, then, did the partitocratic system fare so differently in Italy, Austria, and Belgium? The answer appears to be that, although the three countries can be regarded as partitocratic, the three cases are in reality very different from each other. In Belgium, partitocracy, however 'riddled' with patronage, did function effectively; in Austria, the very idea of a partitocratic system—that is to say of a coalition and of compromises among the parties belonging to that coalition—had begun to be eroded by nearly twenty years in which first the Popular Party and later the Socialist Party had ruled on their own; in Italy, in the 1980s, the partitocratic system had also been undermined, in a somewhat different manner, by the behaviour of the Socialist Party.

The partitocratic system appears able to provide effective government when compromises need to be made to reduce political tension: this did occur in Belgium, admittedly with difficulty and after lengthy debates. The traditional parties steered the country in a federal direction designed to reduce the tension between the two main language communities. The Belgian traditional parties thus proved capable of acting 'programmatically': this occurred in reaction to societal pressure, but, despite other 'patrimonial' aspects, the key issue affecting the country was tackled. In Austria, in contrast, the extensive *proporz* system was not accompanied, especially after the end of the Kreisky era in 1983, by a corresponding programmatic move, in part because there was no dramatic issue on which to focus. Politics could thus return to what it had been before 1966, but, in the interval, the pre-Second World War reasons for the setting up of a 'Grand Coalition' had ceased to be paramount and the legitimacy of that coalition was increasingly in doubt.

The collapse of the Italian 'partitocracy' in the early 1990s resulted ostensibly from the angry reaction of the Christian Democrat Party to what was regarded as the unacceptable challenge which the Socialist Party was posing to the maintenance of the system characterizing Italian politics since the 1940s: the very idea of compromise arrangements on which the 'partitocracy' was based was being put in question. The feud between the two parties was sufficient to make the situation explode, as, in the process, those who had benefited from patronage ceased to be able to defend the system on which they had so far depended. Yet, behind numerous theatrical episodes, the real change which was occurring was the start of the rejection of the partitocracy itself as a governmental arrangement. A partitocratic system of which patronage is a strong component can remain acceptable so long as its protagonists believe that policy decisions must be taken in common on the basis of compromises. If one of the partners challenges this fundamental principle, the basis of the 'contract' no longer exists. Whether that partner uses patronage to help break the 'contract', as was the case with the Italian Socialist Party, is not the key issue, even if the battle took place in Italy over the nature and extent of the illicit deals which had taken place. The key issue was the fact that Italy was moving away from the partitocratic system. Subsequent developments in the politics of the country showed that there was indeed a widespread desire among many groups in the society to move, rightly or wrongly, in the direction of a Westminster-type majoritarian system. Perhaps the Austrian evolution can also be accounted for in this manner, given the twenty years (1966–86) during which the partitocratic system did not fully operate.

The Westminster-Type Majoritarian Polities

In Westminster-type majoritarian polities, patronage is 'normally' limited. It is directed at that fraction of the 'political class' which might be disaffected because it is not in government. What occurred primarily in France, as well as in Spain, was different: it was a change in the function of patronage. From being merely 'a drop of oil' designed to prevent the system from gripping, it became an alternative way of linking government and party. The move towards patrimonialism was thus bringing the political systems of these countries closer to a partitocratic state, but a partitocratic state in which the engine was the government, not the supporting party. Given that the citizenship was not accustomed, as in partitocratic countries, to such a partitocracy, strong negative reactions were to be expected. The result was, especially in France in 1993, but also in Spain in 1996, electoral defeat; a similar reaction had occurred in Greece in 1989–90. Interestingly, by comparison, the British Labour governments had never been able or willing to use patronage extensively, either in the late 1940s or in the late 1970s, when they made changes in policies which some of their rank-and-file supporters found distasteful. This may have been in part because, in both instances, Labour did not stay in power long enough. But this was probably also because the Labour Party was markedly better implanted in the country and therefore less likely to be amenable to the kind of manipulations which are characteristic of patronage. Interestingly, too, but conversely, some increase in patronage did occur on the right in both France and Britain in the 1990s, in combination with what seemed to be both a loss of programmatic fervour and an increased restiveness of the party rank and file.

Patronage in Westminster-type majoritarian systems is thus essentially a substitute or a palliative for policy-making. It does appear to have an effect on the electoral fate of the parties concerned, seemingly because it is regarded as a mere palliative and a distasteful one at that. Yet this effect does not take the form of a blanket rejection of all the traditional parties or even of a permanent change in the party system: it is as if electors assumed that alternation in power would be sufficient to correct the 'ills' which increased patronage had introduced. Patronage thus played a part in the electoral ups and downs of traditional parties, but it was not a direct contributor to the decline of these parties.

PATRONAGE AND THE GENERAL NATURE OF
PARTY GOVERNMENT

Patronage has had a different effect in partitocratic countries from the effect it had in Westminster-type polities. In the latter, the political system is based on the notion that the government is in power to implement a programme and that that programme should be markedly distinct from that of the opposition. Thus, not surprisingly, there is more disillusionment in these systems than in partitocratic systems when the parties in power are unable or unwilling to act 'programmatically'. Patronage can only be a palliative in Westminster-type majoritarian polities; it cannot be a 'way of life'. Yet the danger is that the palliative may well increase the seriousness of the problem which it is introduced to reduce, as discontent with 'sleaze' and 'shady deals' comes to be added to the earlier disillusionment provoked by the reduced programmatic stance of the party in power which patronage was aimed at reducing. The danger is especially large when a party comes to power with an overambitious programme; yet this is an endemic feature of these polities because overambitious programmes give politics an 'exciting' aspect. The 'excitement' is difficult to sustain for long, however, as, to be realistic, parties typically have to be less programmatically adventurous. Support for the government is likely to decline within the supporting party itself as a result, especially where the parties have relatively weak structures and came to power on the basis of a 'miraculously' large and sudden wave of popular support, as was the case in France and to an extent in Spain. The more the strength of the party depends on the programme, the more patronage is necessary if the programme cannot be implemented, but the more, then, party support becomes fragile. A partitocratic arrangement does not constitute a satisfactory alternative, however. Disaffection with the lack of choice is likely to set in and to lead to a gradual decline in party support. This decline is difficult to arrest unless, as in Belgium in the 1980s, a major issue has to be dealt with *and* the party leaders are strong enough to resolve this issue: this is unlikely to occur everywhere, let alone to occur in all circumstances.

One needs therefore to turn to the third type of party government system, that which is based on conciliation, to look for a solution. Party decline may occur also among countries practising conciliation, but the danger of a massive electoral reaction is more limited, as both supporting parties and the government have a genuine authority of their own and can thus maintain enough strength without having to and indeed being able to resort to patronage. The two different forms which these systems have taken seem to be equally effective in this regard. On the one hand, the experience of Scandinavia and that of Finland during the 1980s suggest that a programmatic stance can be combined with a culture of conciliation: conciliation appears better able to sustain long-term change than a system which forces policies through against strong opposition, as is the case in Westminster-type majoritarian systems. These forceful mechanisms often fail because Westminster-like systems become embroiled in a sequence which, in the end, leads to the development of illicit practices, designed in theory to keep supporters loyal but likely to undermine the credibility of both government and supporting parties. Dutch experience suggests, on the other hand, that accommodation is viable if it takes place in the context of a government which, unlike those of Austria or Belgium, maintains a substantial independent authority from that of the supporting parties. In the Netherlands, parties have neither been able nor willing to 'invade' the government: the government has remained somewhat above the parties and that arms-length position has rendered patronage more difficult and thus resulted in the system as a whole being kept above major suspicion. Whether the moderate 'party accommodation' of the Netherlands is preferable to the moderate 'majoritarianism' of the Scandinavian countries cannot be answered in the abstract. But what appears to be the case is that both these forms of party–government arrangements proved less prone to suffer from the problems posed by patronage than partitocratic or Westminster-type majoritarian polities, at least when the latter were also characterized by relatively weakly implanted parties. Whether the Scandinavian or the Dutch arrangements based on stronger parties and on a greater distance between government and supporting parties could easily be introduced in other Western European countries is of course another story.

CONCLUSION

Patronage has manifestly played a part—a negative part—in the life of Western European parliamentary systems in the final decades of the twentieth century. It has not led to the end of parties; nor has it led to a marked change in the nature of party government in the countries concerned. There seemed to be a danger that it might have engulfed parties and party systems. This danger has not materialized as yet. This does not mean, however, that parties will not decline in the future as a result of extensive patronage. The dynamic characteristics of party government are so little known that definite conclusions are precluded in this respect.

While it is therefore still not certain that it contributes directly to party decline, patronage poses major problems for parties and party systems in Western Europe, although these problems are different in the different types of party–government arrangements. The question is therefore not whether countries will ride the storm, but whether it is not better for them to avoid the storm altogether. A little patronage may be inevitable; but it is clearly not healthy for the link between governments and supporting parties to be based markedly on favours and shady deals, either as a matter of course or as ad hoc developments. It is therefore to be hoped that a better understanding of the relationship between the two 'sides' will lead to the progressive discovery of ways of linking everywhere, without an extensive amount of patronage, the representative element which parties constitute to the leadership and decision-taking element which is the *raison d'être* of governments.

NOTES

1. See the summary of this highly complex problem which has given rise to a vast literature in Gallagher *et al.* (1995: 236–7); also Mair (1997: ch. 4), and Katz and Mair (1995).
2. For a brilliant summary of the problem see Mény (1996); see also Della Porta and Mény (1997), and Heywood (1997).
3. The membership of the Spanish PSOE in 1986, after its 1982 electoral victory, was 160.000; in terms of the party voters at this time this represented only 1.8% and 0.6% in terms of the Spanish electorate. See Méndez-Lago (2000: ch. 5).
4. See Blondel and Cotta (1996, 2000) for a more detailed presentation of the characteristics of government-supporting party relationships.
5. On the attachment of electors to parties see Schmitt (1989), who indicates that party attachment did decline by about 10% by the late 1980s, but that the decline was, in broad terms, spread fairly evenly across Western Europe; but also see a more recent analysis in Schmitt and Holmberg (1995).

10

Anti-Party Sentiments in Southern Europe

Mariano Torcal, Richard Gunther, and José Ramón Montero

Over the past two decades, a so-called 'confidence gap' has undermined public support for many public institutions.[1] Popular images of political parties have been especially susceptible to this deterioration (Listhaug and Wiberg 1995). In both the United States and in many European countries, the phrase 'crisis of parties' has become all too familiar, and is often linked with more sweeping criticisms of other democratic institutions, including the government, the legislature, and, more broadly, political elites or 'politicians'.[2] In 1992 the term *Parteienverdrossenheit* ('vexation with parties' or 'crisis of acceptance of parties') was 'the word of the year' in Germany, given its ability to capture the tone of debate concerning political parties (Immerfall 1993; Eilfort 1995). While this term was specifically applied to German parties, it could apply as well to public perceptions in many other countries, where 'parties are seen as overly self-interested, eternally squabbling instead of striving for the common good, incapable of devising consistent policies, and prone to corruption' (Poguntke 1996: 320). More broadly, anti-party rhetoric has become a common element of political discourse in many modern democracies (Poguntke and Scarrow 1996*b*). Accordingly, the alleged decline of political parties has become a preoccupation of journalists, essayists, and social scientists.

Political scientists who have written about this theme fall into two broad categories. One group includes those who focus their analysis on the organizational structures, functions, and membership of parties, and their performance in government and in representative institutions. They have produced an abundant literature based on empirical research, some examples of which appear in this volume.[3] A second group of scholars has been more concerned with citizens' attitudes towards political parties. Their empirical studies, however, have rarely focused on the question of the decline in public support for parties, and have instead been primarily concerned with themes such as the evolution of party identification, electoral participation, and the traditional social ties linking parties to citizens.[4] Despite widespread interest in this theme, there have been surprisingly few empirical studies of the extent and possible origins of anti-party attitudes. In this chapter, we hope to fill this gap in the literature by systematically exploring the hypothesis of 'the decline of parties' from the standpoint of citizen support for these key institutions in four Southern European democracies.

The existing literature on this topic has produced contradictory findings. To some extent, this lack of consistency is the joint product of operationalization and measurement problems. Several such studies, for example, have been based on survey items that are only tangentially related to our central concern: they have used as indicators of anti-party attitudes drawing on related concepts such as the decline of party identification, party membership, voting turnout, and increases in electoral volatility or support for anti-system parties (Poguntke 1996). We concur with Webb (1995: 303) who points out that these behavioural indicators are less reflective of fundamental attitudes towards parties than they are consequences of such factors as the increasing ideological convergence among parties, or a simple process of political dealignment (see also Reiter 1989: 327–8). Accordingly, these studies do not deal directly with citizens' basic approval of political parties as forms of political representation or vehicles for the aggregation of interests (Poguntke and Scarrow 1996b: 259). Indeed, the conceptualization of this phenomenon has been so imprecise that it has not been clearly established that a 'crisis in the approval of political parties' definitely exists, let alone that we understand its possible origins or behavioural consequences.

In this chapter we therefore aim at four complementary objectives: (1) to develop and discuss attitudinal indicators that can serve as adequate measures of anti-party sentiments; (2) to observe the evolution of these indicators over time in a variety of contexts; (3) to discuss their relationship with other aspects of political behaviour; and (4) to speculate about the origins of anti-party sentiments. While most of our analysis will focus on Spain (for which we have a wealth of comparable survey data over a period of two decades), we also explore similar attitudes in Portugal, Italy, and Greece in an effort to determine the extent to which an increase in anti-party sentiments represents a general feature of contemporary West European democracies, and to what extent it may be linked to a broader concept of political disaffection. We shall also examine some of the consequences of this phenomenon with regard to electoral behaviour, to psychological identification of citizens with parties, and to the overall level of involvement of citizens in public life.

THE CONCEPT AND TYPES OF ANTIPARTYISM

During the 1990s, it was commonly argued (often without supporting evidence) that negative sentiments towards political parties had become a widespread feature of politics throughout Western Europe. Although the term *Parteienverdrossenheit* was, for obvious reasons, most commonly used to describe popular irritation with and disaffection from parties in Germany, this and similar terms were often used to capture popular sentiments in other countries. But while many scholars and journalistic observers shared an interest in this phenomenon, they differed substantially with regard to how they conceptualized and measured anti-party sentiments, and they disagreed about how widespread they had become in these countries, as well as about their origins and consequences. German scholars, for example, tended to regard anti-party sentiments as transitory responses by citizens to the political developments of the early 1990s (German reunification, economic crisis, corruption, etc.) (Wiesendahl 1998). A similar interpretation could be derived from a prima-facie examination of the Spanish case: during and shortly after the transition to democracy the popular image of parties was positive;[5] but during the 1980s attitudes towards parties deteriorated rapidly (Wert 1996), at least in part in response to the corruption scandals of the early 1990s.[6]

Other studies, however, reach different conclusions about the nature and possible origins of these clusters of attitudes. Anti-party sentiments in Italy, for example, have been found to be much more stable over time. Sani and Segatti (2001) contend that such attitudes have deep roots in Italy's political culture, and that these orientations were reinforced by socialization during the fascist era. They also conclude that such attitudes helped to undermine support for the parties of the so-called 'First Republic', contributing to their collapse in the 1994 election. Compatible with this country-specific explanation, Reiter (1989: 343) argues that the decline of attitudinal support for parties is specific to political conditions in each individual country. In contrast, other scholars already mentioned assert that the increase in anti-party sentiments is a general, long-term phenomenon that is part of the decline of confidence in all representative institutions in modern democracies, and that is caused by processes of culture change or by the tensions between professional political elites and the individuals and social groups that they are supposed to represent.

Other discrepancies found in this literature involve the consequences of anti-party attitudes. Some have argued that they have contributed to the emergence of populist or xenophobic parties in some countries (Schedler 1996; Mudde 1996), or to the rejection of the major parties and cynicism towards their leaders (Taggart 1994). It is often assumed that increases in anti-party attitudes are closely related to a decrease in general support for the democratic regime, or are linked to anti-system behaviour. In contrast, Sani and Segatti (2001) have demonstrated that anti-party sentiments in Italy coexisted for decades with high levels of party identification, and with strong majority support for the democratic regime. In light of these paradoxes and contradictory conclusions, we believe that a comparative, empirical study of the nature and consequences of anti-party attitudes is long overdue.

Accordingly, we shall analyse this phenomenon using survey data collected in Spain, Portugal, Italy, and Greece over the past two decades. We shall argue that the confusion and inconsistencies among earlier empirical findings have resulted, in large measure, from a lack of awareness that anti-party attitudes are of two distinctly different types, with different origins and different behavioural consequences. We shall refer to these different dimensions as 'reactive antipartyism' and 'cultural antipartyism'. We shall argue that these two dimensions have different origins, attitudinal and behavioural correlates, and evolve over time in distinctly different ways.

Reactive antipartyism is a critical stance adopted by citizens in response to their dissatisfaction with the performance of party elites and institutions. It is the product of inconsistencies between the promises, the ideological labels, and the rhetoric of politicians, on the one hand, and citizens' perceptions of the actual performance of democracy and political elites, on the other. In some respects, it is a logical consequence of 'overpromising' by politicians—of their reliance upon a political discourse that raises expectations among the general public to such a degree it would be difficult to deliver all that was promised. To some extent, however, it is also a response to actual failures on the part of parties and elites. Many social, political, and economic problems are simply not solved, or even satisfactorily addressed; many party leaders may behave irresponsibly, or at least in such a manner as to be regarded as objectionable by many citizens; and some party leaders may misuse their access to government resources and privileges, and engage in corruption, patronage, or other similar practices.

In the case of the four Southern European countries under examination here, it is not difficult to identify patterns of behaviour that could provoke a negative response on the part of many citizens, leading them to adopt a reactive anti-party stance. Portuguese democracy, for example, was born of a highly conflictual and chaotic revolutionary process, only to be followed by more than a decade of extreme governmental instability (see Bruneau 1997; Bruneau *et al.* 2001). In Spain, crises involving corrupt behaviour by government and party leaders repeatedly erupted during the late 1980s and early 1990s (Pradera 1996). In Italy, four decades of government instability, paradoxically coupled with political immobilism and reinforced by dramatic revelations of massive corruption at the highest levels of government, led to a complete breakdown of the party system beginning between 1992 and 1994 (Sani and Segatti 2001). And in Greece, a succession of scandals, demagogic political rhetoric, opportunistic partisan strategies, and irresponsible behaviour plagued the political system until the mid-1990s (Mendrinou and Nicolacopoulos 1997). Under these circumstances, the adoption of anti-party attitudes on the part of citizens could be regarded as little more than an expression of political realism (Poguntke 1996: 327). Since political reality evolves over time, we should expect the extent and intensity of such negative sentiments to fluctuate in accord with the changing conjuncture of political, economic, and social developments. This prediction fits well with the evolution of such sentiments in Germany, where the phenomenon of *Parteienverdrossenheit* was of relatively short duration, and had more modest consequences than had initially been feared (Gabriel 1996: 16–17; Noelle-Neumann 1994: 43–5). Several scholars have asserted that attitudes regarding lack of confidence in representative democratic institutions and political parties should be most commonly found among those who are better educated and politically informed, and more interested and involved in politics—that is, that these sentiments should be more prevalent among those who have high expectations regarding democratic politics, but who are most aware of the shenanigans of politicians and parties (Dalton 1996: ch. 9; Putnam *et al.* 2000).

We can also construct a profile of a very different variety of antipartyism—one that is rooted in the historical traditions and core values of a political culture, and thus independent of short-term changes in a country's political conditions. We shall refer to these kinds of political orientations, which should be expected to remain relatively constant over time in terms of their scope and intensity, as *cultural antipartyism*. Again, the four Southern European cases under examination here provide clear examples of the kinds of socializing factors that are likely to encourage the development and anchoring of such attitudes. As Maravall (1997: 237) has written, these factors include 'a long experience of dictatorships and pseudodemocracies, a history of political turbulence and discontinuities, manipulated elections over long periods, and a prolonged negative socialization into politics. In this sense, citizen's evaluations of politics and their personal influence may be considered simply a rational response, the result of a historical experience which would hardly have encouraged trust in politics'. Parties were obviously an integral part of this picture. In each Southern European case, the country's experiences with liberal democracy in the late nineteenth and early twentieth century represented fertile grounds for the development of cynical attitudes towards parties: their exclusionary 'limited democracies' (Burton *et al.* 1992: 5–6) relied heavily on patron–client relationships, systematic electoral fraud, and outright intimidation as a means of restricting the right of all citizens to participate freely and effectively. Each of these parliamentary but not fully democratic regimes collapsed in the early twentieth century, typically in a political environment characterized by high levels of instability and intense conflict (in the case of Spain, and to a lesser extent of Greece, culminating in civil war), in which political parties often resorted to extra-parliamentary if not downright undemocratic means in their ultimately self-destructive conflicts with one another. Finally, these four political systems fell under the control of right-wing corporatist or quasi-corporatist authoritarian regimes that sought to resocialize their populations, inculcating within them attitudes hostile to the basic notions of competitive parties and liberal democracy. In the course of the regimes' propaganda campaigns, parties and politicians were portrayed as self-serving, and as dividing and weakening what should be a united nation (see e.g. Aguilar 1996; Sani and Segatti 2001). In short, the authoritarian regimes sought to instil anti-party sentiments into their populations through propaganda campaigns and formal socialization by schools, and these efforts reinforced initially sceptical beliefs about the utility of parties and politicians in competitive democratic systems. In so far as late nineteenth- and early twentieth-century experiences with democracy or limited democracy imparted an indirect socialization of cynical attitudes towards parties to the country's population, and the intentional resocialization during the following authoritarian interludes inculcated explicitly antiparty attitudes into significant segments of the populace, such orientations may have become durable features of the political culture of a country. In contrast with reactive anti-partyism, these attitudes should be expected to be stable over time, and, unlike those associated with reactive antipartyism, should not fluctuate in accord with short-term political circumstances.

In this regard, it is not unreasonable to expect that cultural antipartyism might be closely associated with other cynical or negative assessments of various dimensions of democratic politics, forming part of a broader syndrome of political disaffection. As we have argued elsewhere (Montero *et al.* 1997, 1998; Gunther and Montero 2000; Torcal 2000), this syndrome is conceptually and empirically distinct from two other clusters of democratic orientations, one of which involves general support for democracy and is a key element in the legitimation of democratic regimes, while the other reflects political discontent or dissatisfaction with the performance of a regime's political institutions and incumbent officials. Political disaffection, in contrast, includes a subjective sense of distance from politics and political institutions, cynicism and general disinterest regarding politics, and low levels of political participation (Torcal 2000). Accordingly, it is to be expected that this syndrome of disaffection, disinterest, and passivity would include negative attitudes towards political parties.

These two distinct varieties of antypartyism, the cultural and the reactive, should have greatly different behavioural consequences. In so far as reactive antipartyism represents a negative assessment and therefore a series of criticisms against poor performance by party institutions or leaders, it could have the positive result of mobilizing citizens to demand improvement or a change of incumbents in power (Dalton 1999: 75–6; Norris 1999*b*: 263). In contrast, in so far as the cultural variety of antipartyism is a durable characteristic of a political subculture, is not immediately responsive to changes in the performance of parties or their leaders, and is associated with pervasive cynicism and non-involvement in politics. As a critical component of political dissafection, cultural antipartyism may broaden the gap between citizens and their representatives, and reinforce the marginalization of an important sector of the population whose political resources are inferior to others who are better able to defend their interests in a competitive democratic system. Both in terms of democratic theory and of the actual quality of a democracy, the latter would have negative implications.

THE DIMENSIONS OF ANTI-PARTY SENTIMENTS

Let us begin this empirical analysis of antipartyism in Southern Europe by attempting to determine the extent to which attitudes towards parties cluster along two distinct attitudinal dimensions. The survey items that will serve as the initial focus of this study are the following:

1. Parties criticize one another, but in reality they are all alike.
2. Political parties only divide people.
3. Without parties, there can be no democracy.
4. Parties are needed to defend the interests of various groups and social classes.
5. Thanks to parties, people can participate in political life.
6. Parties are useless.

In Table 10.1, we present the results of a varimax rotation of responses to these items in a factor analysis from the mid 1980s. The patterns among these factor loadings are remarkably constant across all four countries and over time, and they clearly reveal the existence of two distinct factors. The first includes indicators that may be regarded as simple rejection of parties in general—'they are all alike' and they 'only divide people'. As we shall argue, these items tap into the *cultural* dimension of anti-party attitudes. The other cluster of items, which we regard as belonging to the *reactive* dimension, consists of more measured affirmations concerning the roles played by parties in modern democracies: they 'defend the interests of the various groups', allow people to 'participate in political life', and are necessary for the functioning of democracy. Only the 'parties are useless' item in the first column does not fit neatly into one or the other of these dimensions: although it is more strongly linked to the cultural dimension, there is also some association with reactive antipartyism. The only exceptions are found in Portugal in 1985 and Greece in 1998, where it is absolutely clear that the 'parties are useless' item belongs to the cultural dimension.[7]

TABLE 10.1. *Factor analysis of anti-party sentiments in Southern Europe, 1985–1998*

Country	Year	Parties useless	Parties alike	Parties divide	Defend interests	Allow participation	No parties, no democracy
Spain	1985	**−.41**	−.19	−.20	**.58**	**.68**	**.66**
		.53	**.60**	**.78**	−.30	−.21	−.17
	1989	**−.40**	.11	−.27	**.57**	**.51**	**.62**
		.53	**.57**	**.62**	−.31	−.26	−.11
	1991	**−.35**	−.17	−.32	**.58**	**.35**	**.44**
		.45	**.52**	**.53**	−.17	−.12	−.00
	1995	**−.50**	**−.01**	−.18	**.74**	**.37**	**.62**
		.42	.50	**.73**	−.12	−.01	−.11
	1997	**−.34**	−.17	−.00	**.74**	**.48**	**.59**
		.52	**.62**	**.62**	−.18	−.15	−.01
Portugal	1985	−.12	.11	.00	**.35**	**.80**	**.62**
		.54	**.70**	**.70**	−.14	−.00	−.22
	1993	**−.44**	−.18	−.28	.06	**.72**	**.75**
		.34	**.57**	**.73**	**.47**	−.07	−.05
Italy	1985	**−.44**	−.01	−.16	**.45**	**.63**	**.64**
		.49	**.66**	**.56**	−.10	−.13	−.13
Greece	1985	−.45	−.00	−.01	**.38**	**.59**	**.38**
		.31	**.73**	**.61**	−.00	−.00	−.00
	1998	−.11	.06	−.02	**.57**	**.62**	**.56**
		.58	**.80**	**.69**	.08	−.05	−.11

Sources: For Spain in 1985, 1989, 1991, 1996, and 1997 Banco de Datos, Centro de Investigaciones Sociológicas (CIS); for all countries in 1985, The Four Nation Study; for Italy in 1990, Sani (1992: 139); for Italy in 1997, Segatti (1998: 5); for Greece in 1998, Greek Study of the Role of Government; and for Portugal in 1993, ESEO, Estudios de Mercado Lta.

First and second factor loadings after varimax votation.

An examination of the survey responses of Southern European citizens interviewed at various times from the mid-1980s to the end of the 1990s (presented in Tables 10.2 and 10.3) reveals that popular attitudes towards political parties are highly ambivalent, if not contradictory. Those citizens simultaneously hold some attitudes that are quite positive (particularly concerning the basic functions played by parties in democratic systems) and others which are decidedly negative (see Sani 1992: 136). When these attitudes are separated into the 'cultural' and 'reactive' categories, however, some clearer patterns begin to emerge. With regard to indicators of reactive antipartyism (see Table 10.3), it is noteworthy that most respondents in all four countries (sometimes overwhelming majorities) have tended to express opinions that were generally supportive of parties. These favourable assessments of parties were by far the weakest in Italy during the 1990s, however, reflecting the restructuring of the party system that was occurring during that period (Sani and Segatti 2001: 178): between 34 and 43 per cent of Italians interviewed between 1990 and 1997 disagreed with statements that parties were needed to defend social interests, enabled citizens to participate in politics, and are necessary for democracy. In contrast, levels of rejection of these survey items in the other countries ranged between 10 and 22 per cent, and even in Italy in 1985 (before the crisis of the Italian party system began) did not exceed 29 per cent. Thus, with the exception of Italy in the 1990s, the overall conclusion to be drawn from these data is that there is significantly less (reactive) anti-party sentiment in Southern Europe than is commonly claimed.

Responses to those items that we regard as indicative of cultural antipartyism, however, reveal a much more negative pattern of attitudes towards parties. As can be seen in Table 10.2, about 40 to 60 per cent of respondents in most of these surveys agreed with the propositions that 'all parties are alike', and that they 'only divide people'. Indeed, as a harbinger of the party-system

TABLE 10.2. *Indicators of cultural anti-party sentiments in Southern Europe, 1985–1998 (%)*

Indicators	Year	Agree	Disagree	Don't know/ no answer	(N)
Parties are all alike					
Spain	1985	49	34	17	(2,505)
	1989	46	34	20	(4,524)
	1991	58	31	11	(2,471)
	1996	57	33	9	(2,498)
	1997	61	30	9	(2,490)
Portugal	1985	60	22	18	(2,210)
	1993*	59	24	3	(2,000)
Italy	1985	62	31	7	(2,074)
	1990	74	26	0	(M.D.)
Greece	1985	48	49	3	(1,998)
	1998	70	18	12	(1,191)
Parties only divide people					
Spain	1985	38	44	18	(2,505)
	1989	31	48	21	(4,524)
	1991	35	51	14	(2,471)
	1996	36	51	13	(2,498)
	1997	36	53	11	(2,490)
Portugal	1985	59	23	19	(2,210)
	1993*	52	29	4	(2,000)
Italy	1985	50	41	9	(2,074)
	1990	51	29	0	(M.D.)
	1997	28	62	10	(4,550)
Greece	1985	66	31	3	(1,998)
	1998	59	19	22	(1,191)

Sources: See Table 10.1.

* The addition of a 'neutral' category in this survey (the results of which are not presented) means that these figures do not total 100%.

TABLE 10.3. *Indicators of reactive pro-party sentiments in Southern Europe, 1978–1998 (%)*

Indicators	Year	Agree	Disagree	Don't know/ no answer	(N)
Parties needed to defend interests					
Spain	1985	65	15	20	(2,505)
	1989	65	13	21	(4,524)
	1991	70	15	15	(2,471)
	1996	72	16	12	(2,498)
	1997	75	13	12	(2,490)
Portugal	1985	59	16	25	(2,210)
	1993*	72	10	5	(2,000)
Italy	1985	63	26	11	(2,074)
	1990	58	41	1	(M.D.)
	1997	51	38	11	(4,550)
Greece	1985	78	13	9	(1,998)
	1998	74	18	8	(1,191)
Parties allow us to participate in politics					
Spain	1985	60	18	22	(2,505)
	1989	61	17	22	(4,524)
	1991	61	22	17	(2,471)
	1996	66	21	13	(2,498)
	1997	67	22	11	(2,490)
Portugal	1985	57	15	28	(2,210)
	1993*	72	9	4	(2,000)
Italy	1985	59	29	12	(2,074)
	1990	56	43	1	(M.D.)
Greece	1985	76	11	13	(1,998)
	1998	63	22	14	(1,191)
Without parties there can be no democracy					
Spain	1985	60	16	24	(2,505)
	1989	62	13	26	(4,524)
	1991	67	15	18	(2,471)
	1996	67	17	16	(2,498)
	1997	70	15	15	(2,490)
Portugal	1985	58	13	29	(2,210)
	1993*	70	10	5	(2,000)
Italy	1985	67	20	13	(2,074)
	1990	65	34	1	(M.D.)
	1997	54	36	10	(4,550)
Greece	1985	85	10	5	(1,998)
	1998	79	13	8	(1,191)

Sources: See Table 10.1.

* The addition of a 'neutral' category in this survey (the results of which are not presented) means that these figures do not total 100%.

crisis that would unfold in Italy beginning in 1992, it is noteworthy that two years earlier fully 74 per cent of Italians stated that they thought there was no difference between parties, and 51 per cent claimed that parties only serve to divide people. In general, we can conclude the sentiments we have referred to as cultural antipartyism are widespread among the citizens of all four Southern European countries.

The considerable differences between patterns of agreement with the cultural and reactive items explains, in part, the inconsistencies in the findings of many previous studies of antipartyism. They also indicate that much more detailed research should be conducted focusing on the behavioural and attitudinal correlates of these orientations (but see also Linz in Chapter 11 below). The first step in this analysis was the construction of two scales measuring the consistency of agreement or disagreement with the items making up the reactive and cultural dimensions of antipartyism. The reactive scale ranges from +3 (reflecting agreement with all three of the positive statements about parties) to −3 (at the anti-party end of the continuum), with scores between +1 and −1 regarded as neutral. The data presented in Table 10.4 clearly show that the great majority of respondents surveyed over the past two decades have held pro-party attitudes, particularly in Spain, Portugal, and, in 1985, Greece. Italians were almost evenly divided in 1985 between those with pro-party and neutral attitudes, while in the case of Greece there was a great decline in pro-party sentiments between the mid-1980s and late 1990s.

Table 10.5 presents the distribution of respondents in accord with their positions on the cultural antipartyism scale, constructed of their responses to the parties 'are all the same' and 'only divide people' items. This scale ranges between +2 (representing a pro-party orientation based on a *negative* response to the two anti-party statements) and −2 (reflecting an anti-party stance). As can be seen, anti-party sentiments of this kind are much higher than was the case with the other dimension, and were especially strong in Portugal and in Greece in 1998. While such negativism is not surprising in the case of Portugal in the early to mid-1980s (given the political instability that characterized the decade following the revolution), it seems certainly to be

TABLE 10.4. *Reactive anti-party sentiments in Southern Europe, 1985–1998 (%)*

	Spain						Portugal		Italy	Greece	
	1985	1988	1991	1995	1996	1997	1985	1993	1985	1985	1998
Pro-party	64	68	58	63	62	62	60	65	48	72	13
Neutral	30	27	37	32	32	32	35	34	43	26	46
Anti-party	6	5	4	4	4	6	5	1	9	2	41

Sources: See Table 10.1.

Don't know and no answer have been excluded from calculation of vertical percentages.

incompatible with the government stability that has characterized Portuguese politics since 1987 (Bruneau and Bacalhau 1978; Bruneau and MacLeod 1986), or with the rapid economic and social development that the country has enjoyed over the past decade and a half. In short, these anti-party attitudes seem to be insensitive to real changes in the Portuguese political environment. The contrary can be seen in Greece, where a substantial increase in anti-party sentiments has taken place between the mid-1980s and mid-1990s. Most of that increase, however, can be accounted for by the much larger percentage of respondents who came to agree with the proposition that all parties were alike, an accurate reflection of the ideological and programmatic convergence between PASOK and Nea Demokratia that began in the mid-1980s during PASOK's second term in office (Diamandouros 1994: 9–20, 34–42; Mendrinou and Nicolacopoulos 1997: 11); the percentage of Greek respondents who thought that 'parties only divide people' actually declined slightly, from 66 to 59 per cent between 1985 and 1998. Spanish survey responses, meanwhile, were remarkably consistent over time. Spanish cultural anti-party attitudes have been almost evenly divided among the pro-, anti-, and neutral categories ever since the mid-1980s.

Aside from the common finding that levels of cultural antipartyism are consistently higher than those of reactive anti-party sentiments, these data reveal that the extent and intensity of such attitudes vary from country to country. Pervasive, negative attitudes towards parties do not appear to constitute a Southern-Europe-wide phenomenon, let alone a general characteristic of politics throughout Western Europe (see Reiter 1989). Instead, these attitudes reflect a great deal of ambivalence among citizens towards their political parties.

THE ORIGINS OF ANTI-PARTY SENTIMENTS

One way of exploring the origins and nature of these two dimensions of antipartyism is to compare the evolution of these attitudes over time among

TABLE 10.5. *Cultural anti-party sentiments in Southern Europe, 1985–1998 (%)*

	Spain						Portugal		Italy	Greece	
	1985	1988	1991	1995	1996	1997	1985	1993	1985	1985	1998
Pro-party	34	35	22	32	32	28	15	22	22	25	8
Neutral	29	32	33	35	33	37	24	24	33	33	18
Anti-party	37	33	44	33	36	35	61	52	44	42	74

Sources: See Table 10.1.

Don't know and no answer have been excluded from calculation of vertical percentages.

different political generations. Depending on the patterns observed, such an analysis should make it possible clearly to separate the effects of different socialization experiences from reactions to short-term developments in the political environment. Given the greater availability of comparable data over an extended period of time, we shall now focus our attention on the case of Spain. The Spanish case is particularly suitable for this kind of analysis, given the great differences in socialization experiences of the various age cohorts in our survey samples: these include the fully democratic but tumultuous regime of the Second Republic, the trauma of the Civil War, the hunger and political repression of the post-Civil War era, the economic development and partial liberalization that took place in the 1960s and early 1970s, and the transition to democracy following the death of Franco. To what extent have these greatly different political and social conditions affected the development of attitudes towards political parties? And how have these positive and negative orientations evolved over the past two decades in response to the major political developments of this most recent period?

While political socialization takes place throughout life (beginning with informal socialization by parents and formal socialization in school, and continuing in response to dramatic political developments, if they should occur), we shall use as the basis of defining the various cohorts the most distinguishing political characteristics that occurred when the respondent was age 17–25. This is the period, according to numerous studies in social psychology (e.g. Newcomb *et al.* 1967; Krosnick and Alwin 1989), when most political attitudes tend to stabilize. Accordingly, age cohort #6 is defined as those respondents who were born before 1914. This group thus includes some individuals who would have passed through their most crucial formative period under the Restoration Monarchy or the dictatorship of Primo de Rivera, but most of them would have matured during the Second Republic (1931–6). Cohort #5 is the Civil War cohort, and includes persons born between 1915 and 1923. The next group, born between 1924 and 1943, is the post-war generation, who would have felt most intensely the harsh period of economic deprivation and political repression that followed the Civil War. In contrast, cohort #3 (born between 1944 and 1957) matured politically during the rapid economic growth and *apertura* (partial liberalization) that characterized the final years of *franquismo*. Respondents belonging to the second cohort (born between 1958 and 1965) passed through their most formative years between 1975 and 1982—the period of transition to and consolidation of the post-Franco democracy. Finally, respondents in cohort #1 (born after 1966) would have been socialized almost entirely in the current democratic era.

An examination of data derived from this type of analysis makes it possible to distinguish among three different kinds of patterns, commonly referred to as cohort effects, period effects, and life-cycle effects. The latter effect is one in which, over a very extended period of time, the effects of ageing influence all cohorts in the same way; they tend to converge on a common point towards the end of their lives, such that trend lines should exhibit an upward slope. Both because of the nature of the hypotheses we are exploring, and because we do not observe life-cycle effects with regard to anti-party sentiments, we will focus our attention on the first two patterns. Cohort effects result primarily from common socialization experiences that impart certain attitudes that continue to influence individuals in the cohort throughout their lives. Accordingly, we should expect to find that individuals socialized under the Second Republic should continue to differ from those whose primary socialization experiences occurred during the current transition to democracy across all of the data points in our time-series analysis. Conversely, period effects should have a similar influence on individuals in all of the cohorts; irrespective of their socialization experiences, they respond in a similar manner to reactive stimuli that occur over the course of the time period surveyed in our analysis. Visually, this should be reflected in simultaneous and parallel peaks and dips in the trend lines for all cohorts.

Figure 10.1 presents the distribution of survey responses to the 'cultural antipartyism' questions over time. The patterns apparent in this graph suggest that the most powerful influence over the anti-party attitudes held by each age group is exerted by a cohort effect. The five age groups arrayed in this figure tend to differ from each other consistently across time, with the older respondents invariably expressing anti-party sentiments. As can be seen, these trend lines are extremely flat, the sole exception being the instability in responses of the oldest cohort during the 1990s. Thus, the strongest influence over these attitudes appears to be related to the primary socialization experiences of the respondent: those individuals who were socialized earlier hold the most negative attitudes towards parties. (It is worthy of mention that these findings also hold for the youngest cohort—socialized since the transition to democracy—whose responses could not be presented in the figure for technical reasons.[8]) This interpretation of the visual presentation of these data is confirmed by a multivariate regression analysis.[9]

In short, these data suggest that the unfortunate earlier decades of the twentieth century in Spain—characterized by electoral manipulation under the Restoration Monarchy, bitterly rancorous partisan conflict under the Second Republic, culminating in Civil War, and followed by decades of anti-party propaganda under an authoritarian regime—left a lasting mark on the political orientations of those older Spaniards who were most exposed to these socializing influences. And the more protracted and cumulative these anti-party cues, the more negative were these attitudes within the cohort. It should be noted that these findings parallel those of a broader study of these and additional variables measuring political disaffection (see Torcal 2000): political disaffection is systematically stronger among the older cohorts of interview respondents.

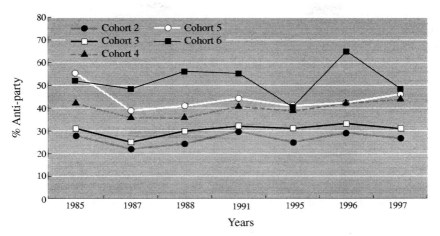

FIG. 10.1. *Cohorts and cultural anti-party sentiments in Spain, 1985–1997*

These data also suggest that cultural anti-party attitudes do not represent a universal or permanent feature of Spain's political culture, but, rather, are a reflection of distinct socialization experiences within different political contexts that have different impacts on the various political generations. Once individuals have acquired such attitudes, however, they are remarkably durable, and the aggregate level of support for such sentiments remains quite stable over time. These attitudes were nearly constant within each of the cohorts, irrespective of occasionally dramatic political developments that one might have expected would lead to an increase in anti-party sentiments, such as the corruption scandals of the late 1980s and early 1990s. Thus, it appears that this 'cultural' variety of antipartyism in Spain is not substantially affected over the short term by the behaviour of party elites or the performance of parties. Instead, such attitudes appear to be the product of socialization experiences that, for many Spaniards, substantially predated the establishment of this democratic regime in the late 1970s. The more pessimistic view of this same finding is that, contrary to expectations that might be derived from Converse (1969) or Schmitter and Karl (1991), the generally successful performance of the current democratic regime has been incapable of erasing these anti-party sentiments among the older cohorts. Instead, it appears more likely that cultural antipartyism will diminish only with the progressive disappearance of the older generations who most strongly cling to such orientations.

Figure 10.2 presents the evolution over time, by age cohort, of the percentage of respondents agreeing with the *pro*-party attitudes that make up the reactive cluster. These patterns are very different from those found in the first graph: rather than being generally stable over time, they fluctuate substantially from one year to the next; and there is no cohort effect that is compatible with what we observed in the previous graph. In sharp contrast with the cultural variety of antipartyism, the older cohorts generally tend to express more pro-party sentiments than do younger respondents. And there is no stable rank-ordering of cohorts; indeed, while the oldest cohort is more pro-party than the others in most years, in 1988 it is the least. Clearly, these data do not indicate the existence of a substantial cohort effect. But their inconsistency also gives very weak support to a 'period effect' interpretation, as is confirmed by an empirical test of a multivariate model.[10]

In general, these reactive anti-party sentiments appear to be associated with a broader 'political discontent' cluster of attitudinal orientations. As we have also argued elsewhere (Montero *et al.* 1997, 1998; Gunther and Montero 2000; Torcal 2000), these attitudes are highly unstable over time. And this instability is a function both of the evaluations of parties and of the respondent's degree of satisfaction with the performance of the incumbent government, which is, in turn, strongly influenced by his/her own partisan preferences. This attitudinal domain is both conceptually and empirically distinct from the political disaffection syndrome, to which the cultural anti-party attitudes appear to be linked, as we shall demonstrate below.

ATTITUDINAL CORRELATES OF ANTI-PARTY SENTIMENTS

In an earlier discussion, it was noted that the distribution of cultural anti-party sentiments among various age cohorts reflected patterns quite similar

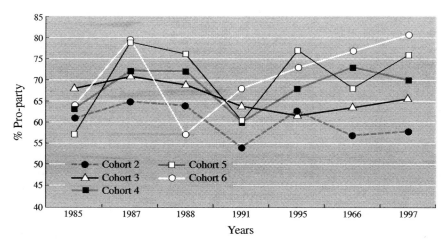

FIG. 10.2. *Cohorts and reactive pro-party sentiments in Spain, 1985–1997*

to other political orientations that we asserted constitute a political disaffection syndrome. In Table 10.6, we present data testing that assertion, revealing the extent to which individuals whose other survey responses are indicative of political disaffection also hold cultural and reactive anti-party sentiments. As can be seen, there is a strong relationship (Tau-b = .31) between cultural antipartyism and the belief that 'Politics is so complicated that people like me cannot understand what is happening.' At the same time, there is absolutely no relationship between this 'internal efficacy' item (a standard measure of one dimension of political disaffection) and reactive antipartyism (Tau-b = .01). There is also a strong relationship between cultural antipartyism, on the one hand, and two standard measures of 'external efficacy': the beliefs that 'Those in power are only looking out for their own personal interests' (Tau-b = .39), and that 'Politicians don't care what people like me think' (Tau-b = .26). While the relationships between these two political disaffection items and reactive antipartyism were statistically significant, they were very weak (Tau-b = .08, in each case). Very similar results are obtained from an examination of the relationships between these two different types of antipartyism and two indicators of political interest which are also intimately linked to the political disaffection syndrome—the respondent's self-described level of interest in politics, and extent to which he/she feels aware about political matters. Neither of these measures of political involvement are statistically associated with reactive antipartyism (Tau-b = −.05 and −.03), while they were much more closely associated with scores on the cultural antipartyism scale (Tau-b = −.28 and −.22); the more aware the respondent, the less likely he or she is to hold antiparty attitudes of that kind.

These findings are of considerable theoretical significance. The linkage between cultural antipartyism and low levels of interest in or awareness of politics provides support for our hypothesis that this variety of negative attitude towards parties is part of the broader disaffection syndrome that we have analysed elsewhere. But the negative finding regarding a possible association between political awareness, on the one hand, and reactive antipartyism, on the other, is also of interest. This finding is inconsistent with claims by scholars (Dalton 1996: 281; Norris 1999*b*: 270) that cynicism, a lack of confidence in institutions, and declining levels of party attachment are characteristic of those who are better informed politically. Indeed, this finding runs counter to that portion of the reactive anti-party model that we set forth at the beginning of this chapter in so far as some scholars predicted that these kinds of anti-party sentiments would be most widespread among those individuals who are most interested in and better informed about politics, and the actual failings of parties and politicians. Instead, we find that there is absolutely no relationship between reactive antipartyism and political interest. In contrast, the association with cultural antipartyism is strongly

TABLE 10.6. *Anti-party sentiments and political efficacy, interest, and awareness in Spain, 1995 (%)*

Efficacy item	Cultural dimension			Reactive dimension		
	Pro-party	Neutral	Anti-party	Pro-party	Neutral	Anti-party
Politics too complicated						
agree	34	56	75	52	53	53
disagree	66	43	25	48	47	47
(N)	(1,034)	(1,115)	(1,065)	(1,877)	(961)	(129)
Tau-b		.31*			.01	
Those in power only look out for their personal interests						
agree	47	83	92	71	76	90
disagree	53	17	8	29	24	10
(N)	(971)	(1,085)	(1,054)	(1,792)	(944)	(126)
Tau-b		.39*			.08*	
Politicians not concerned						
agree	61	77	90	73	78	90
disagree	39	23	10	27	22	10
(N)	(993)	(1,088)	(1,036)	(1,812)	(944)	(127)
Tau-b		.26*			.08*	
Interest in politics						
much and some	43	23	11	30	23	29
little and none	57	77	89	70	77	71
(N)	(855)	(799)	(815)	(1,524)	(604)	(111)
Tau-b		-.28*			-.05	
Political awareness						
much and some	51	35	24	40	36	42
little and none	49	65	76	60	64	58
(N)	(858)	(799)	(813)	(1,520)	(606)	(112)
Tau-b		-.22*			-.03	

Source: Banco de Datos, CIS, #2154.

Significant at .01 level. Don't know and no answer have been excluded from calculation of vertical percentages.

negative, with those who are least interested in and aware about politics being by far the most predisposed to adopt an anti-party stance.

A clue as to the broader meaning of reactive antipartyism can be gleaned from an examination of the partisan preferences of those holding anti-party sentiments. There is very little relationship between cultural antipartyism and the vote (for the PP, the conservative Partido Popular, as compared with the PSOE, the Socialist Partido Socialista Obrero Español) in the 1993 and 1996 elections (Tau-b = .02 in both elections). With regard to reactive antipartyism, however, there is a moderately strong association with a vote for the opposition party. In 1993, when the PSOE was in power, those with reactive anti-party sentiments voted disproportionately for the opposition PP (by a margin of 60 versus 40 per cent). In 1996, when the PP came to power, the relationship was reversed: 62 per cent of anti-party respondents supported the opposition PSOE, while just 36 per cent voted for the PP.

This same pattern can be found when these relationships are re-examined using a generic measure of satisfaction with the performance of the PSOE government in a 1995 survey (CIS survey #2154). Among those who expressed reactive anti-party opinions, 72 per cent disapproved of the performance of the governments headed by Felipe González, while only 41 per cent of those with pro-party attitudes did so (Tau-b = −.12). In this same survey, 60 per cent of pro-party respondents said that they thought things had improved under the PSOE governments that were in power beginning in 1982, while only 27 per cent of anti-party respondents shared these views. Similar patterns can be observed with regard to satisfaction with the state of the economy at that time: 49 per cent of reactive anti-party respondents stated that their personal economic situation was bad or very bad, and fully 80 per cent said that the general economic situation of the country was bad or very bad. Among those who selected pro-party items on the reactive scale, the percentages who gave similarly negative evaluations to their personal and the country's economic condition were 24 per cent and 63 per cent, respectively. In light of these findings, it would not be unreasonable to regard these kinds of anti-party sentiments as being linked to a desire to 'throw the bums out' following an unsatisfactory performance in government. It should be noted that, while responses to the cultural antipartyism items revealed the same general pattern, the relationships between dissatisfaction and anti-party sentiments was much weaker: the 69 per cent of anti-party respondents who were dissatisfied with the general state of the economy was only slightly larger than the 60 per cent of those who have pro-party responses; and a breakdown of cultural anti- and pro-party respondents with regard to a negative assessment of their personal economic situation also produced a narrow margin of 33 versus 23 per cent.

Dissatisfaction inherently involves a desire for change. Not surprisingly, then, reactive anti-party sentiments are also related to both the extent of change desired and to preferences regarding the political means for bringing it about. In a 1995 survey, respondents were asked to choose among the following options concerning the current status of Spanish society: 'It's fine the way it is'; 'it could be improved with small changes'; 'it needs profound reforms'; and 'it should be radically changed'. As can be seen in Table 10.7, those who selected pro-party items on the reactive scale were strongly predisposed towards moderate amounts of change or deeper reforms, while anti-party respondents tended overwhelmingly to prefer more radical changes.

Again, the same general pattern could be observed with regard to cultural anti-party sentiments, but in this case the relationships were extremely weak. With regard to the preferred institutional vehicle for implementing the desire for change, the differences between reactive pro- and anti-party respondents, and between the effects of the cultural and reactive dimensions of antiparty-ism, were even more pronounced. Among those who selected pro-party items on the reactive scale, fully 87 per cent agreed with the proposition that 'Voting is the only way of influencing the government', while reactive anti-party respondents were almost evenly divided, with 49 per cent regarding the vote as the only vehicle for influencing the government, and 51 disagreeing (Tau-b = .23). In sharp contrast, there was virtually no impact of cultural antipartyism on preferences for one or the other of these behavioural prefer-ences (Tau-b = .03).

To this point we have argued that cultural antipartyism is part of a broader syndrome of political disaffection, while reactive anti-party attitudes are conceptually and empirically distinct, and appear to be related to clusters of attitudes associated with political discontent and dissatisfaction with the incumbent government. But what are the origins of these two sets of atti-tudes? We began this exploration of anti-party sentiments in Spain with a comparison of various age cohorts, and we found that cultural anti-party sen-timents were much more commonly found among older Spaniards than among the young. We speculated that these persisting 'cohort effects' were the long-term products of socialization experiences, particularly those encountered during the crucial formative periods of each respondent's life. Indeed, the basic characteristics of these experiences varied greatly among age groups: those individuals in the older cohorts passed through their most for-mative periods of socialization when parties were playing political roles that

TABLE 10.7. *Anti-party sentiments and conservative or reformist attitudes towards Spanish society, 1995* (%)*

	Cultural Dimension			Reactive Dimension		
Attitude towards society	Pro-party	Neutral	Anti-party	Pro-party	Neutral	Anti-party
Fine as it is	5	5	4	5	5	2
Minor reforms	38	30	30	39	25	11
Profound reforms	48	54	48	47	54	59
Radical change	8	11	17	9	16	28
(N)	(1,040)	(1,121)	(1,049)	(1,885)	(971)	(129)
Tau-b		.09*			.17*	

Source: Banco de Datos, CIS, #2154

* Significant at .01 level. Don't know and no answer have been excluded from calculation of ver-tical percentages.

had dramatically negative consequences (especially during the Second Republic and Civil War), or when the Franquist authoritarian regime was systematically disseminating propaganda hostile to parties and liberal democracy in general. In contrast, younger Spaniards' attitudes should be expected to bear the imprint of much more positive images of parties—particularly in light of their constructive roles in the highly successful processes of transition to and consolidation of democracy. But before we conclude that these macropolitical developments were the cause of such sentiments, it is necessary to explore systematically the impact of another powerful socializing agent: formal education. Not only does a country's education system serve as a vehicle for the delivery of a regime's propaganda and self-legitimating messages (which, in the case of Spain, changed dramatically in the 1970s), but it also develops intellectual and technical skills that are relevant to political engagement and participation. In short, it helps to build social capital that facilitates citizen involvement in politics.

Our analysis of survey data collected in 1995 reveals that education is negatively associated with the holding of cultural anti-party attitudes (Tau-b = −.19). Those respondents with low levels of education are far more likely to adopt a cultural anti-party stance: fully 49 per cent of those holding cultural anti-party views had completed the primary level of education or less, while only 30 per cent of those with pro-party attitudes fell into these low-education categories. This finding is compatible with our interpretation of cultural antipartyism as forming part of the political disaffection syndrome. If corroborated by analyses that impose controls for potentially confounding influences, this would suggest that there is a strong social-capital-building effect of education: those individuals who have fewer of the kinds of skills and personal resources relevant to political participation are attitudinally marginalized from involvement in politics, and the holding of cultural anti-party attitudes is one manifestation of this political disaffection.

But before a conclusion of that kind could be justified, it is necessary to attempt to separate two distinctly different socializing influences that in Spain are highly correlated with one another. Educational opportunities for Spaniards were very sharply limited under the Franco regime (in large measure, due to its persistent underfunding of public education, see Gunther 1980: 67–8), but they expanded greatly beginning in the 1970s. Thus, one possible interpretation of the cohort effects that we observed earlier is that older Spaniards may have more negative attitudes towards parties as a by-product of their lower levels of educational attainment. But while older Spaniards may, in the aggregate, have received substantially less formal education than their children and grandchildren, they also passed through their most formative period of life when anti-party messages were either being learnt through the tragic experiences of the Second Republic and Civil War eras, or intentionally disseminated by the authoritarian regime of General Franco. Given the colinearity between educational opportunities and these differing kinds of socialization experience, it is not possible to reach a conclusion about the true nature of these cohort effects without introducing a 'control' variable into the analysis.

In order to separate these two distinctly different kinds of socialization processes, we shall re-examine the relationship between years of education and cultural antipartyism after first dividing the sample into two sets of age cohorts: the younger age group includes those who were most intensively socialized during the final years of *franquismo* (characterized by economic development and partial liberalization) and during the transition to democracy, while the older group includes those whose key formative periods corresponded with the Second Republic and Civil War, as well as the early, harsh period of the Franco regime. The resulting data, presented in Table 10.8, reveal that both types of socialization had an impact on the development of cultural anti-party attitudes, but that years of formal education have by far the more powerful impact. Within each age group, the better educated the respondent, the less likely he/she is to hold cultural anti-party attitudes. This is a particularly interesting finding, since better educated older respondents were less likely to be negative in their attitudes towards parties than the less well-educated, even though they were exposed to more years of anti-democratic and anti-party socialization through the authoritarian regime's education system. This provides some empirical evidence in support of the commonly expressed opinion that most Spanish students (at least in the 1960s and 1970s) refused to take the regime's heavy-handed efforts at socialization seriously. Instead, and somewhat paradoxically, the principal legacy of the former regime in terms of cultural anti-party attitudes appears to result from the fact that Spain's education system under that regime remained seriously underdeveloped until the 1970s, leading to an underdevelopment of social capital among Spain's citizens.

An examination of the relationship between education and reactive antipartyism produces a very different picture. Contrary to the predictions of some scholars, who portray critical attitudes towards parties as the product of greater familiarity with their misbehaviour and shortcomings (and, hence, would expect to find stronger anti-party sentiments among the better educated), the data presented in Table 10.8 revealed that the extent of a respondent's formal education is not consistently or significantly linked to such attitudes. Informal socialization experiences during childhood also differentiate the origins of reactive antipartyism from those of cultural antipartyism. There is a strong negative association between the frequency of discussion of politics within the family when the respondent was a child and the development of cultural anti-party attitudes. A 1997 survey (CIS study #2240) revealed that 59 per cent of those holding cultural anti-party attitudes had 'never' discussed politics with other members as a child, as compared with

TABLE 10.8. *Anti-party sentiments and educational attainment in Spain, 1995* (*horizontal %*)

Education level	Cultural Dimension				Reactive Dimension			
	Pro-party	Neutral	Anti-party	(N)	Pro-party	Neutral	Anti-party	(N)
Younger cohorts								
Uneducated	26	26	47	(49)	62	31	7	(45)
Primary	23	37	40	(419)	65	31	4	(368)
Secondary	30	35	35	(735)	60	35	6	(697)
College prep.	38	36	26	(567)	57	38	5	(554)
University	53	33	14	(390)	61	35	4	(378)
Tau-b	-.20*				.03			
Older cohorts								
Uneducated	18	38	44	(204)	77	21	3	(160)
Primary	27	31	42	(608)	71	26	3	(343)
Secondary	31	33	36	(115)	64	31	4	(112)
College prep.	22	41	37	(82)	70	24	5	(74)
University	44	33	22	(90)	60	38	2	(85)
Tau-b	-.10*				.08*			

Source: Banco de Datos, CIS, #2154.

* Significant at .01.

** Don't know and no answer have been excluded from calculation of horizontal percentages. *Uneducated* includes illiterate, and has never attended school but can read; *Primary* includes complete or incomplete elementary education; *Secondary* includes complete junior-high-school education and elementary professional training; *College prep* includes Bachillerato (university-prepatory high school) and advanced professional training; and *University* includes complete and incomplete university or advanced technical school education.

only 35 per cent of those with pro-party attitudes (Tau-b = −.18). With regard to reactive antipartyism, there is no statistically significant relationship between the two (Tau-b = .02).

Additional indications of the political disengagement of those holding cultural anti-party attitudes can be seen in their low frequency of exposure to political information through the media or discussions of politics with other persons. As can be seen in Table 10.9, there are significant and strong negative relationships between cultural antipartyism, on the one hand, and the frequency with which respondents read newspapers (Tau-b = −.23) and discuss politics with other persons (Tau-b = −.21). Persons holding cultural anti-party attitudes are also significantly less likely to watch television programmes dealing with politics and listen to radio programmes that deal with politics, although the relationships are of more modest strength (Tau-b = −.10 and −.12, respectively). Once again, the correlates of reactive-antipartyism are quite different from those of the cultural variety. Only exposure to television news shares a statistically significant negative association with anti-party attitudes (Tau-b = −.06). The frequency of exposure to other sources of political information are statistically insignificant and, with regard to political discussion and newspaper reading, of the wrong sign.

To what extent are these attitudes linked to support for democracy—a core element of the legitimacy of a democratic regime? In Table 10.10, we present data showing the relationship between both kinds of antipartyism and a questionnaire item that asks respondents to choose among the following options: 'Democracy is preferable to any other form of government'; 'Under certain circumstances, an authoritarian regime, a dictatorship, is preferable to a democratic system'; and 'For people like me, one regime is the same as another'. The most striking conclusion is that overwhelming majorities of Spaniards support democracy irrespective of their attitudes towards parties. It is also clear, however, that both kinds of anti-party sentiments are associated with lower levels of support for democracy (Tau-b = −.20 and −.10, respectively).

ANTI-PARTY SENTIMENTS IN PORTUGAL, ITALY, AND GREECE

To what extent are the attitudinal correlates and the likely origins of anti-party sentiments the same in other Southern European countries? If we were to find these same general patterns in the other three countries in this region, despite their differing historical experiences and political cultures, this would substantially reinforce the construct validity of the attitudinal dimensions that we are exploring in this chapter. In Table 10.11, we present some of the correlates of cultural antipartyism in these three countries. The similarities

TABLE 10.9. *Anti-party sentiments and exposure to political information in Spain, 1995* (%)

Frecuency of exposure	Cultural Dimension			Reactive Dimension		
	Pro-party	Neutral	Anti-party	Pro-party	Neutral	Anti-party
Reads political news in newspapers						
every day or several days per week	37	25	16	27	29	21
once a week	25	22	16	22	24	14
sometimes	11	12	13	12	13	9
never/almost never	27	41	55	39	35	55
(N)	(1,054)	(1,137)	(1,091)	(1,927)	(981)	(131)
Tau-b		−.23*			.01	
Watches television news programs						
every day or several days per week	57	48	44	52	49	38
once a week	20	20	18	20	20	18
sometimes	11	12	12	11	11	13
never/almost never	14	19	25	16	20	31
(N)	(1,051)	(1,136)	(1,087)	(1,921)	(929)	(130)
Tau-b		−.10*			−.06*	
Listens to radio news programs						
every day or several days per week	34	26	22	30	28	21
once a week	16	16	13	15	15	14
sometimes	9	13	11	11	11	13
never/almost never	41	45	54	45	46	52
(N)	(1,053)	(1,135)	(1,091)	(1,924)	(981)	(131)
Tau-b		−.12*			−.02	
Discusses politics						
every day or several days per week	21	11	10	14	16	12
once a week	26	21	13	21	22	24
sometimes	26	25	24	25	28	23
never/almost never	28	43	54	40	33	52
(N)	(1,037)	(1,134)	(1,080)	(1,907)	(971)	(131)
Tau-b		−.21*			.03	

Source: Banco de Datos, CIS, #2154.
*Significant at .01. Don't know and no answer have been excluded from calculation of vertical percentages.

TABLE 10.10. *Anti-party sentiments and support for democracy in Spain, 1995 (%)*

Support for democracy	Cultural Dimension			Reactive Dimension		
	Pro-party	Neutral	Anti-party	Pro-party	Neutral	Anti-party
Democracy is preferable	88	82	66	83	77	61
Authoritarian regime						
sometimes preferable	7	10	14	8	13	21
No difference	5	8	20	9	11	18
(N)	(1,037)	(1,113)	(1,054)	(1,878)	(963)	(124)
Tau-b		−.20*			−.10	

Source: Banco de Datos, CIS, # 2154.
*Significant at .01 level. Don't know and no answer have been excluded from calculation of vertical percentages.

among these relationships (not to mention their compatibility with the Spanish data that we presented above) is most impressive. By far the strongest linkages are between cultural anti-party attitudes and four variables that our already mentioned studies (Montero *et al.* 1997, 1998; Gunther and Montero 2000; Torcal 2000) have demonstrated belong to a broader political disaffection syndrome: these include three measures of 'political efficacy', and the respondent's self-described level of interest in politics. Those who hold cultural anti-party attitudes in all three countries are substantially less interested in politics. Indeed, the differences in level of political interest between anti- and pro-party respondents are quite extreme: 39 versus 77 per cent in Greece; 9 versus 41 per cent in Portugal; and 21 versus 59 per cent in Italy. Those with cultural anti-party attitudes are lower in internal efficacy, more cynical towards politicians, and much less exposed to newspapers. Only the lack of a consistent relationship with television viewing and the weakness of the relationship with radio listening do not fit with our Spanish findings, and this is most likely the result of a significant difference in the wording of questionnaire items.[12] With regard to the origins of these kinds of attitudes, it is noteworthy that there is a strong link in each country with low levels of education and a positive evaluation of the former authoritarian regime. Thus, there is prima-facie evidence that our speculations about the origins of such attitudes in earlier socialization experiences appear to be credible as hypotheses explaining their appearance in these other countries as well.

Similarly, our Spanish findings are also consistent with those from Greece, Italy, and Portugal concerning reactive antipartyism as well. As can be seen in Table 10.12, there is no significant or consistent relationship with regard to exposure to the print or broadcast media, and the link with the respondent's level of educational attainment is extremely weak. The only noteworthy departure from our findings from Spain is that, in Italy, there is a relationship

TABLE 10.11. *Correlates (Tau-b) of cultural anti-party sentiments in Portugal, Italy, and Greece, 1985*

Indicators	Portugal	Italy	Greece
Political efficacy**			
politicians don't care	.23*	.22*	.25*
politics too complicated	.29*	.27*	.31*
those in power only look out for personal interests	.25*	.32*	.38*
Interest in politics	−.30*	−.30*	−.28*
Exposure to political information			
frequency of newspaper reading	−.18*	−.15*	−.15*
frequency of radio news listening	−.08*	−.03	−.01
frequency of TV news viewing	−.09*	.04	.05*
Reformist attitudes towards social change	−.09*	−.01	−.06*
Educational attainment	−.17*	−.18*	−.17*
Support for democracy	−.06*	−.08*	−.10*
Evaluation of former authoritarian regime	.17*	.13*	.32*

Source: The Four Nation Study.

*Significant at .01 level.

** The wordings of the following questionnaire items are: 'Politicians don't care what people like me think'; 'politics is so complicated that people like me cannot understand what is happening'; and 'those in power are only looking out for their own personal interests'.

of moderate strength between this kind of anti-party orientation, on the one hand, low levels of political interest, high levels of political disaffection, and a preference for moderate social and political reforms, on the other. In short, in Italy there is some overlap between the cultural and reactive types of antipartyism. These relationships are much weaker in Greece, and in Portugal they are non-existent. Thus, with the partial exception of the Italian case (which we hypothesize is a product of certain specific features of Italian party politics in the mid-1980s[12]), these findings provide further corroboration that reactive antipartyism is not part of the political disaffection syndrome, and is distinct from cultural antipartyism. Finally, as in the case of cultural anti-partyism, there is a relationship of moderate strength between these negative orientations towards parties and positive assessments of the previous authoritarian regime, as well as lower levels of support for democracy.

In short, these findings provide strong corroboration for our assertion that these two different kinds of anti-party sentiments are both conceptually and empirically distinct. Despite the significant differences among the historical experiences and political cultures of these four countries (and even some questionnaire-item wording differences that weaken our measures of statistical association), the same patterns can be seen consistently across all four countries. These patterns suggest that cultural anti-party sentiments are part of the

TABLE 10.12. *Correlates (Tau-b) of reactive anti-party sentiments in Portugal, Italy, and Greece, 1985*

Indicators	Portugal	Italy	Greece
Political efficacy**			
politicians don't care	.01	.11*	.04
politics too complicated	.00	.03	−.01
those in power only look out for personal interests	.07	.12	.04
Interest in politics	.01	−.11*	−.07*
Exposure to political information			
frequency of newspaper reading	.05	−.01	.01
frequency of radio news listening	.05	−.00	−.03
frequency of TV news viewing	.02	−.04	−.04
Reformist attitudes towards social change	.03	.11*	.08*
Educational attainment	.03	.04*	.05
Support for democracy	−.15*	−.14*	−.06*
Evaluation of former authoritarian regime	.13*	.09*	.09*

Source: The Four Nation Study.

* Significant at .01 level.

** The wordings of the following questionnaire items are: 'Politicians don't care what people like me think'; 'politics is so complicated that people like me cannot understand what is happening'; and 'those in power are only looking out for their own personal interests'.

broader syndrome of political disaffection, while reactive antipartyism appears to be associated with political discontent, and, in particular, dissatisfaction with the performance of the incumbent government.

THE BEHAVIORAL CONSEQUENCES OF ANTI-PARTY SENTIMENTS

It has often been argued that anti-party sentiments, or the broader crisis of confidence in political institutions in modern democracies, can have grave implications for the quality of democracy. Among the various behavioural consequences that have been associated with this cluster of attitudes are the erosion of voters' psychological attachments of parties, decreases in electoral participation, increases in electoral volatility, a decline in the number of party members, and an increase in support for anti-system parties (Poguntke 1996). In light of our findings about the existence of two distinctly different dimensions of anti-party attitudes, let us examine some of the behavioural correlates of these orientations.

Tables 10.13 and 10.14 present data measuring the relationships between anti-party attitudes and three different aspects of political participation. The first of these involves the simple act of voting itself, and separates those who cast a ballot (valid or not) from those who abstained from electoral participation altogether. The next two are based on (1) casting a ballot for or against the incumbent government party (with blank or otherwise invalid ballots counted as votes against the government) and (2) giving electoral support to an anti-system party (the PCP in Portugal, the MSI in Italy, and the KKE in Greece). Closely related to these behavioural manifestations of partisanship is the development of a psychological attachment to a political party—or, as it is more usually described, party identification.[13] An additional dependent variable is membership in various kinds of secondary associations, including cultural, religious, partisan, professional, trade union, or recreational groups. This provides a measure of the degree of active integration of the respondent into civil society and (in some cases) partisan organizations. But electoral participation and membership in organized groups are only two of the several ways in which citizens can participate within their democratic political systems. Since the late 1960s, in particular, non-traditional or unconventional forms of participation have been regarded as significant channels for political activity (see Barnes, Kaase *et al.* 1979; Muller 1979). Some such unconventional arenas for participation are regarded in most democratic countries as entirely proper and legitimate forms of citizen involvement. While peaceful protest demonstrations fall into this category, other forms of non-traditional political participation are not regarded as acceptable forms of behaviour. Illegal sit-ins and occupation of factories, and, especially, engagement in acts of violence, are not only proscribed in most democratic systems, but it can be argued that they represent a violation of democratic rules of the game that can have dangerously polarizing consequences in a democratic system. Thus, Tables 10.13 and 10.14 separate these other forms of political involvement into three categories: conventional participation (including work for a party, participating in party meetings, efforts to convince others how to vote, and attentiveness to politics through the media); unconventional forms of political participation (involvement in strikes, demonstrations, and sit-ins); and illegal protests (consist of blocking traffic, destroying property, and painting graffiti in public places).

Table 10.13 presents Tau-b coefficients measuring the association between these various forms of involvement in politics and the cultural form of antipartyism. As can be seen, cultural anti-party attitudes are associated with each and every form of participation in the table except voting—and the absence of a relationship in that case is somewhat surprising, given the important role that parties play in mobilizing voters during election campaigns. Overall, these findings strongly reaffirm our earlier interpretation of cultural antipartyism as part of a broader syndrome of political disaffection and marginalization from active involvement in politics in all four countries. Respondents with cultural anti-party attitudes tend to avoid the development of a sense of identification with parties, shun involvement with organized secondary associations, tend to vote for anti-system parties, and abstain from both conventional and unconventional forms of political participation and protest. The only significant cross-national difference is that cultural anti-partyism is closely associated with a vote against the incumbent government party in Italy and Greece, but not in the other two countries. Perhaps the most surprising finding to emerge from this analysis is the moderately strong negative association between cultural anti-party orientations, on the one hand, and participation in various non-party forms of political involvement—including conventional, unconventional, and violent protests. These data suggest that, rather than reflecting a preference for other channels for political participation, this kind of anti-party sentiment is indicative of a far-reaching passivity and disaffection from politics in general.

With regard to the reactive form of antipartyism (see Table 10.14), it is much easier to interpret its behavioural consequences: with some exceptions, there are none. Quite surprisingly, in none of these four countries is reactive antipartyism associated to a statistically significant degree with voting turnout, membership in secondary associations, or participation in illegal protests. And with regard to its relationships with our conventional and unconventional participation scales, a statistically significant association is (with the exception of Spain) weak or completely absent. What is perhaps most surprising is the weakness of the relationship between these anti-party sentiments and the respondent's self-described psychological proximity to

TABLE 10.13. *Relationships between cultural antipartyism and forms of political participation in Southern Europe, 1985*

Participation	Spain	Portugal	Italy	Greece
Electoral participation	−.05	−.05	.00	−.07*
Vote for incumbent-government party**	−.02	−.06	−.09*	−.11*
Vote for anti-system party***	—	−.12*	−.08*	−.09*
Party identification	−.09*	−.03	−.12*	−.09*
Secondary association membership	−.11*	−.02	−.12*	−.12*
Conventional participation scale	−.19*	−.25*	−.21*	−.15*
Unconventional participation scale	−.33*	−.24*	−.15*	−.21*
Violent protest participation	−.16*	−.17*	−.01	−.10*

Source: The Four Nation Study.

* Significant at .01 level.
** In Spain, this was the PSOE; in Portugal, the Socialist Party; in Italy, the Christian Democratic Party; and in Greece, the PASOK. Non-voters were excluded from this analysis, although blank and otherwise invalid ballots were counted as a vote against the incumbent party.
*** Excludes non-voters and those who cast blank or otherwise invalid ballots. In Portugal, measures votes for PCP; in Italy, the MSI; and in Greece, the KKE. Spain is excluded because support for anti-system parties is statistically insignificant.

TABLE 10.14. *Relationships between reactive antipartyism and forms of political participation in Southern Europe, 1985*

Participation	Spain	Portugal	Italy	Greece
Electoral participation	−.01	.03	−.02	−.02
Vote for incumbent–government party**	−.13*	−.05	−.01	−.08*
Vote for anti-system party***	—	.05	.02	.00
Party identification	−.08*	−.05	−.11*	−.07*
Secondary association membership	.00	−.04	.03	.04
Conventional participation scale	−.10*	.03	−.05*	−.07*
Unconventional participation scale	−.23*	−.02	−.04	−.02
Violent protest participation	−.04	.01	.06	.08

Source: The Four Nation Study.

* Significant at .01 level.
** In Spain, this was the PSOE; in Portugal, the Socialist Party; in Italy, the Christian Democratic Party; and in Greece, the PASOK. Non-voters were excluded from this analysis, although blank and otherwise invalid ballots were counted as a vote against the incumbent party.
*** Excludes non-voters and those who cast blank or otherwise invalid ballots. In Portugal, measures votes for PCP; in Italy, the MSI; and in Greece, the KKE. Spain is excluded because support for anti-system parties is statistically insignificant.

political parties. Only in the cases of the propensity to vote against the incumbent party in Spain and Greece, and with regard to unconventional participation in Spain,[14] do we see a significant behavioural consequence of the holding of reactive anti-party attitudes. Aside from these two exceptions, the overall impact of reactive anti-party attitudes on the quality of democratic life is virtually nil: individuals who hold such negative attitudes towards parties are no less likely to vote, join social and political organizations, engage in a wide array of both conventional and unconventional forms of political activities, and are only slightly less likely to identify psychologically with political parties.

CONCLUDING OBSERVATIONS

In this chapter we have explored one important aspect of the alleged 'decline of parties': anti-party attitudes among citizens. On the basis of our analysis of over a decade of survey data, we have found that there is no general tendency towards higher levels of anti-party sentiments in Southern Europe. Instead, this appears to be a phenomenon that is specific to each individual country. We have found, moreover, that such attitudes should be separated into two distinct dimensions. We have referred to the first as *cultural antipartyism*, which we found to be quite stable over time, and is linked to low levels of education and political information, and to the broader syndrome of political disaffection. What we have referred to as *reactive antipartyism*, in contrast, does not appear to be rooted in primary socialization experiences, educational attainment, or level of political information, but is related to temporary political circumstances, especially the respondent's level of satisfaction with the government and the incumbent party. Accordingly, such attitudes fluctuate over time, in a manner that stands in contrast with the general stability of the 'cultural' variety of antipartyism.

These two varieties of attitudes towards parties also have differing implications for political behaviour. While reactive antipartyism has only a slight impact on voting turnout, cultural antipartyism has far-reaching effects pertaining to psychological attachments to parties and various forms of conventional participation. What is particularly striking is that, in contrast with the findings of some studies (e.g. Scarrow 1996b), cultural antipartyism in Southern Europe is also linked to low levels of involvement in unconventional forms of political participation. It appears to be part of a general syndrome of apathy and political disaffection, in which certain types of citizens remain marginalized from politics and distant from political elites. In this sense, it can be regarded as potentially undermining the quality of democracy. At the same time, however, it is important to note that anti-party attitudes are not strongly associated with a low level of support for democracy, or with support for anti-system parties. Thus, such attitudes may have significant implications for the quality of the linkages between citizens and political elites, but not for the stability of the democratic regime itself.

NOTES

1. See the classic book by Lipset and Schneider (1983), and also the volumes edited by Klingemann and Fuchs (1995); Nye *et al.* (1997); Norris (1999a); Pharr and Putnam (2000).
2. See Daalder, in this volume; Wattenberg (1990); Aldrich (1995: ch. 1); Mair (1997: ch. 2); Putnam *et al.* (2000); Torcal (2000).
3. Other examples include Lawson and Merkl (1988a); Selle and Svåsand (1991); Müller (1993); Webb (1995); Mair (1995); Strøm and Svåsand (1997); Clarke and Stewart (1998); Dalton and Wattenberg (2000a).
4. See e.g. Dalton *et al.* (1984); Clarke and Suzuki (1994); Schmitt and Holmberg (1995); Miller and Shanks (1996: ch. 7); Dalton *et al.* (2000).
5. Montero (1992); Maravall (1984: 126–7). In 1978, for example, two of every three Spaniards considered parties as useful for bringing about improvements in society, half believed that they were doing a good job in the democratization process, and a third thought that they would help to resolve the economic crisis. Non-responses to these questions included in the July 1978 survey of 5,345 Spaniards undertaken by the Centro de Investigaciones Sociológicas (CIS) ranged from 26 to 34%.

6. In 1992, eight of every ten Spaniards believed that parties lacked internal democracy, and that corruption would inevitably continue to increase (De Miguel 1993: 788 and 796). Similarly, when asked to rank-order various institutions in terms of positive or negative evaluations, survey respondents in the 1990s placed parties in last place (Wert 1996: 135).

7. Because it straddles two attitudinal dimensions in most of these surveys, this item will be excluded from most of the following analyses of these two domains.

8. Specifically, there were too few of these respondents in the earlier surveys included in this study, and the composition of that cohort changed so much over time (with the incorporation of new, younger respondents) that serious problems of comparability would have arisen.

9. In this analysis, the data points used to construct the graph presented in Figure 10.1 serve as the dependent variable, and dummy variables measuring cohort effects (with C_1 representing the Cohort 2, as described above, C_2 Cohort 3, C_3 Cohort 4, and C_4, the oldest age group) and period effects (with T_1 representing 1985, T_2 representing 1987, T_3 for 1988, T_4 1991, T_5 1955, and T_6 representing 1996) were used as independent variables. The results of this analysis are summarized in the following equation:

$$Y = 52.7 - 25.6C_1 + 21.6C_2 + 12.0C_3 - 8.1C_4 + 2.4T_1 - 5.4T_2 - 1.8T_3 + 1.2T_4 - 4.0T_5 + 3.0T_6$$
$$P = (.000)\,(.000)\,(000)\,(.000)\,(.000)\,(.36)\,(.04)\,(.49)\,(.64)\,(.13)\,(.25)$$
$$R^2 = .85$$

These data clearly reveal a strong difference among cohorts, but virtually no period effects. Only the coefficient for 1987 was statistically significant at the .05 level, and that figure was quite weak.

10. As in the previous equation, the data points used to construct the graph presented in Figure 10.2 serve as the dependent variable, and dummy variables measuring cohort effects (with C_1 representing the Cohort 2, as described above, C_2 Cohort 3, C_3 Cohort 4, and C_5, the oldest age group) and period effects (with T_1 representing 1985, T_2 representing 1987, T_3 for 1988, T_4 1991, T_5 1955, and T_6 representing 1996) were used as independent variables. The results of this analysis are summarized in the following equation:

$$Y = 74.3 + 11.1C_1 + 5.1C_2 + 3.1C_3 + 1.0C_4 - 7.6T_1 + 3.2T_2 - 2.6T_3 - 9.0T_4 - 1.6T_5 - 2.4T_6$$
$$P = (.001)\,(.09)\,(.29)\,(.74)\,(.04)\,(.37)\,(.46)\,(.02)\,(.65)\,(.50)\,(.25)$$
$$R^2 = .43$$

11. The relevant questions in the 1985 Four Nation Survey simply asked about the frequency with which the respondent watched television and listened to the radio, not the frequency with which political news was followed on television or radio. Since the great majority of programmes broadcast over both media are non-political, this difference in wording is bound to weaken the relationship. In the case of newspaper reading, this is not much of a problem, since political information dominates the news reported.

12. This may be a product of the fact that, at the time the 1985 survey was conducted, there had been no alternation in government. The DC had governed without

interruption since the 1940s, and opposition parties of the left (the Partito Comunista Italiano) and the right (the Movimento Sociale Italiano) had been permanently excluded from power. Thus, as in the case of supporters of opposition parties elsewhere, their voters should be expected to have adopted conjunctural anti-party attitudes. In the Italian case, however, the electorates of both of these parties included more deeply alienated individuals: the MSI was an explicitly anti-system party, and the PCI had, until quite recently, also maintained an anti-system stance. Thus, the cleavage between supporters of government and opposition parties was deeper, more suffused with additional meaning, and more long-lasting than it was in those countries that had experienced alternations in power and lacked significant anti-system parties.

13. Accordingly, our analysis includes a measure based on a five-point scale, with 1 indicating that the respondent regards him/herself as very close to a political party, and 5 reflecting a great psychological distance from parties.

14. This Spanish finding fits with previous interpretations of the extremely frequent waves of demonstrations, interruptions of traffic, and other forms of protest that have characterized Spain's democracy since the mid-1980s (Orizo 1983: 232; 1991: 163). Accordingly, the frequency of such unconventional protests might be interpreted as a logical response to a lack of confidence in parties as a vehicle for political participation and the expression of demands. This positive finding makes the absence of such a relationship in the other three countries all the more puzzling.

11

Parties in Contemporary Democracies: Problems and Paradoxes

Juan J. Linz

At the turn of the century we face a paradoxical situation. In all societies where people are free to express their preferences there is broad consensus on the legitimacy of democracy as a form of government (Diamond 1999: 24–31, 174–91). There is also considerable agreement, in both established and unconsolidated or unstable democracies, that political parties are essential to the working of democracy. At the same time, however, public opinion in most democratic systems is characterized by pervasive dissatisfaction with and distrust of political parties, and there is much debate in academic circles about the obsolescence or decline of parties—so well summarized by Hans Daalder in Chapter 2 above. Moreover, while critical attitudes are widespread among citizens, we find little echo in public opinion of the powerful anti-party ideologies, sentiments and movements of 'the short twentieth century', as historian Eric Hobsbawm has called the period between 1914 and the end of the Soviet era.

To some extent, these seeming contradictions may be a product of incompatibilities between the Schumpeterian and more participatory conceptions of democracy which many citizens may simultaneously hold. Indeed, those inconsistencies might, themselves, be a significant source of dissatisfaction with parties. Accordingly, a fully satisfactory explanation of these paradoxes would require a great deal more detailed empirical analysis than has been undertaken to date. We would need to know more about how the average voter perceives the need for and the functions of parties. Lacking such studies, we do not know what ideas about the proper functions and structures of parties people have in mind when they express distrust in, and dissatisfaction with, parties. We have not been able adequately to understand these attitudes and their implication—but see the findings analysed by Torcal, Gunther, and

I want to thank my wife, Rocío de Terán, for her collaboration in the writing of this chapter.

Montero in Chapter 10 above. Is their discontent focused on the decay of the mass-membership party, the emergence of the catch-all party, or the contradictions that inevitably surround the role of the party in public office? And the fact that criticisms do appear in so many countries with very different types of parties, taking many different organizational forms, also raises the question of why these sentiments have been so widely expressed, and about what common elements have provoked this distrust. That such negative sentiments are found in both parliamentary and presidential democracies—within which parties play different roles and take different forms—suggests that the reasons may be similar and not directly related to the organizational forms they have taken. Without additional research it is impossible to say if the distrust in parties responds to the same factors or to different causes. We suspect both. In this speculative essay, I will examine some ambiguities in the response to parties in parliamentary systems which I hope will be the focus of future empirical research.

It should be noted at the outset that there are some fundamental differences between the roles played by parties in parliamentary and presidential systems that may give rise to different kinds of criticism of parties. Presidentialism, by its very nature, may generate its own distinctive anti-party sentiment. It reduces the role of parties in producing and sustaining governments, an important function that strengthens ties between the legislature and executive in parliamentary systems. Parties in presidential systems are less likely to articulate government programmes and broad public policies—functions which are more likely to be performed by presidents. To be sure, in the case of 'divided government', Congress can frustrate the policies and ambitions of a popularly elected president, who, in turn, will most likely blame the Congress and the parties for his failure to deliver (Linz 1994). For their part, congressional parties can claim to check the authoritarian or populist policies of a president. In that context, the supporters of a president are likely to be critical of parties, and presidents or presidential candidates may base their campaigns on 'anti-party' appeals.

Aside from this typical dynamic relationship between Congress and presidents, the very nature of presidential elections tends to weaken the standing of parties. The president is not elected as a leader of a party. Candidates might even be outsiders with no link to parties, and even those elected with party support may distance themselves, claiming to be 'above parties'. Some constitutions in post-communist Europe go so far as to stipulate that a president should not have a party identification. But even when a president is elected under the label of a party, he is often, particularly in the United States, not chosen by the party as an organization of elected leaders or members, but by a loosely defined constituency in the primary elections. Such nominations are not the product of the collective efforts of party organizations or members, but of self-promotion, relying on the candidate's own resources and those of a small minority of voters. Once elected, however, he has the legitimacy of the office and an independent constituency. To the extent that voters identify with him, they can regard much of the activity of parties in Congress as an obstacle to the mandate they had given to the president personally. Only those who supported his opponent can see their party in the opposition as responding to their wishes. Legislators, in turn, can represent constituency interests more effectively than in a parliamentary system. But in performing this role, they may represent (or be portrayed as representing) particularistic or 'special' interests, which may conflict with the interests or priorities of parties. It is logical that voters who expect their elected representatives to articulate their particularistic interests may become dissatisfied with party leaders, who must serve more general interests.

In presidential systems, members of Congress can oppose presidential policies, vote with the opposition, and represent their constituency without endangering the cohesion of a party: their actions do not threaten the stability of the executive. The danger is that broad policies of national interest may be compromised by a series of bargains, amendments, and expenditures serving particular constituency interests. The aggregate result of each representative behaving in accord with the notion that 'All politics is local' is that the legislature will consist of ambassadors of a myriad of interests. At the individual level, voters in a particular constituency may feel satisfied that their representative in the House is looking out for their interests—something less likely in European parliamentary systems; but at the aggregate level, the defence of 'special interests' often leads to a neglect of policies with broader social, economic, or political significance. The single-member, majoritarian electoral system in the United States reinforces this defence of particularistic constituency interests, as Shugart and Carey (1992) argue. The resulting lack of cohesion, discipline, and ideological or programmatic commitment of parties emerges as another source of dissatisfaction with parties.

Each type of party system also generates different critiques of parties. Leaving aside polarized multi-party systems with significant anti-system (or perceived as such) parties, any party system will generate hostility to parties for one or another set of reasons. A two-party format of competition will necessarily mean that those rejecting in principle one of the two parties and the candidate to the prime ministership, when alienated or very critical of their own party and its leadership, will feel that the system does not offer any real choice. With a strong left–right dividing line and little chance for inter-bloc volatility, the critique of their own party will lead to a critique of the system that does not allow a choice. A moderate and non-polarized multi-party system—providing more options among parties with real coalition potential and not deeply divided on the ideological spectrum—should be more attractive to voters who feel excessively constrained by a two-party system. However, a multi-party system can mean that the voters lose the control over the ultimate choice of government, which will be determined through negotiations among parties. A coalition may thus represent an 'unethical' bargain not responding to the desires of the voters. Accordingly, many people will feel frustrated with both two-party systems (which provide a stronger link between the casting of popular votes and the formation of governments, but restrict choice) and multi-party systems (which offer a wider range of choices, but less direct voter control over the formation of the government).

These differences among party systems and between presidential and parliamentary democracies notwithstanding, parties everywhere have become the focus of a remarkably similar litany of complaints and criticisms. To what extent do these represent expressions of reasoned concerns over the shortcomings of the actual performance of parties? Conversely, to what extent do they reflect ambiguous, confusing, or even self-contradictory evaluations by citizens based upon unreasonable expectations or a lack of understanding of the complexities and cross-pressures that parties are subjected to in performing their many roles in democratic politics? It is to these questions that we now turn our attention.

ATTITUDES TOWARDS PARTIES: PARADOXES, CONTRADICTIONS, AND AMBIGUITIES

As we have noted, the critique of parties does not reflect a rejection of democracy. In various countries throughout the world people who give their support to democracy, who even consider parties a necessary part of democracy, also express distrust of parties and a wide range of critical and often contradictory attitudes. As we shall see, those attitudes are shared by those giving their electoral support to different parties, even in similar proportions across all major parties from left to right, if the Spanish data presented below can be regarded as generalizable.

Parties may be Necessary, but they are Not Trusted

In Latin America, data from a 1997 Latinobarometer survey show that 62 per cent of the respondents agreed with the statement: 'Without political parties there can be no democracy'; but at the same time, only 28 per cent of these same respondents stated that they had 'some' or 'much' confidence in parties (with 67 per cent responding 'little' or 'none'). It should be noted that there were significant differences among countries on both questions. The percentage of respondents who agreed that parties were necessary ranged from a high of 79 per cent in Uruguay to a low of 44 per cent in Ecuador, and 50 per cent each in Brazil and Venezuela, as can be seen in Table 11.1. But in every instance, the level of confidence in parties was much lower than was the belief

TABLE 11.1. *Belief in the need of parties and confidence in parties in Latin America, 1997*

Belief in the need for parties	Confidence in parties							
	Above average				Below average			
	Country	A	B	(C)	Country	A	B	(C)
Above average	Uruguay	79	45	(17)	Costa Rica	81	26	(35)
	Argentina	75	29	(35)	Peru	63	20	(40)
	Nicaragua	74	35	(35)				
	El Salvador	70	40	(16)				
	Honduras	67	35	(20)				
	Chile	67	35	(25)				
Below average	Mexico	61	31	(22)	Paraguay	55	27	(25)
	Bolivia	60	20	(41)	Guatemala	55	24	(36)
	Panama	56	28	(34)	Venezuela	50	21	(45)
	Colombia	51	42	(40)	Brazil	50	18	(42)
					Ecuador	44	16	(46)

Source: Latinobarometer, 1997.

* In *A*, % who answer 'without political parties there can be no democracy'; average is 62%. In *B*, % who have 'much' or 'some' confidence in parties; average is 28%. And in (*C*) % who answer 'none' to the latter question; average is 33%.

in the necessity of parties: in Uruguay, 45 per cent of respondents said that they had 'some' or 'much' confidence, while in Ecuador, Brazil, and Venezuela it was just 16, 18, and 21 per cent, respectively. Without time-series data it is not possible to say if the distrust in parties led to the low conviction that parties are necessary in a democracy, but we suspect this to be the case in Venezuela (see Meseguer 1998, and in general Mainwaring and Scully 1995).

Even when we distinguish those who express a preference for democracy and those who, under certain circumstances, would prefer an authoritarian government, a significant number of democrats have little or no confidence in parties and the country patterns are similar (Linz 2000: 256—data from Latinobarometer 1996). The same pattern of belief in the 'need for political parties if we want democratic development' and lack of trust in political parties can be found in the data for nine countries of post-communist Eastern Europe (Bruszt and Simon 1991). It is true that anti-party sentiments can be found in every society, but in most consolidated and stable democracies such opinions are held by minorities. In Spain, for example, only 16 per cent agreed with the statement, 'Parties are useless', while 72 per cent rejected that statement.[1] Not surprisingly, anti-party sentiments were stronger among non-voters, 26 per cent of whom agreed with that questionnaire item.

It is striking and disturbing to note that confidence in parties is lower than trust in the armed forces in Latin America. As can be seen in Table 11.2, only in Uruguay do more survey respondents have 'much' or 'some' trust in parties (43 per cent) than in the armed forces (41 per cent), and more citizens claim to have no trust in parties (17 per cent) than in the armed forces (11 per cent). On average throughout Latin America, only 26 per cent of those interviewed in the 1997 Latinobarometer survey have at least some trust in parties (26 per cent), while nearly half (49 per cent) trust the armed forces. In some cases, this confidence gap is enormous: trust in the military exceeds confidence in parties by margins of 16 versus 71 per cent in Ecuador, 21 versus 63 per cent in Venezuela, 18 versus 59 per cent in Brazil, and 21 versus 55 per cent in Colombia. While the percentage of respondents trusting parties in Chile (35 per cent) is second only to Uruguay, the fact that 48 per cent of Chileans express trust in the military is, in light of its recent history, both surprising

TABLE 11.2. *Trust in various institutions in selected Latin American countries, 1997 (%)*

Institution	Uruguay	Argentina	Chile	Ecuador	Venezuela	Mexico
Political parties						
much	11	4	7	6	7	6
some	34	25	28	10	14	20
little	34	32	37	33	32	36
none	17	35	25	46	45	35
The Presidency						
much	19	6	21	13	17	13
some	33	17	40	15	18	24
little	25	27	28	34	37	34
none	19	44	10	33	27	27
Congress						
much	12	6	13	8	11	8
some	33	27	41	12	19	25
little	32	34	33	34	31	36
none	14	28	11	41	37	26
Armed Forces						
much	15	13	21	51	35	23
some	28	21	27	20	28	26
little	25	28	30	21	25	30
none	11	33	21	6	11	18
Television						
much	10	17	13	23	19	14
some	36	35	43	27	28	32
little	33	25	29	28	26	32
none	17	20	11	16	25	19

Source: Latinobarometer, 1997.

and disturbing. Similarly, with the exception of Uruguay, in every country more people claim to have no more trust in parties than in the armed forces. Even if we discount the 'patriotic' dimension of attitudes towards the armed forces, these figures illustrate the problems parties have experienced in overcoming distrust and gaining the confidence of the people. Although less disturbing than the comparison with the armed forces (given its history in many countries of seizing power through *coups d'état*), the comparison with television is also striking. With just two exceptions—Brazil and Mexico—levels of trust in television are higher than trust in parties.

Similar low levels of trust in parties are found in some West European countries (see for instance Torcal 2000). In the 1995 General Election Study of Belgium, for example, only 6 per cent of respondents said that they had 'much' or 'a lot' of trust in parties, while 62 per cent claimed to have little or very little. By way of comparison, 54 per cent expressed trust in the king, while only 11 per cent felt little or very little trust in him.

Competition and Symbols of Unity

Many people are attracted to symbols of the unity of the nation, the state, or the local community. To a considerable degree, this explains the high levels of trust in kings, the armed forces, and the Church (unless it has played a divisive role in the past). It also explains the appeal of leaders who present themselves as 'above parties', and of all-party or grand coalitions, as well as resentment of acrimonious party politics. At the same time, however, people feel that something is wrong when 'all parties are the same', sensing rightly that conflicts in society have to be articulated by parties. Thus, parties inevitably face contradictory expectations on the part of the general public.

Competition, regardless of who wins, disrupts unity and consensus, and the idea that one solution can be good for everyone. In his essay *Soziologie der Konkurrenz*, Georg Simmel (1995 [1908]) analysed the ambivalent sentiments generated by competition. This ambivalence, as Simmel noted, is exacerbated by 'negative competition' when, rather than appealing on the basis of the quality of your product, you attempt to discredit your competitor. In contemporary democracies, where issues are complex, ideologies less binding, and politics personalized, negative campaigning does not necessarily benefit those employing it. Instead, it contributes to cynicism about politics.

Even when people understand the need for competition to achieve collective goals, policy interests, and ideal values, party competition is also competition for power among contenders with a 'selfish' component that is less admirable. Parties are the principal protagonists in that fight, and a negative reaction by many voters, even those supporting one or the other of the contenders, is not that surprising. It is also not surprising that institutions above conflict—non-partisan, neutral, unifying, and integrating, such as heads of state—should be more trusted. Thus, parties may be the victims of the contradictions inherent in the fundamental role they play in democratic regimes: their basic function is to represent the interests of particular segments of society in institutionalized conflict, while most people continue to value unity and cling to the unrealistic notion that there can be a single 'general will' of the people.

The basic notion of representation also entails a tension between the need to maintain party discipline (which is desirable if not necessary for effective governance, especially in parliamentary systems) and the freedom of individual legislators to make up their own minds about policy positions independent from the party leadership. This tension is rooted in fundamental conceptions of representation, as well as in constitutions, parliamentary rules, and the jurisprudence of Constitutional Courts (Presno 2000; Heidar and Koole 2000). There are some interesting data in this regard. A 1997 survey of Spanish voters asked them to choose between the statements that 'within the parties there should be more unity', and 'in the parties there is too much unanimity'. While there was some slight difference between supporters of the different parties as to which of the two options was preferred by a plurality—with those voting for the PSOE (the Socialist Party—Partido Socialista Obrero Español) and PP (Partido Popular, conservative) favouring more unity (by 45 versus 35 per cent, respectively), and IU (a leftist coalition dominated by the Spanish Communist party) voters and non-voters complaining that there is too much unanimity (by margins of 35 versus 50 per cent, and 33 versus 37 per cent, respectively)—the almost even division of public opinion between these two contrary views throughout all subgroups in the sample is most impressive. Overall, 40 per cent of Spaniards preferred greater unity and 37 per cent perceived too much unanimity. These opinions are, in turn, closely linked to preferences concerning more specific norms of parliamentary behaviour, with 52 per cent of those desiring more party unity also favouring party discipline, while 72 per cent of those who complained about too much unity preferred that deputies should be independent to make their own decisions.

The concepts of democratic representation that underpin these differing preferences are also relevant to the processes through which candidates are nominated by parties. One reform that is sometimes proposed as a means of allowing or generating more competition and debate within the parties is to adopt a system of primaries among party members.[2] Such a procedure may respond to the concerns of those who perceive too much unanimity within parties, but its adoption would certainly clash with the views of those who are dissatisfied with what may already be too much division or conflict within parties. For those who see parties as providing a cohesive governing team, the institutionalization of factional disputes would contribute to their dissatisfaction with parties.

Are Parties All the Same, or do they only Serve to Divide the People?

What do people mean when they say that 'parties are all the same'? From one perspective, this could be regarded as a negative attitude, although it could also be a realistic description of growing convergence on many policy issues, as well as on the organization and function of parties. There is considerable agreement with this point of view in many democracies. In Spain, for example, 61 per cent of all respondents (and 71 per cent of non-voters) agreed or strongly agreed with the statement that 'parties criticize each other, but in reality are all the same'. Since support for this assertion was rather uniform among the supporters of all parties, including the major governing parties (58 per cent and 60 per cent among PSOE and PP voters, for example), it would not seem reasonable to interpret this response as anti-democratic or even anti-party.

What about the logical opposite of that attitude—that is, the belief that 'parties only serve to divide the people'? The idea that parties are only divisive probably was stronger in the past with greater party and social polarization than today with catch-all parties and the weakening of ideological passions. And yet such attitudes are widespread among Spaniards (36 per cent agreed or strongly agreed with that statement) and Italians (51 per cent of whom agreed with a similar statement that 'parties create conflicts that don't exist', and 38 per cent agreed that 'parties are all alike': Sani and Segatti 2001: table 4.2). Traditionally an anti-party response of conservatives, in 1997 there was no difference in Spain between supporters of the conservative PP and the socialist PSOE (36 and 37 per cent of whom, respectively, agreed or strongly agreed with this assertion).

The opinions that all the parties are alike and, at the same time, are divisive can easily be interpreted as different ways of expressing a hostility to parties and party politics. What is most surprising is that a significant number of Spanish respondents (30 per cent) simultaneously held both beliefs, despite the seeming contradiction between the two. Consistent with our suspicion that such an orientation represents the most hostile stance towards parties, and that indiscriminate negativism of this kind is most likely characteristic of alienated citizens, it is noteworthy that such seemingly contradictory attitudes were particularly common among non-voters and those casting blank ballots (49 and 50 per cent, respectively); levels of agreement with both of those statements ranged from 34 per cent among IU voters to 39 per cent among both PSOE and PP supporters. The patterns of responses among partisan groups disagreeing with both of those statements (that is, implying that parties don't just serve to divide people, and that they are not all alike) was an exact mirror image, with the lowest levels found among those marginalized from the electoral process (13 per cent among non-voters and 16 per cent among those casting blank ballots), highest among IU voters (36 per cent), with PSOE and PP supporters between those two extremes (22 and 26 per cent, respectively).

And the opposite response pattern—that parties are not the same and don't just divide people—would be the most congruent with democratic values. However, this configuration of attitudes is characteristic of only 17 per cent of Spaniards interviewed in 1997, and even fewer 'blank' voters (16 per cent) and non-voters (13 per cent). Interestingly, the highest levels of such supportive attitudes are found among supporters of IU and the PP (26 per cent).

The second most frequent pattern is to see all parties as the same without being divisive (23 per cent). It could be interpreted as a description of politics in a society where the major parties are catch-all parties whose policies are quite similar, and all of whom place the greatest emphasis on being elected to government. The fact that 35 per cent of non-voters feel that way might reflect some of the alienation generated by that style of party competition. We should not jump to an overly pessimistic interpretation, however, since this is also the opinion of 31 and 29 per cent, respectively, of those who voted for the mainstream PSOE and PP.

The vision of parties generating conflict and not being all the same—a conflictual view of party competition—is not held by many people. We wonder if, in the 1920s and 1930s and in the hot years of the cold war, such attitudes were more widespread. Today, only 4 per cent of Spaniards hold that opinion.

Should Parties be Interested in Opinions or in Votes?

One of the standard indicators of the critical attitude towards parties and politicians is the questionnaire item asking respondents to agree or disagree with the proposition that 'parties are interested in people's votes but not their opinions'. Significant numbers of people in different countries agreed with this statement (Holmberg 1999). While this may be a poorly formulated question, one could also argue that the casting of a supportive or negative vote is a more 'audible' and effective way of conveying a message than merely expressing an opinion. Opinions can be listened to or ignored, but votes cannot be ignored. Why, then, do so many respondents agree with that formulation? Perhaps because opinions can deal with a myriad of problems about which different stands can be taken, while in voting people have to express an opinion on a whole package of issues bundled together by parties and politicians. That package may or may not include the specific issue that concerns a particular individual or a group of people. Parties, by aggregating a large number of issues inevitably have to select the opinions to which they 'listen', while ignoring or downplaying others. If one can imagine ten issues on which citizens might have a clear 'yes' or 'no' option, the possible combinations would be very large. If we were then to attempt to rank those preferences, we can see that only an unwieldy multi-party system would give 'representation', a democratically legitimated voice, to each subset of citizens holding the same configuration of attitudes on these issues. No limited party system, particularly a two-party system, but also a moderate multi-party system, could be attentive to each of these aggregations of citizen opinions. Both parties and citizens have to sort out 'packages', selecting and formulating the issues to offer reasonable but limited choices. For their part, parties assemble 'packages' that would attract the most votes. In so doing, they try to listen to a majority or at least (with proportional representation and multiple parties) to significant groups of citizens. That is different from listening to individual citizens (who might be numerous, but as a percentage of the voters, insignificant), or listening to opinion makers and organized groups that might care intensely about one issue, but have no interest or capacity to aggregate issues to govern. The critique that parties are only interested in votes is implicitly a critique of democracy. Indeed, the interest of parties in attracting votes is linked to the very essence of democracy: votes are necessary to govern or participate in a government coalition, and that is, and should be, the goal of parties in a democracy. Only 'testimonial' parties—which conceive of elections as an opportunity to express their rejection of democracy, the state, and/or the constitution, to propagandize their ideology, to obtain blackmail power, and which have little interest in assuming the responsibility of governing—feel free to reject appeals to groups not defined in principle as their constituency;[3] parties with a calling to govern cannot do so.

Parties should Represent my Interests, But Not 'Special Interests'

Another criticism directed at parties is that 'they do not care about the interests and the problems of people like me'. In short, these critics believe that issues affecting people very directly in a particular constituency are ignored in the policy-making process. Voters expect their representatives to defend their interests and believe that parties are needed to do so, but at the same time are critical of the link between parties and interest groups. Obviously, they have different interests in mind, ranging from the broad interests of a social class, an ethnic group, or a religious community, to very specific interests, like those of a particular industry or some other prominent group in a district. When they affect the individual's own group, there are regarded as 'our interests' or 'the interests of people like me'. When these same kinds of issues involve the interests of others, however, they are pejoratively regarded as 'special interests'.

This inconsistency was less problematic when it was based on an ideological construction or the widely shared values of a Christian society, or when the affected interests—like those of the working class—could be perceived as those of the majority. Under these circumstances, advancement of those interests could be portrayed as progress towards a better society. However, with the fragmentation of interests in a modern society and dissemination of information about how policies affect specific interests (such as the impact of European Union policies on particular industries, fishing rights, and agricultural production), individuals have tended to focus their attention on more specific, particularistic interests. At the same time, catch-all parties cannot identify with particular interests, even of broad categories like workers or farmers, but have to strive for balance among them. And governing parties (in contrast with the greater ability of opposition parties to articulate ideological principles) face a wide variety of conflicting demands and responsibilities that further reduce their ability to defend the interests of their constituents. Thus, a person may blame them for not advancing the interests of their constituents, while at the same time they are criticized for serving the interests of another comparable constituency (never perceived as equally legitimate) or 'special interests'. Thus, it is virtually inevitable that the interest representation function will lead to a critique of parties and politicians.

Some scholars and a significant number of citizens have seen social movements as more attractive than parties and as the wave of the future. This is based on a misunderstanding of their nature and functions. Social movements, generally focused on a single issue, do not have to weigh conflicting demands and make compromises, and can mobilize the enthusiasm of strongly committed minorities, at least temporarily, in a way that less ideological parties, attempting to gain support of large and heterogeneous majorities of voters, cannot. Social movements can criticize parties for their compromises and ambiguities, contrasting their principled or idealistic position with the pragmatism of parties that have to govern or aspire to govern (see Dalton and Kuechler 1990; Giugni 1998).

Corruption: Are the Parties to be Blamed?

Parties are also seen as closely linked with corruption (Del Águila 1995). To be sure, party politicians often are involved in corruption in the most blatant form of personal gain or illegitimate favouring of particular interests. But the ability of parties to prevent such behaviour is sharply limited. Parties have to provide candidates and personnel for a large number of elective and appointed offices, from town council members to prime ministers, and it is obviously impossible for a central party office to acquire full knowledge about the probity of tens of thousands of individual candidates. The party's exposure is further extended by practices intended to further 'democratization' by replacing professional civil servants with party appointees in a wide range of public institutions: judicial councils, supervisory agencies of public broadcasting media, university councils, savings bank boards, consumer watchdog committees, public enterprises, etc. The Austrian *proporz* or the Italian *lotizzazione*, and the whole range of party patronage and clientelism found in other democracies have expanded the presence of parties in many realms of society (see Blondel, Chapter 9 above). Many of these positions offer opportunities for corruption, leading to scandals that are exploited by the opposition and highlighted by the media. Many of these posts are elected positions, presumably assuring democratic control; but voters are uninformed, disinterested, and rely on their party or ideological affinities in voting, rather than the qualifications of the candidates. By default, then, the parties ultimately become responsible for their selection and subsequent behaviour. Thus, the image of the parties as being corrupt, of politicians as corrupt, is almost inevitable. It is partly rooted in reality (particularly given extensive media coverage and exploitation by opposition parties of individuals when they are caught), but uncritical acceptance of this image is far more widespread in public opinion than is warranted. Perhaps only a reduction of the presence of the parties in these institutions, of their hegemony in civil society (in the Gramscian sense) would reduce their exposure to these kinds of accusations.

PERSONALIZATION OF POLITICS AND PROFESSIONALIZATION OF POLITICS

Voters want to know who will be assuming the role of prime minister, and increasingly tend to vote for a party that presents an attractive candidate. They will vote for the party and its candidates while being critical of the party programme and uncomfortable with the local candidate in order to make sure their preferred national leader gains power, or even just to prevent a less liked leader of the other party from being elected. For a variety of reasons, the personalization of political leadership has advanced further than ever, even in parliamentary systems, but at the same time there is a feeling that the concentration of power in the hands of a national leader weakens the internal life of a party, prevents the emergence of alternative leaders, reinforces oligarchic tendencies at the top, and thereby reduces 'democracy'. In this context, the party can be blamed for abdicating its autonomy, its deliberative function, by 'delegating' to the leader. But the leader can also be blamed for 'emasculating' the internal life of the party. Or, conversely, the party can be blamed for internal divisions, for not supporting the leader, at the same time that the leader is criticized for not controlling factionalism within the party. On each of those counts, or perceptions, the party will be criticized by some of its voters.

An additional problem for parties that have spawned and supported a personalized or pseudocharismatic leadership is that even if the leader leaves office, and has lost authority in the eyes of voters and party members, it is difficult (if not impossible) to silence him (e.g. Felipe González) or her (e.g. Margaret Thatcher), and such former leaders continue to have a significant impact on the image of the party. And in cases where there is a division of

labour between party leaders who run for and occupy elective office, and a
leader who dominates the party organization (such as Xabier Arzallus, the
president of the Basque Nationalist Party), a complicated situation may arise
in which the party speaks with two different voices, and often to different
audiences. This not only creates confusion on occasion, but it can also contribute to a lack of accountability: the non-elected leader cannot be made
responsible to voters, and any controversial or irresponsible statements made
by him can be dismissed as merely expressions of his 'private opinions'.

Similar problems occur with the related topic of the professionalization of
politics. It is interesting to note that in a society that believes in professionalism—full and competent devotion to a task, based on knowledge and experience—the expression 'professional politician' has a negative connotation.[4]
There is an implicit notion that the politician should not be just a politician,
someone (to use Schumpeter's graphic expression) 'who deals in votes', but
ultimately an ordinary citizen. The democratic myth that anyone should be
eligible to compete for public office has its symbolic expression in the Greek
election by lot (the *boule*) and the Marxist myth of fishing in the morning and
administering in the afternoon.

The dispensability to engage in politics of which Max Weber wrote has been
reduced by the time demanded by political activity. In the past, many candidates had safe seats, particularly in the case of notables or some trade union
leaders, and therefore did not have to campaign or maintain close contact with
party organizations at the local level. Elections have become more frequent,
moreover, not only national but for regional assemblies, local government, and
European Parliament. This would not involve the national party leadership or
the members of the national Parliament were it not for the fact that voters use
those elections to support or punish the party at the national level. The
demands of the media on the time of politicians have also increased, in addition to the demands of the party organization, local and national committees,
let alone the burdens of holding public office. Only a systematic study of the
increased burdens of such responsibilities on the personal lives and financial
resources of politicians could help us appreciate the difficulty of elective public
service today. Finally, the weakening of the role of the professional independent civil service and the partisan 'colonization' of the administration reinforces
the professionalization of politics and the dependence on the party.

At the same time, the demands of modern professions in the private sector make it difficult if not impossible for an individual to enter politics for a
time and then return to practice. Professions that in the past could be part-
time activities today require full-time commitment. Perhaps only civil servants, teachers, and in some university systems, academics, can return to
their positions after a stint in politics (though a professor who, for four or
eight years, is out of touch with his discipline, is not likely to be welcomed
back to academia). It is impossible to think of the doctor-politician sitting

in Parliament, while continuing to treat patients and teach (as we know occurred in the French Third Republic). The greater professionalization of professions inevitably limits the number of amateur politicians and reinforces the trend to professionalization of politics.

None the less, despite the great difficulty (if not impossibility) of simultaneously pursuing careers in public and private life, the Cincinatus Myth remains strong. Many citizens reject the professionalization of politics and continue to believe in the amateur politician, who serves his fellow citizens for a time but is not ready to give up his other pursuits. This preference requires the existence of skilled persons who have established their careers in private sector professions, who would be willing to suspend that activity for a time to perform public service, and then return to their professions after a period in office. For a variety of reasons, changes in the nature of politics and in the technical demands of many professions make that career trajectory unrealistic. Many individuals enter politics early without having first consolidated a position in the private sector that would provide an income or status comparable to that of a legislator or public official. After an electoral defeat, they would find it difficult to return to a private-sector career; they therefore depend on the party to provide him or her with a 'benefit' (to use Weber's term derived originally from church language) in the party organization, patronage positions, or some public post as ambassadors or appointees to international organizations.

Paradoxically, those opposed to professionalization are ready to support rules which discourage people from entering or staying in politics, reducing directly or indirectly the pool from which to draw the political elite. Among these are rigid rules of incompatibility, designed to 'assure the independence' of politicians from societal interests. Even labour parties, which for so long relied on trade union leaders to become MPs, have now established an incompatibility of union office and parliamentary mandate. A CIS survey reveals broad support for such rules: a majority of Spaniards polled (58 per cent) agreed with the proposition that deputies should stop exercising any type of professional activity because that would make them more independent, while just 27 per cent chose the alternative, 'deputies should not abandon their professional activities and devote themselves exclusively to politics because that way they would know better the problems of common people and would be more connected with society'; 15 per cent had no opinion. One would think that support for incompatibility rules would be strongest among supporters of the left, while the alternative of continuous professional activity would be endorsed by more conservative voters. There is little empirical support for this hypothesis. Although 65 per cent of leftist IU voters favoured exclusive dedication, 59 per cent of PSOE and 59 per cent of PP voters hold that same opinion, and even voters of a bourgeois party like the Catalan CiU (Convergència i Unió, a coalition of two nationalist parties) concur.

But while these rules make it impossible simultaneously to pursue public- and private-sector careers, other populist initiatives undermine the professionalization of political careers through enactment of term limits. This places those wishing to serve in elective office in an extremely difficult situation. Professionalization of politics means that men and women enter politics and seek elective office or party office not as a temporary and/or part-time activity, but as a longer term and almost full-time activity. Some have decided to do so early in life and have not pursued any other professional or career goals. Politics for them is a vocation but also an occupation (*Beruf* in the double meaning of the word in German and the thought of Max Weber 1971*b* [1919]). But the imposition of term limits either terminates political careers after a relatively short period in office, or exposes politicians to enormous risks and insecurity, as they are forced to switch from one elective position to another—in both cases, irrespective of whether their constituents approved of their performance in office or not.

The professionalization of democratic politics is almost inevitable and, within limits, desirable. In light of the self-contradictory positions described above, the critique by some radical democrats must be regarded in many respects as irresponsible. The rules and restrictions that they have proposed and enacted to prevent the professionalization of politics are not only undesirable in their consequences, they are contrary to the basic democratic principle that termination or continuation in elective office ought to be a decision left up to the voters represented by each individual politician.

We have to ask ourselves how parties in the future will be able to serve as a channel for the calling of politics, as a mechanism for elite recruitment, when few people are willing to join them. To be sure, the number of elective offices in any society is relatively small, but we know from elite studies in many fields that there has to be a relatively large pool to produce the few qualified and motivated candidates needed for those posts. Parties can recruit from social movements, but there may be some difficulty for persons committed strongly to a single issue to accept the multiple roles and compromises required by party politics. There is, particularly at the highest levels, the possibility of lateral entry from the professions, the university, the academy, business, interest group leadership, and the bureaucracy on the basis of expertise. Are those so recruited likely to have some of the qualifications we think are needed for political leadership, including the capacity to communicate with the voters, and to articulate the hopes and fears of a society? There is a nursery of politicians in local and regional politics and government, but how many may be reluctant to move outside of such a familiar context to face the uncertainties, challenges, and sacrifices often required of those seeking national-level elective office?

We need to know more about the incentives and disincentives for entering politics in contemporary democracies. We know even less about how these motivations affect the quality of politics. To study this we have to study the individual politicians and the micro-politics at various levels. What image do parties convey to the electorate when they introduce quotas by age, gender, ethnicity, and the like, when it means the displacement or postergation of worthy incumbents and/or experienced party loyalists?

PARTIES, MONEY, AND PARTY DEMOCRACY

Parties Cost Money: But Not Mine, Not from My Taxes, and Not from Interest Groups

The question of money in politics has also generated much hostility towards parties and politicians. Citizens and politicians are reluctant to admit that democratic politics in a mass society is very expensive, and, as with several other points discussed above, citizens have contradictory feelings. People are less willing to become members, give money and services to their parties. But they also complain about how the parties finance their activities, both legally and illegally. Again we find a basic ambivalence. Parties and their activities are regarded as necessary, but the voter is unwilling to support them, and, at the same time, does not like alternative ways of financing parties, especially those involving 'private' funds that might create links with interest groups (and lead to corrupt practices) and by public funding from his taxes.

Are citizens or party members, supporters of one or another candidate or faction in a party, willing to pay for their opportunity to choose? Should the taxpayer who is not a member of a party, who may not be interested in voting, pay for it? If not, then what should be the source of the funds necessary to sustain party activity—dues paid by party members, public subsidies, deductions from salaries of elected officials, 'legitimate' business activities of parties? How can non-oligarchic fairness in access to such funds be guaranteed? Or should such a process be based largely on private voluntary contributions of supporters? Should candidates be allowed to use their own money, which, after all, they should be free to spend for a public purpose, or be involved in raising it?

Survey data from Spain indicate that most people are ready to vote for parties, but when asked, 'What would you do if the party for which you have most sympathy, or that is closer to your own ideas, asks you to contribute economically to some activity proper to the party?', only 22 per cent responded that they would probably contribute, while nearly 68 per cent said that there was little or no possibility that they would support parties financially (with 43 per cent of those respondents replying 'definitely not'). As can be seen in Table 11.3, only among supporters of IU did more than one our of every four voters express a willingness to contribute, while those who had cast ballots for the two

TABLE 11.3. *Readiness to contribute economically to a party in Spain in general elections, by party voted, 1997*

	Party voted in 1996				Did not vote	Total sample
	IU	PSOE	PP	CiU		
With all probability, I would contribute	11	7	6	4	3	6
It is quite probable that I would contribute	25	19	19	17	11	16
There are few possibilities that I would contribute	32	28	26	27	19	25
There is no way that I would contribute	26	36	40	48	56	43
Don't know	6	10	9	4	10	9
(N)	(186)	(663)	(605)	(75)	(268)	(2,439)

Source: Banco de Datos, CIS, # 2240.

major parties (the PP and PSOE) were equally reluctant to support their parties financially. These data clearly reveal that parties may receive electoral support from many voters, but the vast majority of them are free riders!

A slightly different picture emerges when we examine these responses broken down by the respondent's self-placement on the left–right continuum. While only a minority of respondents on each point of the scale expressed a willingness to support parties financially, those at the extreme ends of the scale were somewhat more willing to contribute to parties than those in the middle: 36 and 33 per cent, respectively, of those located at positions 1 or 2 (far left) on the scale and positions 9 or 10 (far right) said that there was a considerable probability or better that they would financially support parties, as compared with just 22 per cent of those in the two positions straddling the middle of the scale. Those responding 'don't know' or refusing to place themselves on the ideological continuum were the least likely of all to support parties (of whom just 10–11 per cent indicated their willingness to do so). These data suggest that, while increased moderation may have contributed to the stability and consolidation of Spain's current democratic regime (in contrast with the ideological polarization that characterized the Second Republic, 1931–6), an unfortunate consequence of the lowering of the ideological heat may be a diminution of economic contributions to political parties.

We know the dangers and abuses connected with money in politics from the American experience. Let us regulate it, limit it under the supervision of state regulatory commissions or the judiciary (albeit at the cost of self-regulation by parties as voluntary free membership organizations). Without such controls, money rather than just votes becomes decisive in determining the outcome of important public policy debates. In the 1920s and 1930s, when issues were highly ideological, matters of life and death, existential conflicts, there was not shortage of volunteers or massive contributions of humble party members. Will that be true in contemporary more rational and less emotional politics? Probably not. But then other motivations of less 'ideological' idealism would become more important.

Parties should be More Democratic; But What does that Mean?

In recent years, numerous vaguely formulated demands for increased intra-party democracy have been set forth whose meaning and implications are most unclear. What do demands for more personalized candidates and the rejection of closed party lists in proportional electoral systems mean, given the low level of knowledge about individual candidates, even of such visible officials as Cabinet members? In the context of large, metropolitan electoral districts, how could voters exercise meaningful choice without additional campaign efforts, entailing considerable expense and television time? Would it really change the behaviour and feelings of voters who are, at the same time, increasingly committed to choose one party and even one particular leader to form the government?

Since the writings of Robert Michels (1962 [1911]), the issue of internal party democracy has been hotly debated. Even constitutions and party regulations include requirements that parties should 'be democratic', meaning democratically governed (Linz 1966). In response to criticism of their oligarchic character, some parties have gone beyond the bounds of representative democracy (such as through elections to congresses and executive bodies) to adopt direct-democracy procedures such as party primaries, in which all members can vote directly for the national leadership of the party (Vargas Machuca 1998; Boix 1998b). Internal party democracy is seen as a cure for the ills of the party, at the same time that the competing candidates affirm they are not creating factions but defending party unity, and that they identify with the party programme. While competition within unity is the *leitmotif*, no one wants a fight among personalities. All of these efforts have been characterized by much ambivalence and little thought about how such competition should be organized without very active members and sufficient funds for the intra-party campaign.

Such changes should provide the party *demos* a role (Hopkin 2001). The problem is that the party *demos* and the *demos* of citizens electing the Members of Parliament are two different *demoi*: one is rather small, the other includes millions of voters. To whom should the party leader be accountable, particularly if he/she is also the head of the government? Either answer is likely to leave large numbers dissatisfied.

Direct democracy inside of the parties is in principle attractive to democrats, but we should not ignore some of the unintended, sometimes dysfunctional, and curiously unanticipated (by most of their advocates) consequences. Why is representative democracy within parties, party conventions, or congresses, being questioned in favour of direct democracy—elections of leaders by party primaries? In addition to the 'anti-politician' affect and 'participatory' appeal of direct democracy, we might find some explanation in the way party congresses have changed. Instead of being arenas for internal debates among middle-level party elites for elections by those familiar with the candidates, they have become a showcase of the party, an opportunity for public expression of solidarity and unity, most prominently featuring speeches by party notables, leaders of friendly parties, and even foreign leaders. The result is a tight schedule well planned in advance which precludes the slow work of committees and prolonged debates that might disrupt the tight timetable. The end result is that what originally had been a deliberative convention has been transformed into a media event. Thus, the convention appears as 'undemocratic' in contrast with direct primaries.

This syndrome also includes distrust of the parliamentary representation of the party, culminating in efforts to limit the influence of parliamentarians in various party organs. The argument against an important role of parliamentarians is that they are nominated by the party machinery. In this view, democracy can only be achieved by democratization of the machinery or bypassing that machine. These sentiments have also led to much debate (dating back to the time of Robert Michels) about whether the parliamentary party and leadership should be subject to control by the party congress. This could imply a form of imperative mandate and even greater enforcement of dependence of the MPs and government on the party, in contradiction with the free mandate which has dominated the thinking and constitutions of modern democracies. To this we have to add the attempt to separate the offices of the leader of the party organization from that of parliamentary party leader or head of government. This separation would establish a diarchy based on different constituencies, creating a structure of accountability to two distinct bodies—party members and voters. We know from history and sociology the problems associated with diarchy.

In their historical origin, parties were groupings of like-minded Members of Parliament; they later developed organizations to assure their election and membership organizations; and finally they evolved into large-scale, more or less bureaucratized and professionalized organizations, whose principal mission was to compete in elections. In the course of the evolution of parties, scholars have focused on different aspects and levels, but increasingly neglecting the parliamentary party (but see Beyme 1983; Bowler 2000; Heidar and Koole 2000). Accordingly, we as scholars need to know more about the nature of the relationships between the party organization and the parliamentary group, about the internal decision-making processes within party organizations, and about the preferences of party members and the electorate at large, before we can effectively explore many of the crucial questions that have emerged from current efforts to 'democratize' political parties.

Democratization of Institutions, But 'No' to Partitocrazia

A central theme in democratic theorizing and more specifically in the debate about parties is that, in order to work, democracy requires more democracy—that is, that democratic control should be established within a wide variety of social institutions. Such demands are formulated with little or no attention to the attitudes and behaviour of citizens and party members, nor much analysis of their implications for democratic governance of the state. Proponents of such viewpoints claim that low levels of participation are simply a reaction to the present state of parties and political institutions, and that citizens would participate more if there were a broader democratization of institutions. In making these assertions, they often contrast the activism and enthusiasm within social movements with political parties, forgetting the very minoritarian and often shifting involvement in social movements.

Let us turn first to the democratization of more institutions, and the making of more positions in state and society elective. Few of the advocates of such processes consider the amount of factual knowledge that is needed to make an informed choice. How and by whom would that information be generated and disseminated, and how ready would citizens be to make the effort to work through this volume of information in order to become sufficiently knowledgeable about the issues at hand? Where would qualified candidates come from—a question that is of considerable significance given complaints about the quality of those presented for a much smaller number of offices? If the candidacies for such newly elected positions were proposed by the parties, and if most people most of the time would continue with their current habit of voting along party lines, would such a democratization merely foster *partitocrazia*, about which so many people already complain? If parties do not play the lead role in nominating candidates, then who would— interest groups, the media, or the candidates themselves (who would almost certainly be individuals with sufficient wealth to mount their own campaigns)? And if voters could not rely upon the party labels of candidates as a cost-effective means of acquiring basic information about where individual candidates are likely to stand on key issues, on what would they base their decisions? Given the extremely low levels of information possessed by most voters about the stands of the vast majority of candidates below the national party leadership,[5] this latter consideration could represent a fatal flaw in proposals for a broader democratization of all kinds of social institutions.

RESPONSIVENESS, RESPONSIBILITY, AND ACCOUNTABILITY

People tend to be disturbed by the fact (or the perception) that politicians structure their campaigns, their positions, and perhaps increasingly their policies, on the basis of public opinion research, focus groups—that is, in terms of what they believe will appeal to the voters. Some find poll-driven democracy disturbing and distasteful. But let us translate it into another language: politicians should express and carry out the will of the people, or at least of those voting for them. They should be responsive. That is democracy! To pursue their own preferences rather than those of the voters has been the basis of the critique of elitist democracy.[6]

What, then, is the origin of this discomfort? The answer is complex but is fundamentally rooted in the fact that responsibility, democratic leadership and commitment to basic values, beliefs, and (heaven forbid) ideology are being sacrificed to responsiveness to a diffuse public opinion. Responsible behaviour implies that due consideration is given to consequences—to the adequate relation between goals and means—and this can imply that the opinions of the electorate might be disregarded. Voters do not have the facts, the technical expertise, the knowledge, nor the experience that we expect (or, at least, hope) politicians to have. Voters respond to an immediate situation, to simple stimuli, not to the complexity of issues, the medium- or long-term consequences. Is this not a critique of democracy? No, because the poll-driven democracy ignores a fundamental element of democratic politics: leaders who shape, change, or resist opinions when they consider them pushing in the wrong direction. To lead does not mean to ignore the people, but to appeal to them, explain, justify policies, and take the responsibility for actions. The voters will have the chance to reward or punish the leaders at the next election. Democracy is ultimately the accountability of those elected to their voters at regular intervals. That general formulation does not tell us much about who is accountable to whom, though party government in parliamentary democracies makes the party and its Members of Parliament accountable for the actions and policies of the government they have supported. However, in practice the party and its national leadership is made also accountable for the actions of a number of those elected in other contexts: regional and local governments and legislatures or city councils presumably not appointed or selected by the national leadership of the party, but by different constituent bodies. To the extent the party is perceived as a whole, however, their actions reflect on the party as a whole. At the same time, those representatives and their constituents are ready to protest any interference with their autonomy. The party and its leadership are therefore blamed for misconduct at the regional or local levels, while also being blamed if it attempts to control those other levels, interfering with free choice of the relevant intra-party or electoral constituencies. Besides, particularly in federal states and now in the European

Parliament elections, the voters do not limit themselves to holding representatives accountable for their performance or qualifications (about which they
may know very little), but use those elections to express their dissatisfaction
with the national government, the central party leadership, and national
Parliament. The frequency of elections at the European, member-state,
regional, and local levels allows the articulation and expression of discontent
without assuming accountability until a later date (Linz 1998*a*). The party
and its leaders can also avoid responsibility and accountability by side-
stepping tough decisions. One way is to shift the decision to the voters by calling for a referendum, in which, it should be noted, voters would most likely
depend on the guidance of parties. An alternative device is to remove the issue
from the democratic decision-making process by letting the courts decide, or
by referring the matter to independent agencies or 'non-partisan' commissions, be they corporative in composition (including representatives of trade
unions, employers' associations, farmers' organizations) or otherwise. It
should be noted that this shift from the vertical accountability of elected
politicians to the horizontal accountability of non-partisan and electorally
unaccountable committees or other agencies runs counter to the basic tenet of
democratic responsibility for the formulation of public policy.

DISTRUST OF PARTIES AND
THE LEGITIMACY OF DEMOCRACY

How does the disturbingly low level of confidence in political parties affect
the legitimacy of democracy? There is some evidence that confidence in parties is linked to greater support for democracy, and that distrust is associated
with less commitment to democracy and somewhat greater readiness to consider authoritarian rule desirable in some circumstances or that it 'does not
make any difference for people like me' (see Torcal, Gunther, and Montero,
Chapter 10 above).

An examination of data from Spain, Chile, and Ecuador tells a complicated
story. In Spain, where the overall belief in democracy is high (81 per cent),
support for democracy declines slightly to 75 per cent among those with no
confidence in parties (see Table 11.4). In Ecuador, where levels of support for
democracy are much lower, there is also a lack of a clear relationship between
attitudes towards democracy and trust in parties. In Chile, however, where
the overall level of support for democracy is 54 per cent and the authoritarian alternative finds favour with 19 per cent of respondents (as compared with
8 per cent in Spain), the differences between those having 'a lot' or 'some' confidence in parties compared to those with 'little' or none are quite significant:
pro-democracy attitudes decline steadily, from 70 to 61 to 55 and to 49 per
cent among subgroups of the sample with decreasing levels of confidence in

TABLE 11.4. *Confidence in parties and attitudes towards democracy in Spain, Chile, and Ecuador, 1997 (horizontal %)*

Confidence in parties		Attitudes towards democracy				
		Democrats	Potential authoritarians	Indifferents	Don't know	(N)
A lot	Spain	82	12	4	3	(109)
	Chile	70	10	2	3	(31)
	Ecuador	54	21	17	7	(84)
Some	Spain	86	8	3	2	(698)
	Chile	61	20	17	1	(302)
	Ecuador	57	11	25	5	(135)
A little	Spain	83	8	6	3	(955)
	Chile	53	22	23	2	(440)
	Ecuador	51	20	22	5	(465)
Don't know	Spain	70	4	8	18	(132)
	Chile	39	6	35	20	(18)
	Ecuador	60	20	—	20	(5)
Total	Spain	81	8	7	4	(2481)
	Chile	54	19	23	3	(1200)
	Ecuador	52	18	23	5	(1200)

Source: Latinobarometer, 1997.

parties. In Chile, where democracy is questioned by a significant part of the population, confidence in parties appears to have an impact on the commitment to democracy. Obviously it could be argued the other way around but we are inclined to think that the attitude towards democracy is prior in time and more salient.

It is important to note that, in contrast with the first half of the twentieth century, we no longer find that critical views of incumbents and parties are accompanied by a radical questioning of core democratic institutions and an embrace of ideological alternatives to liberal democracy. In stable democracies, there are no politically significant advocates of a non-democratic political system; a system without competitive elections, or one with a single or no parties. This may be a positive development from the standpoint of democratic stability, but it also has deprived parties of their traditional defenders. In the past, committed democrats were ready to defend the system and indirectly the incumbents, ignoring their shortcomings; nowadays, the absence of radical ideological challenges to democracy allows for a much more open discussion of the actual shortcomings of democratic institutions.

CONCLUDING OBSERVATIONS

It seems doubtful, in view of our analysis, that the image of political parties and politicians will be substantially improved. The ambiguities can be made more explicit but not eliminated. Reforms can tinker with the problems but, like intra-party primaries, often generate new problems.

How far can dissatisfaction, distrust of parties and politicians (rather than of particular leaders), grow in the population and in intensity without leading to a fundamental questioning of the function of parties in a democracy, without arousing the rejection of representative democracy itself, and without triggering a search for alternative forms of legitimation, as occurred in the 'short twentieth century', thanks to anti-democratic ideological appeals of communism, fascism, corporatism, and military authoritarianism? The appeal of anti- or above-party populist presidentialism is one of those dangers, as we know from some recent developments in Latin America.

There is little discussion and even less research on the roots of dissatisfaction with political parties among those who believe in their necessity and regularly vote for them. Without understanding better the critique of political parties, of representative democracy as it exists, and of politicians, it will be impossible to initiate reforms that would reduce that critical attitude. There has been endless debate about possible reforms of institutions and within the parties without much analysis of their implications. My assumption is that some of the problems with political parties are almost inherent in their nature and therefore difficult, if not impossible, to correct by institutional engineering that often ends up as mere tinkering. Fortunately, the ambivalence toward political parties which we find in our democratic societies, at least for the time being, has not led to their rejection in principle as it did in the first half of the twentieth century. Although politicians are the object of constant criticism, rightly or wrongly, including those for whom the people have themselves voted, the idea that the few elected have the right to govern as a result of the democratic process is less questioned than in the past.

These paradoxes have not been at the centre of the research on political parties with its focus on party systems, electoral systems, and voting studies of different parties, as well as of party organization, party types, and party models undertaken in this volume. This points to the need to expand our focus and research to understand better the working of political parties and the images that citizens have of parties and politicians. We need to know more about politicians than what we can learn from the classical elite studies about the social background and career patterns of those elected, particularly since we have discovered how relatively homogeneous the political elite has become with regard to the characteristics normally studied. We also need to understand better to what extent a typical, if not hostile, climate of opinion about parties and politicians affects the self-selection process of political elites.

In view of the themes I have sketched in this chapter (illustrated by some Spanish and Latin American survey data), we can ask ourselves if it is time to explore new issues in the study of parties in general, rather than of the party the voters vote for. What images do the voters have, what do they expect, what kinds of party behaviour frustrate their expectations, what is their response to different types of party systems and to alternative institutional reforms? These are questions that should be asked without reference to any particular party, though in the analysis we pay attention to differences among the supporters of various parties with regard to the distribution of such attitudes. In designing surveys, we should also try to make it easy for the respondent to express the opinions we would consider contradictory or incompatible from our perspective as outside academic observers. We can expect many debates about how to change parties, many attempts to do so, but it is doubtful that they will be able to do away with the problems and paradoxes with which I began this chapter.

NOTES

This chapter develops themes I have discussed in two previous papers (Linz 2000, 2001), and reflects my long-time interest in the issues raised by Robert Michels (in Linz 1966, 1998*b*). It is largely a think piece whose intent is to stimulate research. I have made no effort to refer to the data that could support my arguments nor to much of the relevant literature, particularly the writings in political theory on representation.

1. The Spanish data used here and elsewhere in this chapter are from the survey # 2240, April 1997, of the Centro de Investigaciones Sociológicas, on 'Ciudadanos y élites ante la política (Encuesta ciudadanos)', that incorporated some questions suggested by the author. I am grateful to the then director of the CIS, Pilar del Castillo, for making these data available to me. Several of the CIS questions we used have been asked over time, as the data used by Torcal, Gunther, and Montero in Ch. 10 above show. Many of the same questions were asked in Portugal and Italy, showing often the same pattern (Bacalhau 1997; Sani and Segatti 2001). I am also grateful to Marta Lagos for the Latinobarometer data that were used in this analysis.

2. This differs from the nomination process in the USA, where all eligible voters (and not just party members) can cast ballots that determine which individuals will represent the various parties in the general election. See Gallagher and Marsh (1988); Scarrow *et al.* (2000).

3. This mode of thinking was characteristic of the orthodox Marxist ideologues of the SPD, who in the late 1920s and early 1930s criticized reformists (like Eduard David) for what they dismissed as *Bauernfängerei* ('catching peasants'). It should be noted that the triumph of the orthodox socialists led to severe weaknesses of the SPD in the countryside, which helped make rural voters available for 'capture' by the Nazi party.

4. The sentiment against the professionalization if politics was captured in Italy by Silvio Berlusconi and Forza Italia when they argued that politics should be 'de-professionalized' and 'entrusted to people who had successfully passed several tests in civil society' (Sani and Segatti 2001).

5. Surveys undertaken in the aftermath of the 1982 and 1993 Spanish general elections, for example, indicated that outside of Madrid (where the heads of the lists were the national leaders of their respective parties) only between 16 and 17% of voters could correctly name the head of the party list for which they had voted for the Congress of Deputies (Montero and Gunther 1994: 50). Further corroboration of the general lack of knowledge about individual candidates below the highest levels of national party leadership can be seen in voting behaviour with regard to elections to the Spanish Senate: by far the strongest predictor of the vote for Senate candidates on open lists was alphabetic order (with strict alphabetic ordering of candidates occurring with regard to 86% of seats allocated in 1993). See Montero and Gunther (1994: 72).

6. For a more extensive discussion the relation between responsiveness, responsibility, and accountability in democratic politics and 'party democracy' see Linz (1998a); see also Przeworski *et al.* (1999).

References

Aguilar, P. (1996). *Memoria y olvido de la guerra civil española*. Madrid: Alianza Editorial.

Aldrich, J. H. (1995). *Why Parties? The Origin and Transformation of Political Parties in America*. Chicago: University of Chicago Press.

Almond, G. A. (1956). 'Comparative Political Systems', *Journal of Politics*, 18: 391–409.

——(1960). 'A Functional Approach to Comparative Politics', in G. A. Almond and James S. Coleman (eds.), *The Politics of Developing Areas*. Princeton: Princeton University Press.

——and Powell, G. B., jun. (1966). *Comparative Politics: A Developmental Approach*. Boston: Little, Brown.

——and Verba, S. (1963). *The Civic Culture: Attitudes and Democracy in Five Nations*. Princeton: Princeton University Press.

—— ——eds. (1980). *The Civic Culture Revisited*. Boston: Little, Brown.

APSA [American Political Science Association] (1950). *Towards a More Responsible Two-Party System*, supplement to *American Political Science Review*, 44.

Attard, E. (1983). *Vida y muerte de UCD*. Barcelona: Planeta.

Bacalhau, M. (1997). 'The Political Party System in Portugal: Public Opinion Surveys and Election Results', in T. Bruneau (ed.), *Political Parties and Democracy in Portugal: Organization, Elections, and Public Opinion*. Boulder, Colo.: Westview Press.

Barnes, S. E. (1997). 'Electoral Behaviour and Comparative Politics', in M. I. Lichbach and A. S. Zucherman (eds.), *Comparative Politics: Rationality, Culture and Structure*. Cambridge: Cambridge University Press.

——Kaase, M., *et al.* (1979). *Political Action: Mass Participation in Five Western Democracies*. Beverly Hills, Calif.: Sage.

Barry, B. (1970). *Sociologists, Economists and Democracy*. Chicago: University of Chicago Press.

——(1975). 'Review Article: "Exit, Voice and Loyalty"', *British Journal of Political Science*, 5: 79–107.

Bartels, L. M. (1992). 'The Impact of Electioneering in the United States', in D. Butler and A. Ranney (eds.), *Electioneering: A Comparative Study of Continuity and Change*. Oxford: Oxford University Press.

Bartolini, S. (1986a). 'La volatilità elettorale', *Rivista Italiana di Scienza Politica*, 16: 363–400.

——(1986b) 'Partiti e sistemi di partito', in G. Pasquino (ed.), *Manuale di scienza della politica*. Bologna: Il Mulino.

——(1996). 'Cosa è "competizione" in politica e come va studiate', *Rivista Italiana di Scienza Política* 26: 209–67.

——(1999). 'Collusion, Competition and Democracy, Part I', *Journal of Theoretical Politics*, 11: 435–70.

——(2000*a*). *The Political Mobilization of the European Left, 1860–1980: The Class Cleavage*. Cambridge: Cambridge University Press.

——(2000*b*). 'Collusion, Competition and Democracy, Part II', *Journal of Theoretical Politics*, 12: 33–65.

——and Mair, P., eds. (1984). *Party Politics in Contemporary Western Europe*. London: Frank Cass.

————(1990). *Identity, Competition and Electoral Availability*. Cambridge: Cambridge University Press.

————(2001). 'The Challenge to Political Parties in Contemporary Democracies', in L. Diamond and R. Gunther (eds.), *Political Parties and Democracy*. Baltimore: Johns Hopkins University Press.

——Caramani, D., and Hug, S. (1998). *Parties and Party Systems: A Bibliographical Guide to the Literature on Parties and Party Systems in Europe since 1945*. London: Sage (on CD-rom).

Beck, P. A. (1996). *Party Politics in America*. New York: Longman, 8th edn.

Beer, S. H. (1982). *Modern British Politics: Parties and Pressure Groups in the Collectivist Age*. New York: W. W. Norton.

Bell, D., and Criddle, B. (1984). *The French Socialist Party: Resurgence and Victory*. Oxford: Clarendon Press.

Belloni, F. P. (1978). 'Factionalism, the Party System, and Italian Politics', in F. P. Belloni and D. C. Beller (eds.), *Faction Politics: Political Parties and Factionalism in Comparative Perspective*. Santa Barbara, Calif.: ABC-Clio.

Berger, S. (1979). 'Politics and Anti-Politics in Western Europe in the Seventies', *Daedalus*, 108: 27–50.

Bergounioux, A., and Grunberg, G. (1992). *Le long remords du pouvoir*. Paris: Fayard.

Bericht zur Neuordnung der Parteienfinanzierung: Vorschläge der vom Bundespräsidenten berufenen Sachverständigen-Kommission. (1983). Cologne: Bundesanzeiger.

Betz, H. G. (1994). *Radical Right-Wing Populism in Western Europe*. Basingstoke: Macmillan.

Beyme, K. von (1983). 'Government, Parliaments, and the Structure of Power in Political Parties', in H. Daalder and P. Mair (eds.), *Western European Party Systems: Continuity and Change*. London: Sage.

——(1985). *Political Parties in Western Democracies*, New York: St Martin's Press.

——(1993*a*) *La clase política en el Estado de partidos*. Madrid: Alianza Editorial.

——(1993*b*) *Die politische Klasse in Parteienstaat*. Frankfurt: Suhrkamp.

——(2000). *Parteien im Wandel. Von den Volksparteien zu den professionalisierten Wählerparteien*. Wiesbaden: Westdeutscher Verlag.

Biezen, I. van (1998). 'Building Party Organisations and the Relevance of Past Models: The Communist and Socialist Parties in Spain and Portugal', *West European Politics*, 21: 32–62.

——(2000). 'On the Internal Balance of Party Power: Party Organization in New Democracies', *Party Politics*, 6: 395–417.

Blondel, J. (1978). *Political Parties: A Genuine Case for Discontent?* London: Wildwood.

Blondel, J. (2000). 'A Framework for the Empirical Analysis of Government-Supporting Party Relationships', in J. Blondel and M. Cotta (eds.), *The Nature of Party Government: A Comparative European Perspective*. London: Palgrave.

——and Cotta, M. eds. (1996). *Party Government: An Inquiry into the Relationship between Government and Supporting Parties in Liberal Democracies*. London: Macmillan.

——— (2000). *The Nature of Party Government: A Comparative European Perspective* London: Palgrave.

Blumenthal, S. (1982). *The Permanent Campaign*. New York: Simon & Schuster.

Boix, C. (1998*a*). *Political Parties, Growth and Equity: Conservative and Social Democratic Strategies in the World Economy*. Cambridge: Cambridge University Press.

——(1998*b*) 'Las elecciones primarias en el PSOE: Ventajas, ambigüedades y riesgos', *Claves de Razón Práctica*, 83: 34–8.

Bowler, S. (2000). 'Parties in Legislatures: Two Competing Explanations', in R. J. Dalton and M. P. Wattenberg (eds.), *Parties without Partisans: Political Change in Advanced Industrial Democracies*. Oxford: Oxford University Press.

Brennan, G., and Lomasky, L. (1993). *Democracy and Decision: The Pure Theory of Electoral Preference*. Cambridge: Cambridge University Press.

Broder, D. S. (1971). *The Party's Over: The Failure of Politics in America*. New York: Harper & Row.

Broughton, D., and Donovan, M., eds. (1999). *Changing Party Systems in Western Europe*. London: Pinter.

Bruneau, T., ed. (1997). *Political Parties and Democracy in Portugal: Organizations, Elections, and Public Opinion*. Boulder, Colo.: Westview Press.

——and Bacalhau, M. (1978). *Os portugueses e a política quatro anos depois do 25 de Abril*. Lisbon: Meseta.

——and MacLeod, A. (1986). *Politics in Contemporary Portugal: Parties and the Consolidation of Democracy*. Boulder, Colo.: Lynne Rienner.

——Diamandouros, P. N., Gunther, R., Lijphart, A., Morlino, L., and Brooks, R. (2001). 'Democracy: Southern European Style?', in P. N. Diamandouros and R. Gunther (eds.), *Parties, Politics and Democracy in the New Southern Europe*. Baltimore: Johns Hopkins University Press.

Bruszt, L., and Simon, J. (1991). *The Codebook of the International Survey of Political Culture: Political and Economic Orientations in Central and Eastern Europe during the Transition to Democracy, 1990–1991*. Budapest: Institute for Political Science of the Hungarian Academy of Sciences.

Bryce, J. (1921). *Modern Democracies*. New York: Macmillan.

Budge, I., and Farlie, D. (1983). *Explaining and Predicting Elections: Issue Effects and Party Strategies in Twenty-Three Democracies*. London: Allen & Unwin.

——and Keman, H. (1990). *Parties and Democracy: Coalition Formation and Government Functioning in Twenty States*. Oxford: Oxford University Press.

Bundesgesetzblatt (Federal Republic of Germany) (1989). 'Gesetz über die politische Parteien', *Bundesgesetzblatt*, 1989/i.

Burke, E. (1861[1770]). *Thoughts on the Case of the Present Discontent*; reprinted in *Works*. London: Bohn's Edition.

Bürklin, W. (1988). *Wählerverhalten und Wertewandel.* Opladen: Westdeutscher Verlag

Burton, M., Gunther, R., and Higley, J. (1992). 'Introduction: Elite Transformations and Democratic Regimes', in J. Higley and R. Gunther (eds.), *Elites and Democratic Consolidation in Latin America and Southern Europe.* Cambridge: Cambridge University Press.

Butler, D. E., and Ranney, A., eds. (1992). *Electioneering: A Comparative Study of Continuity and Change.* Oxford: Clarendon Press.

Calvo-Sotelo, L. (1990). *Memoria viva de la transición.* Barcelona: Plaza & Janés, 4th. edn.

Cameron, D. (1996). 'Exchange Rate Policies in France, 1981–1983: The Regime-Defining Choices of the Mitterrand Presidency', in A. Delay (ed.), *The Mitterrand Era.* London: Macmillan.

Campbell, A., Converse, P. E., Miller, W. E., and Stokes, D.E. (1964). *The American Voter: An Abridgement.* New York: Wiley.

Cansino, C., ed. (1995). 'Party Government: The Search for a Theory', special issue of *International Political Science Review,* 16(2).

Caramani, D., and Hug, S. (1998). 'The Literature on European Parties and Party Systems since 1945: A Quantitative Analysis', *European Journal of Political Research,* 33: 497–524.

Carty, R. K. (1988). 'Three Canadian Party Systems: An Interpretation of the Development of National Politics', in G. Perlin (ed.), *Party Democracy in Canada: The Politics of National Party Conventions.* Scarborough, Ontario: Prentice-Hall.

——(1991). *Canadian Political Parties in the Constituencies.* Research Studies. Royal Commission on Electoral Reform and Party Financing, 23; Toronto: Dundern Press.

——Erickson, L., and Blake, D. E., eds. (1992). *Leaders and Parties in Canadian Politics: Experiences in the Provinces.* Toronto: Harcourt Brace Jovanovich.

Castles, F. G., ed. (1982). *The Impact of Parties: Politics and Policies in Democratic Capitalist States.* London: Sage.

——and Wildenmann, R. eds. (1986). *Visions and Realities of Party Government.* Berlin and New York: W. de Gruyter.

Chamorro, E. (1981). *Viaje al centro de UCD.* Barcelona: Planeta.

CIS [Centro de Investigaciones Sociológicas] (1984). 'La evolución del voto', *Revista Española de Investigaciones Sociológicas,* 28: 305–21.

——(1986). 'La evolución de la intención de voto y otros indicadores políticos: 1979–1982 y 1983–1986', *Revista Española de Investigaciones Sociológicas,* 35: 269–340.

Clark, P., and Wilson, J. Q. (1961). 'Incentive Systems: A Theory for Organisations', *Administrative Science Quarterly,* 6: 129–66.

Clarke, H. D., and Stewart, M. C. (1998). 'The Decline of Parties in the Mind of Citizens', *Annual Review of Political Science,* 1: 357–78.

——and Suzuki, M. (1994). 'Partisan Dealignment and the Dynamics of Independence in the American Electorate, 1953–1988', *British Journal of Political Science,* 24: 57–78.

Coleman, J. J. (1996). *Party Decline in America: Policy, Politics, and the Fiscal State.* Princeton: Princeton University Press.

Converse, P. (1969). 'Of Time and Partisan Stability', *Comparative Political Studies*, 2: 139–71.

Cotta, M. (2000). 'Conclusion: From the Simple World of Party Government to a More Complex View of Party–Government Relationships', in J. Blondel and M. Cotta (eds.), *The Nature of Party Government: A Comparative European Perspective*. London: Palgrave.

Cotter, C., and Hennessy, B. (1964). *Politics without Power: The National Party Committees*. New York: Atherton Press.

Courtney, J. (1995). *Do Conventions Matter? Choosing National Party Leaders in Canada*. Montreal and Kingston: McGill-Queen's University Press.

Cox, G. W. (1997). *Making Votes Count*. Cambridge: Cambridge University Press.

Crewe, I., and Denver, D., eds. (1985). *Electoral Change in Western Democracies: A Framework for Analysis*. New York: St Martin's Press.

Criddle, B. (1987). 'France: Parties in a Presidential System', in A. Ware (ed.), *Political Parties: Electoral Change and Structural Response*. Oxford: Basil Blackwell.

Crotty, W. A. (1984). *American Parties in Decline*. Boston: Little, Brown, 2nd edn.

——(1991). 'Political Parties: Issues and Trends', in W. A. Crotty (ed.), *Political Science: Looking to the Future*, iv. Evanston, Il.: Northwestern University Press.

Daalder, H. (1974). 'The Consociational Democracy Theme', *World Politics*, 26: 604–21.

——(1983). 'The Comparative Study of European Parties and Party Systems: An Overview', in H. Daalder and P. Mair (eds.), *Western European Party Systems: Continuity and Change*. London: Sage.

——(1984). 'In Search of the Center of European Party Systems', *American Political Science Review*, 78: 92–109.

——(1987). 'Countries in Comparative European Politics', *European Journal of Political Research*, 15: 3–21.

——(1992). 'A Crisis of Party?', *Scandinavian Political Studies*, 15: 269–88.

——Mair, P., eds. (1983). *Western European Party Systems: Continuity and Change*. London: Sage.

Dahl, R. A., ed. (1966). *Political Oppositions in Western Democracies*. New Haven, Conn.: Yale University Press.

——(1971). *Polyarchy: Participation and Opposition*. New Haven, Conn.: Yale University Press.

——(1989). *Democracy and its Critics*. New Haven, Conn.: Yale University Press.

Dahrendorf, R. (1980). *Life Chances: Approaches to Social and Political Theory*. London: Weidenfeld & Nicolson.

D'Alimonte, R. (1989). 'Democrazia e competizione', *Rivista Italiana di Scienza Politica*, 19: 301–19.

Dalton, R. J. (1996). *Citizen Politics: Public Opinion and Political Parties in Advanced Western Democracies*. Chatham, NJ: Chatham House, 2nd edn.

——(1999). 'Political Support in Advanced Industrial Democracies', in P. Norris (ed.), *Critical Citizens: Global Support for Democratic Governance*. Oxford: Oxford University Press.

——and Kuechler, M. eds. (1990). *Challenging the Political Order: New Social and Political Movements in Western Democracies*. Oxford: Oxford University Press.

——and Wattenberg, M. P. eds. (2000*a*). *Parties without Partisans: Political Change in Advanced Industrial Democracies.* Oxford: Oxford Universty Press.

———(2000*b*). 'Partisan Change and the Democratic Process', in R. J. Dalton and M. P. Wattenberg (eds.), *Parties without Partisans: Political Change in Advanced Industrial Democracies.* Oxford: Oxford University Press.

——Flanagan, S. C., and Beck, P. A. eds. (1984). *Electoral Change in Advanced Industrial Democracies: Realignment or Dealignment?* Princeton: Princeton University Press.

——McAllister, I. and Wattenberg, M. P. (2000). 'The Consequences of Partisan Dealignment', in R. J. Dalton and M. P. Wattenberg (eds.), *Parties without Partisans: Political Change in Advanced Industrial Democracies.* Oxford: Oxford University Press.

Davis, D. A., Hinich, M. J., and Ordeshook, P. C. (1970). 'An Expository Development of a Mathematical Model of the Electoral Process', *American Political Science Review*, 64: 426–48.

Dawson, R. E., and Robinson, J. A. (1963). 'Inter-Party Competition, Economic Variables and Welfare Policies', *Journal of Politics*, 25: 265–89.

De Esteban, J., and López Guerra, L. (1982). *Los partidos políticos en la España actual.* Barcelona: Planeta.

De Jouvenel, R. (1914). *La République des camarades.* Paris: Grasset.

Del Águila, Rafael (1995). *Crises of Parties as Legitimacy Crises: A View from Political Theory.* Estudio/Working Paper, 75; Madrid: Instituto Juan March.

Del Castillo Vera, P. (1985). *La financiación de partidos y candidatos en las democracias occidentales.* Madrid: Centro de Investigaciones Sociológicas.

Della Porta, D. and Mény, I. eds. (1997). *Democracy and Corruption in Europe.* London: Pinter.

——and Vannucci, A. (1995). 'Politics, Corruption, and the Market for Corrupt Exchange', *Italian Politics Review*, 9: 165–83.

De Miguel, A. (1993). *La sociedad española, 1993–1994: Informe sociológico de la Universidad Complutense.* Madrid: Alianza.

Denver, D. (1985). 'Conclusion', in I. Crewe and D. Denver (eds.), *Electoral Change in Western Democracies: A Framework for Analysis.* London: Croom Helm.

Diamond, L. (1999). *Developing Democracy: Toward Consolidation.* Baltimore: Johns Hopkins University Press.

——and Gunther, R. eds. (2001). *Political Parties and Democracy.* Baltimore: Johns Hopkins University Press.

Diamandouros, P. N. (1994). *Cultural Dualism and Political Change in Postauthoritarian Greece.* Estudio/Working Paper, 50; Madrid: Instituto Juan March.

——and Gunther, R. eds. (2001). *Parties, Politics and Democracy in the New Southern Europe.* Baltimore: Johns Hopkins University Press.

Dittrich, K. (1983). 'Testing the Catch-All Thesis: Some Difficulties and Possibilities', in H. Daalder and P. Mair (eds.), *Western European Party Systems: Continuity and Change.* London: Sage.

Downs, A. (1957). *An Economic Theory of Democracy.* New York: Harper & Row.

Duelo, G. (1977). *Diccionario de grupos, fuerzas y partidos políticos españoles.* Barcelona: Editorial La Gaya Ciencia.

Dunleavy, P. (1991). *Democracy, Bureaucracy and Public Choice*. New York: Harvester Wheatsheaf.

Dunleavy, P. and Ward, H. (1981). 'Exogenous Voter Preferences and Parties with State Power: Some Internal Problems of Economic Theories of Party Competition', *British Journal of Political Science*, 11: 352–63.

Duverger, M. (1954). *Political Parties: Their Organization and Activity in the Modern State*. London: Methuen. Trans. of *Les Partis politiques*. Paris: Armand Colin, 1951.

Edelman, M. (1974). *The Symbolic Uses of Politics*. Urbana, IL.: University of Illinois Press, 6th edn.

EDP [Equipo de Documentación Política] (1977). *Radiografía de las nuevas Cortes*. Madrid: Sedmay.

Eijk, C. van der, and Oppenhuis, E. V. (1991). 'European Parties Performance in Electoral Competition', *European Journal of Political Research*, 19: 55–80.

Eilfort, M. (1994). *Die Nichtwähler: Wahlenthaltung als Form des Wahlverhaltens*. Paderborn: Ferdinand Schöningh.

——(1995). 'Politikverdrossenheit and the Non-Voter', *German Politics*, 4: 111–19.

Eldersveld, S. J. (1964). *Political Parties: A Behavioral Analysis*. Chicago: Rand McNally.

Elkins, D. E. (1974). 'The Measurement of Party Competition', *American Political Science Review*, 68: 682–700.

Epstein, L. D. (1967). *Political Parties in Western Democracies*. New York: Praeger.

——(1968). *Political Parties in the American Mold*. Madison, Wis.: University of Wisconsin Press.

——(1975). 'Political Parties', in F. I. Greenstein and N. W. Polsby (eds.), *Handbook of Political Science*, viii. *Nongovernmental Politics*. Reading, Mass.: Addison-Wesley.

——(1983). 'The Scholarly Commitment to Parties', in A. W. Finifter (ed.), *Political Science: The State of the Discipline*. Washington, DC: American Political Science Association.

Etzioni, A. (1988). *The Moral Dimension: Toward a New Economics*. New York: Free Press.

Evans, G., ed. (1999). *The End of Class Politics? Class Voting in Comparative Context*. Oxford: Oxford University Press.

——and Whitefield, S. (1996). *The Bases of Party Competition in Eastern Europe: Social and Ideological Cleavages in Post-Communist States*. Oxford: Oxford University Press.

Farrell, D., Hollyday, I. and Webb, P. (2002). *Political Parties in Democratic States*. Oxford: Oxford University Press.

Field, W. (1994). 'On the Americanisation of Electioneering', *Electoral Studies*, 13: 58–63.

Figuero, J. (1981). *UCD: la empresa que creó Adolfo Suárez*. Barcelona: Grijalbo.

Finer, S. E., ed. 1975. *Adversary Politics and Electoral Reform*. London: Anthony Wigram.

——(1980). *The Changing British Party System 1945–1979*. Washington DC: American Enterprise Institute.

Flanagan, W., and Fogelman, E. (1967). 'Functional Analysis', in J. C. Charlesworth (ed.), *Contemporary Political Analysis*. New York: Free Press.

Font, J., and Virós, R. eds. (1995). *Electoral Abstention in Europe*. Barcelona: Institut de Ciències Polítiques i Socials.

Fraenkel, E. (1964). *Deutschland und die westlichen Demokratien*. Stuttgart: W. Kohlhammer Verlag.

Franklin, M., Mackie, T., and Valen, H. *et al.* (1992). *Electoral Change: Responses to Evolving Social and Attitudinal Structures in Western Countries*. Cambridge: Cambridge University Press.

Friedrich, C. J. (1941). *Constitutional Government and Democracy: Theory and Practice of Modern Government*. Boston: Little, Brown.

——(1963). *Man and his Government*. New York: McGraw Hill.

Fry, G. K. (1979). *The Growth of Government*. London: Frank Cass.

Fukui, H. (1978). 'Japan: Factionalism in a Dominant-Party System', in F. P. Belloni and D. C. Beller (eds.), *Faction Politics: Political Parties and Factionalism in Comparative Perspective*. Santa Barbara, Calif.: ABC-Clio.

Gabriel, O. W. (1996). 'The Confidence Crisis in Germany', paper presented at the conference on *The Erosion of Confidence in Advanced Democracies*. Society of Comparative Research and the Université Libre de Bruxelles, Brussels.

Gallagher, M., and Marsh, M., eds. (1988). *Candidate Selection in Comparative Perspective: The Secret Garden of Politics*. London: Sage.

——Laver, M., and Mair, P. (1995). *Representative Government in Modern Europe*. New York: McGraw Hill, 2nd edn.

García Guereta, E. (2001). 'Factores externos e internos en la transformación de los partidos políticos: el caso de AP-PP', PhD., Instituto Juan March, Madrid.

Gaxie, D., ed. (1985). *Explication du vote*. Paris: Presses de la Fondation Nationale des Sciences Politiques.

Giblin, B. (1984). 'Stratégies politiques dans le bassin houillier du Nord de la France', *Hérodote*, 33–4: 15–37.

Giugni, M. G. (1998). 'Was it Worth the Effort? The Outcomes and Consequences of Social Movements', *Annual Review of Sociology*, 98: 371–93.

Grabow, K. (2001). 'The Re-emergence of the Cadre Party? Organizational Patterns of Christian and Social Democrats in Unified Germany', *Party Politics*, 7: 23–43.

Green, D. P., and Shapiro, I. (1994). *Pathologies of Rational Choice Theory: A Critique of Applications in Political Science*. New Haven, Conn.: Yale University Press.

Grofman, B., and Lijphart, A., eds. (1986). *Electoral Laws and their Political Consequences*. New York: Agathon Press.

Gunther, R. (1980). *Public Policy in a No-Party State: Spanish Planning and Budgeting in the Twilight of the Franquist Era*. Berkeley, Calif.: The University of California Press.

——(1986a) 'El realineamiento del sistema de partidos de 1982', in J. J. Linz and J. R. Montero (eds.), *Crisis y cambio: electores y partidos en la España de los años ochenta*. Madrid: Centro de Estudios Constitucionales.

——(1986b) 'El colapso de UCD', in J. J. Linz and J. R. Montero (eds.), *Crisis y cambio: electores y partidos en la España de los años ochenta*. Madrid: Centro de Estudios Constitucionales.

——(1989). 'Electoral Laws, Party Systems, and Elites: The Case of Spain', *American Political Science Review*, 83: 835–58.

Gunther, R. (1992). 'Spain: The Very Model of the Modern Elite Settlement', in J. Higley and R. Gunther (eds.), *Elites and Democratic Consolidation in Latin America and Southern Europe*. Cambridge: Cambridge University Press.

——and Blough, R. (1981). 'Religious Conflict and Consensus in Spain: A Tale of Two Constitutions', *World Affairs*, 143: 366–412.

——and Diamond, L. (2001). 'Types and Functions of Parties', in L. Diamond and R. Gunther (eds.), *Political Parties and Democracy*. Baltimore: Johns Hopkins University Press.

——and Mughan, A., eds. (2000). *Democracy and the Media: A Comparative Perspective*. Cambridge: Cambridge University Press.

——and Montero, J. R. (2000). *Legitimacy, Satisfaction and Disaffection in New Democracies*. Studies in Public Policy, 0140–8240; Glasgow: Centre for the Study of Public Policy, University of Strathclyde.

——and Montero, J. R. (2001). 'The Anchors of Partisanship: A Comparative Analysis of Voting Behaviour in Four Southern European Democracies', in P. N. Diamandouros and R. Gunther (eds.), *Parties, Politics, and Democracy in the New Southern Europe*. Baltimore: John Hopkins University Press.

——Sani, G., and Shabad, G. (1986). *Spain After Franco: The Making of a Competitive Party System*. Berkeley, Calif: University of California Press.

——Diamandouros, P. N., and Puhle, H. J., eds. (1995). *The Politics of Democratic Consolidation: Southern Europe in Comparative Perspective*. Baltimore: Johns Hopkins University Press

——Montero, J. R., and Wert, J. I. (2000). 'The Media and Politics in Spain: From Dictatorship to Democracy', in R. Gunther and A. Mughan (eds.), *Democracy and the Media: A Comparative Perspective*. Cambridge: Cambridge University Press.

Habermas, J. (1990 [1962]). *Strukturwandel der Öffentlichkeit*. Frankfurt: Suhrkamp.

Hanley, D. (1986). *Keeping Left? CERES and the French Socialist Party*. Manchester: Manchester University Press.

Harmel, R., and Janda, K. 1994. 'An Integrated Theory of Party Goals and Party Change', *Journal of Theoretical Politics*, 6: 259–87.

——Keo, U., Tan, A., and Janda, K. (1995). 'Performance, Leadership, Factions and Party Change: An Empirical Analysis', *West European Politics*, 18: 1–33.

Haungs, P. (1994). 'Plädoyer für eine erneuerte Mitgliederpartei', *Zeitschrift für Parlamentsfragen*, 25: 108–15.

Heckscher, G. (1957). *The Study of Comparative Government and Politics*. London: Allen & Unwin.

Heidar, K. (1994). 'The Polymorphic Nature of Party Membership', *European Journal of Political Research*, 25: 61–86.

——and Koole, R., eds. (2000). *Parliamentary Party Groups in European Democracies. Political Parties Behind Closed Doors*. London: Routledge.

Held, D. (1987). *Models of Democracy*. Stanford, Calif.: Stanford University Press.

Hendel, C. W., ed. (193)5. *David Hume's Political Essays*. New York: Liberal Arts Press.

Hermens, F. A. (1941). *Democracy or Anarchy? A Study of Proportional Representation*. South Bend, Ind.: University of Notre Dame Press.

Hermet, G., Hottinger, J. T., and Seiler, D.-L., eds. (1998). *Les parties politiques en Europe de l'Ouest*. Paris: Economica.

Herrero de Miñón, M. (1982). *Ideas para moderados*. Madrid: Unión Editorial.
——(1993). *Memorias de estio*. Madrid: Temas de Hoy.
Heywood, P., ed. (1997). *Political Corruption*. Oxford: Blackwell.
Hine, D. (1982). 'Factionalism in West European Parties: A Framework for Analysis', *West European Politics*, 1: 35–50.
Hinich, M. J., and Munger., M. C. (1997). *Analytical Politics*. Cambridge: Cambridge University Press.
Hirschman, A. (1970). *Exit, Voice and Loyalty*. Cambridge, Mass.: Harvard University Press.
Hirst, D. (1975). *The Representative of the People*. Cambridge: Cambridge University Press.
Hofferbert, R., ed. (198)9. *Parties and Democracy: Party Structure and Party Performance in Old and New Democracies*. Oxford: Blackwell.
Holmberg, S. (1999). 'Down and Down we Go: Political Trust', in P. Norris (ed.), *Critical Citizens: Global Support for Democratic Government*. Oxford: Oxford University Press.
Holt, R. E. (1967). 'A Proposed Structural–Functional Framework', in J. C. Charlesworth (ed.), *Contemporary Political Analysis*. New York: Free Press.
Hopkin, J. (1999). *Party Formation and Democratic Transition in Spain: The Creation and Collapse of the Union of the Democratic Centre*. London: Macmillan.
——(2001). 'Bringing the Members Back in? Democratizing Candidate Selection in Britain and Spain'. *Party Politics*, 3: 343–61.
——and Paolucci, C. (1999). 'The Business Firm Model of Party Organization: Cases from Spain and Italy', *European Journal of Political Research*, 35: 307–39.
Hoskin, G. (1995). 'The State and Political Parties in Colombia', paper presented for a conference on The Colombian Process of Reform: A New Role for the State?, Institute of Latin American Studies, University of London, 24–5 April.
Huneeus, C. (1985). *La Unión de Centro Democrático y la transición a la democracia en España*. Madrid: Centro de Investigaciones Sociológicas.
Huntington, S. P. (1968). *Political Order in Changing Societies*. New Haven, Conn.: Yale University Press.
——(1991). *The Third Wave: Democratization in the Late Twentieth Century*. Norman, Okla.: University of Oklahoma Press.
Ignazi, P. (1994). *L'estrema destra in Europa*. Bologna: Il Mulino.
——and Ysmal, C., eds. (1998). *The Organization of Political Parties in Southern Europe*. Westpoint, Conn.: Praeger.
Immerfall, S. (1993). 'German Party Sociology in the Nineties: On the State of a Discipline in Times of Turmoil', *European Journal for Political Research*, 23: 465–82.
Inglehart, R. (1979). 'Political Action: The Impact of Values, Cognitive Level and Social Background', in S. H. Barnes, M. Kaase *et al.*, *Political Action: Mass Participation in Five Western Democracies*. Beverly Hills, Calif.: Sage.
——(1990). *Culture Shift in Advanced Industrial Societies*. Princeton: Princeton University Press.
Janda, K. (1980). *Political Parties: A Cross-National Survey*. New York: Free Press.
——(1983). 'Cross-National Measures of Party Organizations and Organizational Theory', *European Journal of Political Research*, 11: 319–32.

Janda, K. (1993). 'Comparative Political Parties: Research and Theory', in A. W. Finifter (ed.), *Political Science: The State of the Discipline II*. Washington, DC: American Political Science Association.

―― and King., D. (1985). 'Formalizing and Testing Duverger's Theories on Political Parties', *Comparative Political Studies*, 18: 26–43.

Jáuregui, F. (1987). *La derecha después de Fraga*. Madrid: El País.

―― and Soriano, M. (1980). *La otra historia de UCD*. Madrid: Emiliano Escolar Editor.

Jennings, I. (1969). *Cabinet Government*. Cambridge: Cambridge University Press.

Jenson, J., and Subileau, M. (1995). *Mitterrand et les françaises: un rendez-vous manqué*. Paris: Presses de la Fondation Nationale des Sciences Politiques.

Kaase, M., and Klingemann, H.-D., eds. (1990). *Wahlen und Wähler*. Opladen: Westdeutscher Verlag.

Kalyvas, S. N. (1996). *The Rise of Christian Democracy in Europe*. Ithaca, NY: Cornell University Press.

Karvonen, L., and Kuhnle, S., eds. (2001). *Party Systems and Voter Alignments Revisited*. London: Routledge.

―― and Ryssevik, J. (2001). 'How Bright was the Future? The Study of Parties, Cleavages and Voters in the Age of the Technological Revolution', in L. Karvonen and S. Kuhnle (eds.), *Party Systems and Voter Alignments Revisited*. London: Routledge.

Kaste, H., and Raschke, J. (1977). 'Zur Politik der Volkspartei', *Leviathan*, 1, special edn.

Katz, R. S. (1980). *A Theory of Parties and Electoral Systems*. Baltimore: Johns Hopkins University Press.

――(1986). 'Party Government: A Rationalistic Conception', in F. G. Castles and R. Wildenmann (eds.), *Visions and Realities of Party Government*. Berlin: De Gruyter.

――(1990). 'Party as Linkage: A Vestigial Function?', *European Journal of Political Research*, 18: 143–61.

――――and Mair, P. (1992a). *Party Organizations: A Data Handbook on Party Organizations in Western Democracies, 1960–90*. London: Sage.

――(1992b) 'Introduction: The Cross-National Study of Party Organizations', in R. S. Katz and P. Mair (eds.), *Party Organizations: A Data Handbook*. London: Sage.

――――(1992c) 'The Membership of Political Parties in Western Democracies', *European Journal of Political Research*, 22: 329–45.

――――(1993). 'The Evolution of Party Organizations in Europe: The Three Faces of Party Organization', in W. Crotty (ed.), *Political Parties in a Changing Age*, special issue of *American Review of Politics*, 14: 593–617.

――――eds. (1994). *How Parties Organize: Change and Adaption in Party Organization in Western Democracies*. London: Sage.

――――(1995). 'Changing Models of Party Organisation and Party Democracy: The Emergence of the Cartel Party', *Party Politics*, 1: 5–28. (Reprinted in Mair 1997: ch. 5.)

――――(1996). 'Cadre, Catch-All or Cartel? A Rejoinder', *Party Politics*, 2: 525–34.

Kern, R., ed. (1973). *The Caciques: Oligarchical Politics and the System of Caciquismo in the Luso-Hispanic World*. Albuquerque, NM: University of New Mexico Press.

Key, V. O., Jun. (1949). *Southern Politics*. New York: Vintage.

――(1964). *Politics, Parties and Pressure Groups*. New York: Crowell.

——(1966). *The Responsible Electorate*. New York: Vintage Books.

Kies, N. E. (1966). 'A Selected Bibliography', in J. La Palombara and M. Weiner (eds.), *Political Parties and Political Development*. Princeton: Princeton University Press.

King, A. (1969). 'Political Parties in Western Democracies', *Polity*, 2: 111–41.

Kirchheimer, O. (1966). 'The Transformation of Western European Party Systems', in J. La Palombara and M. Weiner (eds.), *Political Parties and Political Development*. Princeton: Princeton University Press.

——(1969). 'Party Structure and Mass Democracy in Europe', in F. S. Burin and K. L. Shell (eds.), *Politics, Law and Social Change: Selected Writings of Otto Kirchheimer*. New York: Columbia University Press.

Kitschelt, H. (1989a). *The Logics of Party Formation: Ecological Politics in Belgium and West Germany*. Ithaca, NY: Cornell University Press.

——(1989b) 'The Internal Politics of Parties: The Law of Curvilinear Disparity Revisited', *Political Studies*, 37: 400–21.

——(1992). 'The Formation of Party Systems in East Central Europe', *Politics and Society*, 20: 7–50.

——(1994). *The Transformation of Social Democracy*. Cambridge: Cambridge University Press.

——(2000). 'Citizens, Politicians, and Party Cartellization: Political Representation and State Failure in Post-Industrial Democracies', *European Journal of Political Research*, 37: 149–79.

——Mansfeldova, Z., Markowski, R., and Toka, G. (1999). *Post-Communist Party Systems: Competition, Representation, and Inter-Party Cooperation*. Cambridge: Cambridge University Press.

Klingemann, H.-D., and Fuchs, D., eds. (1995). *Citizens and the State*. Oxford: Oxford University Press.

Koelbe, T. (1991). *The Left Unraveled*. Durham, NC: Duke University Press.

Kogan, D., and Kogan, M. (1982). *The Battle for the Labour Party*. London: Kogan Page.

Koole, R. (1992). *De Opkomst van de Moderne Kaderpartij: Veranderende partij-organisatie in Nederland 1960–1990*. Utrecht: Net Spectrum.

——(1994). 'The Vulnerability of the Modern Cadre Party in the Netherlands', in R. S. Katz and P. Mair (eds.), *How Parties Organize: Change and Adaption in Party Organization in Western Democracies*. London: Sage.

——(1996). 'Cadre, Catch-All or Cartel? A Comment on the Notion of the Cartel Party', *Party Politics*, 2: 507–34.

Kopecký, P. (1995). 'Developing Party Organizations in East–Central Europe', *Party Politics*, 1: 515–34.

Krockow, C. G. v., and Lösche, P., eds. (1986). *Die Parteien in der Krise*. Munich: Verlag C. H. Beck.

Krosnick, J. A., and Alwin, D. F. (1989). 'Aging and Susceptibility to Attitude Change', *Journal of Personality and Social Psychology*, 57: 416–25.

Kuechler, M., and Dalton, R. J. (1990). 'New Social Movements and the Political Order: Inducing Change for Long-Term Stability', in R. J. Dalton and M. Kuechler (eds.), *Challenging the Political Order: New Social Movements in Western Democracies*. Oxford: Oxford University Press.

Landfried, C. (1990). *Parteifinanzen und politische Macht*. Baden-Baden: Nomos Verlagsgesellschaft.

La Palombara, J., and Weiner, M,. eds. (1966). *Political Parties and Political Development*. Princeton: Princeton University Press.

Laver, M. (1989). 'Party Competition and Party System Change: The Interaction of Coalition Bargaining and Electoral Competition', *Journal of Theoretical Politics*, 1: 301–24.

——and Hunt, W. B. (1992). *Policy and Party Competition*. London: Routledge.

——and Shepsle, K. (1996). *Making and Breaking Governments*. Cambridge: Cambridge University Press.

Lawson, K. (1976). *The Comparative Study of Political Parties*. New York: St Martin's Press.

——ed. (1980). *Political Parties and Linkage: A Comparative Perspective*. New Haven, Conn.: Yale University Press.

——and Merkl, P., eds. (1988*a*). *When Parties Fail: Emerging Alternative Organizations*. Princeton: Princeton University Press.

——(1988*b*) 'Alternative Organizations: Environmental, Supplementary, Communitarian, and Authoritarian', in K. Lawson and P. Merkl (eds.), *When Parties Fail: Emerging Alternative Organizations*. Princeton: Princeton University Press.

Lederer, E. (1973 [1912]). 'Das ökonomische Element und die politische Idee im modernen Parteiwesen', in G. A. Ritter (ed.), *Deutsche Parteien vor 1918*. Cologne: Kiepenheuer & Witsch.

Lehmbruch, G., and Schmitter, P., eds. (1982). *Patterns of Corporatist Policy-Making*. London: Sage.

Leibholz, G. (1966). *Das Wesen der Repräsentation und der Gestaltwandel der Demokratie im 20. Jahrhundert*. Berlin: Walter de Gruyter & Co.

Lepsius, M. R. (1993 [1966]). 'Parteiensystem und Sozialstruktur: Zum Problem der Demokratisierung der deutschen Gesellschaft', in M. R. Lepsius, *Demokratie in Deutschland*. Göttingen: Vandenhoeck & Ruprecht.

Lewis, P. G. (1996). *Party Structure and Organization in East–Central Europe*. Cheltenham: Edward Elgar.

Lewis, S. C. (1993). 'The New Politics in the Old Politics: Institutions and Social Forces in the Remaking of the French Left', book manuscript.

Lijphart, A. (1968*a*). *The Politics of Accommodation: Pluralism and Democracy in the Netherlands*. Berkeley, Calif.: University of California Press.

——(1968*b*). 'Typologies of Democratic Systems', *Comparative Political Studies*, 1: 3–44.

——(1969). 'Consociational Democracy', *World Politics*, 21: 207–25.

——(1977). *Democracy in Plural Societies: A Comparative Exploration*. New Haven, Conn.: Yale University Press.

——(1984). *Democracies: Patterns of Majoritarian and Consensus Government in Twenty-One Countries*. New Haven, Conn.: Yale University Press.

——(1994). *Electoral Systems and Party Systems: A Study of Twenty-Seven Democracies, 1945–1990*. Oxford: Oxford University Press.

——(1999). *Patterns of Democracy: Government Forms and Performance in Thirty-Six Countries*. New Haven, Conn.: Yale University Press.

Linz, J. J. (1966). 'Michels e il suo contributo alla sociologia politica', Introduction to R. Michels, *La sociologia del partito politico nella democracia moderna: Studi sulle tendenze oligarchiche degli aggregati politici*. Bologna: Il Mulino.

——(1967). 'The Party System of Spain: Past and Future', in S. M. Lipset and S. Rokkan (eds.), *Party Systems and Voter Alignments*. New York: Free Press.

——(1992). 'Change and Continuity in the Nature of Contemporary Democracies', in G. Marks and L. Diamond (eds.), *Reexamining Democracy: Essays in Honor of Seymour Martin Lipset*. London: Sage.

——(1994). 'Presidential or Parliamentary Democracy: Does it Make a Difference?', in J. J. Linz and A. Valenzuela (eds.), *The Failure of Presidential Democracies*, i. Baltimore: Johns Hopkins University Press.

——(1998a) 'Democracy's Time Constraints', *International Political Science Review*, 19: 19–39.

——(1998b) *Michels y su contribución a la sociología política*. Mexico: Fondo de Cultura Económica.

——(2000). 'Democratic Political Parties: Recognizing Contradictory Principles and Perception', *Scandinavian Political Studies*, 23: 252–65.

——(2001). 'Some Thoughts on Democracy and Public Opinion Research', in E. Katz and Y. Warshel (eds.), *Election Studies: What's their Use*. Boulder, Colo.: Westview Press.

——Gómez-Reino, M., Orizo, F. A., and Vila, D. (1981). *Informe sociológico sobre el cambio político en España, 1975–1981*. Madrid: Euramérica.

——and Montero, J. R. (2001). 'The Party Systems of Spain: Old Cleavages and New Challenges', in L. Karvonen and S. Kuhnle (eds.), *Party Systems and Voter Alignments Revisited*. London: Routledge.

——and Stepan, A. (1996). *Problems of Democratic Transition and Consolidation: Southern Europe, South America and Post-Communist Europe*. Baltimore: Johns Hopkins University Press.

Lipset, S. M. (1959). 'Some Social Requisites of Democracy: Economic Development and Political Legitimacy', *American Political Science Review*, 53: 69–105.

——(1960a) 'Party Systems and the Representation of Social Groups', *European Archives of Sociology*, 1: 50–85.

——(1960b) *Political Man: The Social Bases of Politics*. New York: Doubleday.

——(1964). 'Ostrogorski and the Analytic Approach to the Comparative Study of Political Parties', Introduction to M. Ostrogorski, *Democracy and the Organization of Political Parties*. New York: Quadrangle Books.

——(1981). *Political Man: The Social Bases of Politics*. Baltimore: Johns Hopkins University Press, expanded and updated edn.

——(1994). 'The Social Requisites of Democracy Revisited', *American Sociological Review*, 59: 1–22.

——and Rokkan, S., eds. (1967a). *Party Systems and Voter Alignments*. New York: Free Press.

————(1967b). 'Cleavage Structures, Party Systems and Voter Alignments: An Introduction', in S. M. Lipset and S. Rokkan (eds.), *Party Systems and Voter Alignments*. New York: Free Press.

——and Schneider, W. (1983). *The Confidence Gap*. New York: Free Press.

Listhaug, O., and Wiberg, M. (1995). 'Confidence in Political and Private Institutions', in H.-D. Klingemann and D. Fuchs (eds.), *Citizens and the State*. Oxford: Oxford University Press.

Lösche, P., and Walter, F. (1992). *Die SPD: Klassenpartei–Volkspartei–Quotenpartei*. Darmstadt: Wissenschaftliche Buchgesellschaft.

Lowi, T. (1963). 'Toward Functionalism in Political Science: The Case of Innovation in Party Systems', *American Political Science Review*, 57: 570–83.

Machnig, M. (2000). 'Auf dem Weg zur Netzwerkpartei', *Neue Gesellschaft/ Frankfurter Hefte*, 47: 654–60.

McKenzie, R. T. (1955). *British Political Parties*. London: Heinemann.

Mainwaring, S. P. (1999). *Rethinking Parties in the Third Wave of Democratization: The Case of Brazil*. Stanford, Calif.: Stanford University Press.

——and Scully, T. R., eds. (1995). *Building Democratic Institutions: Party Systems in Latin America*. Stanford, Calif.: Stanford University Press.

Mair, P. (1987). *The Changing Irish Party System: Organization, Ideology and Electoral Competition*. London: Frances Pinter.

——1990. 'Continuity, Change, and the Vulnerability of Party', in P. Mair and G. Smith (eds.), *Understanding Party System Change in Western Europe*. London: Frank Cass.

——(1994). 'Party Organizations: From Civil Society to the State', in R. S. Katz and P. Mair (eds.), *How Parties Organize: Change and Adaptation in Party Organizations in Western Democracies*. London: Sage.

——(1995). 'Political Parties, Popular Legitimacy and Public Privilege', *West European Politics*, 18: 40–57.

——(1997). *Party System Change: Approaches and Interpretations*. Oxford: Oxford University Press.

——(2001). 'The Freezing Hypothesis: An Evaluation', in L. Karvonen and S. Kuhnle (eds.), *Party Systems and Voter Alignments Revisited*. London: Routledge.

——and Biezen, I. van (2001). 'Party Membership in Twenty European Democracies, 1980–2000', *Party Politics*, 7: 5–21.

——and Smith, G., eds. (1990). *Understanding Party System Change in Western Europe*. London: Frank Cass.

——Müller, W. C., and Plasser, F., eds. (1999). *Parteien auf komplexen Wählermärkten: Reaktionsstrategien politischer Parteien in Westeuropa*. Vienna: Signum Verlag.

Malefakis, E. (1995). 'The Political and Socioeconomic Contours of Southern European History', in R. Gunther, P. N. Diamandouros, and H.-J. Puhle (eds.), *The Politics of Democratic Consolidation: Southern Europe in Comparative Perspective*. Baltimore: Johns Hopkins University Press.

Maravall, J. M. (1984). *La política de la transición*. Madrid: Taurus, 2nd edn.

——(1997). *Regimes, Politics, and Markets: Democratization and Economic Change in Southern and Eastern Europe*. Oxford: Oxford University Press.

——and Santamaría, J. (1986). 'Political Change in Spain and the Prospects for Democracy', in G. O'Donnell, P. Schmitter and L. Whitehead (eds.), *Transitions from Authoritarian Rule: Southern Europe*. Baltimore: Johns Hopkins University Press.

Martín Villa, R. (1984). *Al servicio del Estado*. Barcelona: Planeta.

Martínez, R. (1993). 'The Business Sector and Political Change in Spain', in R. Gunther (ed.), *Politics, Society and Democracy: The Case of Spain*. Boulder, Colo.: Westview.

Matthews, R. C. O. (1985). 'Competition in Economy and Polity', in R. C. O. Matthews (ed.), *Economy and Democracy*. London: Macmillan.

Mayhew, D. (1986). *Planning Parties in American Politics: Organization, Electoral Settings, and Government Activity in the Twentieth Century*. Princeton: Princeton University Press.

Meehan, E. S. (1967). *Contemporary Political Thought: A Critical Study*. New York: Dorsey Press.

Meliá, J. (1981). *Así cayó Adolfo Suárez*. Barcelona: Planeta.

Meltz, D. B. (1973). 'An Index for the Measurement of Interparty Competition', *Behavioral Science*, 18: 59–63.

Méndez-Lago, M. (2000). *La estrategia organizativa del Partido Socialista Obrero Español (1975–1996)*. Madrid: Centro de Investigaciones Sociológicas.

Mendrinou, M., and Nicolapoulos, I. (1997). 'Interests, Parties and Discontent in the Public Mind: Sympathy Scores for Greek Parties and Interest Groups', paper presented at the Joint Sessions of the European Consortium for Political Research, Berne, Switzerland.

Mény, Y. (1996). 'Politics, Corruption, and Democracy', *European Journal of Political Research*, 30: 111–23.

Merkel, W. (1993). *Ende der Sozialdemokratie? Machtressourcen und Regierungspolitik im westeuropäischen Vergleich*. Frankfurt: Campus Verlag

——and Puhle, H.-J. (1999). *Von der Diktatur zur Demokratie: Transformationen, Erfolgsbedingungen, Entwicklungspfade*. Opladen: Westdeutscher Verlag.

Merkl, P. H., ed. (1980). *Western European Party Systems: Trends and Prospects*. New York: Free Press.

Merriam, C. E. (1922). *The American Party System*. New York: Macmillan.

Meseguer, C. (1998). 'Sentimientos antipartidistas en el Cono Sur: un estudio exploratorio', *América Latina Hoy*, 18: 99–112.

Michels, R. (1962 [1911]). *Political Parties: A Sociological Study of the Organizational Tendencies in Modern Democracies*. New York: Free Press.

——(1970 [1911]). *Zur Soziologie des Parteiwesens in der modernen Demokratie*. Stuttgart: Alfred Kröner Verlag.

Miller, W. E., and Shanks, J. M. (1996). *The New American Voter*. Cambridge: Cambridge University Press.

Mintzel, A. (1983). *Die Volkspartei: Typus und Wirklichkeit*. Opladen: Westdeutscher Verlag.

——and Oberreuter, H., eds. (1992). *Parteien in der Bundesrepublik Deutschland*. Opladen/Bonn: Leske Verlag + Budrich.

Montero, J. R. (1981). 'Partidos y participación política: algunas notas sobre la afiliación política en la etapa inicial de la transición española', *Revista de Estudios Políticos*, 23: 33–72.

——(1986). 'La vuelta a las urnas: participación, movilización y abstención', in J. J. Linz and J. R. Montero (eds.), *Crisis y cambio: electores y partidos en la España de los años ochenta*. Madrid: Centro de Estudios Constitucionales.

Montero, J. R. (1992). *Sobre la democracia en España: legitimidad, apoyos institucionales y significados*. Estudio/Working Paper, 39; Madrid: Instituto Juan March.

——(1994). 'Sobre las preferencias electorales en España: fragmentación y polarización (1971–1993)', in P. del Castillo (ed.), *Comportamiento político y electoral*. Madrid: Centro de Investigaciones Sociológicas.

——and Gunther, R. (1994). 'Sistemas "cerrados" y listas "abiertas": sobre algunas propuestas de reforma del sistema electoral en España', in J. R. Montero, R. Gunther, J. I. Wert, J. Santamaría, and M. A. Abad, *La reforma del régimen electoral*. Madrid: Centro de Estudios Constitucionales.

————and Torcal, M. (1997). 'Democracy in Spain: Legitimacy, Discontent, and Disaffection', *Studies in Comparative International Development*, 32: 124–60.

————(1998). 'Actitudes hacia la democracia en España: legitimidad, descontento y desafección', *Revista Española de Investigaciones Sociológicas*, 83: 9–40.

Morlino, L. (1995). 'Political Parties and Democratic Consolidation in Southern Europe', in R. Gunther, P. N. Diamandouros, and H.-J. Puhle (eds.), *The Politics of Democratic Consolidation: Southern Europe in Comparative Perspective*. Baltimore: Johns Hopkins University Press.

——(1996). 'Crisis of Parties and Change of Party System in Italy', *Party Politics*, 2: 5–30.

——(1998). *Democracy between Consolidation and Crisis: Parties, Groups, and Citizens in Southern Europe*. Oxford: Oxford University Press.

——and Montero, J. R. (1995). 'Legitimacy and Democracy in Southern Europe', in R. Gunther, P. N. Diamandouros, and H.-J. Puhle (eds.), *The Politics of Democratic Consolidation: Southern Europe in Comparative Perspective*. Baltimore: Johns Hopkins University Press.

Mudde, C. (1996). 'The Paradox of the Anti-Party Party: Insights from the Extreme Right', *Party Politics*, 2: 265–76.

Mughan, A., Box-Steffensmeier, J., and Scully, R. (1997). 'Mapping Legislative Socialisation', *European Journal of Political Research*, 32: 93–116.

Muller, E. N. (1979). *Aggressive Political Participation*. Princeton: Princeton University Press.

——and Seligson, M. A. (1994). 'Civic Culture and Democracy: The Question of Causal Relationships', *American Political Science Review*, 88: 635–52.

Müller, W. C. (1993). 'After the "Golden Age": Research into Austrian Political Parties since the 1980s', *European Journal of Political Research*, 23: 439–63.

——(1994). 'The Development of Austrian Party Organizations in the Post-War Period', in R. S. Katz and P. Mair (eds.), *How Parties Organize: Change and Adaptation in Party Organizations in Western Democracies*. London: Sage.

——(2000a). 'Political Parties in Parliamentary Democracies: Making Delegation and Accountability Work', *European Journal of Political Research*, 37: 309–33.

——(2000b). 'Patronage by National Governments', in J. Blondel and M. Cotta (eds.), *The Nature of Party Government: A Comparative European Perspective*. London: Palgrave.

——and Strøm, K., eds. (1999a). *Policy, Office, or Votes? How Political Parties in Western Europe Make Hard Decisions*. Cambridge: Cambridge University Press.

————(1999b). 'Conclusions: Party Behaviour and Representative Democracy', in W. C. Müller and K. Strøm (eds.), *Policy, Office, or Voters? How Political Parties in Western Europe Make Hard Decisions*. Cambridge: Cambridge University Press.

————eds. (1999c). *Coalition Governments in Western Europe*. Oxford: Oxford University Press.

Muñoz Alonso, A. (1984). *Las elecciones del cambio*. Barcelona: Argos-Vergara.

Namier, L. B. (1970). *The Structure of Politics at the Accession of George III*. London: Macmillan.

Navalón, A., and Guerrero, F. (1987). *Objetivo: Adolfo Suárez*. Madrid: Espasa Calpe.

Neale, J. E. (1949). *Elizabethan House of Commons*. London: Jonathan Cape.

Neumann, S. (1956). 'Toward a Comparative Study of Political Parties', in S. Neumann (ed.), *Modern Political Parties: Approaches to Comparative Politics*. Chicago: University of Chicago Press.

Newcomb, T. M., *et al.* (1967). *Persistence and Change: Bennington College and its Students after Twenty-Five Years*. New York: Wiley.

Niedermayer, O. (1989). *Innerparteiliche Partizipation*. Opladen: Westdeutscher Verlag.

Noelle-Neumann, E. (1994). 'Left and Right as Categories for Determining the Political Position of the Parties and the Population in Germany', paper presented at the symposium on Political Parties: Changing Role in Contemporary Democracies, Instituto Juan March. Madrid.

Nohlen, D. (1984). *Elections and Electoral Systems*. Bonn: Forschungsinstitut der Friedrich-Ebert-Stiftung.

Noland, A. (1956). *The Founding of the French Socialist Party*. Cambridge, Mass.: Harvard University Press.

Norris, P. (1997). 'Towards a More Cosmopolitan Political Science?', *European Journal of Political Research*, 31: 17–34.

—— ed. (1999a). *Critical Citizens: Global Support for Democratic Governance*. Oxford: Oxford University Press.

——(1999b) 'Conclusions: The Growth of Critical Citizens and its Consequences', in P. Norris (ed.), *Critical Citizens: Global Support for Democratic Governance*. Oxford: Oxford University Press.

Nye, J., Zelikow, P. D., and King, D. C., eds. (1997). *Why People Don't Trust Government*. Cambridge: Harvard University Press.

Offe, C. (1984). *Contradictions of the Welfate State*. Cambridge, Mass.: MIT Press.

Olson, M. (1965). *The Logic of Collective Action*. Cambridge, Mass.: Harvard University Press.

Oneto, J. (1981). *Los últimos días de un presidente*. Barcelona: Planeta.

Orizo, Francisco A. (1983). *España, entre la apatía y el cambio social*. Madrid: MAPFRE.

——(1991). *Los nuevos valores de los españoles. España en la Encuesta Europea de Valores*. Madrid: Fundación Santa María.

Ostrogorski, M. I. (1964 [1902]). *Democracy and the Organization of Political Parties*. London: Macmillan.

Panebianco, A. (1988). *Political Parties: Organization and Power*. Cambridge: Cambridge University Press.

Pasquino, G. (2001). 'The New Campaign Politics in Southern Europe', in P. N. Diamandouros and R. Gunther (eds.), *Parties, Politics and Democracy in the New Southern Europe*. Baltimore: Johns Hopkins University Press.

Paterson, W., and Gillespie, R., eds. (1993). *Rethinking Social Democracy in Western Europe*, special issue, *West European Politics*, 16(1).

Penadés, A. (2000). 'Los sistemas elementales de representación', PhD., Instituto Juan March, Madrid.

Pennings, P., and Lane, J.-E., eds. (1998). *Comparing Party System Change*. London: Routledge.

Perlin, G. (1988). 'Introduction: Party Development and Party Democracy in Canada', in G. Perlin (ed.), *Party Democracy in Canada: The Politics of National Party Conventions*. Scarborough, Ontario: Prentice-Hall.

Pharr, S. J., and Putnam, R. D., eds. (2000). *Disaffected Democracies: What's Troubling the Trilateral Countries?* Princeton: Princeton University Press.

Philippe, A., and Hubscher, D. (1991). *Enquête à l'intérieur du Parti Socialiste*. Paris: A. Michel.

Pierre, J., Svåsand, J., and Widfeldt, A. (2000). 'State Subsidies to Political Parties: Confronting Rhetoric with Reality', *West European Politics*, 23: 1–24.

Pierre, J., and Widfeldt, A. (1994). 'Party Organizations in Sweden: Colossuses with Feet of Clay or Flexible Pillars of Government?', in R. S. Katz and P. Mair (eds.), *How Parties Organize: Change and Adaptation in Party Organizations in Western Democracies*. London: Sage.

Pizzorno, A. (1966). 'Introduzione allo studio della partecipazione politica', *Quaderni di Sociologia*, 3–4: 3–27.

——(1981). 'Interests and Parties in Pluralism', in S. Berger (ed.), *Organizing Interests in Western Europe*. Cambridge: Cambridge University Press.

Poguntke, T. (1987). 'New Politics and Party Systems', *West European Politics*, 10: 76–88.

——(1993). *Alternative Politics: The German Green Party*. Edinburgh: Edinburgh University Press.

——(1996). 'Anti-Party Sentiment: Conceptual Thoughts and Empirical Evidence: Explorations into a Minefield', *European Journal of Political Research*, 29: 319–44.

——(2000). *Parteiorganisation im Wandel: Gesellschaftliche Verankerung und organisatorische Anpassung im europäischen Vergleich*. Wiesbaden: Westdeutscher Verlag.

——and Scarrow, S. E., eds. (1996a). *The Politics of Anti-Party Sentiment*, special issue of the *European Journal of Political Research*, 29(3).

————(1996b). 'The Politics of Anti-Party Sentiment: Introduction', *European Journal of Political Research*, 29: 319–44.

Pradera, J. (1996). 'La maquinaria de la democracia: Los partidos en el sistema político español', in J. Tusell, E. Lamo de Espinosa, and R. Pardo (eds.), *Entre dos siglos: reflexiones sobre la democracia española*. Madrid: Alianza Editorial.

Presno, M. A. (2000). *Los partidos y las distorsiones jurídicas de la democracia*. Barcelona: Ariel.

Preston, Paul (1986). *The Triumph of Democracy in Spain*. London: Methuen.

Pridham, G., and Lewis, P. G., eds. (1996). *Stabilising Fragile Democracies: Comparing New Party Systems in Southern and Eastern Europe*. London: Routledge.

Przeworski, A., and Sprague, J. (1986). *Paper Stones: A History of Electoral Socialism*. Chicago: Chicago University Press.

——Stokes, S. C., and Manin, B., eds. (1999). *Democracy, Accountability, and Representation.* Cambridge: Cambridge University Press.

Puhle, H.-J. (1973). 'Vom Wohlfahrtsausschuss zum Wohlfahrtsstaat', in G. A. Ritter (ed.), *Vom Wohlfahrtsausschuss zum Wohlfahrtsstaat.* Cologne: Markus Verlag.

——(1977). 'Parlament, Parteien und Interessenverbände in Deutschland 1890–1914', in M. Stürmer (ed.), *Das kaiserliche Deutschland: Politik und Gesellschaft 1870–1918.* Düsseldorf: Droste Verlag, 2nd edn.

——(1995). *Staaten, Nationen und Regionen in Europa.* Vienna: Picus Verlag.

——(2001). 'Mobilizers and Late Modernizers: Socialist Parties in the New Southern Europe', in P. N. Diamandouros and R. Gunther (eds.), *Parties, Politics and Democracy in the New Southern Europe.* Baltimore: Johns Hopkins University Press.

Putnam, R. D., Pharr, S. J., and Dalton, R. J. (2000). 'Introduction: What's Troubling the Trilateral Democracies?', in S. J. Pharr and R. D. Putnam (eds.), *Disaffected Democracies: What's Troubling the Trilateral Countries?* Princeton: Princeton University Press.

Rae, D. W. (1971). *The Political Consequences of Electoral Laws.* New Haven, Conn.: Yale University Press, 2nd edn.

Ranney, A. (1954). *The Decline of Responsible Party Government.* Urbana, IL: University of Illinois Press.

——(1965). 'Parties in State Politics', in H. Jacob and K. Vines (eds.), *Politics in American States.* Boston: Little, Brown.

——(1975). *Curing the Mischiefs of Faction: Party Reform in America.* Berkeley, Calif.: University of California Press.

Raschke, J. (1993). *Die Grünen.* Cologne: Bund Verlag.

Reif, K., and Schmitt, H. (1980). 'Nine Second-Order National Elections: A Conceptual Framework for the Analysis of European Election Results', *European Journal of Political Research*, 8: 3–44.

Reiter, H. L. (1989). 'Party Decline in the West: A Skeptic's View', *Journal of Theoretical Politics*, 1: 325–48.

Riker, W. H., and Ordeshook, P. C. (1968). 'A Theory of the Calculus of Voting', *American Political Science Review*, 62: 25–43

————(1973). *An Introduction to Positive Political Theory.* Englewood Cliffs. NJ: Prentice-Hall.

Robertson, D. (1976). *A Theory of Party Competition.* London: Wiley.

Roemer, J. E. (forthcoming). *Political Competition: Theory and Applications.* Cambridge, MA: Harvard University Press.

Rokkan, S. (1966). 'Norway: Numerical Democracy and Corporate Pluralism', in R. A. Dahl (ed.), *Political Oppositions in Western Democracies.* New Haven, Conn.: Yale University Press.

——(1967). 'The Structuring of Mass Politics in the Smaller European Democracies: A Developmental Typology', *Comparative Studies in Society and History*, 10: 173–210.

——(1968). 'Electoral Systems', in *International Encyclopedia of Social Sciences.* New York: Macmillan and Free Press.

——(1970). *Citizens, Elections, Parties: Approaches to the Comparative Study of the Processes of Development.* Oslo: Universitetsforlaget.

Rokkan, S. and Svåsand, L. (1978). 'Zur Soziologie der Wahlen und der Massenpolitik', in R. König (ed.), *Handbuch der empirischen Sozialforschung*. Stuttgart: Enke Verlag, 2nd edn.

Rose, R., ed. (1974*a*). *Electoral Behaviour: A Comparative Handbook*. New York: Free Press.

——(1974*b*) *The Problem of Party Government*. London: Macmillan

——(1984). *Do Parties Make a Difference?* London: Macmillan.

——and Mackie, T. T. (1988). 'Do Parties Persist or Fail? The Big Trade-off Facing Organizations', in K. Lawson and P. H. Merkl (eds.), *When Parties Fail: Emerging Alternative Organizations*. Princeton: Princeton University Press.

Roth, G. (1963). *The Social Democrats in Imperial Germany: A Study in Working Class Isolation and National Integration*. Totowa, NJ: Bedminster Press.

Roucaute, Y. (1983). *Le Parti Socialiste*. Paris: Huisman.

Rustow, D. A. (1956). 'Scandinavia: Working Multi-Party Systems', in S. Neumann (ed.), *Modern Political Parties: Approaches to Comparative Politics*. Chicago: University of Chicago Press.

Sadoun, M. (1988). 'Sociologie des militants et sociologie du parti', *Révue Française de Science Politique*, 38: 348–69.

Sani, G. (1992). 'Comportamientos de masas y modelos de ciudadano', *Revista del Centro de Estudios Constitucionales*, 13: 25–47.

——and Segatti, P. (2001). 'Antiparty Politics and the Restructuring of the Italian Party System', in P. N. Diamandouros and R. Gunther (eds.), *Parties, Politics, and Democracy in the New Southern Europe*. Baltimore: Johns Hopkins University Press.

Santamaría, J. (1984). 'Elecciones generales de 1982 y consolidación de la democracia: a modo de introducción', *Revista Española de Investigaciones Sociológicas*, 28: 7–18.

Sartori, G. (1976). *Parties and Party Systems: A Framework for Analysis*. Cambridge: Cambridge University Press.

——(1977). 'Democrazia competitiva ed élites politiche', *Rivista Italiana di Scienza Politica*, 7: 327–55.

Sawicki, F. (1986). 'Application de la sociologie des organisations à l'étude du PS', Maîtrise de Sociologie, Université de Paris-V.

——(1997). *Les reseaux du Parti Socialiste*. Paris: Berlin.

Scarrow, H. A. (1967). 'The Function of Political Parties: A Critique of the Literature and the Approach', *Journal of Politics*, 29: 770–90.

Scarrow, S. E. (1994). 'The "Paradox of Enrollment": Assessing the Costs and Benefits of Party Memberships', *European Journal of Political Research*, 25: 41–60.

——(1996*a*) *Parties and their Members: Organizing for Victory in Britain and Germany*. Oxford: Oxford University Press.

——(1996*b*) 'Politicians Against Parties: Anti-Party Arguments as Weapons for Change in Germany', *European Journal of Political Research*, 29: 297–317.

——(2000). 'Parties without Members? Party Organization in a Changing Electoral Environment', in R. J. Dalton and M. P. Wattenberg (eds.), *Parties without Partisans: Political Change in Advanced Industrial Democracies*. Oxford: Oxford University Press.

——Webb, P., and Farrell, D. M. (2000). 'From Social Integration to Electoral Contestation: The Changing Distribution of Power within Political Parties', in R. J. Dalton and M. P. Wattenberg (eds.), *Parties without Partisans: Political Change in Advanced Industrial Democracies*. Oxford: Oxford University Press.

Schattschneider, E. E. (1942). *Party Government*. New York: Holt, Rinehart & Winston.

——(1960). *The Semi-Sovereign People*. New York: Holt, Rinehart, an& Winston.

Schedler, A. (1996). 'Anti-Political-Establishment Parties', *Party Politics*, 2: 291–312.

Scheuch, E. K., and Scheuch, U. (1992). *Cliquen, Klüngel und Karrieren*. Reinbek: Rowohlt.

Schlesinger, J. A. (1955). 'Two Dimensional Scheme for Classifying the States According to the Degree of Interparty Competition', *American Political Science Review*, 49: 1120–8.

——(1984). 'On the Theory of Party Organization', *Journal of Politics*, 46: 369–400.

——(1991). *Political Parties and the Winning of Office*. Chicago: University of Chicago Press.

Schmidt, M. G. (1996). 'When Parties Matter: A Review of the Possibilities and Limits on Partisan Influence on Public Policy', *European Journal of Political Research*, 30: 155–83.

Schmitt-Beck, R. (1998). 'Of Readers, Viewers, and Cat-Dogs', in J. W. van Deth (ed.), *Comparative Politics: The Problem of Equivalence*. London: Routledge

Schmitt, H. (1989). 'On Party Attachment in Western Europe and the Utility of Eurobarometer Data', *West European Politics*, 12: 122–37.

——and Holmberg, S. (1995). 'Political Parties in Decline?', in H.-D. Klingemann and D. Fuchs (eds.), *Citizens and the State*. Oxford: Oxford University Press.

Schmitter, P. C., and Karl, T. (1991). 'Modes of Transition in Latin America, Southern and Eastern Europe', *International Journal of Social Science*, 128: 269–84.

——and Lehmbruch, G., eds. (1979). *Trends towards Corporatist Intermediation*. London: Sage.

Schneider, W. (1974). 'Issues, Voting, and Cleavages: A Methodology and Some Tests', *American Behavioral Scientist*, 18: 111–46.

——(1980). 'Styles of Competition', in R. Rose (ed.), *Electoral Participation: A Comparative Analysis*. London: Sage.

Schumpeter, J. A. (1942). *Capitalism, Socialism and Democracy*. New York: Harper & Row.

Sedgwick, R. (1970). *The House of Commons 1715–1754*. London: History of Parliament Trust.

Segatti, P. (1998). 'Gli atteggiamenti anti-partito: un fenomeno evidenti a tutti ma forse non compreso da molti', unpublished manuscript.

Segert, D., Stöss, R., and Niedermayer, O., eds. (1997). *Parteiensysteme in postkommunistischen Gesellschaften Osteuropas*. Opladen: Westdeutscher Verlag.

Selle, P., and Svåsand, L. (1991). 'Membership in the Party Organizations and the Problem of Decline of Parties', *Comparative Political Studies*, 23: 459–77.

Selznick, P. 1957. *Leadership in Administration*. New York: Harper & Row.

Semetko, H. A., Blumler, J. G., Gurevitch, M., and Weaver, D. H. (1991). *The Formation of Campaign Agendas: A Comparative Analysis of Party and Media Roles in Recent American and British Elections*. Hillsdale, NJ: Lawrence Erlbaum Associates.

Sferza, S. (1988). 'Party Building and Rebuilding: The French Socialist Party in the Pas-de-Calais and Ille-et-Vilaine', Ph.D. dissertation.

——(1999). 'What is Left of the Left? More than one would Think', *Daedalus*, 128: 101–26.

Shepsle, K., and Bonchek, M. S. (1997). *Analyzing Politics: Rationality, Behavior and Institutions*. New York: W. W. Norton.

Shugart, M. S., and Carey, J. M. (1992). *Presidents and Assemblies: Constitutional Design and Electoral Dynamics*. Cambridge: Cambridge University Press.

Simmel, G. (1955 [1908]). *Conflict and the Web of Group Affiliation*. New York: Free Press.

——(1995 [1908]). 'Soziologie der Konkurrenz', in *Aufsätze und Abhandlungen 1901–1908, Band, Gesamtausgabe, Band 7*. Frankfurt: Suhrkamp.

Skidmore, T. E., ed. (1993). *Television, Politics, and the Transition to Democracy in Latin America*. Baltimore: Johns Hopkins University Press.

Smith, G. (1989). 'Core Persistence: Change and the "People's Party"', *West European Politics*, 12: 157–68.

——(1990). 'Core Persistence: Change and the "People's Party"', in P. Mair and G. Smith (eds.), *Understanding Party System Change in Western Europe*. London: Frank Cass.

Sorauf, F. J. (1964). *Political Parties in the American System*. Boston: Little, Brown.

Starke, F. C. (1993). *Krise ohne Ende? Parteiendemokratie vor neuen Herausforderungen*. Cologne: Bund Verlag.

Steffani, W. (1988). 'Parteien als soziale Organisationen: Zur politologischen Parteienanalyse', *Zeitschrift für Parlamentsfragen*, 19: 549–60.

Stern, M. (1972). 'Measuring Interparty Competition: A Proposal and a Test of Method', *Journal of Politics*, 34: 889–904.

Stigler, G. J. (1957). 'Perfect Competition, Historically Contemplated', *The Journal of Political Economy*, 65: 1–17.

——(1968). 'Competition', in *International Encyclopedia of Social Sciences*. New York: Macmillan and Free Press.

——(1972). 'Economic Competition and Political Competition', *Public Choice*, 13: 91–106.

Stockton, H. (2001). 'Political Parties, Party Systems, and Democracy in East Asia: Lessons from Latin America', *Comparative Political Studies*, 34: 94–119.

Stokes, D. E. (1966). 'Spatial Models of Party Competition', in A. Campbell, P. Converse, W. Miller, and D. Stokes, *Elections and the Political Order*. New York: John Wiley.

Stokes, S. C. (1999). 'Political Parties and Democracy', *Annual Review of Political Science*, 2: 243–67.

Strøm, K. (1984). 'Minority Governments in Parliamentary Democracies', *Comparative Political Studies*, 17: 199–227.

——(1990a) *Minority Government and Majority Rule*. Cambridge: Cambridge University Press.

——(1990*b*) 'A Behavioral Theory of Competitive Political Parties', *American Journal of Political Science*, 34: 565–98.

——(2000). 'Parties at the Core of Government', in R. J. Dalton and Martin P. Wattenberg (eds.), *Parties without Partisans: Political Change in Advanced Industrial Democracies*. Oxford: Oxford University Press.

——and Müller, W. C. (1999). 'Political Parties and Hard Choices', in W. C. Müller and K. Strøm (eds.), *Policy, Office, or Voters? How Political Parties in Western Europe Make Hard Decisions*. Cambridge: Cambridge University Press.

——and Svåsand, L. (1997*a*). *Challenges to Political Parties: The Case of Norway*. Ann Arbor: University of Michigan Press.

——(1997*b*) 'Political Parties in Norway: Facing the Challenges of a New Society', in K. Strøm and L. Svåsand (eds.), *Challenges to Political Parties: The Case of Norway*. Ann Arbor: The University of Michigan Press.

Subileau, F. (1987). 'Les systèmes de valeurs des militants socialistes français', paper presented at the Joint Sessions of the European Consortium for Political Research, Amsterdam.

——(1988). 'The Strategy of Reconstruction of the French Socialist Party', paper presented at the Joint Sessions of the European Consortium for Political Research, Rimini.

Sundberg, J. (1994). 'Finland: Nationalized Parties, Professionalized Organizations', in R. S. Katz and P. Mair (eds.), *How Parties Organize: Change and Adaptation in Party Organizations in Western Democracies*. London: Sage.

Svåsand, L. (1994). 'Change and Adaptation in Norwegian Party Organizations', in R. S. Katz and P. Mair (eds.), *How Parties Organize: Change and Adaptation in Party Organizations in Western Democracies*. London: Sage.

Taagepera, R., and Shugart, M. S. (1989). *Seats and Votes: The Effects and Determinants of Electoral Systems*. New Haven, Conn.: Yale University Press.

Taggart, P. (1994). 'Riding the Wave: New Populist Parties in Western Europe', paper presented at the Joint Sessions of the European Consortium for Political Research, Madrid.

Tarrow, S. (1990). 'The Phantom of the Opera: Political Parties and Social Movements of the 1960s and 1970s in Italy', in R. J. Dalton and M. Kuechler (eds.), *Challenging the Political Order: New Social and Political Movements in Western Democracies*. Oxford: Oxford University Press.

Thies, M. F. (2000). 'On the Primacy of Party in Government: Why Legislative Parties can Survive Party Decline in the Electorate', in R. J. Dalton and M. P. Wattenberg (eds.), *Parties without Partisans: Political Change in Advanced Industrial Democracies*. Oxford: Oxford University Press.

Thomas, J. C. (1975). *The Decline of Ideology in Western Political Parties*. London: Sage.

——(1980). 'Ideological Trends in Western Political Parties', in P. H. Merkl (ed.), *Western European Party Systems: Trends and Prospects*. New York: Free Press.

Torcal, M. (2000). 'Political Disaffection in New Democracies', unpublished manuscript.

Tusell, J. (1985). 'The Democratic Center and Christian Democracy in the Elections of 1977 and 1979', in H. R. Penniman and E. M. Mujal-León (eds.), *Spain at the Polls, 1977, 1979 and 1982*. Washington, DC: American Enterprise Institute.

UCD [Unión de Centro Democrático] (1978). *La solución a un reto.* Madrid: Unión Editorial.

Vargas Machuca, R. (1998). 'A vueltas con las primarias del PSOE: ¿por qué cambian los partidos?', *Claves de Razón Práctica*, 86: 11–21.

Wagner, A. (1892). *Grundlegung der politischen Ökonomie*. Leipzig: C. F. Winter.

Walter, F. (1995). 'Die SPD nach der deutschen Vereinigung: Partei in der Krise oder bereit zur Regierungsübernahme?', *Zeitschrift für Parlamentsfragen*, 26: 85–112.

Ware, A., ed. (1987a). *Political Parties: Electoral Change and Structural Response*. Oxford: Basil Blackwell.

——(1987b) *Citizens, Parties and the State*. Cambridge: Polity Press.

——(1996). *Political Parties and Party Systems*. Oxford: Oxford University Press.

Wattenberg, M. P. (1990). *The Decline of American Political Parties: 1952–1988*. Cambridge, Mass.: Harvard University Press.

Webb, P. D. (1995). 'Are British Political Parties in Decline?', *Party Politics*, 1: 299–322.

——(1996). 'Apartisanship and Anti-Party Sentiment in the United Kingdom: Correlates and Constraints', *European Journal of Political Research*, 29: 365–82.

Weber, M. (1964 [1922]). *Wirtschaft und Gesellschaft*. Cologne: Kiepenheuer & Witsch.

——(1968 [1922]). *Economy and Society*. Berkeley, Calif.: University of California Press.

——(1971a [1918]). 'Parlament und Regierung im neugeordneten Deutschland', in *Gesammelte Politische Schriften*. Tübingen: J. C. B. Mohr.

——(1971b [1919]). 'Politik als Beruf', in *Gesammelte Politische Schriften*. Tübingen: J. C. B. Mohr.

Wert, J. I. (1984). 'La campaña electoral de octubre de 1982: el camino del cambio', *Revista Española de Investigaciones Sociológicas*, 28: 63–84.

——(1996). 'Sobre cultura política: legitimidad, desafección y malestar', in J. Tusell, E. Lamo de Espinosa and R. Pardo (eds.), *Entre dos siglos: reflexiones sobre la democracia española*. Madrid: Alianza Editorial.

Wheare, K. C. (1954). Review of H. Morrison, *Government and Parliament: A Survey from the Inside*, London: Allen & Unwin, in *The Listener* (25 Nov.).

——(1963). *Legislatures*. Oxford: Oxford University Press.

White, S., Batt, J., and Lewis, P. G. (1993). *Developments in East European Politics*. London: Macmillan.

Wiesendahl, E. (1992). 'Volksparteien im Abstieg', *Aus Politik und Zeitgeschichte*, B34–5/92: 3–14.

——(1998). 'The Present State and Future Prospects of the German *Volksparteien*', *German Politics*, 7: 151–75.

Wildenmann, R. (1989). *Volksparteien: Ratlose Riesen?* Baden-Baden: Nomos Verlagsgesellschaft.

Wilson, J. Q. (1962). *The Amateur Democrat*. Chicago: University of Chicago Press.

Wolinetz, S. B. (1979). 'The Transformation of Western European Party Systems Revisited', *West European Politics*, 2: 4–28.

——(1988). *Parties and Party Systems in Liberal Democracies*. London: Routledge.

——(1991). 'Party System Change: The Catch-All Thesis Revisited', *West European Politics*, 14: 113–28.

——(1993). 'Reconstructing Dutch Social Democracy', *West European Politics*, 16: 97–112.

——ed. (1998*a*). *Political Parties*. Aldershot: Ashgate.

——ed. (1998*b*) *Party Systems*. Aldershot: Ashgate.

——(1998*c*) 'Introduction', in S. B. Wolinetz (ed.), *Political Parties*. Aldershot: Ashgate.

Ysart, F. (1984). *¿Quién hizo el cambio?* Barcelona: Argos-Vergara.

Index

Abril, Fernando 204
abstention 64, 72
accountability 29, 62, 89, 125, 143, 312
    confused 142
    horizontal 313
    lack of 304
    to lower strata 141
activists 127, 153, 162, 169, 171, 196
    left/socialist 173, 175, 176
adaptation 63, 96, 97, 131, 167, 178
ad hoc mechanisms 21, 40, 53, 78, 80, 85, 182, 206
adversarial interaction 29
advertisements 5, 98
    negative 154
affluence 4
Africa 10
agenda setting 62
agglomeration 79, 115, 150
Aldrich, J. H. 3, 6, 11
Alianza Popular 192, 194, 195, 218, 223, 224
alienation 5, 106, 114, 134
alliances 62, 79, 80, 103, 172, 175, 176, 201, 221
    centrist 181
    conservative 222
    elite 213
    standardization of 178
Almond, G. A. 50, 60
Alvarez, José Luis 218
Alwin, D. F. 269
Alzaga, Oscar 204, 217, 218, 223
ambitions 178, 192, 221
American Political Science Association 20, 43
anarchy, *see* 'loosely coupled anarchy'
Andalucía 206–7, 219, 220
Anglo-Saxon system 44, 47, 59
anticipated reactions 89
antipartyism 7, 19, 24, 28, 32, 257–90
    presidentialism and 292
    strongest among non-voters 295
    see also cultural antipartyism; reactive antipartyism

Apparate 66
appointments 240, 241, 242, 245
apprenticeship 180, 202
Areilza, José María de 217
arenas 99
Arias Salgado, Rafael 193, 204, 206, 209, 214
Arzallus, Xabier 304
Asia 10, 58
Australia 138
Austria 29, 50, 123, 236, 255, 302
    catch-all parties 70, 75
    Freedom Party 250
    Great Coalitions 71
    institutionalized patronage 246
    National Liberals 148
    partitocracy 235, 251–2, 253
    see also Haider; Kreisky
Austro-Hungarian empire 238
authoritarianism 42, 70, 75, 87, 163, 172, 193
    anti-party attitudes and 262, 277, 280, 282
authority 92, 99, 102, 115
    collective 199
    institutional 195
autocratic traditions 41
autogestion 171, 172, 173, 174, 180, 182, 184
autonomy 67, 73, 124, 125, 133, 238
    abdication of 303
    factional 218
    institutional 199
    regional 206, 207
    representative elites 214
Autonomy Statutes (Basque/Catalan) 203, 204, 219
availability 22, 89, 91, 93–4, 95, 103
    encapsulation versus 104
    maximization of 105–6
awareness 273, 274

Bacalhau, M. 268
balance of power 23, 113, 116, 120
    internal 123

'balkanization' 106
bargaining 75, 99, 197, 199, 222
   informal 212
   pragmatic 44
Barnes, S. E. 17, 132, 285
Barry, B. 87, 197
Bartels, L. M. 125
Bartolini, Stefano 2, 7, 9, 12, 16, 18, 21, 22, 94, 166
Basque National Party 304
Basque provinces 69, 203, 204, 206, 207, 219, 220
Beer, S. H. 115, 117
Belgium 29, 50, 153, 236, 238, 244, 255
   Flemish Party 250
   General Election Study (1995) 297
   institutionalized patronage 246
   partitocracy 235, 250, 251–2
   patronage 249, 252
   Popular Party 252
   shady deals 234
   Socialist Party 252
Bell, D. 169
Belloni, F. P. 213, 219
benefits 199
Benn, Tony 157
Berger, S. 169
Bergounioux, A. 187
Berlusconi, Silvio 79, 137, 143, 156
BEURS (second generation immigrant youth, France) 188
Beyme, K. von 17, 60, 66, 70, 76, 77, 310
bicameralism 50
Biezen, I. van 126, 128, 144
bigness 73
Blair, Tony 128, 157, 158
blocs 48, 169, 170
Blondel, Jean 7, 18, 24, 28, 29, 161, 177, 198, 242, 303
Blough, R. 192
Blumenthal, S. 106
Boix, C. 309
Bolingbroke, Henry J., Viscount 40
Bowler, S. 310
Brazil 76, 295, 296, 297
Brest Congress (1997) 188
bribes 29, 249
Britain 29, 40, 47, 48, 70, 236
   Conservative Party 143, 156, 157, 195, 243, 251
   Labour Party 128, 156–7, 158, 162, 187, 195, 244, 253
   Liberal Party 191
   once dominant model 43–5, 54

Parliament 41, 44, 45, 49, 242
   party membership 128
   'sleaze' 234
   Social Democratic Party 156
Brittany 180, 181, 183, 184
broadcasting systems 70, 98, 131
Bruneau, T. 260, 268
Bruszt, L. 295
Bryce, J. 3
bureaucracy 41, 62, 71, 85, 131
   representative or elected 146
Burke, Edmund 40, 42, 59
Burton, M. 261
by-elections 220

cadre parties 23, 24, 60, 63, 116, 125, 136, 137, 139, 163
   mass parties and 139, 140–5, 146, 158
   middle and upper level 173
   promotion of 185
Callaghan, James 156
Calvo Ortega, Rafael 223
Calvo Sotelo, Leopoldo 192, 201, 223, 224, 225
Cameron, D. 176
campaigns 5, 24, 59, 74, 75, 106, 143
   capital-intensive 148
   commercialized and professionalized 69
   cost of 92
   emphases on policy during 154
   expenses 131
   individualistic 80
   labour-intensive 152
   leaders declare party policy during 142
   mobilizing voters during 285
   modern 162
   new techniques 125–6
   professionals 160
   propaganda 262
   run by small teams 136
   television 70
   volunteers 152
Canada 25, 138, 142, 143, 144, 146, 161
   Bloc Québécois 157
   Canadian Alliance 158
   intermittently active parties 152
   Liberals 136
   New Democratic Party 164
   Progressive Conservative Party 136, 157–8
   Reform Party 157, 158
   see also Charest; Mulroney

candidate recruitment 141, 152, 162, 173–5
capitalism 53, 71
Caramani, D. 2, 9
Carey, J. M. 293
cartel parties 24, 77, 80, 98, 99, 101, 122, 133, 145, 148–9, 159
  oligopolistic 71
  vulnerability 160
Catalonia 69, 203–4, 206, 207, 219, 220, 305
catch-all parties 18, 23, 52, 66–72, 120–2, 137, 139, 145, 159, 167, 169, 170, 193, 209
  characteristic of 161, 162
  crisis of 20, 59, 72–9
  crystallization of 24
  electoral effectiveness associated with 173
  emergence of 292
  flexible 221
  horizontal growth not synonymous 172
  indiscriminate use of the term 8
  leadership of 219
  modus operandi 148
  multi-party systems and 151
  Panebianco's respecification 146–8
  par excellence 202
  plus' 21, 77, 78
  primacy of 125
  rights and privileges of elites 214
  spread and relevance of 130
  transformation 149, 160
Catholic Church 192, 215
Catholics 60, 67, 68, 176, 213, 222
  progressive 180, 184
  'very good' 215, 216
  see also CFDT; JOC
caucuses 42, 60, 116, 118, 136, 142
Cavero, Iñigo 223
Central and Eastern Europe 42, 59, 76, 295
  post-communist transformations 58, 75
  see also Czechoslovakia; Poland
central committees 122
central office 23, 24, 78, 115, 116, 117, 118
  changed and more professionalized role 126
  election campaigns 136
  strong centralization in 120
centralization 69, 120, 131, 207, 212
centre parties 47, 141, 160, 183
centrifugal forces 47–8
Centro Democrático 200, 201, 202, 204, 217
Centro Democrático y Social 224

CEOE (Confederación Española de Organizaciones Empresariales) 205, 221, 222
CERES (Centre d'Études et Recherches Socialistes) 172, 173, 174, 176, 180–5 *passim*
CFDT (Confederation Democratique du Travail) 173, 174, 181, 182, 184
Chamorro, E. 205
change 275–6
  environmental 130
  programmatic 157
  social 52–3, 132
changeability 102, 103
Charest, Jean 157–8
Chile 296–7, 313, 314
Chirac, Jacques 143, 152
choices 100, 294
  see also rational choice
Christian democrats 21, 74, 151
  Dutch 136
  French 250
  German 152
  Italian 65, 153, 191, 195, 212, 248, 252
  Spanish 201, 204, 205, 209, 213, 215, 216, 220, 223, 224
'civic forum' 75
civil service 70
civil society 58, 59, 61, 64, 66, 77, 79, 244
  state and 148
Clark, P. 197
class 121, 140
  see also middle classes; upper class; working class
cleavages 49, 61, 62, 73, 93, 131
  ethno-national 69
  freezing of 177
  in/out 65
  intra-party 74
  left/right 68, 74
  religious 176
  social 132
clientelism 72, 210, 214, 302
closeness of returns 103, 104
closure 104
coalitions 44, 49, 62, 71, 78, 160, 201, 202, 208, 223
  broad 75, 151, 152
  building 75
  centre-left or five-party 153
  collapsed 218
  consociational 245
  dominant 199
  equal-sized 106

coalitions (*cont.*):
  heterogeneous 170
  leftist 298
  maintaining 162
  'oversized' 242
  parties participating regularly in 153
  process of formation 99
  single-party government replaced by 243
  small 242, 244
  'unethical' bargain and 294
  unfeasible 220
coercion 102
cohabitation 188
collaboration 201, 202, 212, 225
collusion 22, 26, 92, 97, 98, 99
  consequences of 106
  decidability versus 104
  essence of politics 101
  question of 102
Colombia 116, 296
'colonization' 43, 70, 304
Coltivatori diretti 213
commercialization 69, 79
common good 87
communications 5, 54, 125, 132
  mass 24, 114, 131
communists 47, 75, 120, 244
  French 170, 172, 251
  Italian 248
  Spanish 194, 195, 203, 220, 221, 298
communitarianism 43
competence 100, 101
competition 5, 11, 12, 19–23, 24, 61, 62, 71,
    153, 159, 198
  all-out 161
  conditions of 6, 89–104
  democracy and 90–1
  different dimensions of 104–7
  factional 143, 179, 212
  giving participants a sense of 103
  inter-factional 171
  internal 143
  international 73
  inter-party 167
  intra-bloc 171
  intra-left 179, 184, 187
  new 160
  perfect 84, 87, 92
  pressures of 148
  strong 67
  suppressing 119
  two-party 293
  unintended 'social value' of 85–9
  unity and 297–8, 309

compromises 204, 205, 214, 245, 302
concentration 92, 99
conciliation 245, 254
conciliatory interaction 29
confederations 213
Congress of Deputies (Spain) 210, 220
consensual interaction 29
consensus 50–1, 59, 63, 114, 291
  antifascist 71
  building 75
  competition disrupts 297
  cost of 203–7
  lack of 193
conservatives 21, 60, 74, 75
  British 143, 156, 157, 195, 243, 251
  Canadian 136, 157–8
  French 173, 248, 251
  Spanish 205, 224, 274–5, 298, 299, 300,
    308
consociationalism 45, 50, 61, 175, 193, 205,
    215, 244, 245
consolidation 75, 76, 194, 195, 277
constituencies 67, 76, 115, 119, 205
  core 198, 199, 202
  fragmented 79
constitutional monarchy 247
constitutionalization 100–1
constitutions 53, 98, 203, 298
  front benchers' 44
  unwritten 50
consultants 125
contestability 22, 89, 90–3, 95, 103
  closure versus 104
  high 106
  maximization of 105
controversial questions 101
Converse, P. 271
corporatism 61, 62, 70, 76, 79, 201
  right-wing 262
corruption 24, 28, 29, 71, 72, 235,
    302–3
  Italy 116, 234, 249–50
  Spain 116, 259, 271
Cotta, M. 28, 242
Cotter, C. 143
coups d'état 297
Craxi, Betlino 248
Criddle, B. 141, 169
crisis 30, 39, 64
  catch-all parties 20, 59, 72–9
  institutionalization 191–230
Crotty, W. A. 9
cultural antipartyism 30, 31, 260, 261, 264,
    265, 267, 272, 276

disaffection and 262, 263, 273, 277, 282, 283, 285–6
  education and 278
  external efficacy and 273
  political disengagement and 280
  strongly negative 273–4
cultural collectivities 173
cynicism 5, 7, 262, 263
Czechoslovakia 75

Daalder, Hans 7, 8, 18, 19, 20, 23, 43, 44, 64, 134, 138, 139, 166
Dahl, R. A. 61
D'Alimonte, R. 90, 91
Dalton, R. J. 6, 261, 262, 302
decay 6, 292
decentralization 73, 76, 78, 79, 80, 173, 181, 206
  concerns for 180
decidability 22, 90, 95–102, 103
  collusion versus 104
  ensuring 106
  maximization of 106
  minimum 106
  vulnerability and 107
decision-making 40, 41, 53, 58, 60, 75, 106
  coalitional practices in 210, 212
  collective 116
  collegial 213, 217
  critical and divisive 106
  cumbersome procedures 219
  delegitimized 207
  democratic 72
  formal 205
  legitimation of 100, 101
  opening up of procedures 127
  participation in 130, 247
  presidential 204
  recognized role in 198
  spirit in which it occurs 242
decline 3–8, 19, 21, 25, 27, 30, 31, 32, 233–56
  commonly used indicators of 166
decomposition 6
'decoupling' 80
defection 192, 218, 223, 224, 227
Deferre, Gaston 179
De Jouvenel, R. 46
Del Aguila, R. 302
deligitimation 72–4
Della Porta, D. 234
democracy 31, 42, 75, 76
  achievement of 205
  competition and 90–1, 95

  conditions of 90
  consociational 45, 50
  crisis of 30
  defining characteristic of 87, 89, 104–5
  direct 6, 41, 43, 52, 310
  economic and social requisites of 61
  future of 32
  general support for 262
  internal 129, 141, 143, 215
  intra-party 178
  legitimacy of 313–14
  necessary condition of 86
  new 195
  only possible 88
  quality of 263
  support for 280, 283
  theories of 87
  transition to 194, 200–3, 206, 207, 270, 277, 278
  viable 43
democratization 51, 127, 128, 158
  'fourth wave' of 58
  institutions 311
  mass 130
  'Spanish model' of 194
  'third wave' of 5, 14, 18, 25, 58
Denmark 123, 128, 147, 245, 247
deregulation 73, 75, 80
destabilization 177, 222
'destatization' 73
Diamandouros, P. N. 76, 268
Diamond, L. 14, 138, 163, 291
dictatorships 261, 269, 280
disaffection 276, 284
  cultural antipartyism and 262, 263, 273, 277, 282, 283, 285–6
disenfranchisement 106
dissatisfaction 64, 106, 260, 262, 275, 284, 298
  pervasive 291
distribution 73, 100, 103, 104, 130
Dittrich, K. 146
divorce law 205, 214, 222, 223
dogma 43
donations 142
Downs, Anthony 10, 11, 12, 22, 45, 86, 87–8, 93, 95, 151, 154
Duelo, G. 200
Dutch Labour Party (PvdA) 136, 157, 158, 162
Dutch parties, *see* Netherlands
Duverger, M. 2, 9, 14, 42, 44, 46, 47, 48, 115, 138, 194
  see also cadre parties

economies of scale 92, 99
Ecuador 294, 295, 296, 313
education 132, 222, 277–8
Eilfort, M. 257
Ejik, C. van der 94
Eldersveld, S. J. 2, 14, 23, 129
elections 114, 119, 195, 202, 215, 224
    different levels of government 153
    free and fair 75
    frequency of 304
    general 76, 81, 157, 191, 193
    legislative 168
    local 116
    municipal 181
    parliamentary 53–4, 225
    presidential 170
    regional 207, 220
    winner-take-all 151
    see also campaigns
electoral-professional parties 24, 25, 66, 77,
        122, 159–62 *passim*
    characterized 146–7
    multi-party systems and 151
    temptation to become 148
electorates 144, 194, 202, 216
    'betrayal' of 205
    core 199
    heterogeneous 198
    new parties eating into 249
    'opinion' 160
    size and loyalty 159
    sovereignty of 45
    traditional parties and 250
elite parties/elites 8, 22, 30, 50, 60, 63, 76,
        114–16, 118, 121, 130, 145, 159
    accountability of 89
    agreement to share values 101
    autonomous 67, 73
    dissatisfaction with 260
    followers and 44
    heterogeneous 204
    irresponsible 41
    local and regional 69
    motivation of 86
    power 71
    recruitment 78, 207, 208, 212, 217, 306
    responsiveness 104
    rights formerly the preserve of 127
    rival 45
    strategies of 23–4
    transformation to catch-all and cartel
        parties 149
    voters' preferences and 87, 88
encapsulation 104, 105, 117, 121, 130, 132

enfranchisement 106, 130, 148
Epinay Congress (1971) 168, 170, 184
Epstein, L. D. 9, 11, 116, 138, 139
ethnocentricism 10
Etzioni, A. 86
EU (European Union) 48, 302
European Community 156
European Parliament 304, 312–13
exclusion 61
executive 46, 47, 125, 194, 238
    power-sharing 50
'exit' 196, 198, 222
Extraordinary Congress (1979) 195

factionalism 26, 27, 40, 141, 153, 170–86,
        193–4, 217
    comparative advantages of 168
    framework for conflict 156
    internal 143
    unity versus 62
factory groups 185
fascism 41, 70
favours 234, 241, 246, 249
federalism 59, 71, 217
fees 142
Fernández Ordóñez, Francisco 222, 223,
        224, 225
financial resources 123, 142
Finer, S. E. 49
Finland 123, 244, 245, 254
'first-order' parties 127
Foot, Michael 156
Force Ouvrière 183
Forza Italia 137, 143, 156
Fougères 181
Fraenkel, E. 61
Fraga, Manuel 221, 223, 224
fragmentation 47, 49, 50, 65, 72, 74, 80, 92,
        200
    systems that avoid 107
France 29, 47, 49, 70, 145, 244
    Communist Party 170, 172, 174, 175,
        176, 179, 183, 185, 187
    Conservatives 173, 248, 251
    Fifth Republic 46, 53, 169, 170, 243,
        250
    Fourth Republic 45, 46, 48, 50, 141
    Front National 147, 251
    Gaullists 141, 143, 147, 152, 250
    major party collapse 250
    Parliament 45–6
    patronage 247, 253
    RPR 141, 143, 147, 152
    shady deals 234, 235

Socialist Party 8, 25–6, 141, 143, 167–90, 193, 247, 248, 251
Third Republic 45, 46, 48, 50, 141, 305
UDF 141, 143, 144
Vichy 46
see also Chirac; Gaulle; Giscard; Mitterrand
Franco, Gen. Francisco 193, 194, 201, 202, 204, 207, 220, 269, 277–8
Friedrich, C. J. 44, 89
Front National 147, 251
Fry, G. K. 116
Fukui, H. 218, 219
functionalist approach 11
fundamentalists 117
fundraisers 143, 201, 235

Gabriel, O. W. 261
Galicia 206
Gallego 207
García Guereta, E. 218
Gaulle, Charles de 46, 243
Gaullists 141, 143, 147, 152, 250
Gaxie, D. 171
general will 41, 42, 298
German empire 238
Germany 49, 50, 70, 73, 81, 235, 244
    antipartyism 259
    Catholic Centre Party 60
    Christian Democratic Union 152
    federalism 71
    Greens 75
    party membership 126
    Social Democratic Party 40, 60, 65, 67, 80
    Weimar 44, 45, 46–7, 48
    see also Hitler; Kohl
Gestalt 59, 65, 70
Giblin, B. 185
Gillespie, R. 162
Giscard D'Estaing, Valéry 145
Giugni, M. G. 302
Goldwater, Barry 157
González, Felipe 71, 275, 303
governance 167, 175–6, 178, 181
    internal 193
    self 185
government 29
    alternating 48
    alternative channels of access to 122
    approved by the people 88
    'divided' 292
    elections at different levels of 153
    exclusivity of 102

executive 47
feedback on popularity 106
formation of 5–6, 78, 102
majoritarian 50
minority 104
party 233–56
responsibility to Parliament 116
single-party 44, 49, 243
see also coalitions
'governmentalization' 124
Grabow, K. 25
graft 116
Gramsci, A. 303
Greece 70, 80, 81, 251, 253, 304
    anti-party sentiments 31, 260–1, 263, 267, 268, 282, 283, 285, 286, 287
Green, D. P. 12
Greens 74, 75, 124, 143, 150, 151, 188, 233
Grunberg, G. 187
Guesdisme autogestionnaire 185
Gunther, Richard 8, 14, 18, 19, 24, 26, 28, 29, 69, 76, 80, 134, 138, 163, 166, 191, 192, 193, 200, 212, 250, 262, 272, 277, 282, 291, 313

Habermas, J. 67
Haider, Jörg 148
Hanley, D. 176, 179, 180
Harmel, R. 75
Haungs, P. 77
Heath, Edward 157
hegemony 172, 173, 177, 182
Heidar, K. 298, 310
Hennessy, B. 143
Hermens, F. A. 44, 47
Herrero de Miñón, Miguel 204, 217, 222, 223, 224
Hervé, Edmond 181, 183
Hirschman, A. 196–7, 198, 200
Hitler, Adolf 47
Hobsbawm, Eric 291
Hollande, François 188
Holmberg, S. 300
Hopkin, Jonathan 8, 18, 26, 80, 137, 166, 250, 309
horizontal growth 172, 173, 174, 178, 179, 180
Hoskin, G. 116
Hubscher, D. 177, 180, 184
Hug, S. 2, 9
Hume, David 39
Huneeus, C. 193, 213, 217
Hunt, W. B. 62
Huntington, S. P. 58, 196

hypotheses 49
  middle-range 14
  testing 12, 15, 17, 19, 23, 163, 164

identity 69, 79, 184
  collective 202
  ideological 225
  national 98
ideology 41, 48, 52, 62, 74, 118, 121
  abandonment of 162
  clear and consistent 195
  eclectic 202, 209
  end of 138
  heterogeneous 192, 194, 195, 200, 201, 212, 225
  homogeneous 200
  incompatible 212
  polarization of 106
  revitalization 26, 172–3
  vague 209
  well-articulated 150
Ille-et-Vilaine federation 179, 180–3
illegal practices 28, 234, 235, 251, 285, 286
image 5, 69, 277, 303
  charismatic 204
  conservative 224
  popular 259
  sectarian 214
Immerfall, S. 257
incentives 118, 119, 130, 192, 199, 201
  powerful 218
  selective 159, 197
  solidary 160, 197, 201, 203, 225
inclusion 61
income 127
'independents' 202, 203, 209, 213
industrialization 53, 130
Inglehart, R. 166
instability 92, 178, 224, 260, 261, 270
institutionalization 6, 27, 53, 58, 75, 87, 153
  crisis of 191–230
  factional disputes 298
  goal 100
  lack of 250
  patronage 245, 246
institutions 10, 23–4, 71, 76
  decision-making 58
  democratization of 311
  executive 107
  intermediary 73
  reform of 78
interest groups 4, 68, 72, 76, 121, 146, 166
  increased reliance on 160
  influence and action 159

major parties' relationship with 198
  party links with 214
  right-wing 223
interests 58, 78, 80, 146, 195, 301–2
  business 214, 221
  individual 199
  particularistic 210, 293
  perceived 198
  personal 273
  plasticity of 167
  private 41
  sectional 53
  societal/social 71, 265
  special 32, 293, 301, 302
intermediaries 53, 54, 73
intermediation 64
  corporatist 79
  enlarged 76–8
internal conflict 8, 207, 215, 220–7
interventionism 73, 80
investigative journalism 79
Ireland 50, 123
  see also Northern Ireland
Israeli Labor Party 217
issues 101, 171, 172, 176
  economic 214
  emphasis on 160
  environmental 150
  ideological 107
  major and divisive 107
  position 100
  religious 192
  salience of 99, 100, 106
  valence 100
Italy 29, 45, 47, 48, 49, 70, 74, 78, 81, 244, 302
  anti-party sentiments 259–60, 264–5, 267, 282–3, 285, 286, 299
  Christian Democratic Party 65, 153, 191, 195, 212, 248, 252
  Communist Party 248
  corruption 234, 249–50
  'First Republic' 212, 259
  institutionalized patronage 246
  Leghe 75
  managing elections and suppressing competition 119–20
  Partito Socialista Italiana 191
  partitocracy 235, 250, 251–2
  patrimonialism 248
  PLI, PRI and PSI 153
  Socialist Party 153, 217, 248, 249
  trasformismo 116, 118
  see also Berlusconi

Janda, K. 17, 138
Japan:
  Liberal Democratic Party 193, 195, 212, 217, 218, 250
  Socialist Party 217
Jáuregui, F. 202
Jennings, I. 116
Jenson, J. 172
JOC (Jeunesse Ouvrière Catholique) 181
John Paul II, Pope 192
Jospin, Lionel 188
judiciary 41

Kaase, M. 132, 285
Karl, T. 271
Kaste, H. 209
Katz, Richard S. 7, 14, 20, 25, 113, 123, 124, 125, 129, 131, 134, 138, 141, 236, 237
  see also cartel parties; catch-all parties
Kern, R. 116
Key, V. O. 11
Keynesian policies 73
Kies, N. E. 10
Kinnock, Neil 156
Kirch, Leo 78
Kirchheimer, O. 2, 8, 14, 21, 25, 60, 63–4, 65, 113, 146, 147, 154, 160, 167, 208
  see also catch-all parties
Kitschelt, H. 14, 26, 167
Kogan, D. & M. 187
Kohl, Helmut 71
Koole, R. 24, 25, 77, 113, 122, 124, 129, 137, 141, 143, 144, 298, 310
Kopecky, P. 128
Kreisky, Bruno 244, 252
Krosnick, J. A. 269
Kuechler, M. 6, 302

Labour Party (Britain) 128, 156–7, 158, 162, 195, 244, 253
  factionalism 187
labour unions 75, 120, 213
laicité 172, 173
laïque 181, 183
La Polambara, J. 2
Latin America 31, 58, 69, 163
  see also Brazil; Chile; Colombia; Ecuador; Mexico; Uruguay; Venezuela
LAU (Ley de Autonomía Universitaria, Spain) 205, 214
Laver, M. 62
Lavilla, Landelino 224, 225

Law for Political Reform (Spain, 1976) 200, 220
Lawson, K. 5, 9, 77, 164, 167
leadership 27, 41, 44, 69, 94, 115, 121, 136
  allocation of resources 185
  baronial 224
  catch-all party 219
  collective 215, 217
  collegial 146, 210
  competing for votes on the basis of 148
  deference to 129
  dissatisfaction with 293
  excess 182
  factions among 200
  federal 184
  'fusion' between government and 243–4
  ideological commitments abandoned by 195
  ineffectual 192
  influence of 132
  instability of 178
  insulated from members' pressures 161
  internal protest against 198
  key channel of communication between voters and 125
  laïque 181
  legitimacy 128
  member support 246
  'newsworthy' 131
  party a vehicle for 156
  personalization of 303
  power and 127
  presidential 212
  professional 141
  real 122
  regular turnover in 212
  relations between members and 149
  renewal 171, 175
  responsiveness 95
  selection of 142
  substantive and ideological differences 133
Lederer, Emil 60
left-wing parties 53, 120, 150, 157, 169–70, 201
  economic policy 222
  libertarian 151
  see also communists; socialists
legislation 102
legitimation/legitimacy 73, 80, 87, 100, 101, 119, 201, 217, 252, 313–14
  ad hoc 85
  broad consensus on 291
  ideological 182

legitimation/legitimacy (*cont.*):
  key element in 262
  leadership 128
  problem in 134
  self 277
Lehmbruch, G. 61
Leibholz, G. 66, 70
Lepsius, M. R. 60
liability 177–8
liberalization 75
liberals 60, 74, 114, 115, 120, 151
  British 191
  Canadian 136
  Italian 153
  Spanish 201, 205, 208, 210, 213, 223
Liévin Congress (1994) 180
Lijphart, A. 29, 45, 50, 51, 61, 193, 216,
    242, 244
linkages 64, 74, 77, 125
  societal 176
Linz, Juan J. 7, 19, 31, 32, 195, 267, 292,
    295, 309, 313
Lipset, S. M. 2, 51, 60, 61, 130
Listhaug, O. 257
local parties 129
Locke, John 58
'loosely coupled anarchy' 78
Lösche, P. 78
loyalty 69, 119, 120, 159, 167, 208
  elite 215
  exit, voice and 196–7
  factional 175, 212
  organizational 201
  territorial 175
  traditionally strong 246

McGovern, George 157
Machnig, M. 77
McKenzie, R. T. 44, 118
Mackie, T. T. 6, 166
MacLeod, A. 268
Mainwaring, S. P. 76, 163
Mair, Peter 3, 6–7, 14, 20, 25, 51, 94, 113,
    122–6 *passim*, 128, 129, 133, 138, 141,
    144, 160, 166
  see also cartel parties; catch-all parties
majoritarian polities 29, 50, 107, 244–7
    passim, 250–5 *passim*
Malthusianism 177, 182
mandates 45, 87, 118, 305
manifestos 142
Maravall, J. M. 221, 261
market forces 52
markets 11, 22, 70, 90, 99, 197

open 91
Martín Villa, R. 200
Martinez, R. 221
Marxists 53, 176, 195, 220, 221, 304
mass parties 19, 21, 23, 24, 42, 43, 60, 65,
    68, 116–20, 137, 166
  autonomy 133
  cadre parties and 139, 140–5, 146, 158
  class 64, 167, 170, 172
  decay of 292
  emergence and character of 130
  nationalist 67
  parties seem to want to maintain image
    of 128
  primacy of 125
  transformation 149, 160
Matthews, R. C. O. 107
Mauroy, Pierre 173
Mayhew, D. 143
mayoría natural strategy 221, 222
mayors 202
means of production 195
media 53, 69, 70, 76, 78, 96, 154
  electronic 54
  mass 5, 101, 125, 131, 132
  political information through 280
  shock orchestrated by 233–4
  written 98
Meltz, D. B. 103
Mendrinou, M. 261, 268
Merkl, P. 5, 77
Merriam, C. E. 2
Meseguer, C. 295
Mexico 297
Michels, R. 2, 14, 19, 23, 40, 41, 60, 67,
    133, 213, 309, 310
middle classes 4
migration 4
militancy 129, 174, 194
militantes 73
minorities 207, 295
Mitterrand, François 26, 171, 172, 173,
    177, 184
mobilization 62, 73, 74, 78, 117, 126, 171,
    176
  ad hoc 80
  anti-political 169
  catch-all vote 195
  decline of 177
  grass-roots 181
  mass 51–2
  social 170
models 17, 20, 23–7, 178–86, 207–20
  catch-all 193, 207, 208, 209, 214

consensus 50
consociational 213, 215, 217, 245
  factional 193, 207, 208, 213, 215
  holding-company 193, 208, 213, 214, 215, 217
  incompatible 194
  mass-party 24
  once dominant 43–5
  rational-choice 13, 22
modernity 64, 73
modernization 63, 65, 66, 67, 72, 79, 80
  societal 169
monarchy 247, 269, 270
money 127
monopoly 75
Montero, José Ramón 7, 19, 24, 28, 29, 81, 134, 195, 227, 262, 272, 282, 292, 313
morality 98
Morlino, L. 74, 76, 81
Mosca, Gaetano 102
Mudde, C. 134, 259
Mughan, A. 124
Muller, E. N. 60, 285
Müller, W. C. 2, 3, 17, 24, 25, 28, 124
Mulroney, Brian 157
multi-party systems 20, 151, 152, 293–4
  moderate 301
  re-evaluation of 48–51
  rejection of 45–8
municipalities 183, 185

national committees 143
National Movement (Spain) 201
nationalization 173, 174, 178
Nea Demokratia (Greece) 268
negative reference groups 199
neocorporatism 52, 53, 71
neoliberals 73
neopopulism 74
Netherlands 25, 29, 50, 60, 69, 71, 234, 235
  cadre parties 141, 142, 143
  CHU/CDA 153
  coalitions 244
  consociational model 245
  Dutch Labour Party 136, 157, 158, 162
  government distance from Parliament 238
  moderate 'party accommodation' 255
  parliamentary office staff 123
  power of the monarch 247
  primacy of party in public office 128
networks 5, 14, 77, 94, 178, 183
  ancillary organizations 132
  associational or personalistic 202

corporatist 76
  factional 172, 174, 175
  fragmented and overlapping 76
  patron-client 152
  personal 115
Neumann, S. 2, 14, 21, 23, 42, 60, 67, 138, 139, 140, 145, 146, 148
New Labour (Britain) 157
New Politics 6, 51, 169, 171, 188
new politics parties 77, 137, 139, 160
New Zealand 138
Newcomb, T. M. 269
newspapers 280
  'independent' 131
Nicolapoulos, I. 261, 268
Noelle-Neumann, E. 261
Noland, A. 187
nomenklatura system 244
nominations 152
Nord 185
norms 86, 194
Norris, P. 262
Northern Europe 114, 116, 151, 164
Northern Ireland 69
Norway 123, 147, 245

occupational collectivities 173
OECD (Organization for Economic Cooperation and Development) 48
office-seeking parties 13, 61, 149, 152–3, 154–5, 158, 161, 162
  patterns of transformation 159
  primary interest 150
oligarchic rule 60, 67, 72, 118
oligopolies 71, 79
'on the ground' parties 23, 78
openness 91
operationalization 10, 153–9
opinion leaders 5
opinions 300–1, 304
  see also public opinion
Oppenhuis, E. V. 94
opposition 62, 71, 104, 142, 157, 184, 244
  articulation of ideological principles 302
  exploitation by 303
  'irresponsible' 47
  moderate 201
  reactive antipartyism and vote for 274–5
  'tolerated' 204
Ordeshook, P. C. 95
organization 62, 65, 79, 113
  contemporary 122–6
  models of 114–22

organization (*cont.*):
performance and 166–90
re-examining 23–7
Ostrogorski, M. I. 2, 19, 40, 41, 115

PACs (Political Action Committees, US) 143
Panebianco, A. 14, 118, 122, 124, 125, 145, 146–8, 173, 188, 197, 199
see also electoral-professional parties
Paolucci, C. 137
Parliament 53–4, 104, 114, 115, 123, 125, 126, 155, 313
arms-length relationship between government and 247
government responsibility to 116
Members of 117, 118, 119, 120, 246, 309, 310, 312
party outside of 136
see also Britain; France; Netherlands; Portugal; Scandinavia
parliamentarianism 43
'parliamentarization' 124
parochialism 175
Parteienverdrossenheit 257, 259
participation 4–5, 117, 130, 177, 199
anti-party attitudes and 284–7
lack of 240
popular 247
Partienstaat 20, 41, 47, 62, 64, 65, 66–72, 76, 79, 80, 81
legitimation of 73
parties:
alternative politics 160
anti-democratic 140
'anti-party' 134
anti-system 285, 286
ascendancy of 113–35
attitudes towards 5, 27–32, 262, 294–303
bourgeois 117
business firm 137
Catholic 60, 67, 68, 173, 174
caucus 42, 60, 116, 118, 136
cell-based 167
charismatic 147
contemporary democracies 291–317
denial of 39–42, 43
denominational 60, 64
distrust of 313–14
'established' 243
extremist 134, 147
faction-ridden 193, 195, 212, 217
growing literature on 2–3
highly centralized 203

intermittently active 152
irrelevance of 166
leader-centred 146, 148
marginalizing 126–9, 146, 157, 185
money and 307–11
nationalist 67, 203, 204, 250, 304, 305
new style 75, 249
'omnibus' 206
patrimonial 177, 248
programmatic 159, 177
protest 160
reconceptualizing 19–23
redundancy of 20, 39, 51–4
rejection of: multi-party systems 45–8; selective 39, 42–3
revisiting linkages 27–32
section-based 167
selective appraisal of particular systems 43–5
strengthening theory 8–15
total integration 42, 139
trust in 294–7
waning of 52–4
working-class 4, 67, 68, 117
xenophobic 259
see also authoritarianism; cadre parties; cartel parties; catch-all parties; centre parties; Christian democrats; conservatives; electoral- professional parties; elite parties; Greens; left-wing parties; liberals; mass parties; office-seeking parties; policy-seeking parties; right-wing parties; social democrats; socialists; totalitarian regimes; vote-seeking parties
partis-comité 42
partitocratic polities 29, 64, 70, 235, 237, 245, 246, 250, 251–3
move away from 249
party-building 172, 181, 194, 195, 209, 217, 218
party membership 126–8, 133, 152, 162, 175
dues 307
grass-roots 131
mass 129, 130, 143
relations between leaders and 149
size of 141, 144, 236, 247
social solidarity of 132
Party Politics (journal) 3
Pas-de-Calais federation 179–80, 183–6
PASOK (Greek democratic socialist party) 268
Pasquino, G. 69

Paterson, W. 162
patrimonialism 177, 248
patronage 24, 60, 71, 155, 236–55
  access to 150, 152, 161
  cross-national differences 28–9
  distribution of 207, 212, 246
  struggle over dispensation of 212
  voter mobilization through 117
PCF (Parti Communiste Français) 170,
    172, 174, 175, 176, 179, 183, 185, 187
peasants 173, 181, 182
Percheron, Daniel 184, 185, 186
performance 7, 24, 29, 30, 60, 61, 95, 205
  anticipated 100
  evaluation 107
  organization and 166–90
  policy 48–9
  shortcomings of 294
  unsatisfactory 275
performance sensitivity 102
Perot, Ross 156
personalismo 163
personalities 160
personalization 69
  and professionalization 301–7
Philippe, A. 177, 180, 184
Pierre, J. 128
Pizzorno, A. 159, 174
Plataforma Moderada 193, 213, 217, 224
PLP (Parliamentary Labour Party,
    Britain) 156
pluralism 44, 47, 61, 86, 105, 244
  corporate 53
  endangered 104
  internal 174
  moderate and extreme 48
pocket boroughs 116
Poguntke, T. 30, 74, 134, 257, 258, 261,
    284
  see also new politics party
Poland 75
policy:
  agendas 4, 5, 167
  economic 222, 249
  financial 249
  formulation 11, 62
  implementation 62, 102
  public 52
policy-making 53, 205, 251, 301
policy-seeking parties 13, 61, 150–1, 153,
    155, 158, 161
  primary emphasis 149, 154
  programmatic party a variant of 159
  'stickiness' of programmatic change 157

'political class' 71, 72, 73, 76, 79, 253
Political Council (Spain) 209, 219, 225
political families 212, 213, 216
politicians:
  centrist 192
  images of 5
  'professional' 72, 121
  public opinion polls and 106
  self-seeking/serving 46, 262
  shenanigans of 261
politics 43, 45, 47, 75
  active participation in 117
  adversarial 106, 242, 244
  alternative 160
  chaos in 92
  collusion the essence of 101
  consensus 194, 203, 205, 206
  conspiratorial 182
  discussion within family 278–80
  economic theory of 61
  'fluid' 42
  internal 130
  inter-party, intra-party resources and 26
  intra-party 166, 167, 173, 177
  less organized 79–81
  mass 66
  national 186
  notable 70
  personalization of 301–7
  post-modern 80
  professionalized 78, 301–7
  'seniority' in 209
  spatial dimension of 104
populism 73
Portugal 69, 80
  anti-party sentiments 260, 263, 267–8,
    282, 283, 285
  Parliament 76
post-materialism 166
postal ballots 127, 129
power sharing 153
preferences 22, 72
  behavioural 276
  intra-party 131
  party 11, 102
  policy 88, 166, 224
  see also voter preferences
presidentialism 292
'presidentialization' 204, 209, 210, 212
Presno, M. A. 298
press 131, 192
pressure groups 66, 76
Primo de Rivera, Miguel 269
privatization 73, 80

privileges 71, 134
product differentiation 95, 97
professionalization 69, 73, 78, 79
  personalization and 301–7
Progress Parties 147
promises 142
propaganda 62, 184, 262, 277
proportional representation 47, 50, 70, 119
proportionality 210
Protestants 117
Przeworski, A. 169
pseudodemocracies 261
PSOE (Partido Socialista Obrero Español)
  192, 195, 205, 206–7, 220–4 *passim*,
  274–5, 298, 299, 300, 305, 308
public office 23, 24, 26, 78, 224, 292, 304
  ascendancy of the party in 113–35
public opinion 69, 99, 106, 176, 217, 291
Puhle, Hans-Jürgen 8, 18, 20, 21, 24, 59,
  65, 67, 68, 80
Putnam, R. D. 261

'qualified entry' 174

racism 134
radio 5, 280
Ranney, A. 2, 11, 103
rapprochement 173
Raschke, J. 209
rational choice 11, 13, 15–16, 17, 22, 62, 95
reactive antipartyism 30, 31, 260, 264, 267,
  273, 276, 283
  discussion of politics and 278–80
  education and 278
  political discontent and 284
  vote for opposition 274–5
recruitment 121, 171, 176, 177, 184, 202
  candidate 141, 152, 162, 173–5
  elite 78, 207, 208, 212, 217, 306
  vertical 182
Rédon 181
re-equilibration 21, 64, 72, 78–9, 80, 81
referenda 54, 200, 203, 206, 207, 219
reforms 78, 178, 179, 200, 218
  decentralizing 181
régime censitaire 119
Reiter, H. L. 258, 268
Rennes 181, 183
  Congress (1990) 178, 180
representation 298
representativeness 74
repression 75, 269
Republicans:
  American 144

  French 172
  Italian 153
responsibility 88, 107, 313
responsiveness 79, 87, 88, 89, 90, 312
  elite 104
  leadership 95
resurgence 6
returns 103
revitalization 6, 169, 183, 184
  ideological 26, 172–3
right-wing parties 4, 74, 134, 141, 158,
  201
  authoritarian 262
  extreme 147
  hard-line attitude 222
  new 150–1, 157, 160
  notabilaire tradition 180
  see also conservatives; Front National;
    Vlaams Blok
Riker, W. H. 95
rivalries 178
Rocard, Michel 172, 173, 176, 180, 181,
  182, 183
Rodríguez Shagún, Agustín 223
Roemer, J. E. 12
Rokkan, S. 2, 7, 14, 51, 53, 54, 60, 130
Rose, R. 6, 166
Roth, G. 117
Roucaute, Y. 187
Rousseau, J.-J. 41, 42
RPR (Rally for the Republic, France) 141,
  143, 147, 152
ruptura pactada 205–6
Rustow, D. A. 48

Sadoun, M. 179
salaries 131
Sani, G. 259–60, 264, 299
Santamaria, J. 221
Sartori, G. 2, 9, 44, 47, 48, 60, 68, 89,
  169
Sawicki, F. 178, 180
scandals 234, 249, 260, 271
Scandinavia 29, 48, 80, 234, 235, 254
  moderate majoritarianism 255
  parliamentary system 242
  single-party government 244
  see also Denmark; Finland; Norway;
    Sweden
Scarrow, S. E. 30, 73, 134, 162, 257, 288
Schattschneider, E. E. 2, 3
Schedler, A. 259
Schlesinger, J. A. 11, 17, 102–3
Schmitter, P. C. 61, 271

Schneider, W. 100
Schumpeter, J. A. 11, 22, 42, 45, 61, 86–7, 88, 90, 291, 304
Scully, T. R. 163
secondary organizations/associations 214, 285, 286
secularization 4, 169, 173
Segatti, P. 259–60, 264, 299
segmentation 65
selection 142, 159
self-interest 43, 121
Seligson, M. A. 60
Selznick, P. 27, 196, 198
separation of powers 238
Sferza, Serenella 8, 18, 25–6, 141, 143, 170, 172, 179–80, 181
SFIO (Section Française de L'Internationale Ouvrière) 179, 180, 181, 183, 187
shady deals 234–5, 236
Shapiro, I. 12
short-termism 21, 27, 30, 80
Shugart, M. S. 293
Simmel, Georg 22, 85–6, 297
Simon, Herbert 204
Simon, J. 295
single-issue associations 40, 73–4, 159
'sleaze' 234, 251
Smith, Adam 85
Smith, Gordon 66, 146, 160
Smith, John 156–7
sociability 177, 186
social contract 87
social democrats 21, 74, 120, 151
  British 156
  Dutch 136, 162
  German 40, 60, 65, 67, 80
  Spanish 201, 209, 213, 222, 223
social divisions 50–1, 215
social movements 6, 62, 73, 76, 79, 160, 166, 181
  efforts of factions to capture 188
social psychology 269
social values 85–9, 90
socialists 53, 74, 75, 162
  Belgian 252
  French 8, 25–6, 141, 143, 167–90, 193, 247, 248, 251
  German 47
  Greek 80, 251, 268
  Italian 153, 217, 248, 249
  Japanese 217
  Portuguese 80

Spanish 80, 158, 192, 195, 206, 236, 247, 248, 251, 274–5, 298, 299, 300, 305, 308
  see also Labour Party (Britain)
socialization 30, 78, 124, 171, 174, 261, 271
  formal 262, 269
  heavy-handed efforts at 278
  indirect 262
  informal 269, 278
  primary 270
solidarity 132, 160, 175, 184, 186
Solidarnosc 75
Sorauf, F. J. 2, 11
Soriano, M. 202
South America, *see* Latin America
Southern Europe 59, 164
  anti-party sentiments 7, 257–90
  characteristic of socialist parties 162
  'third wave' of democratization 58
  see also Greece; Italy; Portugal; Spain
Soviet era 291
Spain 29, 69, 70, 80, 81, 244, 298, 307
  anti-party sentiments 31, 261, 267, 269–82, 287, 295, 299
  caciquismo 116, 118
  Communist Party 194, 195, 203, 220, 298
  Constitution (1978) 203, 205
  election (1992) 81
  managing elections and suppressing competition 119–20
  overall belief in democracy 313
  Pactos de la Moncloa (1977) 75–6, 203, 219
  Partido Popular 274–5, 298, 299, 300, 308
  patronage 247, 253
  Restoration Monarchy 269, 270
  Second Republic 269, 270, 308
  'sleaze' 234
  Socialist Party 80, 158, 192, 195, 205, 206–7, 220–4 *passim*, 236, 247, 248, 251, 274–5, 298, 299, 300, 305, 308
  UCD collapse 26–7, 80, 191–230, 250
sponsor organizations 199
Sprague, J. 169
stability 5, 106, 191, 192–3, 196, 198
Stamokap 53
statism 70, 172, 182
Stern, M. 103
Stigler, G. J. 91, 92
Stokes, D. E. 100
Stokes, S. C. 3

stratarchic organization 129
strategies 154, 155
structural-functionalism 10, 15
Ström, K. 2, 4, 13, 17, 25, 62, 149, 150, 240
Suárez, Adolfo 13, 27, 193, 200–7 *passim*,
    209, 210, 212, 214, 215, 218–25
    passim, 250
subcultures 68, 120
Subileau, M. 172, 173
subnational level 179–80
subsidies 123, 127, 131, 132, 142, 147, 160,
    161, 307
    reliance of parties on 133
suffrage 67, 89, 115, 116, 117, 130
    extension to working class 120
    restricted 114
Sundberg, J. 127
Svåsand, L. 4, 51, 121
Sweden 128, 245, 247, 249
Switzerland 48, 50

Taggart, P. 259
Tarrow, S. 6
teledemocracy 54
telemarketing 154
television 5, 69, 70, 98, 125, 131
    news programmes 280
tenure 104, 106
territorialism 170–8, 179–80
    reformed 183–6
terrorism 192
TGV supertrain 186
Thatcher, Margaret 156, 157, 303
theory-building 12, 15, 17, 20, 23, 163
Third World 42, 181, 237
Torcal, Mariano 7, 19, 24, 28, 29, 134, 262,
    272, 282, 291, 297, 313
totalitarian regimes 42, 47
trade unions, *see* labour unions
transactions 91
transcourants 188
transparency 234
trasformismo 116, 118, 182
Tusell, J. 201
two-party system 47, 48, 250
    American 11, 102, 293
    British 20, 44, 45, 49
tyranny 41

UCD (Spanish Union of Democratic
    Centre) 26–7, 80, 191–230,
    250
UDF (Union of Democrats for France)
    141, 143, 144

uncertainty 58, 101, 102, 306
    organizational, zone of 130
unicameralism 50
United Kingdom, *see* Britain
United States 14, 20, 25, 40, 47, 49, 103,
    116, 138
    'anti-party parties' 134
    candidates with policy positions outside
        'mainstream' 157
    catch-all parties 60, 64, 69, 70, 146
    Democrats and Republicans 144
    fluid politics' 42
    governmental autonomy 238
    images of politicians 5
    PACs 143
    particularistic interests 293
    policy outcomes 52
    presidential candidates 292
    term limits 32
    two-party system 11, 102
    voter mobilization 117
unity 62
    competition and 297–8, 309
upper class 120
Uruguay 71, 294, 295, 296, 297

Vannucci, A. 234
Vargas Machuca, R. 309
Venezuela 294, 295, 296
Verba, S. 60
vertical growth 171–2, 179
violence 285, 286
Vlaams Blok 250
'voice' 196, 197–8, 203, 205, 221
volatility 22, 73, 74, 106
    aggregate measures of 94
Volkspartei 66, 67, 209
voluntary contributions 131
volunteers 152
vote-seeking parties 13, 61, 146, 149–50,
    151–2, 157, 158, 161
    central preoccupation 154
    opportunistic 160
    patterns of transformation 159
    policies 153
    underlying orientation 157
voter preferences 21, 87, 88, 93, 94, 95–6,
    97
    distribution of 100
    partisan 11, 102
    vague, inchoate 202
voters 90, 141, 160
    available 93
    'blank' 300

canvassing 142
exit-prone 198
informed 93
key channel of communication between
  leaders and 125
marginal 198, 199
median 106
mobilizing, during campaigns 285
moderate 170
non-religious 214
opinion 93
potential reactions of 101
rational 93
votes 61, 300–1
competing for, on the basis of leaders
  148
maximizing 67, 69, 87, 151, 154, 162,
  194, 199, 212, 213
protest 64, 72
punishment 191
standard deviation of 103
symmetry of distribution of 103, 104
vulnerability 22, 89–90, 95, 102–4, 160, 179
decidability and 107
early, surviving 197
high 106
'perfect' 106
versus safety of tenure 104

Wagner, A. 52
Walter, F. 77, 78
Ware, A. 9, 25, 139, 143, 144, 145, 148
Wattenberg, M. P. 6
Webb, P. D. 166, 258
Weber, Max 2, 59–60, 140, 305, 306
Weiner, M. 2

welfare state 52, 70, 73, 120, 132
desirability and necessity of 114, 156
Weltanschauungen 60, 67
Wert, J. I. 259
Western Europe 3–8, 14, 19, 21, 25, 27,
  138
catch-all parties 66, 67, 69, 70, 74, 137
literature 2
organizational development 114
party government 233–56
party membership 126
patterns of change in 159–62
substantial or enduring parties 214
transformation and change 162
trust in parties 297
Volkspartei 66, 67
see also under individual country names
Westminster-type polities 29, 48, 50, 142,
  244–7 *passim*, 250–5 *passim*
regard for 249
'wets' 157
Wheare, K. C. 48
Whitelaw, Sir William 157
Wiberg, M. 257
Widfeldt, A. 128
Wiesendahl, E. 259
Wilson, J. Q. 197
Wolinetz, Steven B. 7, 9, 13, 17, 18, 24, 25,
  77, 146, 157
women 172, 173
in labour force 4
working class 4, 67, 68, 117, 173, 181
extension of suffrage to 120
renewing links to 184

xenophobia 4, 134, 259